After the Deluge

After the Deluge

Regional Crises and Political Consolidation in Russia

Daniel S. Treisman

Ann Arbor
THE UNIVERSITY OF MICHIGAN PRESS

To Susi

First paperback edition 2001
Copyright © by the University of Michigan 1999
All rights reserved
Published in the United States of America by
The University of Michigan Press
Manufactured in the United States of America
♾ Printed on acid-free paper

2004 2003 2002 2001   5 4 3 2

No part of this publication may be reproduced, stored in a retrieval system, or transmitted in any form or by any means, electronic, mechanical, or otherwise, without the written permission of the publisher.

A CIP catalog record for this book is available from the British Library.

Library of Congress Cataloging-in-Publication Data

Treisman, Daniel.
    After the deluge : regional crises and political consolidation in Russia / Daniel S. Treisman.
      p. cm.
    Includes bibliographical references and index.
    ISBN 0-472-10998-7 (alk. paper)
    1. Federal government—Russia (Federation)   2. Central-local government relations—Russia (Federation)   3. Russia (Federation)—Politics and government—1991–   I. Title.
JN6693.5.S8T74   1999
351.47—dc21   99-37664
                                                                         CIP

ISBN 0-472-08831-9 (pbk. : alk. paper)

Contents

List of Figures vii

List of Tables ix

Acknowledgments xi

Chapter 1. Introduction 1

Chapter 2. Center and Regions in Russia 28

Chapter 3. Fiscal Transfers and Fiscal Appeasement 47

Chapter 4. Public Spending and Regional Voting 81

Chapter 5. Political Strategies of Regional Governors 120

Chapter 6. Yugoslavia, the USSR, Czechoslovakia—and Russia 137

Chapter 7. Conclusion: Democratization and Political Integration 161

Appendix A 181

Appendix B 189

Appendix C 209

Appendix D 216

Notes 221

References 241

Index 259

Figures

3.1. "Winners" and "losers" from fiscal redistribution, 1992	56
4.1. Regional vote for Yeltsin in 1991 presidential election	83
4.2. Vote of trust in Yeltsin, April 1993 referendum	84
4.3. Change in regional vote for Yeltsin, 1991 election to April 1993 referendum	85
4.4. Vote for the three most pro-reform blocs in December 1993	86
4.5. Vote for major pro-reform blocs and for Communists, December 1995	87
4.6. Second-round vote for Yeltsin in 1996 presidential election	88
A1. The threshold function for regional rebellion	183
A2. Threshold function and cumulative density of σ	184
A3. Increasing tax	185
A4. Tax increase with selective appeasement	186
A5. Appeasement with imperfect information	187

Tables

2.1. Elections of Regional Leaders, January 1991 through June 1996 — 32
3.1. Estimated State Budget Revenues and Expenditures in Russia in the Early 1990s — 50
3.2. Estimated Fiscal and Financial Transfers from Center to Regions, 1992–96 — 53
3.3. What Explains the Pattern of Net Center-to-Region Transfers in Russia, 1992–96? — 61
3.4. What Explains the Pattern of Particular Transfers and of Regional Tax Retention, Russia 1992? — 68
3.5. Change in Ranking of Regions in Terms of Net Central Transfers, 1988–92 — 76
4.1. Relationship between Central Transfers and Regional Budget Spending — 93
4.2. Voting for Yeltsin and Incumbent Pro-Reform Blocs — 95
4.3. The 1996 Presidential Election: Voting for Yeltsin in Rounds 1 and 2 — 101
4.4. Why Did Different Regions Support Different Political Blocs in the December 1993 Parliamentary Election? — 104
4.5. Independent Variables Correlated with the (North-South) Latitude of Regions' Capital Cities — 109
4.6. Logistic Regression of Whether the Incumbent Governor Was Reelected if Regional Election Held — 114
4.7. Logistic Regression of Whether the Most Senior Regional Executive Official Running in December 1993 Federation Council Election Was Elected — 116
5.1. Which Regional Chief Executives Opposed Yeltsin at Moments of Constitutional Crisis? — 126
5.2. Which Regional Chief Executives Supported Yeltsin During 1996 Presidential Election Campaign? — 130
5.3. Aid, Voting, and Governors' Strategies in Three Russian Regions — 133
6.1. Federal Own Revenue in Three Reforming Communist Federations and Russia — 140

Tables

6.2. Federal Expenditures in Three Reforming Communist Federations and Russia — 141
6.3. Consolidated Budget Revenues in Three Reforming Communist Federations and Russia — 143
6.4. Federal Budget Balance in Three Reforming Communist Federations and Russia — 145
6.5. Grants from Federation to Czech and Slovak Governments, in Percent of Czechoslovakia GDP — 146
6.6. Yugoslavia, Financing the Federation — 147
6.7. Republic Budget Expenditure per Capita in Czechoslovakia 1989 and 1992 — 149
6.8. Expenditures of State (Federal + Republic) Budgets on Social Security Benefits, Czechoslovakia — 149
6.9. Growth of M1 in Czech and Slovak Republics, 1991–92 — 150
6.10. Domestic Credit Growth in Czech and Slovak Republics, 1991–92 — 150
6.11. Estimated Interrepublican Redistribution in Yugoslavia, 1986 — 153
6.12. Operations of the Yugoslav Federal Development Fund in the Late 1980s — 154
6.13. Access to Concessionary Loans and Money Creation of Three Yugoslav Republics, 1987 — 154
6.14. Net Budget Transfers from the Union — 156
6.15. Estimated Net Indirect Transfers to Republics as Result of Underpriced Exports/Imports of Oil and Gas, and Overpriced Exports/Imports of Non–Oil-and-Gas Goods, 1990 — 158
B1. Center-to-Region Transfers and Regional Tax Share, Russia 1994 — 190
B2. Regions' Ranks in Net Transfers Received — 194
B3. Index of Social Infrastructure Underdevelopment — 200
B4. Index of Pace of Economic Reform — 202
B5. Sovereignty Declarations, August 1990–May 1991 — 203
B6. Characteristics of the Independent Variables Used in Final Regressions — 204
B7. Correlation Coefficients for Independent Variables Used in Same Long Regression in Table 3.3 — 207
B8. Breakdown of the Dependent Variable, 1992 — 207
B9. Breakdown of the Dependent Variable, 1994 — 208
C1. Characteristics of Russia's Regions — 214
D1. Which Regional Delegations to the 1993 Congress of People's Deputies Voted with Yeltsin's Side? — 217

Acknowledgments

I have accumulated debts—intellectual and otherwise—to many people in the course of researching and writing this book. Peter Hall, Andrew Walder, and especially Tim Colton provided insightful suggestions and generous encouragement during the period of its germination as a Ph.D. dissertation in the Government Department at Harvard. Andrei Shleifer has been a source of intellectual stimulation throughout, as well as penetrating comment on the current state of Russian politics. Jim Alt, Robert Bates, Robert Conrad, Tim Frye, and Joel Hellman read earlier versions of parts of the book and offered useful insights. Phil Roeder read the manuscript in its entirety and provided invaluable criticism. His careful reading forced me to clarify my thinking on various points and has greatly improved the final product. Deborah Treisman, Michel Treisman, and Hans Landesmann also read parts of the final manuscript and made valuable suggestions. Other colleagues swapped insights into the current state of Russian politics; I would like to thank in particular Michael McFaul, Steve Solnick, Yitzhak Brudny, and Robert Moser.

I am more than grateful to my colleagues in the political science department at UCLA for the atmosphere of intellectual curiosity and good humor in which the final manuscript took shape. Lev Freinkman, of the World Bank, has been more than generous with his expertise on numerous occasions. I am grateful also to participants in seminars and workshops where I presented earlier versions of parts of the argument, at Harvard, Yale, UCLA, the University of Pennsylvania, and the U.S. Institute of Peace, as well as at the American Political Science Association 1995 and 1996 annual meetings and the American Economic Association 1998 annual meeting.

In Russia, I have trespassed on the patience of more people than can be listed here. Leonid Smirnyagin and Aleksei Lavrov generously shared their data and insights over the course of several years. Others have found the time to provide their own perspectives on Russia's emerging politics. I am grateful in particular to Ramazan Abdulatipov, Aleksandr Belousov, Yuri Blokhin, Viktor Filonov, Boris Fyodorov, Sergei Ignatev, Gabibulla Khasaev, Mikhail Leontev, Aleksandr Morozov, Oleg Morozov, Mikhail Motorin, Vitali Naishul, Valery Pavlov, Sergei Shatalov, Sergei Sinelnikov, Viktor Stepanov, Andrei Yakovlev, and Mark Yanovsky. Mark Bond, Konstantin Borovoi, Ruslan Shamurin,

Mikhail Zhivilo, and Yuri Zhivilo provided broader insight into the world of Russian business and politics, and Sergei Lazaruk into the Moscow cultural *tusovka*.

Charles Myers at the University of Michigan Press shepherded the manuscript through the editorial process with patience and dedication. I am grateful also to anonymous readers of the mansucript—some for valuable comments and suggestions, others for securing the additional time necessary to see my arguments confirmed by subsequent developments. I would like to acknowledge financial support from the Harvard University Russian Research Center, which provided a summer grant and a postdoctoral fellowship at crucial periods, as well as the UCLA Academic Senate and Center for European and Russian Studies. My understanding of center-region relations was enhanced toward the end by participation in a technical support project offering advice on fiscal federalism to the Russian Ministry of Finance, funded by USAID under the direction of Robert Conrad. No part of the argument in this book should, of course, be attributed to USAID or any other funding organization.

Chapter 3 draws upon my earlier work in "The Politics of Intergovernmental Transfers in Post-Soviet Russia," *British Journal of Political Science* 26 (1996): 299–335, and "Fiscal Redistribution in a Fragile Federation: Moscow and the Regions in 1994," *British Journal of Political Science* 28 (1998): 185–200. I am grateful to the *British Journal of Political Science* and Cambridge University Press for permission to excerpt.

On a personal note, I am grateful to my parents, Anne Kahneman and Michel Treisman, and my stepfather, Danny Kahneman, for the constant support, interest, and understanding they have shown through the years as this project took form. Hans and Elaine Landesmann, my mother- and father-in-law, invited me along to some of the most conducive spots for writing that I can imagine. My wife, Susan Landesmann, to whom the book is dedicated, put up with it—and me—for so long that she deserves a medal. Instead, she will have to settle for my love.

CHAPTER 1
Introduction

In Russia, writes the literary critic Vyacheslav Ivanov, "we are consumed with geography, and we have no real history" (quoted in Layard and Parker 1996). Perhaps more precisely, for Russians the two long ago became indistinguishable. Centuries in Russia divide not into years but into miles, the miles of the expanding frontier. Unlike European powers, which went abroad to colonize, Muscovy began at home and progressed outward, gradually "colonizing itself," transforming disparate Eurasian peoples into "Russians" (Klyuchevsky 1995). Just where the country lies remains a question for philosophers as much as for surveyors. Not only do its borders move, even its center will not hold still: to redirect their country's destiny, both tsars and commissars began by moving the capital.

More recently, Russia's geography has fused with its politics. The flood unleashed by Gorbachev's reforms left Russians of all descriptions by the early 1990s poking around in the political debris. As they tried to piece together a new order—one that was democratic, market-oriented, and modern—the main divisions that emerged between them were often less ideological or socioeconomic than geographical. Where economics or ideology did shape debate, there usually was a territorial subtext. This, more than anything else, complicated Russia's efforts at self-reinvention and distinguished its experience from that of most other postcommunist states.

Most postcommunist transitions—whether in Eastern Europe or the former Soviet Union—started out more or less alike. First came a brief and apparently universal moment of euphoria. Those who took to the streets of Budapest or Prague to demonstrate against tottering Soviet-style governments seemed, in the words of one observer, to be simultaneously healing "divisions in their society" and "divisions in themselves," nurturing "solidarity both within and between nations" (Ash 1990a, 138, 145). The same could be said of the crowds in Moscow after the 1991 August coup collapsed.

However, civic enthusiasm soon gave way to a more complicated disenchantment. Everywhere unity was replaced by a consciousness of difference. Abstract commitments dissolved into concrete interests, as anticommunist coalitions splintered into scores of tiny parties. In the article from which this book borrows its title, Timothy Garton Ash described how the former dissidents of Poland, Hungary, and Czechoslovakia made this jump from moral absolutes to presidential suites, quarreling among themselves along the way (Ash 1990b). But similar divisions emerged at all levels of state and society. A superficial cohesion was replaced by what Václav Havel labeled a "wild and shameless squabbling over purely particular interests" (quoted in Jacques Rupnik 1995, 61).

The return to particularity occurred everywhere, usually within months. But in different countries it focused on different divisions. In Russia—a country the size of 54 Polands or 133 Czechoslovakias—it crystallized around geography. As elites fumbled for a new set of political arrangements, the interactions of regions and center came to occupy an ever larger place in constitutional debates. Results of early elections showed a country with a political spectrum that ran not so much from left to right as from North to South. The ultimate— though still unlikely—political danger feared by observers turned out to be not social revolution or civil war but territorial disintegration.

One by one, different ethnic republics within the Russian Federation declared themselves sovereign states, adopted constitutions, flags, and even national anthems, announced that their laws took precedence over federal law, asserted rights over resources in their territory, and refused to remit the taxes Moscow demanded (see Treisman 1997). To wring concessions out of the center, republic leaders threatened general strikes and regional tariffs, the confiscation of federal property, local states of emergency, and even terrorist attacks. Chechnya, after a coup in which the nationalist leader Dzhokhar Dudaev came to power, announced its complete independence. In Tatarstan, 61 percent voted in favor of republic sovereignty in a referendum held by the republic's leadership in March 1992, and Russia reportedly moved troops up to the region's border.[1]

If at first this looked like a specifically ethnic uprising, it soon turned out to be something more general. By 1993, demands for greater autonomy had spread to numerous ethnically Russian regions.[2] Oblasts from Sverdlovsk in the Urals to Vologda, a backwoods region in Russia's North, had declared themselves republics and asserted new rights. Most alarming was a growing regional tax revolt, disconcertingly reminiscent of the one that had finished off the USSR in late 1991, at the height of which about one-third of the country's regions were withholding some or all of their assessed taxes. The finance minister, Boris Fyodorov, accused the country's regions of trying to destroy the central government by means of "financial asphyxiation."[3]

Such tax revolts are known to create a particularly dangerous dynamic of "contagion."[4] As more regions revolt, it becomes increasingly illogical for others to continue to pay an ever larger share of the cost of public goods. The logic is that of a bank run, in which the depositors' fear of finding themselves last in line leads even those eager to help the bank survive to join the stampede to withdraw funds after panic reaches a critical point. A few refusals can thus prompt spirals of defection. Such situations often exhibit the structure of a "tipping" game, with two equilibria—one at a very high rate of compliance, the other at complete fiscal collapse.[5]

Newspaper articles around this time echoed Fyodorov's concern. As early as October 1991, the Russian political scientist Aleksandr Tsipko warned that if the Soviet Union disintegrated Russia would itself dissolve into "many new sovereign Russian states" (Tsipko 1991a, 1–4). Headlines ranged from the inquisitive—"Can Yeltsin's Russia Survive?"—to the openly alarmist—"The Country Will Collapse," or "Russia's Disintegration is Inevitable" (Yemelyanenko 1993; Antonov 1993; Migranyan 1991). Various Western observers also took this possibility seriously. According to one scholar writing in 1994, "the process that led to the breakup of the Soviet Union is continuing within the Russian Federation itself." The same author wrote of a "cohesiveness vacuum" and warned that "little is left to hold the country together" (Stern 1994, 40, 54). Another outlined both "explosion" and "implosion" scenarios for disintegration (Gouré 1994; see also Rupnik 1994).

Yet, for all the conflicts and crises, Russia did remain intact. From the centrifugal political jockeying a precarious but surprisingly enduring stability emerged. By 1997 the country had not disintegrated and actually appeared to most observers to be more geopolitically stable than in previous years.[6] With the exception of Chechnya, each of the most severe conflicts between the center and individual regions of the early 1990s had been contained and apparently alleviated. As I argue later, that the center could *conceive* of a military intervention in Chechnya in 1994 and did not back down as it had in late 1991 owed much to the knowledge that the threat of defiance spreading to other regions had been greatly reduced.

The aim of this book is to explain this experience. What underlay the dynamic of escalating and then subsiding regional protest in the early 1990s? What can account for the Russian Federation's fragile cohesion? How did the introduction of democratic institutions and elections interact with territorial divisions of interest? What does this experience reveal about the evolving logic of power in the Russian political system? And does Russia's recent history cast light upon the logic of conflict and accommodation within other ethnically or regionally divided states?

While many factors contributed to restoring Russia's territorial equilibrium, the argument I make in this book places particular emphasis on a certain fiscal policy that central officials stumbled into as they struggled to deal with looming regional crises. This policy was one of selective fiscal appeasement. Central authorities directed budget transfers and tax breaks disproportionately toward regions where disenchantment with Moscow threatened to escalate into strikes, separatist gestures, or other acts of protest. These fiscal benefits—when they financed higher rates of regional government spending—tended to buy electoral support for central incumbents and pro-reform forces. The decrease in public hostility toward Yeltsin and his central allies in those regions reduced the incentive for their political leaders to exploit tensions with Moscow for personal political gain. Central authorities thus prevented bandwagons of opportunistic protest and tax-withholding from escalating and preserved the power of their weak enforcement resources to keep less obstreperous regions in line.

To be clear: I do not claim that the center's fiscal policy was the only factor that explains Russia's survival. Many factors contributed to this outcome. I do argue, however, that Moscow's policy of selective fiscal appeasement played a crucial and hitherto poorly understood role in preserving the state's integrity. And, paradoxically, many of the features of this policy that I claim helped to alleviate political crises were themselves viewed by many at the time as dangerously destabilizing.

This argument about internal political dynamics in Russia suggests new perspectives on some other parts of the world and historical periods. For other weak central states in territorially divided societies, similar methods of economic appeasement aimed at the most credible protesters may at times greatly enhance the effectiveness of existing enforcement powers. What generally appear to be policies of weakness may at times be rational attempts to husband strength. To prove this more generally, or to define in precisely which circumstances such appeasement strategies will be sufficient to prevent territorial disintegration, would go far beyond the evidence I can muster in this book. I therefore offer only speculative hypotheses about how the logic might apply to a number of past and contemporary cases. The most natural comparison is with the three other ethnically divided and nominally federal communist states that *did* disintegrate—Yugoslavia, the USSR, and Czechoslovakia. While a policy of fiscal appeasement sufficient to contain centrifugal strains may or may not have been available to central authorities in these three countries, I do show in chapter 6 that in none of the three was such a policy attempted. For a variety of reasons, the leaders of Yugoslavia, the USSR and Czechoslovakia chose quite different responses to separatist challenges.

The rest of this chapter reviews what political science and economics suggest about why states sometimes disintegrate territorially and sometimes remain intact. It examines alternative possible explanations for Russia's experience in the 1990s. I argue that while various factors emphasized by previous accounts did play a part in shaping this experience, they do not convincingly explain Russia's survival unless one incorporates the dynamic of fiscal appeasement previously mentioned.

Integration and Disintegration

Why do states sometimes disintegrate along territorial lines and sometimes remain intact? Understanding the forces that underlie cohesion or disintegration in regionally divided states has rarely been more relevant than at the turn of the twenty-first century.[7] In countries across the globe tensions have erupted recently between center and periphery. More than once, the integrity of long-established states has fallen into doubt. In China and India in the 1990s, relations with the regions were a crucial but volatile term in the central leadership's political equation (see Shue 1988; Shirk 1993; Huang 1995; Mitra 1992). In Mexico, a peasant rebellion in Chiapas forced the PRI leadership to confront its disgruntled hinterlands. Regional identities and political movements also emerged with unexpected force in some of the advanced democracies of Western Europe—Spain, France, and Britain, among others (see Hueglin 1986; Judt 1994; Woods 1995). In the Po Valley of northern Italy, advocates of an independent Padania gathered surprising support in the mid-1990s. Meanwhile, a referendum on secession in Quebec in 1995 failed to pass only by the slimmest of margins.

Political scientists have struggled to keep pace. As the tectonic plates beneath states shifted, debates broke out over the causes of minority nationalisms, the stability of federations, and the political economy of secession. At the same time, new studies of the rise and decline of historical empires suggested original perspectives on the causes of cohesion or disintegration. From these and earlier strands of inquiry, a variety of theories emerged about what holds divided states together. These theories can be classified by the approach they take toward differences of interest between central and regional actors.

A first school of thought, developed in the 1950s and 1960s, viewed integration as essentially a *technological* problem. Differences of interest between central and regional actors were, for the most part, ignored. Territorial cohesion was described as a result of "social communication"—an image that implicitly assumed a harmony of interests between "speaker" and "listener." In Karl Deutsch's well-known formulation, integration was equated with a high volume of transactions between members of different political subunits (Deutsch 1964). In his words, the degree of "cohesiveness among individuals and among communities of individuals can be measured by—and is probably promoted by—the extent of mutual relationships or interaction among them" (Deutsch, quoted in Muir and Paddison 1981, 159). Preventing splits depended on the quantity—not the content—of communications sent and received. States disintegrated under the pressure of regionalist or nationalist revolts when the state's size exceeded the scope of its currently available "equipment and technology" of communications (Deutsch 1966, 149). "Messages" linking the units were drowned out by "noise" (Deutsch 1964, 49).

This view of states as telephone lines seemed counterintuitive to various students of political development who saw far more conflict in the process by which states emerged. For these scholars, state building was an exercise of central power: integrative institutions were constructed out of intrusions by central elites and defensive reactions by peripheral actors. Such institutions cemented the dominance of central interests over those of actors in the regions.

Three modes of central penetration were often singled out (see Rokkan and Urwin 1983; Tarrow 1977, chap. 1). First, central elites imposed values and symbols on regional populations, introducing cultural standardization by means of a written script. Integration occurred as values diffusing from the center overcame the local "tenacity of prior attachments" and "reluctance to accept strange gods" (Shils 1975, 11). Second, central armies, police forces, and other administrative bureaucracies incorporated regions into a centralized system of legal order and enforcement.[8] And third, the center could integrate regions through economic relations. Two possible methods were promotion of interregional markets and central extraction and redistribution of resources—both of which typically involved the imposition of centrally controlled money.[9] Each of these penetrations changed the periphery and created kinds of dependence that made separation harder.

These three channels imply several pathways by which state disintegration might come about. It might result from a breakdown in the cultural authority of the center and a movement by local populations to reclaim their "old gods." It might follow a crisis of central political authority, or a reduction in the ability of bureaucratic principals to monitor, reward, and punish their agents in the field. Similarly, it might reflect a growing failure of the center to defend the national currency and infrastructure of interregional markets, or an erosion of the center's capacity to extract and redistribute local resources.

Where center-periphery theorists saw the causes of state integration in the domination of central actors over regional ones, a third view with roots in both the economics of public finance and the political theory of federalism drew a path of causation from the bottom up. Integration was the result of a voluntary contract between regional actors to pursue a collective goal jointly. Free regions chose to confederate or federate, and central actors were faithful and tightly controlled agents of the regional actors. What held large states together, in this view, was the recognition by regional actors that public goods such as military defense could be provided more efficiently at larger scale. The benefits of economies of scale in public good provision were balanced against the likelihood of receiving a bundle of public goods further from the particular preferences of the region.[10] The relative size of these two effects determined the optimal level of centralization.[11] The implicit explanation for state disintegration would be a sudden increase in divergence of regional preferences over public goods, an increase that was sufficient to outweigh any economies of scale.

Stated so baldly, each of these perspectives sounds incomplete. States are neither telephone lines, nor prisons, nor clubs, but something that contains elements of each of these. The interests of central and regional actors are clearly relevant, yet it is an oversimplification to assume that either central or regional interests always dominate. Most states are neither the European Union nor empires of slave dependencies. The important analytical question is how these interests interact. Almost always, *both* economies of scale in public good provision *and* the potential for exploitation by the center exist. Some scholars have argued that particular institutional arrangements can secure the former while restraining the latter.

Two sets of institutional arrangements have been suggested. First, institutions of consociational democracy are argued to preserve integration even in deeply divided societies. Such institutions represent a set of bargains between elites of ethnically, regionally, religiously, or linguistically defined segments of the population that protect the autonomy of minority segments more reliably than majority rule does. While issues of common concern are decided by a grand coalition of the leaders of the subcommunities, questions of internal governance are left to each segment to decide for itself. Proportionality is formally guaranteed in public appointments and spending, and each group retains a minority veto (Lijphart 1993). The great devolution of powers to the subcommunities limits the ability of the center to impose unpopular policies. Still, it is not clear what would prevent a central actor from abusing the subcommunities, or one subcommunity from capturing the central institutions and upsetting the previous bargain. As advocates of consociational democracy acknowledge, such arrangements sometimes work but sometimes break down into civil war or secession. While consociational institutions have helped preserve stability in Belgium, Switzerland, the Netherlands, and Malaysia during various periods, such systems fell apart dramatically in Cyprus in 1963 and Lebanon in 1975 (Lijphart 1993).

Second, some scholars have emphasized the utility of federalism for accommodating territorially diverse populations within a single state.[12] In Weingast's model of federalism, subnational actors can coordinate in repeated play to punish a central attempt to exploit one of them (1995). The potential for central abuse is restricted by this institutionally rooted logic. Yet, as in the case of consociationalism, it is easier to identify possible cases of "market-preserving federalism" than to predict how long the useful balance of power between center and regions will last. In practice, central actors sometimes strike deals with some regional or ethnic subgroups at the expense of others—federal institutions have not, for this reason, prevented ethnic conflicts in postcolonial Africa. And the ability of regional actors to coordinate—useful for preventing central incursions—may also be used to prevent the center from preserving economic integration or enforcing contracts. One condition likely to limit this danger, though not to limit central abuse, is the existence of a large number of small subunits (Riker and Lemco 1987). But a large number of subunits, while increasing the costs of "bad" regional coordination, would also increase the costs of the "good" variety. How effectively particular institutions integrate a country depends in part on what actors do to preserve or undermine those institutions and on the relative power of the actors.

Explaining Russia's Experience

From these various theoretical perspectives, a number of possible explanations for Russia's cohesion in the 1990s emerge. The center's ability to contain centrifugal pressures might be due to cultural and ethnic ties between center and regions, effective vertical administrative hierarchies, the threat of force, economic integration, economies of scale in public good provision, political institutions, or the large number and relatively small size of regional units. As I shall argue, however, existing explanations that incorporate these features leave puzzling questions unanswered. Understanding the ways in which these factors interacted with a particular central fiscal policy is essential to explaining the outcome.

Culture and Ethnicity

Just as cultural, linguistic, and ethnic divisions provide fault lines along which states can fracture, cultural, linguistic, and ethnic homogeneity are often thought to enhance a state's cohesion. In Kedourie's rendition of the argument: "Those who speak the same language are joined to each other by a multitude of invisible bonds by nature herself, long before any human art begins. . . . From this internal boundary . . . the making of the external boundary by dwelling place results as a consequence" (1961, 5; quoted in Woolf 1996). Ties of "blood, speech, custom, and so on" have an "ineffable, and at times overpowering, coerciveness in and of themselves" (Geertz 1963, 109). And this sentiment of loyalty to members of one's kinship, language, and cultural groups strengthens the political fabric of administrative units that have borders more or less congruent with these divisions.

Even though Russia is home to more than 120 nationalities, 81.5 percent of the population as of 1989 was nevertheless ethnically Russian. Some have seen in this relative homogeneity and the long history of assimilation it represents a reason for the country's resilience (Lapidus and Walker 1995, 87). Peter Rutland, for instance, notes: "Russians share a strong sense of cultural homogeneity, and have four centuries' experience of life in a common state" (1994).

This undoubtedly *did* simplify the task for those seeking to ensure that the Russian center "held" in the early 1990s. However, there are many reasons to doubt claims that cultural or ethnic factors are by themselves enough to explain why Russia has survived. Such arguments consist of several steps. They assume that: (1) those who share ethnic, cultural, or linguistic attributes feel a powerful and relatively constant sense of loyalty to each other that overrides other possible economic or territorial conflicts of interest, (2) this loyalty translates into a preference for a shared political unit, and (3) individuals will be able to establish or preserve a political unit on the basis of their shared identity. Each of these is at times problematic—and particularly so in 1990s Russia.

First, are ethnic, national, or cultural identities clearly bounded, coherent, relatively permanent packages of attributes and values that unite individuals into stably defined groups and override other divisions of interest? An emerging consensus among political scientists, sociologists, and anthropologists suggests not.[13] In fact, cultural and ethnic identities are multiple, overlaid, and elastic; their boundaries are hard to define and often change; and individuals switch between definitions of their identity, at times rapidly.[14] All cultures contain various, often contradictory, sets of values and definitions, which facilitate a redrawing of boundaries and loyalties should occasion arise. Furthermore, cultural identities have been "engineered" and traditions "invented," often in relatively short periods of time.[15]

Where economic interests or mutual suspicions divide the populations of adjacent territories, a sense of distinctive identity is often "rediscovered." There are always alternative historical narratives that could be told about any adjacent territories, either emphasizing commonalities or emphasizing differences. If a history of Padania could be constructed, so could a history of Siberia's distinct development. The intensity of cultural attachments is hard to measure, rendering cultural explanations of cohesion somewhat post hoc. It is not always clear whether cultural factors were the cause or merely a tool of other disintegrative or integrative projects.

All of these features of the plasticity of cultural and ethnic identity are evident in republics of the former Soviet Union, including Russia. Opinion polls in the last years of Soviet rule found that Russians were actually more likely to define themselves as Soviet people than as Russians.[16] It was certainly possible by this time for them to view their homeland as "Russia." Yet from 63 to 81 percent of ethnic Russians said instead that their homeland was "the USSR." "Neither language, nor the past, nor culture, nor traditions had a significance comparable to their perception of themselves as citizens of the Soviet state" (Gudkov 1994; quoted in Dunlop 1997, 55). Within a few years, the majority had changed their definition of identity: according to one survey, the proportion of Russian residents identifying their homeland as the "Soviet Union" had dropped to about 29 percent by 1993, while 50 percent now chose "Russia" (55 percent among ethnic Russians; Hough, Davidheiser, and Lehmann 1996, 45). That Russians could move so rapidly from one basis of self-identification to another suggests that perhaps they could have adopted yet another definition of their identity had circumstances developed differently. In fact, many did. By 1995, only 39 percent of Russian residents (41 percent of ethnic Russians) said that "Russia" was their homeland, while those "rediscovering" their Soviet nationality rose from 29 to 39 percent. In addition, between 1993 and 1995 the percentage answering that their "homeland" was the particular subnational region in which they lived doubled, from 12 to 23 percent (Hough, Davidheiser, and Lehmann 1996, 45). Given that as of 1995 three out of five ethnic Russians did *not* consider their homeland to be Russia, it seems hard to argue that ethnic and cultural loyalty were reliable guarantors of the country's cohesion.

More than most peoples, Russians have been plagued by the question who they, as a nation, are. All nationalities define themselves in part in opposition to an "other." But it has been argued that to an unusual degree Russians' sense of nationhood emerged as a reaction to preexisting Western models, fueled by a kind of Nietzschean *ressentiment*—"a psychological state resulting from suppressed feelings of envy and hatred . . . and the impossibility of satisfying these feelings" (Greenfeld 1992, 15). As late as the turn of the twentieth century, Russian identity was linked to being a subject of the tsar, and usually to a religious commitment, rather than to any particular ethnic heritage: it remained a nationality of politics rather than of blood. "Thus, the formation of the Russian nation by the time of the revolution was not yet accomplished . . . it remained unclear who was a Russian even in ethnic terms" (Khazanov 1995, 237). Continual and extensive ethnic intermingling and intermigration across the Eurasian plains meant that most claims of simple ethnic identity were spurious.[17]

The reconstruction of historical narratives to fit particular objectives remains a major industry in Russia, a country that, in the historian Yuri Afanasiev's phrase, has been blessed with an "unpredictable past" (Matlock 1995, 3). One Western scholar visiting Russia in late 1994 found "no small amount of more or less deliberate myth-making going on" (Urban 1996, 147). Another analyst, extrapolating from the experience of the mid-1990s, predicted that "across Russia's political landscape we can expect to see a kaleidoscope, spatially varied at any moment, and fluid in time, of asserted identities, aboriginal and otherwise. Communities 'imagined' to pursue a goal of greater local power will likely dissolve once that power is achieved. . . . Identities incapable of effectively contesting power relations will be abandoned, and new communities constructed to pursue alternative paths to power will emerge" (Fondahl 1996, 14). In Russia, communities were not just "imagined," they were continually *re*-imagined.

At the same time, some observers did see the first traces of a redefinition of identity in terms of *regional* loyalties and attachments. Associations of regions of the Far East and Siberia had formed and seemed at times to pose a potential separatist threat. Among Russian inhabitants of Siberia concerned about Moscow's extraction of natural resources, a "Sibiriak" cultural identity was "rediscovered" (Rupnik 1994, 101). New "histories" of the independent Far East

Republic of the early 1920s became a staple of conversation in the eastern provinces.

Second, even if the vast majority of Russians did feel strong cultural or ethnic bonds, did that necessarily translate into a reliable preference for united statehood? In some other parts of the world economic or political conflicts have prompted threats of secession even among relatively ethnically homogeneous populations. Such threats emerged, for instance, in the American colonies in the eighteenth century, in the southern United States in the nineteenth,[18] in western Canada and northern Italy in the late twentieth century. Despite relative cultural homogeneity, the West Indies Federation disintegrated in the 1960s. In 1933, Western Australia proposed to secede from the Australian federation, and a two-thirds majority of the state's voters voted for secession in a referendum.[19] The split was only prevented by an extremely accommodating response on tax issues from the other Australian states.

Third, even if a majority might prefer to preserve a united state—for ethnic or other reasons—history suggests that it will not always be able to do so. Some states have dissolved even though a majority would probably have preferred otherwise. The danger for Russia was not that numerous regions would declare independence and seek to separate because of non-Russian ethnicity. Rather, it was that a few adamant nationalist regional leaders might act as "detonators," setting off a broader brushfire of insubordination that would undermine the center's capacity and credibility. In the absence of institutional firebreaks, the combination of minority nationalisms, economic divisions, local political ambitions, and general suspicion could prove a highly flammable mixture.

One need look no further for an example than the Soviet Union's own disintegration. In the late 1980s, many observers had been skeptical about threats to Soviet cohesion precisely because of the small number and size of republics whose population seemed positively to favor independence. As late as 1989, this probably included only the Baltic republics and Georgia, which together accounted for only 4.6 percent of the Soviet population. What observers then did not realize was how easily these relatively tiny detonator republics, by exposing the emperor's nakedness and trying to shift economic burdens to other republics, could create a spiral of defection that increasingly drew in far less separatist republics by appealing to the ambitions of the republic-level politicians and the suspicions of the populations.

To return to the financial metaphor, a bank run does not require a large number of depositors who positively *desire* to bring down the bank in order for the bank to fold. A few who spread panic can quickly change the logic of the situation, and the fear of ending up empty-handed can overwhelm depositors' sentiments of loyalty or mutual responsibility. Even if the central state could "invest" their contributions far more efficiently in production of public goods, the fear of instability and the opportunity to score personal gains might override such considerations when regional leaders tried to decide how to respond to a mounting crisis. It is far easier in retrospect to find reasons why Chechnya did not become the Russian Lithuania than it was in 1992 to predict just where the cycle of regional mobilization would end.

The blow that ended the Soviet Union was delivered neither by the earliest, most dedicated nationalists nor by the most distinct and unassimilated ethnicities. Some had predicted that Moscow would face the greatest challenges from the Central Asian republics, based on precisely such a notion of their cultural remoteness from the Russian metropole.[20] In fact, it was the failure of the large *Slavic* republics—the most culturally similar—to join forces in late 1991 that made Soviet disintegration inevitable. Among the Central Asian republics, there seems to have been remarkably little enthusiasm for closing up the USSR. Even larger majorities had voted for preserving the Union there in a Union-wide referendum held in March 1991 than in Russia, Ukraine, or Belarus—more than 93 percent in each of the Central Asian republics.[21] Nursultan Nazarbayev, the Kazakh president, was reportedly stunned when he heard of the CIS's creation (Olcott 1997, 556). Had the Slavic republics not made this decision—itself predetermined by the overwhelming vote for independence by Ukraine's voters—some version of the Soviet Union minus the Baltics and probably the Transcaucasus republics might well have survived.

If Yeltsin could so easily reach agreement with the leaders of Ukraine and Belarus to separate their states, it seems plausible that under different circumstances some of Russia's regional leaders might have done the same. Belarus had been part of the Russian empire for longer than some regions of the present Russian Federation—Tyva, Ingushetia, Dagestan, and Balkaria, for instance (Dmitrieva 1996, 9–11). In Belarus, a higher proportion had been in favor of preserving the Soviet Union in March 1991 than in many of Russia's autonomous republics. Such shared history and cultural affinity mattered surprisingly little, however, when the three leaders met in the woods near Minsk.

The argument of this book is not that cultural affinities are unimportant. Indeed, they make it natural that Belarus and Russia later took steps toward reintegration. However, such historical or cultural glue may come unstuck when economic, strategic, or political factors pull in the opposite direction. Major economic divisions or spirals of dissolution often seem to be stronger than ethnic or cultural ties.

Administrative Structures

Even ethnically divided societies may be integrated by powerful administrative structures that stretch from center to periphery. Two kinds of vertical hierarchy are often thought to create incentives for cohesion that can counteract the disruptive impulses of regionalist politics. The first is the administrative bureaucracy. Appointed regional officials who hope to advance to higher posts may associate their advancement with resisting the demands of local politicians. And regional politicians may themselves hope later to receive appointments in administration, should they lose elective office. The second is the national party.[22] Regional politicians who hope later to seek national office must cultivate support of the current national leaders of their party. This will at times require subordinating immediate electoral concerns to acquiring goodwill in the central party organization.[23]

This argument is theoretically plausible and supported by the experience of other countries. However, it does not fit the evidence of this case. Both disciplined parties and bureaucracies were largely absent in post-Soviet Russia. Under the old order, the two had been fused in the party-state. The Communist Party's collapse left the political landscape bereft of nationwide integrating hierarchies. Newly formed national parties had minute followings, fluid and highly personalized identities, and little leverage over supporters in the regions or incumbent officials. They came and went with astonishing speed.

Vertical administrative control within branches of the state had been severely weakened by the decentralization, reform, and organizational decay of the previous ten years. While regional branches of federal agencies such as the state security service, police, procuracy, tax inspectorate, and antimonopoly committee remained formally subordinated to the center, their apparatus had become "intertwined with the regional elite at both personal and institutional levels" (Gelman and Senatova 1995, 218). Each region contained from 36 to 53 branches of federal agencies, ranging from the Ministry of the Interior to the sanitary inspectorate.[24] By 1995, according to two regional specialists, "all federal agencies in the provinces receive money, including salaries, from regional budgets (which are reimbursed from the federal budget) and therefore cannot be independent of the regional executives" (Gelman and Senatova 1995). Federal appointments or dismissals in the regions often required the governor's agreement. Perhaps most telling, a decree issued by Yeltsin in February 1993 created a "two-level system of police, federal and municipal" and subordinated special police troops (OMON) to regional chief executives (Gelman and Senatova 1995). Even *army* commanders in different regions could not always be relied on to follow the center's orders rather than their own wishes or those of regional leaders (Thomas 1995b; see the discussion in the following section).

Some have suggested that the enactment of the December 1993 "Yeltsin Constitution," with its expanded presidential powers, may explain the apparent increase in cohesion. Yet it is quite unclear why this would be the case, since the changes after December 1993—while weakening parliament—also increased the power of regional executives. Regional governors were encouraged to run for relatively safe seats in the upper house of the national parliament, the

Council of Federation, a body that came to represent the regional elites and give them a far more direct role in vetting legislation. The regional legislatures were weakened vis-à-vis the governors. More and more often, regional governors were elected, rendering it politically harder for Yeltsin to dismiss them for insubordination. Furthermore, the constitution left many of the most important issues of center-region relations unresolved, and a process of negotiation leading to individual bilateral power-sharing agreements began almost immediately after its enactment. In fact, most observers would probably agree that the main trend in center-region power relations in the 1990s was not a strengthening of the center because of the new constitution but a strengthening of the regions at the expense of the center.

Fear of Central Use of Force

The fear of central military action to prevent secession, as used in Chechnya, might be what restrained separatist regional leaders within Russia. This was almost certainly a background consideration. Any isolated separatist region that tried to go much too far too fast risked a forcible response. Some have also suggested that President Yeltsin's storming of the parliament in October 1993 may have had a chilling effect on potential regional opponents, who might have inferred that the risk of military retaliation was substantial (e.g., Payin 1995, 198).

Again this argument is theoretically plausible and supported by other cases. Yet there are serious reasons in the case of Russia to doubt that the center's deterrent was sufficient by itself to explain the return to stability. Even if the center's resolve to use force was boosted by the events of 1993–94, its capacity to do so was visibly dwindling. Central leaders could no longer take for granted the cohesion of the army. Regional governors had for several years been forging close relationships with local military commanders, trying with some success "to establish contacts with the generals Soviet-style—at the bathhouse, on hunting or fishing trips, or simply over dinner" (Felgengauer 1994). As central defense allocations were being cut, military detachments were coming to depend materially on their regional political hosts. According to one analyst writing in 1993,

> local authorities are 'luring away' the troop commanders and military district commanders. People in the military realize that it isn't from the center that they're getting their apartments, kindergartens and food. And therefore, if they have to make a choice, they will carry out the orders of the local authorities. (Antonov 1993)

According to another analyst in mid-1994, the "failure to pay servicemen's wages in three military districts—the Far East, Siberia, and Transbaikal—has obliged regional leaders to assume full responsibility for the upkeep of the military on their territory" (Teague 1994b, 7). Rather closer to the Kremlin, Moscow mayor Yuri Luzhkov was said to have established particularly close relations with the capital's military and security leaders through the distribution of patronage. On the eve of the October 1993 crushing of the parliamentary revolt, "Luzhkov offered 500 officers in the elite Taman and Kantemir divisions vouchers for housing in the capital" (Yasmann 1995). Yeltsin subsequently dismissed several leading Moscow security force leaders who had close personal ties to Luzhkov. As the interior minister, Anatoli Kulikov, put it in early 1996: "The army is being ruined just as in February 1917. But then it was done by the Bolsheviks; now it is broken up by nonpayments" (Gordon 1996a).

This general trend toward greater military dependence on regional leaders would erode Moscow's ability to use the army to threaten or subdue such leaders (see also Thomas 1995b). The army's effectiveness in putting down regional rebellions might be further hindered by the fact that, with falling discipline and only a small fraction of conscripts reporting for duty, draftees were serving much closer to home than in the past (Clark and Graham 1995, 346). Their willingness to fire on protesters might be correspondingly diminished.

Did Yeltsin's use of force to crush the parliamentary rebels in the White House in October 1993 cause a subsequent retreat on the part of regional leaders? In the aftermath of the conflict, the president issued a number of decrees removing regional, republic, and local heads of administration who had sided with the parliament, and he dissolved the regional soviets, ordering new elections. Such actions might have intimidated the governors.

However, the evidence does not seem to fit this interpretation. In fact, the months right after Yeltsin's military victory saw a *heightening* of separatist challenges from some quarters—and a rather confused set of responses on the president's part. It was precisely in October 1993 that the leadership of Sverdlovsk Oblast, visibly uncowed by recent events, decided to push ahead with plans to create a "Urals Republic" in the region. That month, the oblast adopted a Urals Republic constitution, and the governor, Eduard Rossel, proudly announced the new state's formation.[25]

Yeltsin eventually dismissed Rossel on November 11. But before that the president *himself* sounded like the intimidated party. At a meeting with regional leaders on November 2, Yeltsin reportedly "stressed that in spite of the desire by certain Moscow politicians to preserve full powers it [was] necessary to separate the powers of the federal government and the regions." The president reportedly added that "the regions have to deal with their own problems on their own, by, among other things, raising their own status because the government has no coherent regional policy."[26] This remarkably conciliatory stance so surprised the prime minister, Viktor Chernomyrdin, that he was seen hastily scratching out part of the text of his own prepared speech.

Other regional leaders also seemed unabashed by Yeltsin's recent use of force. On November 3, the Tatar president, Mintimer Shaimiev, publicly reasserted his republic's sovereignty. And the population in the republics did not rally behind Yeltsin after his show of political muscle. In the December 12 referendum, voters in three-quarters of the republics either rejected the constitutional draft outright, boycotted, or failed to reach the 50 percent quorum (Solnick 1994, 5–6). Overall, no crisis of regional nerves is detectable.

Was Chechnya's unenviable fate what deterred subsequent regional challenges? In fact, the return to quiescence *preceded* the invasion. It seems more reasonable to conclude that the center dared to act forcefully against Chechnya because it had already managed to stabilize relations elsewhere so successfully. What was distinctive about the Chechnya operation was that, despite the explicit rationale, it came at a time when few republics were simultaneously pressing claims against the center and when several of the main "troublemakers" (Tatarstan, Bashkortostan) had actually negotiated agreements with Moscow. Some other factor already seemed to have slowed the sovereignty drive. There is little evidence that, at moments of intense, multilateral regional mobilization, the center's military threat was a credible deterrent. At such moments, Moscow seemed extremely reluctant to use or even threaten military force.

Indeed, the central hard-line advocate of force in Chechnya, Minister for Nationalities Nikolai Yegorov, admitted as much in an interview in March 1995. As reported by the agency Interfax, Yegorov said that

> federal authorities could not have used force against Chechnya three years ago. After the collapse of the Soviet Union, many of the Russian republics and regions began declaring sovereignty . . . At that time, the use of force against the Chechen leadership could have caused an explosion throughout the Northern Caucasus as well as in other parts of the country. According to Yegorov, Chechen leader Dzhokhar Dudaev understood the state of affairs at the time, but did not take into account that the situation in Russia would eventually change, and one republic could not continue to test the strength of the entire country. (*OMRI Daily Digest,* March 29, 1995)

Had Yeltsin exerted force earlier, in Ramazan Abdulatipov's view, he would have faced "several Chechnyas."[27] The president's adviser on political geography, Leonid Smirnyagin, in explaining the decision, pointed out that "the situation is much better than two years ago" (quoted in Thomas 1995a, 6). Recent treaties signed with other Muslim regions had reduced the likelihood that they would take Chechnya's side. After its demoralizing experience in Chechnya, the army's desire to get itself involved in another attempt to crush regional rebellions must have been minuscule—and its deterrent power highly weakened.

Economic Integration or Public Goods

One source of cohesion in divided states may be a high level of economic integration between different regions. Regions that depend on each other for essential goods and resources are less likely to risk creating obstacles to trade flows. Reliance on the center to provide a common currency for such trade may also reduce the appeal of separatism. In fact, the pattern of industrial development in the Soviet Union from Stalin on was designed with precisely such considerations in mind. The economies of different territories were deliberately concentrated in a few sectors to increase their dependence on other parts of the country. The centralized economy, with planning from Moscow, was considered an important source of integration. This type of interregional economic dependence might explain why regions of Russia have generally not pushed separatist demands too far.

A major problem with this argument is that such interregional dependence did not prevent the Soviet Union from disintegrating. As of 1988, the average level of trade between Soviet republics came to about 21 percent of republican GDP—slightly higher than the level of trade between Canadian provinces in 1988 (19.7 percent).[28] This was not far from the degree of integration of Russia's 11 macroregions in the late 1980s. As of 1987, seven of the 11 regions imported 25 percent or less of goods domestically consumed from outside the region, and all imported less than 32 percent. In each case, more than two-thirds of the goods consumed were produced within the macroregion (Matsnev 1996, 37).

The economic and communications sinews that had linked Russia's regions under Soviet rule were themselves increasingly dislocated in the 1990s by the shock of economic reform and decay. Russian interregional trade fell sharply—in some cases to extremely low levels—and the monetary system weakened. With prices moving toward market levels, the traditional supply chains designed by the planners were no longer economically rational and financially sustainable for the enterprises involved. Rising energy and transport costs undermined long-established relationships between geographically distant producers and suppliers, and prompted enterprises to reorient their trading patterns, looking for suppliers and clients closer to home. Foreign trade liberalization encouraged them to shift where possible to export markets. In the words of one analyst, "the absence of efficient domestic transport and communications, along with high freight prices, pushes the outlying regions to seek economic contacts abroad rather than with remote parts of Russia" (Starovoitova 1993, 107). So to the extent that the inefficient structure of economic transactions established under the

Soviet order was what was integrating the country, the change to market principles eroded this.

Regional governments responded to the crises of their local economies with policies of protection and deliberate autarky. By September 1992, 22 regions had "introduced restrictions on trade with other areas and set up export quotas and duties on imports and exports" (Gouré 1994, 405). In Tatarstan, Mordovia, Buryatia, Primore, Amur, Ryazan, Tula, Belgorod, Nizhny Novgorod, Bryansk, and Tver, regional officials restricted the import of vodka from other regions to protect local distilleries.[29] One region even set up a customs post on its border. Foreign trade liberalization meant those with internationally demanded products—oil, gas, diamonds, and so forth—could do far better by exporting than serving traditional customers in other parts of the country. And as rising transport costs drove up domestic prices, raw-materials-producing regions in the Urals, Siberia, and the Far East, in turn, cut their imports of food and consumer goods from other parts of Russia, replacing them with foreign imports. At the same time, complaints of excessive monetary austerity led to the creation of regional bills of exchange and other monetary surrogates, and, in Sverdlovsk Oblast, even to the introduction of a "Urals franc."

The results of these trends were probably most dramatic in the Far East, where rising internal transportation costs helped stimulate a shift in trade toward the Pacific Rim. By 1996, the cost of a round-trip air ticket from Vladivostok to Moscow—about $450, or more than twice the average monthly wage—was beyond the means of most local residents, and more than 40 percent of the Far East's food requirements were now imported from the Pacific Rim countries (Moltz 1996, 182). According to one economist quoted in *Izvestia*, by 1996 it was "cheaper to deliver a shipment of fish from the Far East to Novorossiisk if you sen[t] it by ship through the Indian Ocean and the Atlantic to St Petersburg and then by rail than if you sen[t] it overland across Siberia" (Satter 1996). As two analysts put it, "the Far East is quickly dropping out of the Russian economic space" (Nobuo Arai and Tsuyoshi Hasegawa, quoted in Moltz 1996, 182). One survey found in 1996 that nearly 87 percent of Primore residents favored the creation of a new Far Eastern Republic (Satter 1996). Though the growth of the region's foreign trade moderated in the mid-1990s, the trend of economic distancing from other parts of Russia continued. As of 1995, only 15 percent of all products produced in the territory of Primore went to other parts of Russia—compared to 29 percent exported to other *countries*. By September 1996, only 9 percent of regionally produced goods went to other parts of Russia, compared to 31 percent exported (Kirkow 1997a).

Similar problems could be observed in the Siberian region of Irkutsk. Transport to and from the oblast dropped sharply—river freight transport by 33 percent in 1992, and rail transport by 12 percent (Kirkow 1997a). Siberian residents apparently came to rely more and more on their own private plots for agricultural produce (Kirkow 1997a). In short, available evidence suggests an at least temporary fall in interregional economic integration in Russia in the 1990s, prompting some to predict a "further weakening of the Russian economy's integrity" (Matsnev 1996, 50).

Could the return to greater stability in Russia have reflected a change in regional tastes for public goods or in the technology of public good provision? Had the central Russian state become better able to satisfy local demands for public goods such as economic regulation or law and order, rendering regional attempts to provide such services inefficient by comparison? The more common view was just the opposite: the center was increasingly *failing* to provide basic public goods, forcing regional and local level governments to try to fill the gap even at the cost of considerable economies of scale. Observers complained of a fragmentation rather than a centralization of public good provision.

The example of money is most striking. Economies of scale in the use of a national currency as a means of exchange are universally recognized. Transaction costs for all economic actors are reduced if all use a single, centrally provided money. Yet, in Russia in the late 1990s, an increasing proportion of transactions were being financed by regional surrogate currencies—bill of exchange (*vekselya*), municipal bonds, other securities—or conducted as barter (see Woodruff 1995; Kirkow 1997a). The center's ability to provide even such an essential public good as this was apparently in question. Similarly, many doubted the effectiveness of federal law enforcement—or even external defense. By April 1997, Siberian regions were banding together to guard the Russia-Mongolia border themselves, since the federal government was failing to protect them from horse thieves from across the frontier.[30] Moscow's ability to attract its regions to stay within the federation thus did not seem to have much to do with an increasing capacity to provide public goods.

Political Institutions or Large Number of (Relatively Small) Units

Could distinctive features of Russia's political institutions have enabled it to withstand the regionalist pressures of the early 1990s? Consociational power-sharing arrangements and federal institutions have helped to contain such divisions in other places. Russian politics in the 1990s certainly exhibited elements of center-region power sharing. But the nature of institutions did not match Lijphart's definition of consociationalism. While subcommunities and regions had representation in central political decision making, they did not individually have a veto. Nor was there any sense in which the central government represented a grand coalition of all subcommunities or regional subgroups. Ethnic minorities had some rights—and considerable de facto power—over regional cultural policies, the language of education, and so on, but certainly not complete autonomy on such matters. And there were no guarantees of ethnic or regional proportionality, either formal or informal, in central bureaucratic appointments or spending.

As for federalism, while nominally federal structures existed in Russia, the way they operated violated just about every precept of Weingast's "market-preserving federalism." Under market-preserving federalism, subnational governments "have primary regulatory responsibility over the economy," cannot use this regulatory authority to set up interregional trade barriers, and face a hard budget constraint—that is, are not bailed out by the central government when they face fiscal problems (Weingast 1995, 4). In Russia in the early 1990s, both levels had extensive authority to regulate and often exceeded it, interregional trade barriers were common, and the center both informally and formally (through subventions and payments from a special fund after 1994) bailed out regions facing fiscal problems. In fact, it is doubtful that Russia even met Weingast's requirements (based on Riker) to be classified as a *federal* political system. Few observers would have said that in Russia "the *autonomy* of each government is institutionalized in a manner that makes federalism's restrictions self-enforcing" (Weingast 1995, 4). These institutional arguments, therefore, seem unable to explain how Russia managed to contain its centrifugal pressures.[31]

Another possibility is that Russia's cohesion is explained by the large *number* of regions. Riker and Lemco have argued that the stability of federations increases with the number of their units: "the fewer the units, the more unstable is the federation" (Riker and Lemco 1987). In Riker's formulation, this reflected the calculation of states in a large federation that they would be much more militarily insecure outside than inside the federation. So the logic might not apply so well to regions that are not under military threat. As usual, counterexamples to the general rule can be found. Some federations with few units have survived (Australia), while some with a relatively large number of units have undergone civil wars of secession (the United States, which in 1860 had 32 states). While a large number of units may complicate the task of coordinating a protest against the center, such coordination problems can be overcome.

A second possibility is that the key factor is not the total number of units, but the size of the largest unit relative to the whole. One "oversized" unit might have an encompassing interest in organizing and enforcing collective action by the states against central authority. In the Soviet Union's disintegration, Russia clearly played a coordinating role toward the end.[32] By contrast, among the Russian regions, the largest, the city of Moscow, was tiny relative to the total, containing only about 6 percent of the country's population.

Yet, in other recent cases of state disintegration, it was clearly *not* the largest unit that fought the hardest to secede: indeed, the largest unit sometimes vigorously opposed the state's disintegration. In Yugoslavia, the most ardent separatist was Slovenia, the fifth largest of the six republics, with only 8 percent of the total population, and the largest, Serbia, attempted to use force to *prevent* secession. In the USSR, while Russia's eventual pressure on Gorbachev in late 1991 catalyzed opposition by the other large republics, it was the tiny Baltic states that had blazed the way. Lithuania's share of the Soviet population (1.3 percent) was barely half Tatarstan's share of the Russian population (2.5 percent); even if all three Baltic republics are lumped together, their populations come to only 2.7 percent of the Soviet total.

While Russia's constituent units are relatively small, they were by no means too small to be viable as independent states. Bashkortostan and Tatarstan—the two largest, after the cities of Moscow and St. Petersburg—each have populations greater than 70 existing countries, ranging from Ireland and New Zealand to Panama and Uruguay. More important, the potential for secession by the early 1990s focused not only on separate republics or oblasts but on broader associations of regions. By 1991, 11 regional organizations had been set up to coordinate local economic policy and lobby Moscow on issues of common concern. They were largely non-overlapping, covered most of the country, and corresponded closely to the economic region boundaries of the former RSFSR (Petrov, Mikheyev, and Smirnyagin 1993). Some of these at different times adopted separatist rhetoric, others denied that they wished to secede though sometimes seeming to protest a little too much (see Radvanyi 1992). The development was noted by Ruslan Khasbulatov, the speaker of the Russian parliament, who warned in mid-1992: "Separatism in Russia . . . has taken not only a national but also a regional character. Regional separatism is clearly behind the idea of creating a Siberian, Far Eastern, or Urals republic, and the difficulties which arose with a number of Russian regions at the time of the signing of the Federal Treaty" (Khasbulatov 1993, 250–51).

Perhaps the most likely secessionist was the large Siberian Agreement association formed in 1990, which came eventually to include all 19 of the West and East Siberian regions. At its height, the association's constituent members contained a population of 24.4 million, or about one-sixth of all Russian citizens. Some of its members talked of establishing an independent "Siberian Republic" (Petrov et al. 1993; Tolz 1993a). Siberian regionalism was taken particularly seriously by politicians at the center because of the apparent cohesion of the various leaders, the atmosphere of cooperation between Siberian legislative and executive branches, and the protogovernment structures the association began to set up (Hughes 1994, 1137).

At a conference of Siberian deputies held in Krasnoyarsk in March 1992 some overtly advocated separation. A deputy from the Tyumen Oblast soviet, B. Perov, argued that "the congress should adopt a manifesto on independence, declare itself the supreme authority in Siberia and at the same time dissolve on the spot all the colonial organs of Russian power" (quoted in Sakwa 1993, 191). The meeting's final resolution demanded that the Russian Supreme Soviet and the president "take urgent and comprehensive measures for the decolonisation of Siberia." Had such regionalist claims hardened and multiplied, the danger of disintegration would have been more than hypothetical.

Selective Fiscal Appeasement: The Argument in Brief

Some of the factors previously discussed may indeed have contributed to Russia's survival. But, by themselves, they do not add up to a convincing explanation. Even those that do sound like part of the story raise additional puzzles. If cultural and ethnic identities are not primordially fixed determinants of political preferences but relatively fluid and rearrangeable sets of values and narratives, why did regional identities not crystallize more sharply as the economic and political interests of Russia's regions diverged? Why does ethnic or cultural "glue" stick in some settings but not in others? If it is harder to coordinate rebellions when the number of units is large, what explains why interregional associations set up to overcome such coordination problems failed to make headway? And if fear of the application of central force helped deter regional defections, how did the center manage to keep this deterrent credible and effective even as its control over enforcement agencies in the regions and over governors was so evidently shrinking?

Besides these factors, some additional source of cohesion must have helped to contain the centrifugal forces that seemed to various observers to threaten the Russian state's survival. I argue that the missing element—which conditioned how ethnic identity, central administrative resources, and federal institutions interacted—was a particular fiscal policy on the part of central authorities. By using subsidies and tax breaks to selectively accommodate those regions most prone to stage disruptive protest actions, the center managed to defuse crises in many potential hotspots before they could spread. Central fiscal policy was used to prevent bandwagons of protest from gathering speed.

Furthermore, the dramatic confrontations between center and regions that aroused such alarm were themselves an essential element in this integrating mechanism. Amid the uncertainty that accompanied democratization, regional protests became the only way to communicate credibly a certain type of information. Paradoxically, the signals that anticenter protests provided were of great value to the center itself. Such signals made it possible for the federal government to consolidate its power by targeting its limited fiscal resources in a politically prudent way. An interactive feedback of elections, regional protest, and fiscal redistribution compensated at least temporarily for the absence of vertical integrating institutions such as national parties and disciplined hierarchical bureaucracies, and helped to keep Russia intact.

Regional political leaders revolt against central authority for one of two reasons. They may do so strategically, judging that such revolts will increase the benefits that they can expect to receive from the center. Or they may do so because such revolts—regardless of whether they elicit central concessions—serve a political purpose within the regional leader's own constituency. They may enhance the leader's local support, encouraging constituents to rally behind him, or may help him to outmaneuver local rivals. I argue that regional leaders balance the expected benefits of revolt—both material and mobilizational—against the expected costs of central sanctions.

The ultimate central sanction, of course, is force. But few regimes have the resources to suppress rebellions in more than a few of the country's regions at once. Therefore, the risk of—or expected "pain" from—such sanctions decreases as more regions simultaneously rebel. Because of the limited enforcement resources of the center, each region that openly defies Moscow reduces the risk for others to do the same. As more regions join a bandwagon of protest, the "pain" the center can inflict on an additional rebel rapidly falls to a very low level, and all who could benefit from defying the center will do so. Those that previously paid positive net taxes to the center will not be willing to continue. Even if the central state provides public goods valuable to the regions, the free-rider logic will tend to prevail, leading to rapid collapse of the central state's fiscal powers. Even those that benefit from centrally provided public goods will prefer to shirk on contributions. When a central government cannot raise revenue, it ceases to exist.

Preventing federal disintegration, therefore, means preventing such a bandwagon from picking up momentum. And in order to keep its deterrent powerful and credible, the center must prevent the most determined rebels from opening the way for others. The most determined rebels will be those regional leaders with the greatest local *mobilizational* motive to defy the center, because they also have any strategic incentive to rebel that the others have: the same instrumental logic applies to all. If such leaders have sufficiently strong domestic political reasons to wish to turn themselves into anticenter local heroes, it may be impossible for the center to deter them with threats of sanctions. Even the certainty of being "punished" may not be enough—and punishment may itself even increase their mobilizational gains, reinforcing the tendency of local constituents to rally behind them.

Yet, while the threat of force is ineffective, increasing net transfers to such a regional leader will at times be enough to dissuade him from launching a public revolt. Why would appeasement work where deterrence alone fails? The answer suggested by empirical analysis of Russian politics is that material benefits to a potentially rebellious region can reduce the mobilizational gains a strategy of revolt offers to its political leaders. The degree of anticenter sentiment among the population is reduced by greater transfers to—and state spending in—the region. In Russia in the early 1990s, when regional leaders increased local spending in order to buy themselves support this also appears to have reduced local antipathy to the central government in Moscow. And when antipathy to the central government fell, the regional leaders became, in turn, less likely to protest against the center, presumably out of fear that their constituency would no longer support such a risky approach.

At the same time, the center's example of appeasing one rebellious region may give other regions a strategic incentive to rebel opportunistically in the hope of also being appeased. But these opportunistic rebels will be deterred by the knowledge that because the *non-opportunistic* rebels have already been demobilized they will be isolated and subjected to more severe punishment. By demobilizing the most determined protesters, the center increases the force of its deterrent against the less determined ones.

The logic of this argument—formalized in appendix A—suggests that the optimal central strategy for preserving a federation at moments of crisis will often be to extract relatively higher net taxes from those with a low mobilizational incentive to revolt—regions where the local population is unlikely to rally behind a rebellious leader—and use them to appease the regional leaders with a high mobilizational incentive to challenge the center. By doing this, the central regime can conserve the deterrent necessary to keep the state from disintegrating in a race for the exit.

But in periods of democratization, the center will not necessarily know which regions have the greatest mobilizational incentive to revolt—and which should therefore be appeased. Such incentives may change from period to period in response to changes in the region's internal political balance and other factors. All governors learn to arrive at the president's office with chilling tales and warnings of social explosions. Central policymakers have no way to be certain which are bluffing. Each period, they can only guess which are sincere on the basis of regions' past behavior and characteristics, set tax and transfer rates accordingly, and hope for the best. If a region nevertheless rebels, this will credibly signal that its net tax assessment was above the threshold at which rebellion becomes rational even given the risk of punishment, and the center should reduce its assessment before the next round if it wants to avoid another challenge. (It must also carry out whatever threats to punish it has made, in order to keep them credible.) By a process of *tâtonnement,* the center can move toward the set of tax and transfer assessments that maximizes the center's net tax surplus while inhibiting all rebellions—if there *is* such an equilibrium set of assessments that yields a positive central surplus.

In Russia in the early 1990s such a policy of central fiscal appeasement was carried out, and it does appear to have helped stabilize a federation under extreme stress. Larger net transfers were channeled to regions with a demonstrated ability and resolve to challenge central incumbents through separatist gestures, strikes, or protest voting. Increases in net fiscal transfers led to subsequent increases in regional government spending. Such increases in spending were, in turn, associated with a more favorable local trend in voting for Yeltsin and associated central parties of reform. And where votes for Yeltsin increased more than average, regional leaders were more likely subsequently to take his side and less likely to oppose him publicly at moments of national crisis. In short, by shifting fiscal resources around, the center was able to prevent spirals of protest from escalating to a point at which they would have undermined the federation's cohesion.[33]

However, the center's ability to redistribute in a way that defuses regional crises does not mean it necessarily has the resources to buy a stable electoral majority. Economic reform itself sharply redistributed income between sectors, in ways that were exacerbated by the general drop in economic performance. Agriculture suffered, while raw-materials-producing and exporting regions were major gainers. While the center's strategy for redistributing between regions bought incumbents some votes in the more depressed regions, it blunted and disorganized protests rather than securing widespread positive support. And the additional votes were not sufficient to compensate for those lost to the discontent over the costs of economic reform and depression. The central government's ability to use fiscal transfers to soften the blow for politically important constituencies and preserve its national electorate was limited by the lack of central resources and erosion of the tax collection system.

The linked successes and failures of this policy suggest one explanation for the disastrous decision to launch a military operation against Chechnya in late 1994. In part, Chechnya had become increasingly isolated in the previous two years, as one by one the other separatist regions had been bought off with federal concessions and had signed separate agreements with Moscow.[34] At the same time, Yeltsin's eroding popularity among his own past supporters may have helped lure him into a tragically misguided attempt to reforge his charismatic appeal through decisive but risky action. The invasion of Chechnya was not necessary to prevent the state's collapse as was claimed at the time. The immediate threat of disintegration had been far greater in 1992 or 1993, yet military force had been rejected. Rather, it was the decline of this threat that made invasion more conceivable.

Yet, Chechnya was exactly the region where sanctions—even military force—were least likely to work. First, the leader, Dzhokhar Dudaev, was a "mobilizational" rather than a "strategic" separatist. Indeed, he was the only head of executive in an ethnic republic within Russia in the early 1990s who had come to power as leader of a nationalist movement.[35] And historical and cultural factors strongly predisposed the population to rally behind local leaders in conflicts with Moscow. War, while imposing horrendous costs on the population, served to boost Dudaev's popularity rather than Yeltsin's.

By the 1996 presidential election campaign, Yeltsin appeared to be desperately trying to win back the ground he had lost in the electoral popularity game. Central policy aimed at reorienting spending toward constituencies, both regional and social, where votes were needed and could presumably be bought most cheaply. By mid-February 1996, the president had promised increases in social spending amounting to an estimated 41 trillion rubles (or $8.6 billion), designed to raise pensions, student stipends, benefits for miners, and defense spending and to rebuild Chechnya.[36] As the evidence in chapter 4 will suggest, he had some success in winning votes in regions by reducing wage arrears and signing special decrees conferring aid (see also Treisman 1996a).

Paradoxically, Yeltsin found himself supported during the 1996 campaign by the leaders of some of the most vigorous autonomy-seekers of the previous five years. Tatar President Mintimer Shaimiev endorsed him in February, saying that Yeltsin "adheres to democracy more than others, and guarantees the current relationship between Tatarstan and the center."[37] He was joined a week later by the Bashkir president, Murtaza Rakhimov, who told the news agency Interfax that despite the Russian president's "numerous blunders" he intended to stand by him. "It was with Yeltsin that Bashkortostan signed an historic power-sharing agreement. It was with Yeltsin that we embarked on the road to reform and it is with Yeltsin that we intend to walk the road of reform to its logical end."[38] Perhaps the height of absurdity came when Alla Dudaeva, whose husband, the Chechen president, had been assassinated by a Russian missile, also announced that she planned to vote for Yeltsin.[39] And even Eduard Rossel—the politician who had made his career by demanding the creation of a "Urals Republic" in Sverdlovsk, had been fired by Yeltsin, but then had been popularly reelected first to the regional parliament, then as the region's governor—had changed his tune since the center signed a special agreement with the oblast transferring to it various economic rights. "Our province's new possibilities can be realized only if Russia's top state leadership remains stable," he told an interviewer as early as January 1996. "Therefore, if Russian President Boris Yeltsin decides to run in the forthcoming election for head of state, I, as governor of his native province, will do everything I can to promote Boris Nikolayevich's victory."[40]

Plan of the Book

A formal model that demonstrates the logic of the argument sketched in this chapter can be found in appendix A. The following chapters establish different parts of the argument empirically. Chapter 2 reviews the main developments in the history of center-region relations in Russia during the early 1990s, providing historical background. Chapter 3 analyzes the pattern of fiscal redistribution between Russia's 89 regions and the central state in the early 1990s. It examines why some regions received large net transfers from Moscow while others paid large net tax remittances into the central state's coffers. It demonstrates the first element of the argument outlined in the previous section: *fiscal redistribution in Russia in the early 1990s favored those regions with the capacity and resolve to make credible threats to disrupt economic or constitutional order.* The next chapter examines whether such net fiscal transfers—when they increased or decreased local state spending—affected the trend in public opinion and voting in the subsidized or taxed regions. It demonstrates the second key element of the book's argument: *increases in regional spending (themselves related to increases in central transfers) led to higher levels of voter support for central incumbents.* Chapter 5 analyzes whether regional trends in voting were, in turn, related to the strategies of regional political leaders in their interactions with Moscow. It finds, among other things, that *executives of regions where the vote of support for Yeltsin had been rising were more likely to support him at moments of crisis.* Putting together the results of the three empirical chapters suggests the interpretation already outlined: by extracting and redistributing fiscal resources from docile to rebellious regions, the center managed to demobilize bandwagons of local protest and preserve its political control. Though costly in terms of social equity and economic efficiency, this pattern of politicized redistribution helps to explain why Russia in the early 1990s survived the serious threats to its integrity.

The argument so far has been specific to Russia. But, if correct, it has implications for many other cases of territorially divided states. Can policies of selective fiscal appeasement explain survival of other troubled federations? Can the lack of such policies explain why some divided states have collapsed? I do not try to answer these questions in this book, though I sketch out some speculative hypotheses in the concluding chapter. In chapter 6, though, I address a different, narrower comparative question. If the argument helps to explain Russia's experience, is it at least consistent with what we know of similar cases? Besides Russia, three other communist or former communist states had nominally federal structures and ethnic minorities. Each of these—Yugoslavia, Czechoslovakia, and the Soviet Union—disintegrated. Chapter 6 examines the pre-dissolution fiscal history of each of these. It argues that in none of these was a comparable central attempt made to appease the most likely separatist regions. Whether or not such a policy might have delayed or prevented disintegration remains a matter for speculation. But experiences of territorial disintegration in these countries appear quite consistent with the explanation given for Russia's cohesion. Finally, the concluding chapter examines the book's implications for understanding of Russian politics in the 1990s as well as for theoretical debates over the causes of state disintegration, ethnonationalist activism, and the implications of ethnic divisions and federal structure for implementing economic reforms.[41]

CHAPTER 2

Center and Regions in Russia

This chapter reviews the historical background to Russia's struggle in the 1990s to reconcile politics and geography. In the following sections the focus moves from the country's territorial structure to its changing constitutional arrangements, and then to the political battles and bargaining that intertwined with the constitutional debate. I describe the rise of conflict between center and regions in 1992–93 and the unexpected easing of tensions in 1994. Finally, I examine the course of events that led to the military intervention in Chechnya later that year.

Changing Maps

During the past century, maps of Russia's internal divisions have been redrawn a number of times. As of the late 1990s, the country was divided into 89 "subjects of the federation." Among these were 21 republics, named after one or more non-Russian ethnicity; 49 *oblasts,* or provinces; and six *krais,* or territories. The two capital cities of Moscow and St. Petersburg also had the status of federation subjects. So did 10 "autonomous *okrugs*" and one "autonomous oblast," located within various oblasts and krais, each of which was, like the republics, named after one or more non-Russian "titular nationality."[1]

This structure was the latest in a series of arrangements by which successive Moscow-based regimes had governed the provinces. The administrative architecture of imperial Russia reflected the tension between the court's desire to centralize authority and the practical difficulties of doing so in a vast country with an undeveloped state apparatus. As new territories were brought into the empire, Muscovite and imperial Russian governments often retained the existing local administrative structures, permitting limited self-government in some areas. Under Alexander I, Poland and Finland had constitutions and national diets with the right to legislate on internal matters, Courland and Livonia had their own charters, and the nomads of Central Asia and Siberia, as well as the Jews, enjoyed considerable autonomy. However, as the bureaucracy developed toward the end of the imperial era, most local autonomy was curtailed and replaced by centralized administration (see Pipes 1974, 250–51).

The heartland of imperial Russia was divided into *guberniyas,* each of is administered by a governor appointed by the tsar. These administrative divisions were initially retained after the revolution. But in the 1920s and early 1930s Stalin experimented with new administrative units, consolidating some smaller guberniyas into larger "oblasts." Between the mid-1930s and mid-1940s, however, these were split once again into smaller units—also called "oblasts"—which roughly corresponded in size to the imperial guberniyas.[2]

Meanwhile, considerable change was occurring in the status of regions with large non-Russian populations. During the early postrevolution years Moscow, now under Bolshevik rule, found itself once again struggling to control distant and restive provinces. Tatar and Bashkir republics were created on the Volga and in the Urals in 1919–20, and the Dagestan and Gorno republics were set up in the North Caucasus in 1921.[3] Autonomous oblasts appeared in other areas, named after the Chuvash, Mari, Adygei, and other ethnic groups. During the 1920s and early 1930s, some of these were upgraded to the status of autonomous republics. From the late 1920s, autonomous okrugs began to be set up to host smaller nationalities—the Nentsi, Khanti, Mansi, and others.

Despite their earlier opposition to the principle of federalism, the Bolsheviks in power found federal structures a useful expedient to contain and gradually reverse the spontaneous decentralization occurring during the revolution and civil war years. Formal rights were issued to republics and lower-level regions, and supreme legislative authority was entrusted to the soviets at each level. The Russian republic was itself given a nominally federal structure and christened the Russian Soviet Federative Socialist Republic (RSFSR). Yet these concessions were rendered moot in practice by the personnel power and administrative dominance of the Communist Party, which became increasingly centralized (Pipes 1957, chap. 6).

The administrative architecture crystallized with the enactment of the 1936 constitution, which defined 15 autonomous republics within the RSFSR. After this, changes in national-territorial units occurred only when foreign territories were annexed (Simon 1991, 147). A sixteenth republic was added to the RSFSR when the previously independent Tuva People's Republic on the border with Mongolia was incorporated, first as an autonomous oblast in 1944 and later as a republic. The same structure of oblasts, krais, and 16 autonomous republics was inherited by Gorbachev at the beginning of perestroika.

The 16 autonomous republics in Russia under the Soviet regime had had their own constitutions, but, unlike the Union republics, not even a formal right of secession (Sakwa 1993, 115). Autonomous oblasts and okrugs had no constitution and few rights of self-government. They were subordinate both to the central authorities and to those of the oblast or krai in which they were located.[4] The rights of such lower-level units were highly circumscribed even in the legal framework. The 1978 Russian Constitution assigned to the federal leadership responsibilities for the all-inclusive residual category of "other issues of republican significance" (Tolz 1993b).

Reforming the System

This was the order—nominally federal but in practice highly centralized and controlled by the party—that existed when Gorbachev came to power. Four autonomous oblasts—Adygeia, Karachaevo-Cherkessia, Gorno-Altai, and Khakassia—were elevated to the status of autonomous republics in 1991. The next year, Ingushetia, formerly part of the Chechen-Ingush Republic, was recognized as a separate republic. The status of Chechnya remained uncertain throughout the mid-1990s.

Perestroika weakened party control and led to a decentralization of power in practice, which accelerated a spontaneous devolution of control that had begun under the Brezhnev regime (Bahry 1987a). During the late Soviet years, mafias of party, state, and economic leaders had crystallized at the regional level, linked by mutual protection societies and informal networks.[5] In a radical departure, Gorbachev attempted from late 1988 to transfer power from the local party committees to the system of legislative bodies (*soviets*) and their executive committees (*ispolkomi*), which had always performed the functional roles of administration, under the ideological tutelage and personnel control of the party. In part to rejuvenate the membership of these soviets, in part to give them greater legitimacy, he introduced the first competitive national elections—first for the Union-level parliament in 1989, then for Union republic and regional legislatures in 1990.

These elections, held in conditions still biased in favor of local party elites, did not see a radical shift of governing personnel in most regions. The old party leaders were generally elected to the soviets and then chosen by the rank and file to head their ispolkom. But the elections created a new system of authority in which legitimacy depended in part on local support as well as central favor. At the same time, the elections opened up a mechanism for rehabilitating locally popular leaders who had fallen out with the central party bosses. Boris Yeltsin's reviving fortunes symbolized this change. Thrown out of the Politburo by Gorbachev in 1988, he was elected to the Soviet Congress of People's Deputies in 1989, then to the Russian Congress of People's Deputies in 1990, and in May 1990 the body elected him its chairman. In June 1991, he was popularly elected Russia's first president.

In August 1991, after the collapse of the attempted coup, the central party's control over political events in the regions crumbled. The victorious Russian authorities set about building a new basis for administering the provinces. The Supreme Soviet passed a decree creating the post of "head of administration" (or governor) in the 55 oblasts and krais. These were to replace the ispolkom chairmen and were to be accountable to both the president and regional legislatures. A law passed by the Supreme Soviet in October specified that the heads of administration would be popularly elected by the end of 1991. But Yeltsin asked that the elections be postponed until December 1992, and the Congress of People's Deputies acquiesced. In the meantime, Yeltsin appointed heads of administration by decree, often after consultation with the regional soviet leadership or using a shortlist the soviet leadership provided.[6] In December 1992, the Supreme Soviet again put off most elections for governors, this time until 1995 (Wishnevsky 1994, 8). In 1995, Yeltsin postponed such elections again, until late 1996.

But in specific cases, elections were permitted. Mayors had been elected in Moscow and St. Petersburg at the same time as the presidential election of June 1991. Some oblasts were allowed to elect their governors in April 1993, around the time of a national referendum on Yeltsin's rule. Such exceptions were made when the oblast soviet demanded such an election, or when it was considered necessary to break a deadlock between the oblast soviet and the appointed governor.

Those regional elections that were held in 1993–94 were generally disappointing for reformers. In April 1993, Yeltsin appointees lost to communists in Orel, Smolensk, Lipetsk, Penza, Chelyabinsk, and Bryansk oblasts (Wishnevsky 1994, 8). Yeltsin seems to have been aware of the leverage that popular election gave unsympathetic regional governors against him. After October 1993, he passed a decree "giving him exclusive authority to appoint and dismiss regional governors" (Paretskaya 1996, 35). In 1996, he passed another decree on increasing discipline in the executive branch, which asserted the president's right to dismiss governors even if they had been elected.[7]

In the ethnic republics, by contrast, elections for president or head of government were the norm from the start. The first such vote took place in Tatarstan, where Mintimer Shaimiev was elected president at the time of the Russian presidential election of June 1991. Soon after this, elections were held in Chechnya, Mari El, Sakha, and Mordovia. By June 1996, 16 of the 21 republics had elected presidents or heads of state, while 22 of the oblasts and krais had elected governors (see table 2.1).

After the 1991 coup, Yeltsin also created the institution of president's representative in the region, with the mission to report to him and monitor implementation of federal laws and decrees. However, these representatives often came into conflict with local soviets or governors. When Yeltsin increasingly took the governors' side, the institution atrophied.

The other main focus of regional politics was the regional legislatures, or soviets. Before August 1991 these were large and unwieldy bodies. Soviets at different levels contained about 1.4 million members—or about 1 percent of the population (Sakwa 1993, 187). After the coup attempt, regional soviets were in-

TABLE 2.1. Elections of Regional Leaders, January 1991 through June 1996

Region	Election Date[a]	Winner
Moscow City	12.6.91	Popov
St. Petersburg	12.6.91	Sobchak
Tatarstan	12.6.91	Shaimiev
Chechen-Ingush Rep.	27.10.91	Dudaev
Mari El	8–14.12.91	Zotin
Sakha	20.12.91	Nikolaev
Mordovia	22.12.91	Guslyannikov
Kabardino-Balkaria	5.1.92	Kokov
Adygeia	5.1.92	Dzharimov
Tyva	15.3.92	Oorzhak
Ingushetia	28.2.93	Aushev[b]
Kalmykia	11.4.93	Ilyumzhinov
Orlovskaya Obl.	11.4.93	Stroyev
Penzenskaya Obl.	11.4.93	Kovlyagin
Lipetskaya Obl.	11.4.93	Narolin
Amurskaya Obl.	25.4.93	Surat
Bryanskaya Obl.	25.4.93	Lodkin
Krasnoyarsky Krai	25.4.93	Zubov
Chelyabinskaya Obl.	25.4.93	Sumin
Smolenskaya Obl.	25.4.93	Glushenkov
Bashkortostan	12.12.93	Rakhimov
Chuvashia	26.12.93	Fyodorov
North Ossetia	16.1.94	Galazov
Ingushetia	27.2.94	Aushev
Irkutskaya Obl.	27.3.94	Nozhikov
Karelia	17.4.94	Stepanov[b]
Komi	8.5.94	Spiridonov
Buryatia	30.6.94	Potapov
Sverdlovskaya Obl.	20.8.95	Rossel
Kalmykia	15.10.95	Ilyumzhinov[b]
Moskovskaya Obl.	17.12.95	Tyazhlov
Nizhegorodskaya Obl.	17.12.95	Nemtsov
Novgorod Obl.	17.12.95	Prusak
Novosibirskaya Obl.	17.12.95	Mukha
Omskaya Obl.	17.12.95	Polezhaev
Orenburgskaya Obl.	17.12.95	Yelagin
Tomskaya Obl.	17.12.95	Kress
Tverskaya Obl.	17.12.95	Platov
Tambovskaya Obl.	17.12.95	Ryabov
Belgorodskaya Obl.	17.12.95	Savchenko
Yaroslavskaya Obl.	17.12.95	Lisitsyn
Primorsky Krai	17.12.95	Nazdratenko
St. Petersburg	2.6.96	Yakovlev

Source: compiled from McFaul and Petrov (1995) and from press reports.
[a]Date is days.month.year.
[b]Ran unopposed.

structed to form a "small soviet," one-fifth the size of the full body, to act as a working legislature. Then, after the crisis of October 1993, Yeltsin ordered the regional soviets completely dissolved. In their place, smaller dumas were created. This remained the basic architecture of regional government as of late 1998.

Constitutional Debate

Throughout the reform period, the constitutional division of powers and responsibilities between regional and central government remained a focus of continual debate. The first Russian Congress of People's Deputies, which met in June 1990, decided to work on a new constitution to replace the 1978 RSFSR Constitution as well as a federal treaty to define relations between Moscow and the regions (Sheehy 1993, 38). Responsibility for producing a draft fell to the Supreme Soviet's Constitutional Commission, initially chaired by Yeltsin himself, and later led by its executive secretary, Oleg Rumyantsev. In November, the first version was published (Teague 1994a, 43, 30).

This draft would have reduced the ethnoterritorial hierarchy to two levels: on the one hand, "national and territorial state formations, having the status of equal republics"—that is, the former autonomous republics—and, on the other, "federal territories"—that is, the oblasts and krais (Teague 1994a, 31). But this was intended as only a temporary accommodation. Ethnic territorial definitions were to be gradually phased out and replaced by about 50 new territorial units with equal rights and status, similar to Germany's *Länder*.

Such territorial units were to go by the name of *zemli,* or "lands." During his presidential campaign in the spring of 1991, Yeltsin supported even more fundamental consolidation, advocating the division of the country into eight to ten large economic regions (Sakwa 1993, 199). However, after a second draft of the Rumyantsev constitution was published in October 1991, still incorporating the notion of *zemli,* intense opposition emerged among the autonomous republics. Sakha and Tatarstan "threatened to leave the Federation if the proposal was not dropped" (Solnick 1995, 57). The word *zemli,* Rumyantsev said later, had served as "a red flag to the autonomies."[8] Such proposals to de-ethnify Russia's administrative architecture were subsequently abandoned.[9] But the effort to build consensus on a new draft bogged down.

Amid the confusion left by the Soviet Union's disappearance, some central actors came to consider it crucial to reach at least a temporary constitutional agreement with the leadership of the republics and other regions. In March 1992, three versions of a "Federation Treaty" were signed—with the leaders respectively of the republics, of the autonomous okrugs and autonomous oblast, and of the oblasts, krais, and capital cities.

The Federation Treaty gave the republics various attributes of statehood that were not shared by the other units. These included the right to have a constitution, to elect a president, and to have a supreme court. The treaty also expanded republics' rights over natural resources, budgets, and foreign trade (Sakwa 1993, 129). Populations of the republics were assigned property rights in the "land, minerals, water, flora, and fauna" on the republic's territory, but those of oblasts and krais were not (Teague 1994a, 37). (Nevertheless, the "possession, use, and disposal of land, minerals, water and other natural resources" was to be regulated by both republic and federation laws, which limited such rights in practice.) The treaty also required the consent of republican authorities before Moscow could impose a state of emergency in a republic; no such regional consent was required in oblasts and krais. Unlike the republics, the other units were not recognized as "sovereign states."

The treaty defined which powers were reserved for the center, which jointly exercised by center and subjects of the federation, and which reserved for the subjects. It stated that disputes over jurisdiction between the center and the subjects were to be settled by the Constitutional Court. (Reports suggested, however, that such conflicts continued to go unresolved and to unfold chaotically; Teague 1994a, 36.) Various issues were, perhaps deliberately, left vague. The distribution of profits from exports, relative tax rates, and levels of federal subsidies to local budgets remained to be determined by negotiation or federal resolutions.

That this treaty was signed at all seems in retrospect quite surprising. Central support for it was less than solid. According to Ramazan Abdulatipov, then the chairman of the Supreme Soviet's Council of Nationalities, President Yeltsin had initially wanted to sign individual agreements with each of the republics in turn and had had to be convinced of the need first to sign an overarching federal treaty with all subjects.[10] Enthusiasm on the part of the republics was also initially muted. Tatarstan and the Chechen-Ingush Republic categorically refused to sign. Bashkortostan bargained for a special appendix giving it greater rights over foreign trade; Kalmykia also insisted on special amendments; and Sakha received additional rights over natural resources (Solnick 1995; Teague 1994a, 35). Karelia obtained special guarantees (Slider 1994, 247). In all, nine of the 18 republics that signed the Federation Treaty attached special conditions (Teague 1994a, 38).

As conflict developed between Yeltsin and the Supreme Soviet during 1992, the constitutional process itself became caught up in this struggle. According to the 1978 RSFSR Constitution, the parliament was the only organ that could amend it (Teague 1994a, 44). Yeltsin sought nevertheless to wrest control of the drafting process from Rumyantsev's commission. In the spring of 1992, he encharged his aide Sergei Shakhrai with coming up with a new version.

Then, in the summer of 1993 the president convened an ad hoc "constitutional convention" in the Kremlin, made up of regional leaders, public figures, lawyers, and various other notables. The participants discussed constitutional drafts, but agreement proved elusive. The most significant bone of contention turned out to be the relative rights of republics, on one hand, and oblasts and krais, on the other. The republics objected to the lack of explicit recognition of their "sovereignty," and in the end the compromise draft approved by the convention on July 12 did declare the republics "sovereign states within the Russian Federation." This was not enough to satisfy the leadership of Tatarstan, whose delegation walked out. And the draft still ran into numerous problems when it was circulated to regional legislatures and executives.

As tension between the president and parliament escalated in Moscow, Yeltsin tried once again to reach agreement with the regional leaders, proposing the creation of a "Federation Council" to serve as the upper house of a new national parliament, made up of the heads of executive and legislature of each of the 89 federation subjects (see Solnick 1994). It was hoped that this Federation Council could give legitimacy to the new draft constitution, bypassing the Supreme Soviet. But regional and republic leaders rejected this plan in mid-September.

The next twist in the constitutional saga came on September 21, when Yeltsin issued a decree dissolving parliament and calling new elections. Simultaneously, a referendum on a new constitution was to be held, substituting popular legitimacy for the old parliament's approval. But members of the parliament refused to dissolve it and leave the building. A standoff developed. After the parliamentary leadership incited armed mobs to attack the Moscow mayoralty building and the Ostankino television center, Yeltsin ordered troops to storm the parliament, under artillery support from tanks which set the White House on fire.

During the buildup of this confrontation, both the parliamentary leadership and the president appealed to the regions for support. Most regional legislature leaders took the side of the national parliament, while most governors stood by Yeltsin. On September 30, parliamentary leaders from 15 Siberian regions met in Novosibirsk at the invitation of the oblast's governor, Vitali Mukha. The assembled leaders threatened to create a Siberian republic, to withhold all taxes from Moscow, and to cut communications along the Trans-Siberian Railway if the president did not rescind his decree (Teague 1994a, 47). Around the same time, the president of Kalmykia, Kirsan Ilyumzhinov, along with the chairman of the Constitutional Court, Valeri Zorkin, set up a "Council of Subjects of the Federation," which itself declared the presidential decree void (Payin 1995, 196).

Yeltsin's eventual victory over the parliament permitted him to retake the constitutional initiative. A rapidly assembled draft was presented to the public in a referendum in December at the time of the new parliamentary elections and was officially declared to have received 58.4 percent of the votes. This constitution reduced some of the disparities in status between republics and oblasts and krais. It dropped the definition of republics as "sovereign states" and eliminated separate republican citizenship (Tolz 1996, 42–44). Republics were still allowed to have a "constitution" and to elect their own presidents, however, while nonrepublics could only have a "charter." Throughout the early 1990s, most of the republics had been adopting their own constitutions, which often contradicted the federal one. Many of these asserted the supremacy of republican law over federal legislation. And Tyva's constitution, for instance, explicitly allowed the republic to secede from Russia (Slider 1994, 248).

The 1993 Constitution is often viewed as less pro-republic than the Federation Treaty. Yet, in fact the Constitution explicitly incorporated the Federation Treaty (Article 11). Another article (Article 1 of Section 2) added, nevertheless, that in the case of any inconsistency between the Constitution on the one hand and the Federation Treaty (or bilateral treaties between the center and regions) on the other, the federal Constitution would prevail. The lingering ambiguity was probably deliberate.

At first glance, the enactment of this constitution might seem like the logical end to Russia's constitutional process. In fact, activity continued with hardly a break. Almost immediately, Yeltsin began to negotiate and sign bilateral agreements with individual republics (and later oblasts) defining the division of powers more concretely. In part, such agreements were considered necessary because the constitution enumerated many "shared responsibilities," without explaining how these responsibilities should be shared.

But the agreements also provided specific benefits. The first, signed with Tatarstan in February 1994, gave the republic additional control over natural resources, permitted it to create a national bank, gave greater autonomy in foreign trade, and allowed it to "exempt its young men from military service in the Russian army" (Teague 1996). A treaty with Bashkortostan later that year affirmed the republic's "independence" and gave it control over its budget, judiciary, and prosecutor (Solnick 1994, 55). After September 1995, Yeltsin began negotiating similar agreements with oblasts and krais (Hughes 1996, 41–42). By mid-1996, 24 of these had been signed.

Such a differentiated approach to the regions has proved controversial. Perhaps the most virulent critic has been Aleksandr Solzhenitsyn, who declared the signing of such treaties to be "just a form of direct capitulation by the center before the autonomies and a violation of the rights of the remaining oblasts of Russia" (1996). The chairman of the Federation Council, Yegor Stroyev, said he found it painful to consider these agreements, which in practice were pulling the country apart (Medvedev 1996, 16–18). They were also criticized by the Russian foreign minister, Yevgeny Primakov (Hughes 1996, 43). According to President Yeltsin's adviser on political geography, Leonid Smirnyagin, the idea for such agreements had originally been proposed by Sergei Shakhrai, who initially envisioned just three—with Tatarstan, Chechnya, and the enclave of Kaliningrad.[11]

Those involved in the process tended to view these treaties as temporary expedients, essentially political documents rather than durable additions to the constitutional architecture. According to an adviser to the head of Karelia, such agreements were "political rather than legal acts."[12] The deputy governor of Tambov Oblast called them a "temporary compromise."[13] Smirnyagin pointed out that they were mere agreements on division of powers between the *executive* branches at central and regional levels, but had not been ratified by the legislatures. Still, few regions were ready to give up the contest to extract such temporary benefits.

Political Struggle

For all the tortuous debate they generated, the constitutional negotiations were only one arena—and at times just a sideshow—in a far broader political struggle between central and regional authorities. Officials at the two levels bargained continuously, threatened each other, and probed each other's strength at several margins. Relative status, powers, and revenues were all contested.

Divisions at the center gave regional leaders leverage. Indeed, central politicians, caught up in political battles among themselves, sometimes encouraged subnational leaders to assert greater privileges as a way of weakening their central rivals. In 1990, as the newly elected Russian parliament began discussing sovereignty, Gorbachev tried to raise the status of the autonomous republics within the RSFSR. A Soviet law of April 26, 1990, granted the autonomous republics the status of "subjects of the [Soviet] federation." All were invited to participate in negotiations over a new Union treaty, along with the Union Republics (Lowenhardt 1995, 85).

Yeltsin, elected chairman of the Russian parliament in late May, at first resisted this enlargement of the powers of Russia's autonomous republics. But he quickly shifted to a strategy of accommodation, outbidding Gorbachev in his own gambit. The Russian Federation's Declaration on State Sovereignty of June 12, 1990, affirmed in point 9 the need for a "material broadening" of the rights of autonomous republics and lower level administrative units (Lowenhardt 1995, 84). In August, Yeltsin encouraged the Tatar authorities to "take as much sovereignty as you can swallow," and he spoke of the need to turn Russia into not a federation but a confederation (Laba 1996). For Yeltsin, regional autonomy came to supplement economic and political reform as foci around which he could build a supporting coalition.

With the collapse of the Soviet Union in late 1991, the nature of competition at the center changed. Conflict between Yeltsin and Gorbachev was soon replaced by confrontation between the Russian presidency and parliament, under its speaker, Ruslan Khasbulatov. Again, this led to a competitive courting of the regional elites, though with an institutional division of labor: Yeltsin tended to appeal to regional executive leaders, Khasbulatov to the regional soviet chairmen.

This need to find allies for the political contest in Moscow seemed to soften Khasbulatov's initially severe view of center-region relations, just as it had done for Yeltsin earlier. Early on, the Supreme Soviet speaker espoused a tough policy toward separatism in Tatarstan, opposing election of the Tatar president and change in the republic's status. "There will not be any independent states on the territory of the RSFSR," he is quoted as saying (Sakwa 1993, 123). But soon, according to his colleague Abdulatipov, Khasbulatov gravitated to a more flexible position, supporting signing of the Federation Treaty.

Abdulatipov, then head of the Supreme Soviet's upper house, was a strong advocate of accommodating regional demands. In February 1992 he blamed the failure of Gorbachev's efforts to save the USSR on the grudging nature of central policy: "the Union center made only as many concessions as were won by the republics. The Union center was always bringing up the rear." He added that, in some respects, Moscow should perhaps even infringe "on overall federal interests . . . for the sake of preserving the federation. Perhaps it is better to overdo it in the sense of making some concessions to the regions than to go too far in exercising leadership over them."[14]

The collapse of the Soviet Union in late 1991 initiated a process of internal fragmentation and regional protest that some thought could lead directly to the disintegration of Russia itself (see chap. 1). Even before the Union's demise, one Russian scholar warned that "the Russian SFSR government's struggle with the center is undermining the foundations of its own federal existence" (Tsipko 1991b). In 1992 and 1993, an ever-growing number of the leaders of ethnic republics demanded sovereignty, asserted greater rights, and began to withhold taxes from the center and to challenge Moscow's authority over local branches of the state. Chechnya, under General Dzhokhar Dudaev, declared complete independence, and in Tatarstan a referendum elicited majority support for republic sovereignty.

Ordinary oblasts and krais soon began to join the republics in pressing Moscow for concessions. Leaders in Primorsky Krai threatened to reestablish a Far Eastern Republic like the one that had existed in the early 1920s before Bolshevik rule had been consolidated (Teague 1994a, 32). Some spoke of a "United States of Northern Asia," stretching from the Urals to the Pacific (Teague 1994a, 32). In July 1993, a series of regions announced they were unilaterally upgrading their status. Vologda Oblast to the north of Moscow declared itself the Vologda Republic, and Sverdlovsk announced it had become the Urals Republic on July 1. A few days later, Primorsky Krai decided to become a "state-territorial formation within the Russian Federation," and

Voronezh's small soviet adopted a resolution equating its rights to those of the republics.

As well as making such declarations, a growing number of regions simply stopped remitting tax revenues in full to the center. Chechnya ended all tax payments. Tatarstan and Bashkortostan asserted control over locally collected tax revenues and said they would make only voluntary transfers to Moscow in the future. In their defense, various regions blamed the center for not providing adequate funds to pay for federal programs, local education, and police. By September 1993, 31 republics and provinces were reportedly withholding tax from Moscow, and the number was rising (Teague 1994a, 42).

This development was particularly alarming because it had been the refusal of a string of Soviet republics to finance central agencies and programs that had ultimately undermined Gorbachev's attempts to keep the Union intact.[15] Various writers began comparing Russias condition to the situation in the last months of the Soviet Union. According to Elizabeth Teague, Yeltsin found himself "facing the threat that the Russian Federation like the USSR before it, might fall apart" (Teague 1994a, 30).

Were such comparisons overstated? Did Russia face a genuine danger of complete federal collapse? The return to relative calm in center-region relations after 1993 made it easy to underestimate in retrospect how serious earlier tensions had been. From the perspective of the late 1990s, it was not difficult to find reasons why the Soviet disintegration had been inevitable, while Russia's survival was never seriously threatened. However, both outcomes had seemed far more uncertain just a few years earlier. In a book published in 1990, one leading Sovietologist argued that the danger of Soviet disintegration had been greatly exaggerated.

> Least of all should it have been assumed that the country was about to fly apart. Americans have had little experience with ethnic unrest based on linguistic demands, and they have grossly overreacted to what they have seen in the Soviet Union.... From a comparative perspective the Soviet Union looks like one of the more stable multinational countries. (Hough 1990, 206)

This was not an unusual view, at least until 1989. Alexander Motyl argued in 1987, quite reasonably, that the repressive capacity of the KGB along with the successful cooptation of non-Russian political elites made it unlikely that the non-Russian nationalities would rebel (Motyl 1987).

On the other hand, politicians from across the political spectrum seemed to take the prospect of Russian disintegration in the early 1990s seriously, both at the time and in retrospect. Boris Fyodorov was not alone in his concern. As Yeltsin himself put it in 1996: "I would be sinning against truth if I were to claim that the threat of disintegration of the Russian Federation did not exist. Four years ago it was rather serious."[16] According to Ramazan Abdulatipov, a definite danger of disintegration existed at two moments—in early 1992, between the Soviet Union's collapse and the signing of the Federal Treaty, and then in 1993 in the period before Yeltsin's storming of the White House.[17] Oleg Rumyantsev, executive secretary of the Supreme Soviet's constitutional commission, warned in March 1992 that unless the deputies adopted a draft constitution he was proposing, Tatarstan and Sakha would try to separate and "the Russian Federation will be destroyed from within" (Teague 1994a, 33). Making allowance for rhetorical excess and political motivation, their alarm does seem to have been genuine and quite widely shared.

Paradoxically, the greatest danger of disintegration did not come from the multiethnic nature of Russia, with its more than 120 nationalities. As discussed in chapter 1, though numerous, these minorities were relatively small, and 81.5 percent of the population was ethnically Russian. Even in the republics, the "titular" nationalities outnumbered Russians in only a minority of cases. Each region was small in relation to the total population.

Rather, what created the danger was the competition between individual regions and republics to assert greater rights. In such situations, disintegration does not necessarily occur because of a genuine desire by all units to secede. It can emerge from a spiral of reactions by individual regions, each of which might prefer the state to survive but which fear to be left paying the entire cost of supporting it. As argued in chapter 1, the dynamic is that of a bank run, in which it becomes increasingly irrational to keep depositing in the bank as the risk of breakdown rises.

While each region is individually small, the logic of contagion is dangerous. Explaining the collapse of the Soviet Union, Roman Laba quotes a Lithuanian poet who in 1988 asked at the first meeting of the Lithuanian national movement Sajudis: "Can a mouse defeat an elephant?" The poet's answer: "Yes, one only has to wait for the moment when the elephant is balancing itself on its little toe."[18] Arguably, only a few "mice" within the Soviet order—the Baltic republics and Georgia—actually wanted complete independence before the general disintegration took hold. Yet, as more and more insisted on leaving, support for independence grew even in Ukraine and Belarus. In Russia in mid-1993, according to one analyst, separatist declarations by some of the more rebellious provinces could have "provoked a general stampede and the collapse of the Russian Federation" (Teague 1994a, 51).

At the same time, the troubled early 1990s witnessed the growth of broader regional associations, including both republics and oblasts, which could have posed a far more credible threat of secession. A united Siberian or Far Eastern Republic could have threatened to redirect sales of raw materials to the Pacific region even more than was already occurring because of the breakdown of economic relationships. By 1991, 11 regional organizations had been set up to coordinate local economic policy and lobby Moscow on issues of common concern (see chap. 1). Had they lived up to the hopes of their founders, Russias subsequent history might have been quite different.

Back from the Brink

Whatever the extent of the danger it faced in the early 1990s, Russia has remained—with one important exception—a single state. The scores of local challenges and crises never quite coalesced into a general revolt. In fact, most of 1994 saw a relative cooling of passions in center-region relations and the emergence of a new pragmatism. A "Pact on Civic Accord" was signed by numerous politicians, both central and regional, in April at Yeltsin's prompting.

Such a stabilization was puzzling given the previous experience. It even took some top officials dealing with regional and ethnic issues by surprise. Sergei Shakhrai in early spring had warned, "The year 1994 will be a year of inter-ethnic and regional frictions and conflicts . . . this process is unfortunately inevitable," and predicted that "inter-ethnic relations will deteriorate in the future. Local governments will pursue a policy of separatism under the flag of defending national interests" (quoted in Gouré 1994). The previous chapter discussed the main explanations that have been suggested for this apparent stabilization.

This book contends, as outlined in the introduction, that one key force for cohesion was a policy on the center's part of selective accommodation—in particular, fiscal accommodation—that prevented bandwagons of protest or regional tax revolt from gathering speed. Instead of relying only on intimidation, the center's strategy was to negotiate a kind of asymmetric federal order comparable to that of Spain. According to one constitutional scholar, "a decision was made to allow the specifics of Russia's new federation to be determined gradually, by political means, and ad hoc negotiations, and not by a rigid, legal instrument with rules set in stone" (Walker 1995, 60). According to another, it was "precisely the asymmetric nature [of the power-sharing treaty process] that has restrained secessionist tendencies, allowing Moscow to negotiate on the basis of the particular interests of each republic and region" (Hughes 1996, 43). Through this policy, the tottering central "elephant" managed to prevent the regional "mice" from ganging up to topple it.

This strategy of bilateral negotiation and selective accommodation also helps to explain why the regional associations such as Siberian Agreement never developed a significant capacity for collective action against the center. Siberian Agreement was hampered by large differences of economic interests between its member regions and, equally importantly, by the center's success in exploiting these differences to create internal political divisions.

Whatever politicians might say about Siberia's shared destiny, the range of economic profiles of the regions was quite extreme. While some were agricultural, others focused heavily on military industry or on raw materials and energy. At the same time, institutional starting points were quite different: some were republics while others were ordinary oblasts and krais. According to the mayor of Novosibirsk city, Siberian Agreement was "riddled with disagreements over political and economic issues and, in the final analysis, each member attempted to maximize its own parochial interests by using 'its own special door to the centre'" (Hughes 1996, 1148). It helped that officials in Moscow made sure that each of these doors was kept conveniently ajar.

The rich had little interest in sharing their wealth with their poorer Siberian neighbors. When the chairman of Siberian Agreement, Vitali Mukha, suggested consolidating the budgets of the association's members, the chairman of the Krasnoyarsk soviet declined on the grounds that his region was thinking of itself becoming an independent republic (Hughes 1993, 33). The subregional elites appeared to one Western observer "as disconcerted by the idea of control of economic resources by Siberian Agreement . . . and by a more equitable regional redistribution of wealth as they are by Moscow's control and draining of Siberia's resources" (Hughes 1994, 1148). While Tyumen's average wages soared after central economic reforms were enacted—as the prices of oil and gas rose and the region acquired a greater share of profits—there was no spillover to Novosibirsk, where wages were depressed by the collapse of military orders.

These differences made it easy for Moscow to divide the leaders of the Siberian regions through a policy of selective cooptation. By rewarding individual regions for bargaining with the center directly, Moscow created incentives for them not to surrender their leverage to the Siberian Agreement leadership. And many showed little reluctance to be coopted. As the chairman of the Krasnoyarsk Krai soviet, Vyacheslav Novikov, demanded with surprising candor of visiting Russian ministers: "Your bureaucrats live on bribes, so let our bureaucrats live on bribes also" (quoted in Hughes 1993, 30). Yet, the concessions the center made to the Siberian regions favored the raw materials and fuel producers disproportionately. In 1992, Moscow delegated some control over export quotas and licenses to members of Siberian Association. Chernomyrdin, a figurehead of the gas and oil industry, was taken into the government, later to become prime minister, and the Tyumen regional leader Yuri Shafranik was made minister of fuel and energy in Moscow.[19]

The distance between the political interests of Siberian regions can be seen particularly sharply in the contrasting histories of Novosibirsk and the oil-producing Khanti-Mansiisky Autonomous Okrug. Novosibirsk, hit hard by economic depression was aided little by central transfers—it received only about 5,000 rubles per inhabitant in 1992 compared to a mean of 14,000 for the Siberian regions. The result was one of the largest drops in per capita real regional government spending in the area. Funding of public services fell about 60 percent that year. This appears to have translated into public discontent—the oblast was the only Siberian region where support for Yeltsin in the April 1993 referendum was actually *lower* than in the June 1991 election. During the September crisis, Mukha, who was not just the chairman of Siberian Agreement but also the governor of Novosibirsk Oblast, emerged as one of Yeltsin's most outspoken regional opponents, not only openly supporting the parliament but threatening that anyone in the province who followed Yeltsin's orders rather than those of the rebel vice president Alexander Rutskoi would be subject to criminal proceedings (Teague 1993, 20).

In the Khanti-Mansiisky Autonomous Okrug, by contrast, soaring oil revenues led to an actual increase in real regional spending of 23 percent in 1992. Support for Yeltsin in April 1993 jumped 15 percentage points from its already high 1991 level. When the regional council of Tyumen Oblast, administratively superior to the okrug's institutions, declared Yeltsin's September 1993 decree to be unconstitutional in Khanti-Mansiisky AO, the leaders of the okrug nevertheless managed to wriggle around the higher command. The members of Siberian Agreement, thus, did not sustain the kind of united position that would have given them bargaining power against the center.

War in Chechnya

The general calming of relations between the center and regional governors in 1994 renders the one major exception all the more anomalous and tragic. On November 28, 1994, the Russian Security Council decided to use force to try to remove the Chechen president, Dzhokhar Dudaev. The Chechen question had become a live issue since the spring, when advocates of a tough line against the republic managed to convince Yeltsin to use the Russian secret services to support centers of anti-Dudaev resistance that had appeared in the Upper Terek and Urus Martan districts of the republic (Eismont 1996). These centers had been involved in armed clashes with the Dudaev forces since the summer and had been joined by the former parliament speaker, Ruslan Khasbulatov, who in the fall set up a headquarters in the village of Tolstoi Yurt.

The Russian government decided, in a secret resolution, to support one of the resistance leaders, Umar Avturkhanov, based in the Upper Terek district, and started supplying him with arms and ammunition, including heavy armored vehicles and artillery. Moscow also began paying wages and pensions to the inhabitants of the Upper Terek and Urus Martan districts, though the allocations were "frozen" by the Dudaev government (Eismont 1996). In preparation for a planned assault on the capital Grozny, tanks were provided by Russia, and crews for them were recruited (reportedly with the participation of the Russian Federal Counterintelligence Service), offered high wages, and equipped with fake documents. In late November, a convoy of Russian armored vehicles was sent into Chechnya to reinforce the resistance settlements of Tolstoi Yurt and Urus Martan.

Four days later, at dawn, the opposition forces attempted to storm Grozny. Secrecy had been completely neglected by the rebel commanders, and the resistance turned out to have only small and poorly trained infantry units. These forces were routed by Dudaev's defenders, who in a 10-hour battle managed to destroy or seize more than half the opposition's 47 tanks (Eismont 1996).

This humiliation, along with the impossibility of keeping the participation of the Russian security forces secret, seems to have convinced Yeltsin to raise the stakes of the gamble. Two days later, on November 28, an emergency meeting of the Russian Security Council adopted a secret decision to draw up a plan for a military operation in Chechnya, and Russian planes destroyed Dudaev's aircraft and bombed the runways of two airfields near Grozny. On December 11, 1994, two tank units containing several hundred armored vehicles crossed into Chechnya, beginning the full-scale war (see also Thomas 1995a).

Whatever the arguments used to justify this action, it seems to have been chosen as a consequence of incremental decisions, based on overconfidence and poor information.[20] Unexpected failures and humiliations led to attempts to regain the initiative. The minute size of Chechnya made it almost inconceivable that the Dudaev forces could hold out for long. And yet, the war proved once again the advantages that guerrilla fighters enjoy in mountain terrain even against heavily armed opponents.

The puzzle remains: why was Chechnya different? Why did Dudaev push harder than his counterparts in Tatarstan or Tyva? In part, his vehemence can be explained as an extreme reaction to factors that also led to activism in other places. Leaders of Muslim republics tended to be more separatist than those with predominantly Christian or Buddhist populations (see Treisman 1997). However, Tatarstan and Bashkortostan, for instance, were Muslim republics, yet were more willing to compromise with Moscow on independence. What may have been more significant were some particularities of Dudaev's position.

He was both the leader of a nationalist organization and a virtually complete outsider—both among the republic's political elite and among its nationalist opposition. An airforce officer resident in Estonia, Dudaev had not lived in Chechnya for 20 years before he came to be its president (de Waal 1995). Indeed, according to the analysts Emil Payin and Arkady Popov, Dudaev owed his nomination as leader of the nationalist organization in large part to his nonnative status and long absence from the republic. The leaders of the Chechen political clans had not been able to agree on the division of power, and so they had compromised on Dudaev, who belonged to a small clan with little influence, "a person without contacts, unrooted, who would be easy to push aside when the time came" (Payin and Popov 1995).[21]

Lacking a secure base of either elite or popular support, Dudaev was domestically vulnerable. In order to outmaneuver rivals in the nationalist movement, he may have been forced to adopt an intransigent stance. His widow, Alla Dudaeva, has claimed that "Dzhokhar, especially in the first years, often became a hostage of his surroundings" (Dudaeva 1996). President Shaimiev of Tatarstan expressed a similar view: "Dudaev ended up a hostage of the policy of complete independence, and of the head of the security services [*Komitet Bezopasnosti*] there. He ended up a double hostage." Either he had to achieve the independence he had promised or "he would have been overthrown by his own people."[22] Abdulatipov, who visited Chechnya at various points during the evolving crisis, says that Dudaev complained that there was no single, authorized figure on the Moscow side with whom he could negotiate. Abdulatipov also blames Dudaev's miscalculations. "Once he started accumulating weapons, Dudaev's position hardened. He thought he would bring Russia to its knees, and invited me to join him. He believed that with such a lot of arms and a warlike people, he could defend the republic."[23]

Equally puzzling is why the Russian leadership chose to take such a risk in late 1994. This marked a complete reversal for Yeltsin, who as late as August 1994 had announced that "forcible intervention in Chechnya is impermissible. . . . we in Russia have succeeded in avoiding interethnic clashes only because we have refrained from forcible pressure. If we violate this principle with regard to Chechnya, the Caucasus will rise up. There will be so much turmoil and blood that afterwards, no one will forgive us."[24]

Some explanations have focused on the economic costs of uncertainty over the oil pipeline running through the republic or of the organized crime located there. Yet, the costs of a military operation and occupation could have been expected to be enormous. Chechnya's domestic oil production was minute—3.6 million tons of crude oil in 1992 out of the Russian output of 354 million tons—and the Grozny oil refinery was bombed by the Russians soon after the operation started (Khazanov 1995, 219). Some have seen the military operation as an attempt to deter other regions from seceding. But, as previously argued, the danger of this had already largely passed—and the central authorities had not chosen to invade at earlier moments when the risk of separatism spreading was much higher. On the contrary, by late 1994 a greater danger seemed to be that a *failure* of Russian force could "restart the stalled engines of disintegration" (Shoumikhin 1996, 4).[25] Another theory views the action as an attempt to rekindle popular support for Yeltsin; yet a poll published a few weeks before the military operation found only 20 percent supported the use of force.[26] If this was the motivation, it was irrationally pursued.[27]

In the event, opposition to the war from the presidents of Muslim Tatarstan and Bashkortostan was astonishingly muted. Both were critical, but offered to mediate and later supported Yeltsin in his reelection campaign. Immediately after the invasion, Moscow launched a charm offensive to shore up its support among regions that might be inclined to side with the Chechens. Heads of the North Caucasus regions were invited to meet with Prime Minister Chernomyrdin in January 1995. According to Ingushetia's President Aushev, "economic and financial problems of members of the Federation in connection with the events in Chechnya" were discussed, and Chernomyrdin offered the leaders "priority in financing their needs" in exchange for loyalty on the issue of Chechnya. Leaders of Dagestan, Ingushetia, North Ossetia, and other regions were invited to submit to the government lists of expenditures that "they have incurred and expect to incur" in connection with the Chechnya operation.[28] No stampede of regions to secede followed. Shortly after the 1996 election, with the intervention of General Aleksandr Lebed, a truce was signed between Moscow and the Chechen rebel forces under which the question of the republic's independence was put off for five years and Russian troops withdrew from the republic.

CHAPTER 3

Fiscal Transfers and Fiscal Appeasement

Moscow's regional fiscal policy in the early 1990s had few admirers. The way transfers and tax breaks flowed to different regions struck most experts as haphazard, unpredictable, and economically inefficient—if not outright corrupt. Charitable observers complained merely of randomness: one compared the distribution of funds to the aimless collisions of particles and gas molecules in Brownian motion.[1] Others saw in the process the more unsavory work of individual lobbyists cashing in on personal connections and access. Regional lobbyists rarely seemed to leave the capital's hotels. In 1992, the federal budget was revised quarterly because of unpredictable inflation rates, prompting seasonal influxes of regional representatives. In the June 1992 round, 85 of the 89 regions sent delegations to Moscow to protest their assigned spending levels and to press for changes (Wallich 1994, 45–46). The next year, all 89 regions reportedly obtained some sort of special fiscal arrangement, through tax breaks or dispensations.[2]

Nor did the policymakers responsible for such allocation have much to say in their own defense. "In 1992," the prime minister Viktor Chernomyrdin told reporters the following year, "there was no regional policy in Russia" (Vetrov and Shmarov 1993). In early 1994, President Yeltsin was still apologizing. "Relations with the regions are acutely in need of a strategy," he acknowledged. "Hitherto we have continued papering over the cracks" (*Trud* 1994, 1).

Were the results of this process as random as many observers thought and as policymakers themselves seemed to admit? Did fiscal outcomes reflect only the relative persistence and connections of lobbyists reaching agreements in back offices around the capital? This book argues that, on the contrary, a clear political logic underlay the pattern of central fiscal redistribution to the country's regions. The results were neither random nor predominantly shaped by personal connections. To a considerable extent, fiscal benefits were used to appease regions where leaders, the population, or both were prepared to challenge the existing constitutional or economic order in potentially threatening ways. This chapter presents the evidence on which this claim is based. Subsequent chapters argue that this strategy of selective appeasement—messy, nontransparent, economically inefficient though it was—did serve an important political purpose. It knit regions to the center, defused most threats of territorial secession or other major political challenges, and helped to preserve the fragile cohesion of the Russian federal state.

The next section describes the system of fiscal redistribution that evolved in Russia in the 1990s. I then go on to examine the pattern of aggregate net transfers that resulted. I discuss the possible explanations suggested by economic and political science theory for why some regions might benefit more from central fiscal policy than others, and use multiple regression to test how well such hypotheses fit the evidence.[3]

Fiscal Redistribution in Russia

As in most federal states, large amounts of money flowed back and forth between regional and central governments in Russia in the 1990s. Each region was required to remit a portion of the tax revenue collected on its territory to the center, at rates determined by bilateral negotiation.[4] Central state bodies, in turn, provided the regions with a range of different types of transfer—subventions, budgeted investment grants, subsidized central credits, off-budget fund payments, and discretionary benefits such as exemptions to export duties.

Unraveling this complex network of financial and tax flows is difficult. One has to appreciate the paradoxes of the Soviet order in order to understand the hybrid fiscal system that evolved out of its decay. The Soviet regime was organized as a centralized, redistributive system, in which the production and distribution of goods and materials were centrally planned. In Moscow offices, bureaucrats set quantities to be produced and prices to be charged for hundreds of thousands of commodities, based on their estimates of productive capacity and on the economic priorities approved by the Supreme Soviet and party leadership. Then the national plan was translated into the necessary orders and materials allocations for particular ministries and enterprises.

That, at least, was how the process was supposed to work. In fact, by the late Brezhnev period an "administrative market" had evolved within the architecture of the centralized command system. In this sphere, official positions and connections functioned as a form of capital (Naishul 1991, 1993; Kordonsky 1991, 1992; Aven and Shironin 1987; Aven 1992; Grossman 1990). Favors were traded between party officials and industrial directors; plan directives were bent; and numerous black and "gray" markets existed to trade everything from rare books to foreign currency. In part, such informal bargains provided the flexibility necessary to fulfill the goals of the planners in the face of unforeseen bottlenecks; in part, they subverted central aims, subordinating them to the material interests of local party leaders or underground businessmen.

The plan became an arena for bargaining, with enterprise directors and regional party officials traveling to Moscow to enlist the aid of their ministry in lobbying party officials and planners to increase their allocations. A large, cyclical system of group pressures, focused on the party Central Committee, periodically shifted the priorities of the plans between developing agriculture, military industry, the energy complex, and other sectors (Kordonsky 1992; Neshchadin 1995). A smaller-scale but constant process of individual lobbying shaped the way each annual plan's targets were allocated among the thousands of enterprises. Assignments were negotiated and renegotiated, sometimes as late as December of the planned year (Winiecki 1991, 33).

Within this system of decayed administrative planning, budgets and money played a relatively unimportant role, essentially as accounting tools. The key objects of trade—both official and unofficial—were either physical goods themselves or the administrative authorizations to buy them, known as *fondi*. Money flows were calculated to meet the needs of the physical plans, at all levels of the system. Central Bank credits were automatic, small, and of limited significance since in conditions of endemic shortage, without *fondi* money could buy little (IMF et al. 1991, 107; Garvy 1977; Gregory and Stuart 1990).

Budgets were centralized and disaggregated like other parts of the planning system. Local budgets were part of the "unified" All-Union budget, assembled largely by Gosplan in Moscow, approved by the Supreme Soviet, and implemented by the Finance Ministry (Berkowitz and Mitchneck 1992; Wallich 1994, 27–29). Tax revenues collected locally were shared "upward" between different levels of government (Wallich 1994, 10). Some entered the local budget directly (e.g., profit remittances from enterprises and organizations under local jurisdiction); others were split on the basis of formulas negotiated between lower and higher level officials (e.g., turnover tax, profit tax on republican enterprises and organizations).

The economic reforms of the late 1980s and early 1990s changed this system in three fundamental ways. First, measures to give individual enterprises greater autonomy critically weakened the industrial ministries, which had served as the key channel of bids and pressures between the enterprises and the planners. Planning and budgeting had traditionally been oriented far more toward industrial sector needs than geographical concern (Bahry 1987a, 35). With the weakening of the ministries, the central role in lobbying passed to the enterprise directors themselves, who started knocking directly on the doors of the prime minister and other government officials. And, increasingly, they were assisted by regional political leaders, who were themselves lobbying Moscow ever more insistently for particular regional benefits and privileges.

The second, even more revolutionary change came with price liberalization in 1992. Instead of lobbying for materials, plan targets, or *fondi,* industrialists began to lobby for monetary prizes—budget allocations, tax breaks, central credits. Many of the techniques and procedures were taken over directly from the "administrative market," but the market had become monetized. The offices of Gosplan (rechristened the Ministry of Economics) became a less essential stop for regional lobbyists than those of the Central Bank—and later, as the Central Bank was increasingly domesticated by the government, than those of the Finance Ministry.

Third, in part by central design, in part as a result of lobbying by regional officials for central aid, more and more tax revenues and spending responsibilities were devolved to the regional governments (Wallich 1994, 6).[5] While federal state spending dropped from 23.4 percent of GDP in 1992 to 18.6 percent in 1994, regional and local spending rose from 12.7 percent to 17.5 percent (see table 3.1);[6] and while central budget revenues fell from 15.9 to 13.3 percent in the same period, those of the regions rose from 12.8 to 14.6 percent.

TABLE 3.1. Estimated State Budget Revenues and Expenditures in Russia in the Early 1990s

	GDP (%)				
	1992	1993	1994	1995	1996
Revenues	46.1	39.4	37.8	33.9	32.3
Federal	15.9	11.8	13.3	13.7	12.5
Regional + Local	12.8	15.0	14.6	12.4	12.3
Off-budget funds	17.4	12.6	9.9	7.9	7.5
Expenditures	62.9	47.9	45.1	37.8	35.0
Federal	23.4	17.2	18.6	15.7	12.3
Regional + Local	12.7	17.0	17.5	14.6[a]	15.0
Off-budget funds	26.8	13.8	9.1	7.5	7.7
Industrial Off-Budget Funds					
Revenues	5.8	4.2	2.5	1.5	n.a.
Expenditures	3.6	3.3	2.3	n.a.	n.a.
Central Bank Directed Credit[b]	15.5	5.0	1.9	n.a.	n.a.
Memo: GDP (trillion rubles)	18.1	162.3	630.0	1,659.2	2,256

Source: Revenue for all years calculated from World Bank operational data, April 1997. Expenditures: 1992–94: Le Houerou 1995, calculated from tables 1.1, A1–A3; Andrei Illarionov, "Attempts to Carry Out Policies of Financial Stabilization in the USSR and Russia," *Problems of Economic Transition,* June 1996, 39 (2): 5–48. State budget revenues and expenditures exclude intergovernmental transfers. 1994 without Chechen republic. Cash not commitment basis. 1995: *Russian Economic Trends,* 1996, 5 (2), calculated from 11, 12, 22, 28–29. Figures have been adjusted where appropriate to exclude intergovernmental transfers, using data from Lavrov 1996, in table 2. 1996 expenditures from Institute for the Economy in Transition, *Economic Trends and Perspectives,* February 1997. Off-Budget Fund 1996 revenues and expenditures from *Russian Economic Trends,* 1997, 3: 28. Industrial off-budget funds: figures from Le Houerou 1995 and World Bank operational data (for 1995).

[a]Assuming RET's figure of 30.3 percent GDP for consolidated budget expenditures does not double count the 1.8 percent intergovernmental transfer.

[b]Estimate from Le Houerou 1995 and Illarionov 1996, 32; includes directed credit for investment and conversion.

Subnational governments were responsible for most social spending, infrastructure, consumer subsidies, housing, heating, and other communal services (Le Houerou 1993, 8). Their share in both economic and social spending soared in the early 1990s. By 1994, the regions and localities were responsible for 80 percent of consolidated budget spending on education, 88 percent of spending on health, 64 percent of spending on culture and the mass media, 74 percent of spending on social protection, and 71 percent of spending on the national economy (mostly capital investment and subsidies) (Le Houerou 1995, 22).

Fiscal decentralization also reflected the centrifugal pressures of many of Russia's regions and ethnic republics, which picked up the separatist banner after the Soviet Union collapsed (see chap. 2). A few—Bashkortostan, Chechnya, Tatarstan, and Sakha (Yakutia)—stopped or greatly reduced remittances of tax revenue to the Russian budget. No overarching organization had replaced the Communist Party, previously the institution that had resolved interregional or interindustry conflicts. Fiscal rights and responsibilities became a key arena of center-region competition.

In short, Russia's fiscal institutions and traditions in the early 1990s resembled a monetized and decentralized version of the "administrative market" of the Brezhnev era. Budgets were negotiated upward, from the smallest rayon to the federal Finance Ministry. Each unit bargained intensely with its superior, strategically distorting the upward flow of information in order to get a favorable spending ceiling, revenue share, and, if necessary, subvention. Norms of provision, while used as reference points, served more as arguments in the interlevel trade than factors in their own right.[7] As a result, in one analyst's view, the budgetary system of the mid-1990s was "not truly a 'system', but rather a series of ad hoc bargained agreements, nontransparent at best, whose effects and incentives are not well understood" (Wallich 1994, 33).

Legislatures at each level had authority to approve the budget and revenue-sharing rates. But in practice it was largely officials of the finance department who prepared and implemented them. At the central level, parliamentary deputies were often viewed by regional or industrial lobbyists as a means to gain access to or put pressure on the government officials who did the actual allocation. According to Mark Yanovsky, a department head at the Ministry of Economics, "the role of parliament is that of a hammer which beats through" (Yanovsky 1993).

Several attempts were made to rationalize the legislative and administrative framework of intergovernmental finance. But most were only implemented partially, or not at all. The "Basic Principles of Taxation" Law, passed in December 1991, assigned different taxes exclusively to different levels of government (corporate and personal income taxes to the regions; VAT, export taxes, and certain excise taxes to the federal government). In practice, however, the regions resisted and revenue sharing survived. Corporate income or profit tax and VAT continued to be divided between the federal and regional governments, at changing, bilaterally negotiated rates. A law on subventions, passed in 1992, was never implemented (Wallich 1994, 56).

The greatest apparent victory of the central rationalizers came in 1994, with the introduction of a system to finance aid to ostensibly needy regions through a redistributional Fund for Financial Support of the Subjects of the Federation, which made payments based on publicized formulas. Simultaneously, most soft credits previously handed out by the Central Bank were made part of the budget. However, despite these efforts, "the systemless distribution of benefits and subsidies to different regions continued" (Lavrov 1995a). Expenditures from the Support Fund were dwarfed by other uncoordinated and unregulated budget payments, and, as will be demonstrated, the results of allocation even from the explicitly need-oriented Fund were themselves politicized. The system, as of 1995, remained "unsettled—and unsettling" (Le Houerou 1995, ii).

Tracing these tangled trails of money is difficult—what one hand gave, another seemed often to be reclaiming, redirecting, or misappropriating.[8] But the total amounts were quite large. According to one analyst's estimates, total federal transfers to the regions along with federal off-budget fund spending came to about 29 percent of GDP in 1992.[9] If one includes all Central Bank credits, the total rises to nearly 34 percent. Tax and off-budget fund revenues remitted by regions to the center, meanwhile, came to 26 percent of GDP. The total flows (for which data are available) had fallen substantially by 1994, but still remain sizable. Transfers from center to region that could be identified plus spending of federal off-budget funds came to 15.7 percent of GDP.[10] Meanwhile, tax and off-budget fund contributions remitted to the center in 1994 totaled about 19 percent.[11]

Four main categories made up the bulk of center-region transfers (see table 3.2). First, *budget transfers* of different kinds (subventions, payments from the regional support fund, net mutual payments, and short-term budget loans) occupied a growing share of the total—1.5 percent of GDP in 1992 but 3.4 percent in 1994.[12] These were also becoming increasingly important for financing regional spending. In 1992, federal budget transfers constituted about 10 percent of regional revenues, but by 1994 their share was 19 percent. Besides transfers to lower level budgets, the federal budget contained various spending programs with regionally focused impact: for instance, centrally financed investments (2.4 percent of GDP in 1992 and 2.3 percent in 1994) and budget subsidies to agricultural producers and the coal industry (1.9 percent of GDP in 1992).[13]

Such fiscal flows emerged from a complicated interaction of government and parliament. The initial budget draft was prepared by the Finance Ministry in Moscow, on the basis of "bids" by the large enterprises, regional officials, and remaining industrial ministries. Once approved by the government, it was submitted to the parliament where it was given several readings and amended. Finally, after the parliament voted for it, the budget was signed into law by the president. Thus, the process admitted numerous points of pressure in the ministries, government, and parliament for different lobbyists to get details changed.

TABLE 3.2. Estimated Fiscal and Financial Transfers from Center to Regions, 1992–96

	1992		1994		1995	1996
	bn Rs	%GDP	tr Rs	%GDP	%GDP	%GDP
1. Direct transfers from federal budget, total	263.8	1.5	21.4	3.4	1.5	1.9
• Subventions and/or payments from RSF	142.5	0.8	4.9[c]	0.8	1.0	0.8
• Net mutual payments	105.8	0.6	16.4	2.6	0.4	0.8
• Short-term budget loans	15.5	0.1	0.1	0.0	0.1	0.3
1A. Indirect transfers by increasing region's share of VAT	n.a.	n.a.	3.4	0.5	0.3	0.4
2. Subsidy to "closed cities"	n.a.	n.a.	0.6	0.1	0.1	0.1
3. Budget investments[b]	442.6	2.4	14.6	2.3	n.a.	n.a.
4. Budget subsidies to agriculture[b]	168.0	0.9	n.a.	n.a.	n.a.	n.a.
5. Budget subsidies to coal industry[b]	180	1.0	n.a.	n.a.	n.a.	n.a.
6. Conversion program[b]	63.0	0.4	0.7	0.1	n.a.	n.a.
7. Directed credits for inv. and conversion[b]	204.0	1.1	1.4	0.2	n.a.	n.a.
8. Central bank directed credits[b]	2,595	14.4	10.5	1.7	n.a.	n.a.
9. Fed. off-budget fund expenditure[d]	1,730	9.6	49.9	7.9	7.6	7.7
10. Discretionary benefits	451.2[a]	2.5	n.a.	n.a.	n.a.	n.a.
Total (1–10, but not 1A)	6,097	33.7	99.2	15.7		
Memo: GDP	18,100 bn Rs		630 tr Rs		1,659.2 tr Rs	2,256 tr Rs

Source: 1992, 1994: Freinkman and Titov 1994, 15 and World Bank operational data; IMF Economic Reviews, *Russian Federation* 1994; Le Houerou 1995. 1995–96: Lavrov 1996, 37, World Bank operational data, *Russian Economic Trends* 1997, 3: 28; (8) from Illarionov 1996, 32.

[a]First 9 months.

[b]To enterprises, not regional governments; figures for 1994 budget investments, calculated from Goskomstat Rossii 1995, 842, 848; those for 1994 investment and conversion credits, from Sinelnikov (1995, table 5-4).

[c]Of this, 2.3 trillion was direct payments from the Support Fund, 2.6 trillion was a subvention to Moscow.

[d]Not including import subsidies; for 1992, 1994, calculated from Le Houerou 1995, table A4. 1995–96 from *Russian Economic Trends* 1997, 3: 28.

The second category of center-region transfers was *directed credits*, allocated by the Central Bank in collaboration with the Ministry of Finance and Ministry of the Economy, to support agriculture, grain procurement, conversion, working capital, and the needs of the northern regions, among other programs. Total estimated Central Bank directed credits came to 15.5 percent of GDP in 1992 and 5 percent in 1993 (Le Houerou 1995, tables A1, A2). Since repayment of these credits was often uncertain, at times they resembled subsidies.[14] While the Central Bank insisted on its autonomous right to decide to whom to issue such credits, it generally responded to requests of an interdepartmental Commission on Credits Policy, which included representatives of the Economics, Finance, Agriculture, and other ministries, as well as the Central Bank (IMF 1995, 30; Ignatev 1993; Yanovsky 1993).

Third, money was transferred by federal *off-budget funds* (the pension fund, road fund, etc.). Estimated spending by federal off-budget funds came to about 10 percent of GDP in 1992, and 8 percent in 1994. Unfortunately, information about the regional distribution of such spending has not been available. Fourth, *discretionary benefits* of various kinds (export privileges, hard currency allocations, etc.) were assigned by the central government and parliament to regions on an ad hoc basis under individual resolutions. For the first nine months of 1992, such benefits were estimated at 2.5 percent of GDP.[15] Unfortunately, no accounting is available for subsequent years.

Meanwhile, resources flowed from the regions to the center in the form of tax remittances (13.5 percent of GDP in 1992 and 9.4 percent in 1994) and payments to federal extrabudgetary funds (12.3 percent of GDP in 1992 and 9.3 percent in 1994). While VAT, corporate profit tax, and some excises were shared between the two levels at negotiated rates, personal income tax went entirely to regional budgets in 1992–93 and almost entirely to them in subsequent years. Overall, after subventions and net mutual settlements are included, the federal government ran a deficit of about 21 percent in 1992 and of about 10 percent of GDP in 1994, while the regional governments ran a surplus of 1.6 percent of GDP in 1992 and just balanced their budgets in 1994 (Le Houerou 1995, tables A1–A3).

"Winners" and "Losers": Uncovering the Pattern

The first thing that strikes an observer of the outcomes of intergovernmental tax and transfers policy in the early 1990s is the apparently huge disparity between favored and less favored regions.[16] In 1992, the average region remitted to Moscow about 60 percent of the tax revenues collected on its territory. But while Tyumen (including its two autonomous okrugs) passed on 80 percent, Tatarstan and Bashkortostan sent the federal authorities just about nothing. In 1994, a typical region remitted about 35 percent, but the rates ranged from 48 percent to zero. Meanwhile, transfers flowing in the other direction also varied widely. While many regions received no subventions at all, the Koryaksky Autonomous Okrug was supported to the tune of 50,000 rubles per capita in 1992.[17] Central investment grants that year ranged from 950 rubles per capita in Bashkortostan to 12,000 in the Far Eastern region of Magadan.

These different types of transfer might, of course, even out in the aggregate, reducing the total interregional variation. But even in the aggregate the disparities are striking. While the coefficients of variation for the different types of per capita transfers for which 1992 data were available ranged from .55 to 3.3, the coefficient of variation for aggregate center-region transfers was 1.14.[18] Total center-to-region transfers for which data were available ranged from about 1,000 rubles per capita (for Bashkortostan) to 96,000 (for Komi) in 1992. Net transfers, from which tax payments to the center have been subtracted, ranged from −58,000 rubles per capita (in Tyumen) to 64,000 rubles per capita (in Komi).

To those familiar with Russia's geography, it might not seem surprising that Tyumen paid far more in taxes to the center than it received in transfers: it is the country's leading oil-producing region. It is harder to explain, however, why the Komi Republic, Russia's fourth largest oil-producing region, would be right at the other end of the scale, with the highest net transfer *from* Moscow, or why Tatarstan and Bashkortostan, the second and third largest oil producers, would be allowed the most generous tax retention deals.

Nor are there any obvious geographical explanations. Figure 3.1 shows the 23 regions that received positive net transfers from Moscow in 1992, along with the 18 that paid the largest net tax to the center (i.e., all that paid more than 10,000 rubles per capita). While the biggest "losers" from central redistribution appear generally to lie to the west of the Urals, the 23 biggest "winners" are spread out across the whole country—from Bryansk in the west to Kamchatka in the east. There are clusters of "winners" in Eastern Siberia and the Far East, in the North Caucasus, on the Volga, and in the North. But in some cases, the biggest "winners" lie right next to the biggest "losers." Chelyabinsk Oblast in the Urals received four times as much per capita in transfers from the center as neighboring Perm Oblast. (Both paid about the same per capita in tax to the center.) Equally puzzling, Dagestan, in the North Caucasus, got to keep 56 percent of the tax collected locally, while neighboring Stavropol Krai retained only 38 percent. (At the same time Dagestan was receiving about 70 times as much in central subventions as Stavropol.)

The levels of regional government spending that these transfer flows helped finance were also highly disparate. Per capita spending by regional governments in 1992 ranged from about 7,000 rubles per capita (in Stavropol Krai) to about 85,000 (in Sakha-Yakutia). The coefficient of variation for per capita regional spending in Russia's regions was .83 in 1992, and 0.77 in 1993, com-

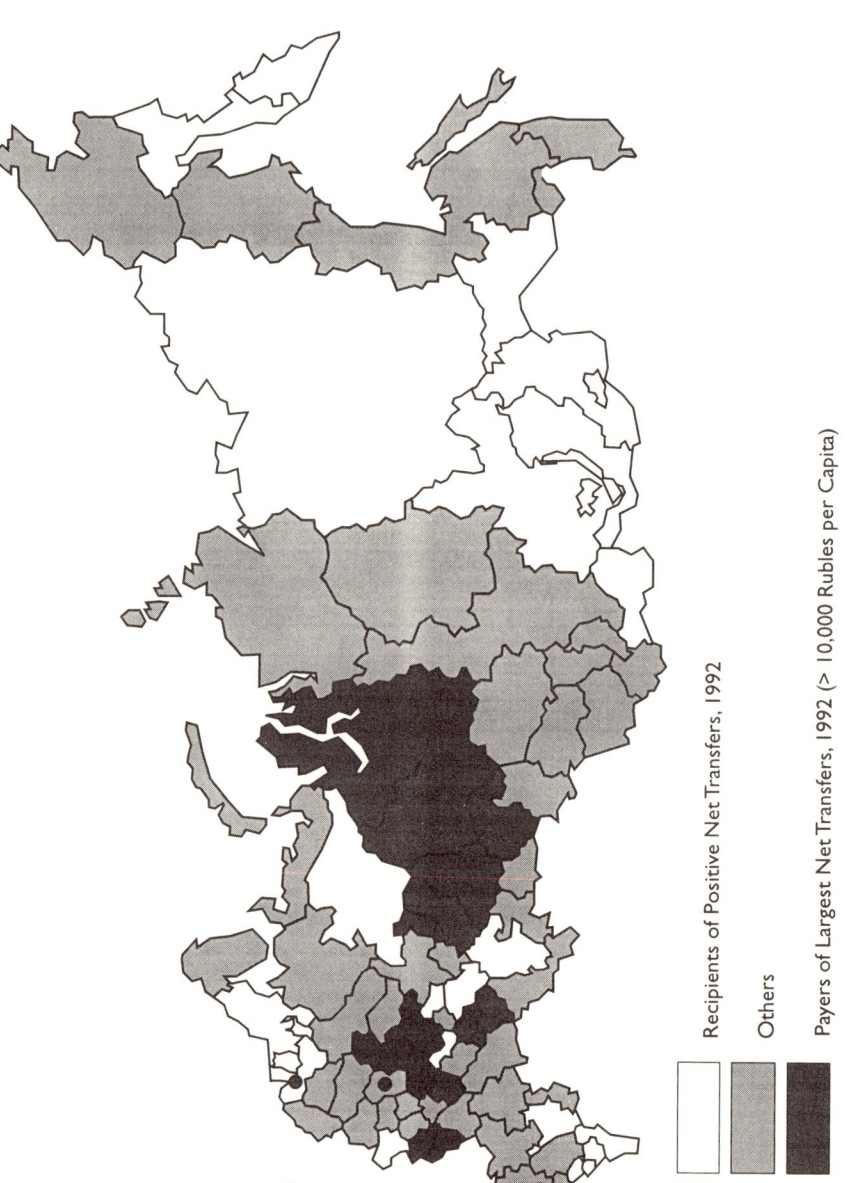

Fig. 3.1. "Winners" and "losers" from fiscal redistribution, 1992. (Based on data provided by Leonid Smirnyagin.)

Recipients of Positive Net Transfers, 1992

Others

Payers of Largest Net Transfers, 1992 (> 10,000 Rubles per Capita)

pared to about .42 for per capita state-local spending in the United States in the mid-1980s (Fisher 1991, 265).[19] To compare Russia with another reforming communist order, in China the coefficient of variation for provincial per capita spending was closer to that in Russia—increasing from .66 in 1980 to .72 in 1985, while then declining to .57 in 1991 (Tong 1994, 12). But the extremes were less unequal. In China in the mid-1980s, the highest spending region outspent the lowest by a factor of about eight; in Russia in both 1992 and 1993, there was a 12-fold difference.

Possible Causes

Were these inequalities as haphazard as has often been believed? Statistical analysis suggests some regularities beneath the surface. The next two sections will demonstrate these regularities. The first step is to identify what factors might explain why some regions received larger net transfers than others. Various possibilities suggest themselves, both from the pronouncements of those in positions of power and from established theories of intergovernmental fiscal politics.

First, the pattern of net transfers might reflect particular objectives of the central allocators. Certain regions might receive more generous transfers to alleviate greater *need* or especially dire inability to pay for public services. In Western states, many government programs aim to target developmental or welfare aid to regions unable to provide basic services to their inhabitants.[20] Need has been measured in a variety of ways, some focusing on general characteristics of the community (population change, employment change, per capita income change, etc.), others focusing on particular characteristics relevant to specific federal programs (e.g., proportion of dilapidated housing, for urban renewal grants). In Russia, one element of intergovernmental transfers— subventions, and later payments from the Regional Support Fund—was explicitly designed to assist needy regions with insufficient budget resources. Such channeling of aid to less well-endowed regions would continue a practice noted in the Soviet era. Donna Bahry found that allocation of investment funding led then to "a mild form of redistribution, allotting slightly more to less developed regions than would otherwise be the case" (Bahry 1987a, 164).[21]

Yet, in 1991 an economically radical team of politicians had taken charge of the central economics ministries, led by vice premier Yegor Gaidar, with the announced goals of establishing market institutions and privatizing state enterprises. Their conception of the role of the state was rooted in the classical welfare economics tradition: interventions should promote *efficiency* (Baumol 1952; Stiglitz 1989). At times, members of this group spoke of using state fiscal policy to create incentives for rapid reform. Deputy Premier Anatoli

Chubais, for example, announced in August 1993 that financial aid to regions should be made conditional on progress in privatization (Todres 1993). Thus, a second hypothesis is that central allocators distributed revenues and tax obligations in such a way as to support efficient forms of economic organization and to stimulate *economic reform.*

Redistributive outcomes might also reflect other objectives of central allocators. These might include encouraging regional governments to improve their *tax collection* by rewarding regions that made the greatest "tax effort."[22] Or allocators might wish to support particular *economic sectors.* In Russia, two sectors (agriculture and the fuel and raw materials sector) are often accused of having disproportionate power and reaping excessive rewards from the budget and credit-allocation process.[23]

Besides the objectives of central politicians—whether social, economic, or other—fiscal outcomes might reflect differences in the capacity of regions and their leaders to lobby for aid or privileges.[24] This depends, first, on the regional leaders' degree of *access* to central officials. In the United States, two studies suggest that both city and state governments that employ a Washington lobbyist or consulting firm receive more in federal grants than those that do not (Pelissero and England 1980; Cingranelli 1984). Other scholars have noted that a city or state government's capacity to make formal applications for aid is itself an important determinant of grant receipts (Stone and Sanders 1987, cited in Rich 1989). In Russia, regions that have a permanent representative in Moscow might be expected to have greater access and thus greater success. A second mode of access believed to be important is the contact with central policymakers that comes with an official visit to the region. One might expect visited regions to have received a fiscal premium.[25] Third, regions whose representatives occupied leading roles within the parliament, whose representatives served on the budget committees, or that had a disproportionately large number of parliamentary representatives might be able to use this leverage to extract greater budget concessions.

However, lobbying capacity depends not just on getting into an official's office, but also on having sufficient *bargaining power* once one is admitted. In part, bargaining power is likely to be a simple function of the political importance of the region—populous, economically weighty regions and those with the higher administrative status of republics may find it easier to get the finance minister's attention. But in a more important sense, bargaining power depends on the ability to make credible threats to disrupt central priorities if regional demands are not met.[26] In 1992–94, the key central concerns in federal relations were defusing separatist momentum, avoiding regionwide strikes, preventing public hostility toward central incumbent politicians from reaching extreme levels, and securing the loyalty of regional leaders at moments of political crisis in Moscow.[27] The threat of a region to disrupt these aims would be more credible if the region had in fact taken disruptive action in the recent past. Such actions—strikes, separatist declarations, and so on—could credibly signal relatively high disagreement utility levels.[28] If the region's voters had signaled extreme discontent with central incumbents by voting strongly against them, this might also suggest a threat to the central regime's political future.

It is these last factors that are critical to the argument of this book. I argue that, though the center's objectives of supporting needy regions, encouraging reform, or favoring particular sectors may have been important at times, and greater access or representation at times bore fruit for the overrepresented region, the bargaining power of regions—in particular, their blackmail potential—was significant in determining the pattern of net transfers. Regions with a greater capacity and resolve to disrupt central priorities—whether economic, political, or constitutional—were able to pressure the center into providing greater benefits in the hope of preventing disruptive protests.

Explaining the Pattern

One method to assess which of the listed factors best correspond to the actual patterns of fiscal transfers in 1990s Russia is the statistical technique of ordinary least squares regression. If a factor is important in explaining the pattern of transfers, one would expect its estimated regression coefficient to be significant.

Regressions were run for a variable measuring the net center-to-region flow of transfers (net of tax remittances) for each of the years 1992, 1994, 1995, and 1996.[29] The explanatory factors included reflect the different hypotheses outlined in the previous section.[30]

As already mentioned, no comprehensive accounting of all center-region financial flows is available. The subsets of transfers for which figures were available were somewhat different in the different years. The 1992 data contained a broader range of different types of central fiscal and quasi-fiscal transfers.[31] In part because the role of quasi-fiscal transfers such as subsidized directed credits had diminished by 1994, the data for that year focus more on official budget transfer flows, as do those for 1995 and 1996. Data for central credits in these years were not available.[32]

One might expect the results of the analyses for these years to be quite different. While 1992 was the first, tumultuous year of independent statehood and radical economic reform in Russia, 1994 was a postelection year of consolidation, during which a rationalized system of center-region fiscal relations was introduced. This new system inspired high hopes. According to President Yeltsin in an interview soon after the Regional Support Fund's initiation:

> We are leaving behind forever the practice of endless haggling between the center and the regions whereby each party tries to get a bigger share.

60 After the Deluge

> This has generated enormous resentment, suspicion, and abuses. Now things will be different. (*Trud* 1994)

The last two years, 1995 and 1996, were election years, and one might expect to see changes in the way fiscal transfers were allocated. That somewhat different sets of transfers were analyzed for the various years also renders it particularly unlikely that similar results would emerge by chance.

In order to avoid concluding too much on the basis of a particular incomplete selection of transfer flows, besides analyzing the aggregate flows variable I also ran regressions to analyze the pattern of allocation of particular transfer streams (e.g., investment grants, net mutual payments, special benefits) in 1992 and 1994, the years for which detailed data were available, and to explain differences in the share of total revenues that the region was permitted to retain. If the same factors appeared to influence not just the aggregate results but a range of different individual transfers in the same way, this would constitute additional evidence of their importance. For instance, one might reasonably expect efficiency criteria to influence the allocation of investment grants. But if the same criteria also explained the allocation of subventions, as well as the aggregate flow of transfers to the regions, one would be more convinced of a general efficiency-related logic not unique to the investment process but found also in other institutional subchambers of the fiscal system.

The results for the aggregate net transfers regressions are shown in table 3.3. Each coefficient listed in the table estimates the size of the change in net center-to-region transfers associated with a one-unit change in the given independent variable, holding constant all the other independent variables included in the regression. A positive coefficient suggests that an increase in the independent variable is associated with an increase in the dependent variable—for example, an early sovereignty declaration (coefficient of 19.80 in 1992 column 1) was associated with a higher net center-to-region transfer in 1992. A negative coefficient suggests a negative relationship—for example, the higher the recent vote for a pro-reform candidate (coefficient of $-.33$ in 1992 column 1), the *smaller* the net transfer the region received. Asterisks indicate the degree of statistical significance of the coefficient estimate: for instance, we know that for those with two or more asterisks the probability that the true coefficient is actually zero is less than .05 or one in twenty.

To show how well each hypothesis holds up when one controls for the others, I include first in column 1 regressions the estimates when the full range of explanatory factors is included. Many of the coefficient estimates, however, are not significant, indicating a lack of support for the corresponding hypotheses. I therefore also present a shorter model in column 2, which gives the estimates after all those variables have been excluded from the model for which in the first stage of analysis an *F*-test at the .10 level indicated that the variable did not

TABLE 3.3. What Explains the Pattern of Net Center-to-Region Transfers in Russia (1992–96)?

	1992		1994		1995		1996	
	(1)	(2)	(1)	(2)	(1)	(2)	(1)	(2)
A. Bargaining Power								
Recent Protest or Opposition								
Recent vote for pro-reform party or presidential candidate[a]	−.33** (.15)	−.43*** (.11)	−10.69** (4.14)	−9.06*** (2.68)	−22.77*** (8.40)	−16.65** (6.65)	−39.26* (20.40)	−26.51* (14.19)
Region declared sovereignty 1990	19.80*** (4.78)	19.55*** (2.87)						
Governor opposed Yeltsin Sept. 1993			83.55** (34.86)	72.39** (32.02)				
Governor did not actively support Chernomyrdin's OHIR 1995[b]					125.56*** (46.83)	123.06*** (43.71)	157.73 (100.73)	173.90* (91.00)
Log 1,000 man-days lost to strikes previous year	8.76*** (1.95)	8.43*** (1.58)	56.28 (36.61)		−5.07 (46.95)		39.90 (106.01)	
Political Weight								
Population	−.003* (.002)	−.002*** (.001)	−.03** (.01)	−.02** (.01)	−.05* (.03)	−.06** (.02)	−.21*** (.06)	−.21*** (.05)
Estimated economic output	−.01 (.01)		.15* (.08)		.05 (.12)		.88*** (.26)	.85*** (.17)
Republic			−78.65* (43.79)		31.41 (86.51)		26.17 (178.92)	

(continued)

TABLE 3.3.—Continued

	1992		1994		1995		1996	
	(1)	(2)	(1)	(2)	(1)	(2)	(1)	(2)
B. Alleviating Need								
Social infrastructure underdevelopment[c]	−2.53 (2.08)		−2.66 (1.61)					
Proportion of population under 16	.51 (1.20)		23.20* (12.94)		4.78* (2.59)	4.36* (2.20)	20.79*** (7.66)	20.49*** (6.51)
Proportion of population of pension age	.04 (.80)		−11.14 (8.35)	−26.29*** (3.50)	57.68** (26.41)	55.01*** (13.48)	41.58 (60.56)	
Profits per capita previous year	4.20 (3.96)		−1574.03*** (238.56)	−1216.88*** (126.00)	23.91 (17.18)	21.58** (8.96)	33.17 (39.15)	
Est. avge. real income previous year[d]	.03 (.03)		.31* (.18)		−1.04*** (.17)	−.97*** (.13)	−.83*** (.16)	−.76*** (.12)
Degrees latitude north	−.90** (.36)	−.86*** (.25)	−3.33 (3.68)		−1.02* (.55)	−1.22*** (.44)	−4.37** (1.71)	−4.33*** (1.45)
					15.33** (6.73)	12.60** (5.86)	12.11 (14.88)	
C. Other Central Objectives								
Advanced economic reform[e]	−2.11 (1.40)	−1.82* (1.09)	7.83** (3.68)	6.95** (3.24)	7.91 (7.50)		23.97 (16.13)	30.76** (13.92)
Percent of work force in agriculture	−.48 (.31)	−.61*** (.18)	−4.02 (3.60)		−4.92 (6.99)		−20.70 (17.10)	
Region's share in RF raw materials output	−1.57*** (.48)	−1.41*** (.25)	5.24 (4.69)	11.88*** (3.83)	−8.47 (9.91)		63.39*** (22.99)	63.43*** (19.42)
Index of "tax effort"[f]	−5.62 (6.49)		−35.48 (40.05)		−117.79 (72.62)	−130.65** (62.52)	−82.61 (88.26)	−105.80 (78.22)

D. Access and "Pork"

	(1)	(2)	(3)	(4)	(5)	(6)	(7)	(8)
Visited by President that year[g]	-2.13 (3.39)		-15.27 (33.75)				442.79*** (151.28)	402.27*** (137.63)
Visited by Prime Minister that year	-.85 (4.53)		52.48 (40.08)	68.37* (36.15)				
Region had member on parliament's budget committee[h]	2.15 (4.54)							
Chairman of parliament's budget committee (or deputy) from region			-9.82 (65.05)	90.26 (132.93)			-406.95 (294.53)	
Chairman (or deputy) of one house of parliament from region			9.77 (54.36)	-73.50 (105.66)			-33.09 (205.45)	
Parliament deputies per capita elected in single-mandate districts[i]	-.87 (1.25)		99.03** (42.65)	138.67*** (32.47)	181.42*** (53.52)	191.59*** (44.04)	6.67 (170.06)	
Region had perm. rep. in Moscow	1.05 (3.57)		-50.94 (32.90)	-72.49** (29.87)	97.28 (80.27)		-125.57 (197.02)	
Constant	57.26 (49.07)	75.73*** (16.36)	128.22 (470.46)	854.68*** (115.64)	-2050.49** (984.69)	-1768.98*** (621.01)	256.66 (2445.20)	2086.48*** (320.39)
R^2	.78179	.74182	.88955	.86193	.91434	.90690	.89250	.88501
Adj. R^2	.67534	.70740	.84095	.83966	.88202	.89039	.84643	.86122
N	61	68	72	72	73	73	70	70

Note: OLS Regression Coefficients; dependent variable is center-to-region fiscal transfers net of region-to-center tax remittances, in 1,000 rubles per capita; standard errors in parentheses. Column 2 contains all variables from

(continued)

TABLE 3.3.—Continued

column 1 that significantly improve the fit of the regression, as judged by an F-test at the .10 level. One extreme outlier, the Koryaksky Autonomous Okrug, was excluded from the data for the 1994 regressions since its value on the dependent variable was more than five standard deviations greater than the mean. The Koryaksky Autonomous Okrug, a sparsely inhabited North-Eastern Territory of 35,000 inhabitants, received more than 6 million rubles per capita in 1994 central transfers.

[a]1992: vote for Yeltsin in 1991 presidential election; 1994 and 1995: vote for Russia's Choice in 1993 parliamentary election; 1996: vote for Yabloko or Russia's Choice in 1995 parliamentary election.

[b]Variable = −2 if the governor himself ran on the "OHIR" list in 1995 election; −1 if he did not but a high official from the regional administration did; 0 if neither the governor nor a high official agreed to be on the list.

[c]In each case, an index of social infrastructure underdevelopment (see app. B for derivation) was tried, as well as the elements of this index, and some additional indicators of social infrastructure underdevelopment. The one most significant was used in the final specification. 1992: index; 1994: telephones (or access to them) per 100 urban families in 1992; 1995: telephones (or access to them) per 100 urban families 1995; 1996: doctors per 100,000 residents 1994. Variables adjusted so that high value always indicates underdevelopment.

[d]In 1994–96 regressions, two specifications were tried (1) average monthly money income previous year as percent of cost of 19 basic food commodities, and (2) average monthly money income previous year as percent of subsistence minimum. The more significant one was chosen. 1994: (1); 1995: (2); 1996: (2). Data were only available for (1) in 1992. In this case, same year income was used.

[e]In each case, an index of advanced economic reform was tried first (see app. B for derivation). The elements and some other indicators of advanced economic reform were tried and used instead if more significant. 1992: index; 1994: percent of 285 goods with controlled prices; 1995: private farms per 1,000 rural inhabitants; 1996: percent of 285 goods with controlled prices. Variables adjusted so that high value always indicates advanced economic reform.

[f]Constructed by method of Roy Bahl (1994).

[g]1996: visited by president during first six months leading up to first round of presidential election.

[h]Region had representative on Supreme Soviet Commission on Budgets, Planning, Taxes and Prices.

[i]1992: Supreme Soviet representatives per million inhabitants; 1994–96: State Duma representatives elected in single-member constituencies per million regional inhabitants.

* $p < .10$ ** $p < .05$ *** $p < .01$

significantly improve the fit of the regression. The models in column 2 thus represent estimates with less "noise" coming from probably unimportant factors.

What do the regressions show? First, they identify a pattern that is far less haphazard than casual observers had assumed. In each case, a small number of theoretically plausible factors (those included in the column 2 models) can explain about three-quarters of the variation in net transfers. The same or similar factors are often significant in more than one year.

The regressions provide some powerful evidence for the argument about fiscal appeasement advanced at the beginning of the chapter. Those regions that had demonstrated discontent with the central regime—by voting against Yeltsin or his pro-reform allies, declaring sovereignty, staging major strikes, or not supporting Yeltsin and his allies at moments of heightened political competition—did better in the fiscal transfers game than their more complaisant counterparts. The ability and resolve to disrupt central priorities served as a powerful lever for extracting benefits.

This pattern showed up in several ways. First, net transfers were significantly related to regional voting patterns in previous years. The larger the regional vote *against* leading pro-reform parties or candidates in the most recent national election, the more generous was that region's subsequent allocation. This result is highly significant in 1992, 1994, and 1995, though only marginally so in 1996 (at the .07 level in a two-tailed test).[33] These results are still significant controlling for the full range of other plausible determinants of fiscal transfers. For instance, anti-Yeltsin regions did not receive higher transfers because they tended to be less developed, because they had greater social need, or because their leaders had better access to the central decision makers (the results hold *controlling* for indicators of each of these alternative hypotheses).[34]

Shunning the incumbent pro-reform parties and candidates in national elections was not the only way in which regions could win themselves more generous fiscal treatment. More overt challenges to central order—whether by mass or elite—also earned a premium. It is difficult to construct indicators of such protest actions, but I was able to devise a number of measures relevant to the different years. The budget negotiations of 1992 followed some of the most turbulent years in Russia's recent history. In 1990, a series of regions within Russia, most ethnically distinct, had declared themselves sovereign in what became known as the "parade of sovereignties" (see chapter 2). Their claims represented an obvious challenge to the existing constitutional order. The following year, 1991, had seen a wave of strikes mobilize workers in different regions of the country to demand both economic and political changes. Both of these actions turn out to be closely related to the subsequent pattern of fiscal transfers. If a region's leaders had been among those who declared sovereignty in the first outburst of demands in late 1990, their province received nearly 20,000 rubles per inhabitant more in additional transfers and tax breaks in 1992—more than one standard deviation in the level of net transfers. Regions that had staged major strikes in 1991 also received a significant payoff the next year.[35]

That central policy had yielded to such blackmail tactics in 1992 would not surprise Russia's leaders, who had been intensely aware of the precariousness of their position and their lack of resources to deter or repress revolt. But by 1994, with the dissolution of the old parliament and enactment of a presidential constitution, the government seemed to have greater ability to resist regional pressures. The new Regional Support Fund had an explicit mandate to target fiscal aid to those regions with greatest need. Did the logic governing central redistribution shift between 1992 and 1994 from one based on the politics of protest to one based on economic efficiency or social need?

The regressions in table 3.3 suggest that in later years threats to central order remained a powerful lever. For 1994, an indicator of loyalty to the Russian president is provided by the responses of governors to Yeltsin's decree dissolving the parliament in September 1993. Almost all the heads of regional executives made some public statement at that time, either supporting the president, indicating a neutral position between president and parliament, or, in 15 cases, explicitly opposing Yeltsin. As history records, the president ultimately won this particular test of wills, dissolved the old parliament, and confirmed the ground rules by which its successor was elected.

One might expect the loyal governors to receive a reward in the 1994 budget. In fact, just the opposite occurred. Regions where the governor had supported Yeltsin during his critical showdown with the parliament—or at least remained neutral—seem to have come out *worse* financially than those whose leaders overtly opposed him. Overall, supporting Yeltsin at his moment of vulnerability or remaining neutral appears to have cost a regional governor about 70,000 rubles per inhabitant in net transfers (about one-eighth of a standard deviation). Once again, aggressive anticenter statements were met with central generosity.

Another indication of governors' attitudes toward the central "party of power" can be gauged from whether the governor chose to join Prime Minister Viktor Chernomyrdin's "Our Home is Russia" bloc, set up in early 1995. Those governors who chose *not* to join OHIR or to encourage a deputy to join thus sent a clear message about where they stood politically and where their loyalties lay. This message was apparently worth a considerable sum of budget money. Those governors not affiliated with the prime minister's party received larger net transfers for their region in 1995 and possibly in 1996 (the latter result is significant at only $p < .07$). Again, all of these results hold controlling for the full range of possible alternative causes (except for 1996, where the significance of a governor not supporting "Our Home is Russia" falls to $p < .15$ when the full range of variables is included).

Furthermore, as tables 3.4 and B1 (in appendix B) show, these regional discontent variables were not just significant in explaining the aggregate pattern of net transfers: they were also significant predictors of receipts from several of the transfer streams taken separately. In these tables, different transfer streams and the share of tax revenue retained are regressed separately on the independent variables, using the same procedures as before. The lower the vote for Yeltsin in 1991, the higher the share of tax revenue that a region was able to retain, and the higher were central transfers per capita. In particular, anti-Yeltsin regions seem to have received significantly higher special benefits conferred by discretionary presidential or government decrees. An early sovereignty declaration was associated with both a higher share of tax revenues retained in the region and significantly higher central transfers—in particular, higher special benefits and transfers from the government's reserve fund. (These were compensated slightly by lower subventions in the sovereignty-declaring regions, but the positive benefit far outweighed this.) More man-days lost to strikes were followed in 1992 by higher transfers—though they were actually associated with a smaller retained share of total tax revenues (perhaps the regions most likely to strike were those that traditionally retained a smaller share of revenues). The increased transfers came in the form of higher investment grants, special benefits, payments from the government reserve fund, and possibly also larger central credits.

In 1994, regions that had returned a lower vote for the progovernment Russia's Choice bloc the previous year received higher federal transfers, in particular from the Regional Support Fund. Strikes by this point did not have any clear effect, though greater strike losses may have been associated with larger Regional Support Fund transfers (significant at $p < .08$). Governors who opposed Yeltsin at his moment of weakness in the September 1993 confrontation with parliament were permitted to retain about 4 percent more of total tax revenues in their region. One interpretation might be that this represented not so much a central policy of appeasement as a central inability to implement *any* policy. It might be argued that such governors were not beneficiaries of central largesse so much as exploiters of central weakness, readier than their colleagues to cut tax payments unilaterally. Such ambiguities are inherent in any policy of appeasement, which is of essence reactive. But there is also some evidence of a central appeasement policy of commission as well as omission. The recalcitrant governors were rewarded with greater direct payments from the Regional Support Fund (significant, however, only at $p < .10$, in a two-tailed test). Taken together, these findings reinforce the story told so far of the importance of regional discontent—made credible both by elite and mass past actions—in extracting greater federal allocations.[36]

The significance of an early sovereignty declaration in the 1992 regressions raises additional questions. Was it the declaration itself that elicited central aid, by credibly signaling resolve on the part of the region's leadership to challenge the constitutional status quo? Or was it some other characteristic of

TABLE 3.4. What Explains the Pattern of Particular Transfers and of Regional Tax Retention, Russia

	Regional Tax Share		Central Transfers		of which: Subventions	
	(1)	(2)	(1)	(2)	(1)	(2)
A. Bargaining Power						
Recent Protest or Opposition						
Vote for Yeltsin 1991	−.35**	−.35**	−.16	−.28**	.02	
	(.16)	(.14)	(.18)	(.12)	(.03)	
Region declared	15.15***	13.66***	14.29**	13.99***	−.90	−1.49***
sovereignty 1990	(5.15)	(3.59)	(5.80)	(3.21)	(.84)	(.54)
Log (1,000 man-days lost	−4.91**	−4.75**	10.97***	8.86***	.50	
to strikes 1991 + 1)	(2.10)	(1.90)	(2.37)	(1.82)	(.36)	
Political Weight						
Population	.003*	.004***	−.003	−.002**	−.00*	
	(.002)	(.001)	(.002)	(.001)	(.00)	
Estimated economic	.01*	.01***	−.01		.00	
output	(.01)	(.00)	(.01)		(.00)	
B. Alleviating Need						
Social infrastructure	−.76		−1.88		.31	
underdevelopment	(2.23)		(2.52)		(.38)	
Proportion of population	3.25**	3.52***	−.98		−.32	
under 16	(1.29)	(1.00)	(1.46)		(.22)	
Proportion of population	.93	1.18*	−.52		−.35**	−.20***
of pension age	(.86)	(.64)	(.97)		(.15)	(.05)
Profits per capita 1991	−5.14		5.75		−.83	−.80**
	(4.26)		(4.79)		(.73)	(.32)
Est. avge. real income	.03		.02		−.01	
1992	(.03)		(.04)		(.00)	
Degrees latitude north	.09		−.92**	−.58**	−.04	
	(.38)		(.43)	(.27)	(.07)	
C. Other Central Objectives						
Advanced economic	−.64		−2.10		−.04	
reform	(1.51)		(1.70)		(.26)	
Percent of work force in	−.61*	−.58**	−.45	−.81***	.09	.07**
agriculture	(.33)	(.27)	(.38)	(.21)	(.06)	(.03)
Region's share in RF	−1.58***	−1.68***	.09		.12	
raw materials output	(.52)	(.37)	(.59)		(.09)	
Index of "tax effort"	4.96	−2.23	−6.53		.95	
	(6.99)	(4.59)	(7.86)		(1.21)	
D. Access and "Pork"						
Visited by President	−7.74**	−7.84**	−.01		.70	
	(3.65)	(3.21)	(4.11)		(.63)	
Visited by Prime Minister	3.14		−3.05		.15	
	(4.88)		(5.49)		(.84)	

1992? (OLS regression coefficients)

	Budget Investment		Government Reserve Fund		S. Soviet Reserve Fund		Special Benefits		Credits	
	(1)	(2)	(1)	(2)	(1)	(2)	(1)	(2)	(1)	(2)
	.00		.001		−.00		−.20	−.23**	.02	
	(.03)		(.001)		(.00)		(.18)	(.11)	(.02)	
	.05		.07*	.07**	−.01		14.65**	12.95***	−.00	
	(1.06)		(.04)	(.04)	(.03)		(5.74)	(3.18)	(.60)	
	.82*	.79**	.08***	.07***	.01		9.15***	6.67***	.44*	.37*
	(.46)	(.35)	(.02)	(.02)	(.01)		(2.34)	(1.77)	(.25)	(.19)
	−.00	−.00**	−.00**	−.00***	−.00		−.00		−.00	
	(.00)	(.00)	(.00)	(.00)	(.00)		(.00)		(.00)	
	−.00		−.00**	−.00***	−.00		−.00		−.00**	−.00*
	(.00)		(.00)	(.00)	(.00)		(.00)		(.00)	(.00)
	.43		−.04**	−.04***	.02		−2.63		.12	
	(.48)		(.02)	(.01)	(.01)		(2.49)		(.26)	
	−.05		.02**	.01***	−.01		−.36		−.28*	−.29***
	(.28)		(.01)	(.00)	(.01)		(1.44)		(.15)	(.07)
	−.24	−.21***	.01		−.01**	−.00***	.29		−.22**	−.19***
	(.19)	(.06)	(.01)		(.01)	(.00)	(.96)		(.10)	(.05)
	1.00		.05	.06**	−.00		5.75		−.13	
	(.92)		(.03)	(.03)	(.02)		(4.75)		(.50)	
	−.00		.00		.00		.03		.00	
	(.00)		(.00)		(.00)		(.04)		(.00)	
	−.05		−.01***	−.01***	.00*	.00***	−.81*		−.03	
	(.08)		(.00)	(.00)	(.00)	(.00)	(.43)		(.04)	
	−.32		−.02	−.02	.02*	.01*	−1.64		−.15	
	(.32)		(.01)	(.01)	(.01)	(.01)	(1.68)		(.18)	
	−.02		−.00		.00*	.00***	−.51	−.49***	−.02	
	(.07)		(.00)		(.00)	(.00)	(.37)	(.18)	(.04)	
	.09	.11*	.00		−.00		−.31		.19***	.18***
	(.11)	(.06)	(.00)		(.00)		(.58)		(.06)	(.04)
	−1.33		−.05	−.04	.08*		−7.37		1.21	
	(1.51)		(.06)	(.04)	(.04)		(7.79)		(.82)	
	1.89**	1.56***	.00		.02		−2.89		.36	
	(.79)	(.58)	(.02)		(.02)		(4.07)		(.43)	
	1.57		−.03		−.02		−4.66		−.06	
	(1.06)		(.04)		(.03)		(5.44)		(.57)	

(continued)

TABLE 3.4.—Continued

	Regional Tax Share		Central Transfers		of which: Subventions	
	(1)	(2)	(1)	(2)	(1)	(2)
Region had member on parliament's budget committee	−.39 (4.89)		.90 (5.51)		−.52 (.84)	
SS deputies per capita	−1.49 (1.35)		−.08 (1.52)		.83*** (.23)	.97*** (.13)
Region had perm. rep. in Moscow	−.47 (3.85)		−.10 (4.33)		.50 (.66)	
Constant	−36.86 (52.84)	−46.57 (33.62)	105.53* (59.48)	68.94*** (17.93)	17.13* (9.11)	4.64*** (1.49)
R^2	.63778	.59415	.60037	.52542	.69603	.72356
Adj. R^2	.46109	.50830	.40542	.48092	.55129	.70382
N	61	63	61	70	62	75

Note: standard errors in parentheses; column 2 contains all variables from column 1 which significantly add to the fit of the regression, as judged by an *F*-test at the .10 level.

the more separatist regions? Most of these were republics, with some degree of non-Russian ethnic population. Further analysis suggests that a region's ethnic balance, per se, played little role. Neither a measure of the regional concentration of non-Russians nor one measuring the proportion of inhabitants who were of the region's specific titular nationality was at all significant when added to the regression.[37] (In both cases, sovereignty declarations remained significant.) It is harder to separate out the effects of sovereignty declarations from those of administrative status of the region because of the high overlap between republic status and an early sovereignty declaration. (Among the 22 regions that declared sovereignty in 1990 were 13 of the 16 republics then in existence, 8 autonomous okrugs, and one ordinary oblast, Irkutsk.)[38] Because of the high overlap between these two variables, they are not included together in the regressions reported. If a dummy variable for republic status *is* included alongside the sovereignty declaration variables in model 1, the republic status variable is completely insignificant (at $p = .79$); because of the high overlap, the sovereignty declaration variable's significance drops to the .19 level and its estimated coefficient falls from 19.8 to 16.7. If the republic status dummy is substituted for the sovereignty declaration variable, it is less significant and the regression's adjusted R^2-value falls. In short, if one knows that a region declared sovereignty in 1990, knowing its ethnic makeup or administrative status reveals little more information about its access to fiscal benefits in 1992.

How large were these effects? How large a payoff could a region earn through such gestures of disenchantment? One can gauge this by comparing the estimated impact of fiscal factors with the apparent impact of other factors. In

Fiscal Transfers and Fiscal Appeasement 71

Budget Investment		Government Reserve Fund		S. Soviet Reserve Fund		Special Benefits		Credits	
(1)	(2)	(1)	(2)	(1)	(2)	(1)	(2)	(1)	(2)
−.78		.00		−.02		2.07		.20	
(1.06)		(.04)		(.03)		(5.45)		(.57)	
.02		−.02	−.02**	.04***	.04***	−.65		−.22	
(.28)		(.01)	(.01)	(.01)	(.00)	(1.50)		(.16)	
−1.72**	−1.97***	−.05		.00		1.30		−.17	
(.83)	(.53)	(.03)		(.02)		(4.29)		(.45)	
13.77	9.06***	−.12	.30	.13	−.21**	61.02	19.03**	14.38**	13.57***
(11.43)	(1.27)	(.43)	(.19)	(.31)	(.10)	(58.89)	(7.64)	(6.18)	(2.79)
.49643	.39482	.67025	.62313	.76344	.73119	.52281	.41388	.55056	.43137
.25664	.34142	.51323	.54340	.65079	.71019	.29004	.37836	.33133	.38763
62	74	62	63	62	69	61	70	61	70

*$p < .10$ **$p < .05$ ***$p < .01$

1992, for instance, regions in the south received considerably more in net central transfers than their counterparts to the north. For each 10 degrees latitude further south a region's capital was located, it received about 8,600 rubles per capita more in net transfers (or a little more than half a standard deviation; see table 3.3, 1992, column 2). But for each 10 percent of the vote that had gone to candidates *other* than Yeltsin in 1991, the region could expect to get about 4,300 rubles per capita more—and an early sovereignty declaration was associated with more than 19,000 additional rubles per capita in net transfers. In other words, a republic like Karelia, about 7 degrees north of Moscow, might expect to get about 6,000 rubles per capita less than the country's capital in net transfers because of its northerly location. But this loss would be completely wiped out if the total vote for Yeltsin the previous year in Karelia had been 14 percentage points lower than in Moscow (in fact it was nearly 19 points lower). If the leader had declared sovereignty in 1990 (in this case, he had), this would not just compensate for the republic's location but net it an additional 13,000 rubles per capita.

In 1994, more profitable regions received smaller net transfers than less profitable ones. For every 1,000 rubles per capita in profits earned in the region the previous year, net transfers in 1994 were about 1,200 rubles per capita lower. Bryansk Oblast in 1993 had profits per inhabitant nearly 60,000 rubles higher than Tomsk Oblast and could expect therefore to get about 72,000 rubles per capita *less* in net 1994 transfers. However, if the governor of Bryansk had the nerve to oppose Yeltsin in his September 1993 conflict with the parliament (he did), or if the vote for Russia's Choice in Bryansk had been 8 percentage points lower than in Tomsk (in fact it was 10 points lower), this would more than make up the difference (it did: Bryansk actually received about 177,000 rubles per inhabitant *more* than Tomsk).

While public expressions of discontent or disloyalty continued to earn regions a fiscal premium over the years, the relative role of different kinds of protests changed in some interesting ways. One notable difference is the weakened influence of the strike weapon. Whereas 1991 had been the height of a wave of labor mobilization, with political strikes frequently shutting down coal mines and other enterprises, 1993 saw a dramatic decrease in the number of strikes and in their impact—the total level of strike losses in that year was only *one-tenth* of that in 1991. By 1994, the relationship between strikes and transfers had disappeared. It is tempting to view the replacement of strikes by voting and political declarations as an institutionalization of the politics of protest, perhaps comparable to the institutionalization of conflict observed in other cases of democratization (see Rustow 1970). However, the change may merely have reflected the particular circumstances in 1994–96, a time at which frequent elections provided clear measures of regional opinion, and labor mobilization had abated for a variety of reasons.

At the same time, the disaggregated regressions of table 3.4 suggest that different pressure tactics may have worked best in different institutional settings. Since disbursements from the government's reserve fund were controlled, obviously enough, by the government, while transfers from the Supreme Soviet's reserve fund were decided by the parliamentary leadership, differences in the pattern of allocation from these two sources may indicate different priorities of the institutions' leaders. While strikes and sovereignty declarations both led to significantly higher government reserve fund payments in 1992, neither had a significant impact on Supreme Soviet fund transfers. Thus, these signals of discontent seem to have been more effective at blackmailing the government than at pressuring parliament.

The tables also reveal much about the context in which such political factors operated. Besides public expressions of discontent, certain other variables appeared to earn regions larger net transfers. Were "needy" regions favored? Those recording higher profits per capita (and thus lower need in one sense) did receive lower net transfers. This is not surprising since higher profits would mean larger payments of profit tax to the federal budget and thus automatically smaller *net* transfers from the center. Other indicators of "need" tell a changing story. While there was just about no significant evidence of net transfers favoring regions with greater social need in 1992 and 1994 (when the larger the elderly population, the *smaller* were net transfers), in 1995 and 1996 fiscal benefits *did* go disproportionately to regions with greater evidence of need. Regions with a less developed social infrastructure (poorer provision of telephones or doctors) received significantly larger net transfers in 1996 and (marginally) significantly larger net transfers in 1995. In 1995, regions with larger dependent populations of old and young received more, as did regions further north facing harsher climatic conditions. In both years, regions where real incomes were lower enjoyed significantly higher net transfers. Such results suggest a trend toward greater use of transfers to alleviate pockets of hardship or underdevelopment.

Particularly interesting are the disaggregated regressions for transfers under the Regional Support Fund in 1994, its first year (see table B1 in appendix B). Did it successfully channel funds to regions in greatest need? I included dummy variables here to capture the explicit criteria for allocation under the Fund—whether or not the region had been classified as "needy" or as "especially needy."[39] "Especially needy" regions *did* receive significantly larger fund transfers—on average about 60,000 rubles per capita, including additional VAT exemptions (see table B1).[40] However, political factors also show up, even in this area designed to isolate allocation decisions from the pressures of politics. The higher the vote for Russia's Choice in 1993, the lower the amount received even by "needy" and "especially needy" regions under the Fund in 1994.[41] Established precisely to remove the appearance of injustice and illogicality, the Fund appeared to have achieved only a partial success in the first year. Its criteria, while significant, were evidently supplemented in their implementation by the political rationales of the past.[42]

In both 1994 and 1996, regions that were more advanced in economic reform received significantly larger net transfers, perhaps suggesting that rewarding faster reform was another motivation of central policymakers. (However, that regions received these funds in 1994 apparently in the form of direct transfers from the Regional Support Fund—an unlikely sponsor of economic reforms—raises the possibility that this result reflects some other correlated factor.) While both agricultural and raw-materials-producing regions fared worse than average in 1992, the raw-materials-producing regions received larger net transfers in 1994 and 1996, suggesting that they benefited not just from economic reforms but also from state aid.[43] It is tempting to read into the emerging fiscal payoffs to raw materials regions evidence of the political bargain struck from 1994 on between the Yeltsin-Chernomyrdin regime and the oil and gas barons. One way in which the administration partially compensated fuel and energy enterprises for continuing to supply insolvent clients and thus forestalling political crises was to temporarily tolerate high rates of nonpayment of federal taxes by these energy sector firms (see Treisman 1998a). Such nonpayment of taxes to the federal budget would increase the region's net fiscal transfer.

With one exception, I did not find much evidence that access to central officials or parliamentary pork-barrel politics influenced the pattern of allocation. Having a permanent representative in Moscow, a representative on the parliament's budget committee, a representative serving as budget committee chair or deputy chair, or a representative serving as speaker or deputy speaker of parliament did not yield significantly greater net transfers. These results are surprising because the conventional wisdom paints Russian politics as a murky world of backroom bargains, in which access and contacts are crucial and political positions are used to milk cash from citizens and the state. Considerable evidence, both judicial and anecdotal, suggests a high degree of corruption and favoritism in the allocation of state benefits (see, e.g., Treisman 1992, 1995). It is possible that this is, in fact, true of fiscal allocation—the contacts necessary may be far less formal than merely having a permanent representative in Moscow or being visited by a high official.[44] But the evidence was harder to find.

The one major exception, though, is striking. Those regions that Yeltsin personally visited during the first six months of 1996, as the presidential campaign unfolded, received more than 400,000 rubles per capita more in net transfers that year (about one-eighth of a standard deviation). Previous visits by high officials had not been associated with discernible outpourings of cash—but evidently presidential election years are somewhat different.[45] Though evidence that parliamentary pork-barrel politics reshaped the overall results of allocation is scanty, such factors did appear to influence at least one particular transfer stream. Regions lucky enough to have a representative serving as chair or deputy chair either of one of the parliamentary budget committees or of one house of parliament did receive a significantly higher allocation of investment funds in 1994. Perhaps this is the preferred channel for such parliamentary handouts.

Nevertheless, the opportunities for wheeling and dealing by well-placed parliamentarians seem somewhat dwarfed by the sheer power of numbers. Regions that had more representatives per capita in the State Duma because of having single-member constituencies with smaller populations received significantly larger net transfers in 1994 and 1995.[46] In 1994, these included direct payments from the regional support fund and possibly also from net mutual payments. Regions represented by the chairman of one of the houses of parliament or his deputy could expect to receive about 55,000 rubles per capita more in investment grants in 1994 (table B1). But for every additional representative a region had per million inhabitants, it could count on nearly 140,000 additional rubles per capita in net transfers (see table 3.3). To have one extra deputy per million inhabitants would apparently help a region more in extracting benefits than having one of the most senior parliamentary leaders in its delegation.[47] At the same time, less populous regions, which would tend to have greater proportional influence in government and in the Council of Federation because of their entitlement to a minimum number of representatives, received significantly larger net transfers in all years, and in particular larger mutual payments in 1994.[48]

These results may suggest a rather more open and mechanical system of lobbying than would be consistent with the conventional view of long-established contacts, backroom favors, and individualized corruption. Tiny, sparsely inhabited territories are represented officially at central meetings by a governor who has most of the same formal rights as the leaders of densely populated urban centers. Part of a region's benefits may simply stem from this access and formal consultation. If so, these benefits would go much further in per capita terms in the less populated regions. The parliamentary variable suggests that the sheer number of deputies a region had in the State Duma increased the amount that they could together extract. Regions that had more deputies per capita received more rubles per capita. If correct, such an interpretation would imply a surprisingly unstructured and egalitarian system of power in the parliament and in region-center relations.

From accounts of participants, the competition involved in lobbying parliament for budgetary benefits for a particular region is intense. Ramazan Abdulatipov, the chair of the upper house from 1990–93 and then a Federation Council deputy from Dagestan from 1994–95, argued that such lobbying was largely ineffective. Even though parliament voted on the budget, he said, the complicated process of getting legislation passed made it very difficult for deputies to sneak in special benefits for their regions.

> I tried myself to lobby on behalf of Dagestan during voting on the budget for 1993. I had one article on aid to Dagestan. I succeeded in getting the organizers to include it in a block of 100 articles which were supposed to be voted on together, as a package. But then somebody found out about it and started arguing from the microphone—why should Dagestan be favored? There is also lobbying from that side.[49]

As a result, parliamentary leaders often sought to extract localized benefits through the executive branch rather than through their own institution.

In short, these results suggest a consistent logic. While other factors also help to explain the outcomes of central allocation, the politics of regional appeasement played an important role. Regions where the population or leadership had recently expressed opposition toward the central regime fared particularly well in the division of central largesse in the early 1990s. Challenging Moscow—whether by elite declaration, mass industrial action, or public voting—paid off far better than complaisance.[50] The regional politics of protest appears to have been richly rewarded.

Changing Patterns

So far, I have analyzed the relationship between regional characteristics and absolute levels of fiscal transfers. But an equally interesting question is whether we can see the same effects in short-run *changes* in the level of fiscal transfers. The most protest-prone regions may receive greater benefits year after year. But does an increase in the level of hostility toward the central regime in a particular year translate into an increase in central funds?

76   After the Deluge

This is hard to test systematically given the limited data available. Nevertheless, the evidence does support such a hypothesis. An estimate of net center-region per capita fiscal transfers for 1988, as a percentage of total revenue collected in the region, is available (see Dmitrieva 1996, 31–32). Though comparing this directly to the net transfer figures for 1992 (expressed here as a percentage of total revenue collected regionally) is problematic, the relative ranking of regions in terms of their net gains or losses from fiscal redistribution can be compared to the 1992 rankings. (The 1992 net transfers aggregate variable contains a wider range of different types of fiscal flows—largely because of the increasing significance of these flows after the perestroika changes already discussed.) The size and direction of change in the ranking of regions between 1988 and 1992 is instructive. While some regions shot up the scale of central redistributive priorities, others sank into neglect. The number falling was about the same as the number rising. While one region dropped 53 places in the rankings (Novosibirsk Oblast), another rose 60 places (Tatarstan).[51]

Ideally, one would want to see how such changes in redistributive ranking relate to *changes* in plausible independent variables—separatist activism, voting, access, and so on. Lack of data makes this just about impossible. Yet, since overt anticenter protests essentially began in the years after 1988, it may be reasonable to take the initial (1990–91) readings as an indicator of change. I there-

TABLE 3.5.   Change in Ranking of Regions in Terms of Net Central Transfers, 1988–92

	(1)	(2)
A. Bargaining Power		
Recent Protest or Opposition		
Vote for Yeltsin in 1991 pres. election	−.11	
	(.21)	
Declared sovereignty by Jan. 1991	15.91**	19.22***
	(6.92)	(4.10)
Log man-days lost to strikes, 1991	7.94***	7.40***
	(2.91)	(2.24)
Political Weight		
Population	−.00	−.00***
	(.00)	(.00)
Estimated economic output per capita	−.00	
	(.01)	
B. Alleviating Need		
Social infrastructure less developed	4.52	
	(3.06)	
Profits per capita 1990	4.67	
	(15.13)	

TABLE 3.5.—*Continued*

	(1)	(2)
Percent of population under 16	1.79	2.28***
	(1.77)	(.61)
Percent of population of pension age	.15	
	(1.34)	
Estimated real income 1992	.02	
	(.05)	
Degrees latitude north	−1.06*	−.75**
	(.55)	(.36)
C. Other Central Objectives		
Index of advanced pace of economic reform	−3.51*	−3.14**
	(2.03)	(1.56)
Index of region's effort at tax collection	−5.01	
	(7.74)	
Percent of work force in agriculture	−.86*	−.56**
	(.49)	(.25)
Share of RF total raw materials output	−1.13	−.87**
	(.79)	(.40)
D. Access and "Pork"		
Region had representative on parliament's budget commission	−2.04	
	(6.64)	
Representatives per capita in Congress of People's Deputies	1.19	
	(1.80)	
President visited region 1992	3.88	
	(4.85)	
Prime Minister visited region 1992	4.99	
	(6.63)	
Region had permanent representative in Moscow	3.95	
	(5.20)	
Control Variable: 1988 Ranking	.79***	.80***
	(.16)	(.08)
Constant	−5.08	−33.93
	(71.70)	(30.32)
R^2	.74629	.72683
Adjusted R^2	.61309	.68516
N	61	68

Note: standard errors in parentheses; column 2 contains all variables from column 1 which significantly add to the fit of the regression, as judged by an F-test at the .10 level. A change in rank from 20th to first is classified as a *rise* of 19, etc.

*$p < .10$ **$p < .05$ ***$p < .01$

fore look for a relationship between declaring sovereignty early and change in subsequent redistributive rank. The hypothesis is that regions that declared sovereignty would tend to rise in the center's redistributive priorities relative to those that did not.

As can be seen from table 3.5, the same bargaining power factors that predicted a high relative level of net center-region transfers in 1992 also predicted a big rise in the redistributive rankings between 1988 and 1992. Regions that declared sovereignty in the first wave rose on average almost 20 places. Strikes also led to a rise in a region's rank on the list of the center's redistributive priorities. Apart from this, less populous and less resource-rich regions became relatively more favored by central policy, and the pattern exhibited strong regression to the mean. Those regions ranked higher tended to drop more subsequently, and those that started lower tended to rise.

What about the subsequent change? Such a result might follow from a one-time shift of priorities at the beginning of Russia's independence, a durable recasting of the balance between regions' redistributive positions. Reasonably comparable data exist for the main budget transfer items for 1993 and 1994, making possible analysis of the nature of change in the pattern of redistribution between these two years. Unfortunately, constructing indicators of the change in the degree of separatist assertiveness of regions during 1993–94 is even more difficult than in the previous case. The most assertive regions had declared sovereignty months or years before, and no ready way to measure subsequent increments in assertiveness suggested itself.

However, measuring the change in mass voting patterns is somewhat easier, since roughly comparable elections or referenda were held at convenient intervals. Though no two elections in a country without a structured party system are directly comparable, a rough measure of the change in support for Yeltsin and his allies can be formed from the 1991 presidential and 1993 parliamentary election results. A variable was constructed measuring the difference between the vote for the three most pro-reform parties in the December 1993 election (Russia's Choice, the Russian Movement for Democratic Reform, and Yabloko) and the vote for Yeltsin in June 1991. Based on the previous analysis, we would expect a negative relationship between the change in the level of pro-reform voters and the subsequent change in fiscal transfers—a region where support for reformers was dropping fastest would get the largest increases in redistributed cash.

Bivariate correlations suggest exactly such a relationship with the change in transfers and net transfers between 1993 and 1994. The correlation between the change in pro-reform votes (1991–93) and the change in central transfers (1993–94) was $-.21$, significant at $p < .05$; and the correlation between the change in pro-reform votes and the change in *net* central transfers (from which tax remittances have been subtracted) was $-.40$, significant at $p < .001$. Relatively larger drops in regional support for Yeltsin and his allies were rewarded with larger increases in central largesse the next year. Regression analysis found that this negative relationship also held up controlling for other plausible independent variables.

Conclusion

The politics of taxation and fiscal transfers in Russia in the early 1990s struck observers as haphazard, ephemeral, and devoid of any underlying logic. To participants and experts, monetary allocations seemed to result from the clash of lobbyists, rebounding like billiard balls between a dozen centers of power in the capital, deflecting each other at numerous junctures. About all that seemed certain was that the outcome would be complicated and irrational.

But the trajectories of billiard balls, though hard to predict before play begins, are actually highly ordered. They can be understood in terms of the laws of physics, the skill of the players, and the rules of the game. This chapter has tried to trace the aggregate paths of a subset of state money during the early years of Russia's postcommunist transition. Admittedly the data is partial and imperfect, and can only suggest patterns rather than prove causal relationships. But, even given its flaws, it seems to tell a fairly consistent and intelligible story, one that is far less random than it might at first appear.

Among phenomena that may explain why some regions do better and others worse in the competition for transfers and tax revenues, the politics of regional protest occupies a prominent place. In 1992, 1994, 1995, and probably 1996, regions that had recently voted more heavily *against* Yeltsin or his political allies received more generous shares of a range of different central transfers and tax benefits. Regions where the local leadership had made separatist gestures or opposed the president or his central allies at moments of crisis also seemed to be favored. And in 1992, as a dramatic wave of labor mobilization tapered off, those regions that had suffered major losses to strikes in the previous year were also treated to larger benefits by the government.

Central policy seemed aimed to appease regions with a demonstrated capacity and resolve to challenge Moscow, whether by elite declaration, voting, or mass action. The patterns created by such a politics of blackmail stand out more sharply than any associated with uneven access, institutional power, or pork-barrel spending. While disruptive action appears to earn rewards for politicians, behind-the-scenes strategies of influence (such as infiltrating key committees or parliamentary leadership posts and associating with top officials during visits to the provinces) seem, with a few exceptions, either not to be independently effective in the fiscal arena or else to yield results too small or private to feature in what figures are published. While corruption, personal connections, and clique rivalries characterize the conventional—and partly justified—image of recent Russian politics, such features of political life occur within a far more openly competitive and apparently precarious process of threats, pressures, and political brinkmanship.

This casts a rather unexpected light on the periodic conflicts and crises between Moscow and the provinces in the early 1990s. Protests that came clothed in the trappings of nationalism or labor militancy may at times have been acts in a more prosaic drama. A couple of examples suggest the contradictory mix of separatism, protest, and bargaining that infused Russia's center-region relations. In the spring of 1993, a young businessman from Kalmykia, Kirsan Ilyumzhinov, was elected that republic's president. His campaign, playing upon Kalmyk cultural distinctness, had asserted the need for economic independence from Moscow. Shortly after his victory, he sent a letter to the Russian Minister of Finance, Boris Fyodorov, declaring his commitment in the interest of greater independence to reducing the need for subventions from the Russian budget (Ilyumzhinov 1993). In the next sentence, he requested that "in order to resolve this question already in the second half of this year" the Finance Ministry issue Kalmykia an interest-free budget loan of 90 billion rubles.

One example of the subsidy-seeking strike occurred in Primore in the summer of 1993. In August, the region held a one-day, general work stoppage. The strikers' demand was not for an increase in wages, but for a lowering of electricity and fuel prices, a reduction of the territory's payments to the federal budget, and control over import and export fees. The region's governor, Yevgeny Nazdratenko, said he did not call for a strike "but did not persuade people to return to work either" (Todres 1993). The newspaper *Kommersant* noted that the strike was supported by the region's corps of deputies and industrial directors, along with the largest seaports (Vetrov 1993). Nazdratenko happened to be in Moscow at the time, where he was making similar demands to the central government. Soon afterward, a delegation including the prime minister, Viktor Chernomyrdin, visited Primore and promised various kinds of assistance. In October, Chernomyrdin signed a resolution permitting Primore to reduce remittances to the federal budget, providing 55.5 billion rubles in additional credits for the rest of the year, and establishing fixed prices for electricity, which, according to the newspaper *Segodnya,* would require 143 billion rubles in subsidies for coal purchases (Bekker 1993b).

Such strategies of simultaneous negotiation, rhetorical hostility, and implicit threats of disruption seem rational given the logic of fiscal policy already noted. But why did the center yield to such blackmail? Appeasement is generally considered a self-destructive and destabilizing policy, likely merely to encourage aggressors to increase their demands. Rewarding the recalcitrant seems calculated to increase their number. Yet despite a central policy of rewarding the most voluble troublemakers in 1992–93, tensions between Moscow and the regions subsequently abated. Explaining this paradox is the goal of the next two chapters.

CHAPTER 4

Public Spending and Regional Voting

Chapter 3 uncovered a puzzling logic in the way that central authorities allocated fiscal transfers among Russia's 89 regions. Redistributing resources from the loyal to the rebellious would seem to risk merely feeding the fires that some thought threatened the federation's cohesion. To observers like Boris Fyodorov, the finance minister, rewarding the assertively disobedient governors appeared a strategy calculated to encourage a broader revolt. And yet it did not. This chapter and the next attempt to explain why.

The answer I suggest has to do with the consequences of fiscal transfers when they filtered through into higher rates of public spending. When government spending increased in a region, this apparently influenced how residents voted in elections and referenda. Where regional government spending increased relatively more, the vote was subsequently higher for Yeltsin and his reformist allies, controlling for the previous level of regional support for them. Thus, larger central transfers, when they boosted spending, appear to have bought votes for central incumbents. This chapter presents the evidence for this claim. It shows that the relationship between spending and votes held in a series of different elections and years, even controlling for the various other possible causes of regional voting patterns.

Patterns of Regional Voting

To look at maps of how Russia voted in the early 1990s is to see a political society taking form. Before 1989, Russias regions voted more or less alike. In the 1984 Supreme Soviet election, for example, more than 99.9 percent of voters nationwide endorsed the single list of approved candidates—a total that leaves little room for regional variation (White, Rose, and McAllister 1996, 21). But as Gorbachev's experiment with competitive elections pried the ballot boxes loose from the party's embrace, new patterns started to emerge. First in the Soviet Union, then in Russia itself, geography began to impose itself on the electoral returns. Different regions expressed different political identities.

Trying to make sense of the evolving patterns has much in common with waiting for a Polaroid photograph to develop. The first nationwide poll that offered Russian voters a clear choice between divergent candidates was the presidential election of June 1991. Boris Yeltsin, promising radical economic reform and greater autonomy from the Soviet center, easily defeated a field of candidates that ranged from communist apparatchiks to one hypernationalist extremist. The results showed major regional differences, but no clear geographical pattern (see fig. 4.1). Some of Yeltsin's greatest successes—78 percent of the valid vote in Chelyabinsk Oblast, for instance—came in regions adjacent to his relative failures—48 percent in Bashkortostan. In general, he did slightly better in the west than the east, and about equally well in north and south.[1]

By the next nationwide poll—a referendum held in April 1993 on support for Yeltsin or the parliament—a far clearer pattern had emerged (see fig. 4.2). Almost all the president's strongest supporters now lay to the north of the 60th parallel, while the heavily anti-Yeltsin regions lay to the south, in a band crossing from Smolensk and Dagestan to Amur Oblast in Siberia. The change is even more strikingly visible in figure 4.3, which shows the regions where the *drop* in support for Yeltsin was greatest. Most of these regions lie in a more or less contiguous band to the south and southwest of Moscow, stretching from Bryansk to Novosibirsk.

The same north-south split occurred in party-list voting in the December 1993 parliamentary election (see fig. 4.4).[2] The three most clearly pro-reform blocs among the 13 running—Russia's Choice, Yabloko, and the Russian Movement for Democratic Reforms—together polled highest in the north and Far East, and lowest in the same crescent crossing the southwest and south. Again in the 1995 parliamentary election, the most pro-reform blocs did best in the north and the Communists in the south; and the same division appeared in the voting for president in July 1996 (see figs. 4.5 and 4.6).

In brief, a dramatic polarization occurred in the geography of support for Yeltsin and his allies in the years following his election as president of Russia. A growing number of voters in the south and southwest began to desert pro-reform groupings and seek out more conservative or populist alternatives. But voters in the north and east became ever more attached to the radical reformers.

Explaining Regional Voting

What can explain this emerging variation? Why are southern voters so much more conservative than their northern compatriots?[3] Why within both north and south do some regions give much higher and others much lower votes to the reformers? Once again, the statistical technique of multiple regression can be used to seek an answer.[4] The hypothesis of this chapter is that interregional differences in regional government spending—themselves the result in part of differences in central transfers—explain part of the variation. Voters support in-

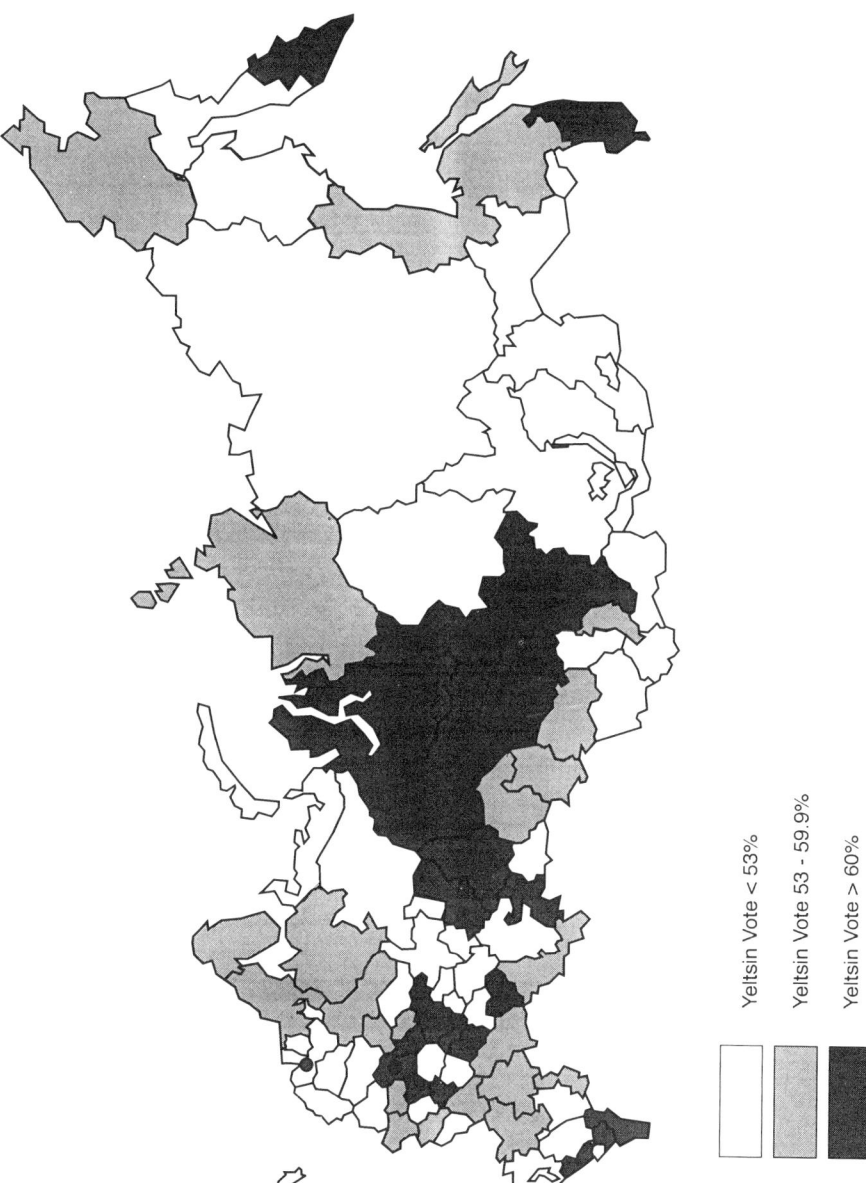

Fig. 4.1. Regional vote for Yeltsin in 1991 presidential election. (Data from McFaul and Petrov 1995, 655–56.)

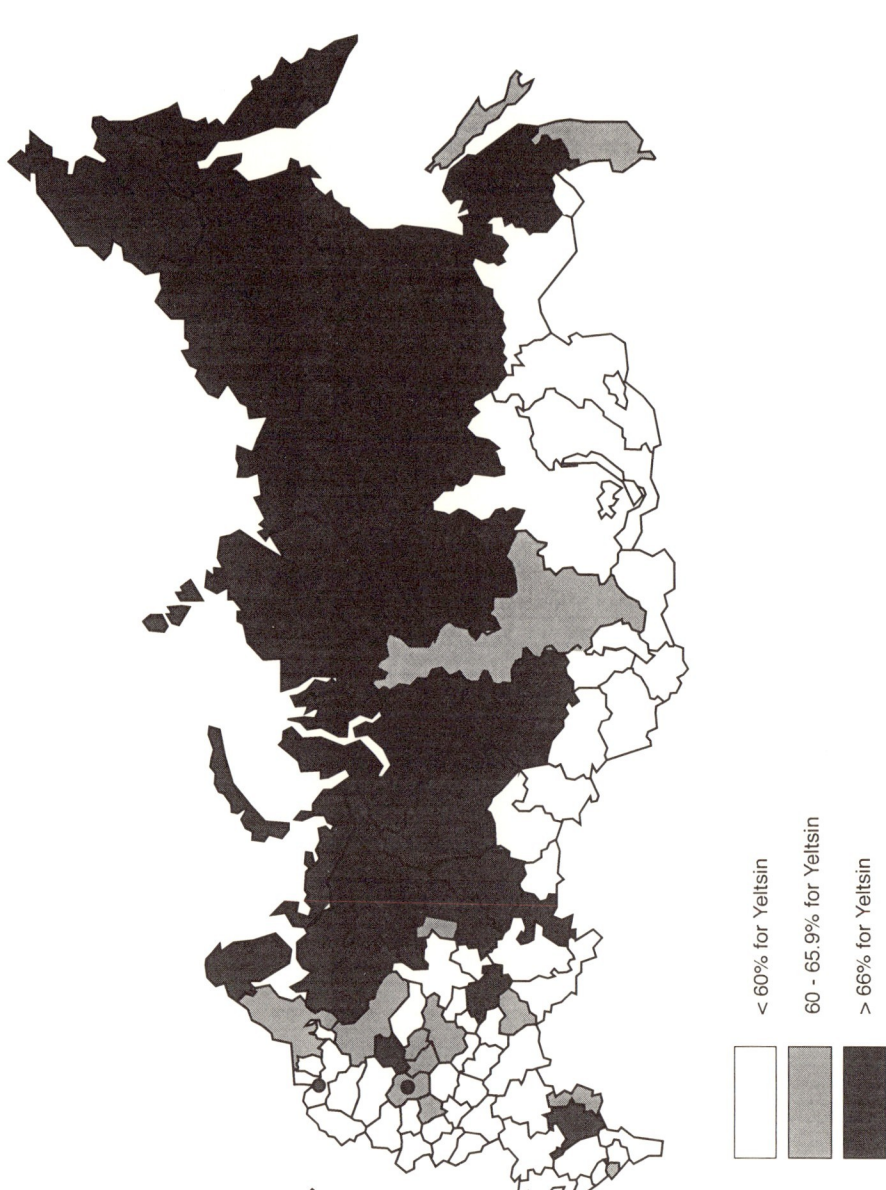

Fig. 4.2. Vote of trust in Yeltsin, April 1993 referendum. (Data from McFaul and Petrov 1995, 657–58.)

< 60% for Yeltsin
60 - 65.9% for Yeltsin
> 66% for Yeltsin

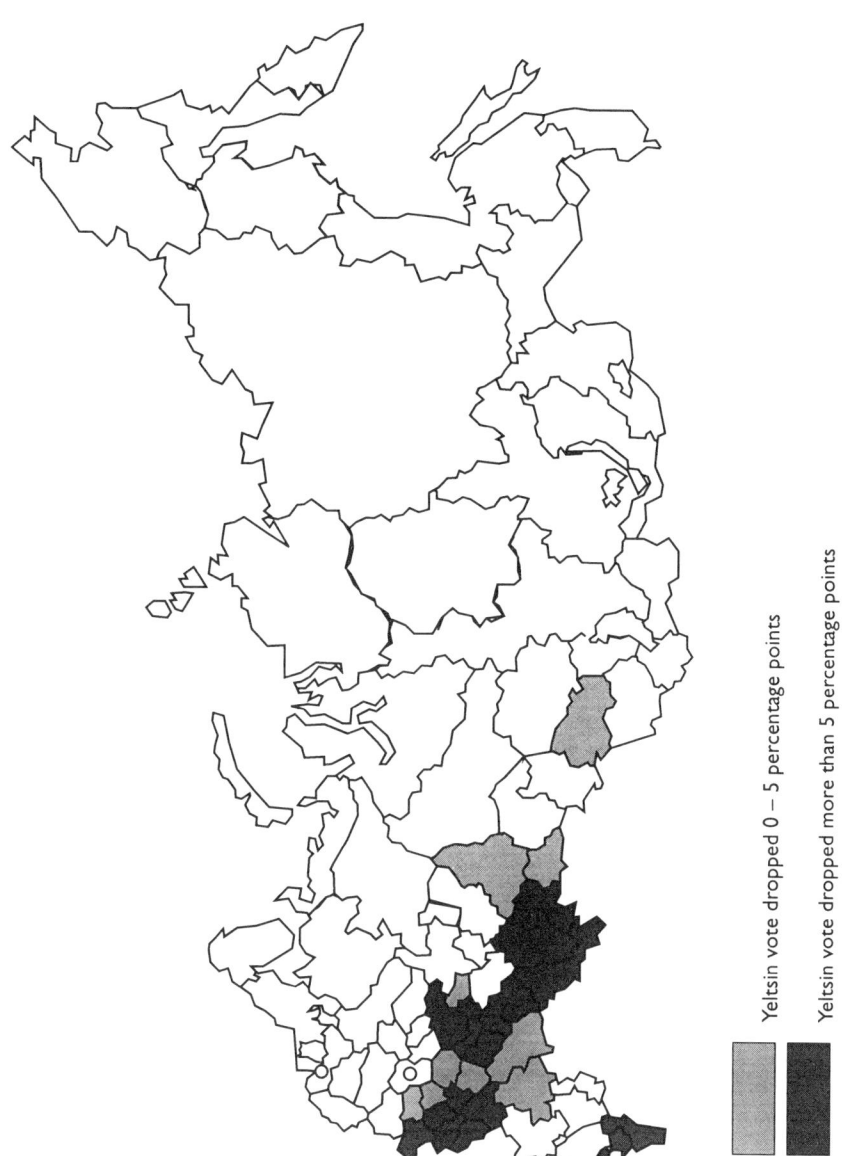

Fig. 4.3. Change in regional vote for Yeltsin, 1991 election to April 1993 referendum. (Data calculated from McFaul and Petrov 1995.)

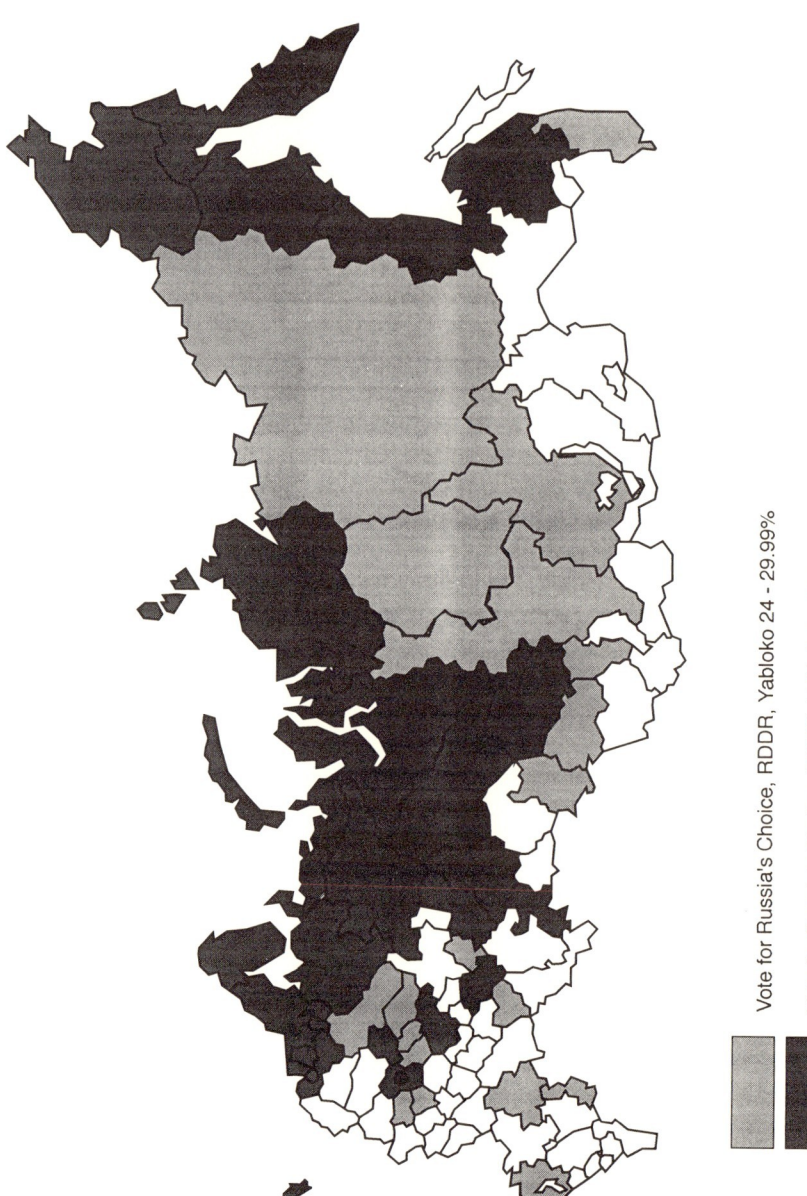

Fig. 4.4. Vote for the three most pro-reform blocs in December 1993. (Data from McFaul and Petrov 1995.)

Vote for Russia's Choice, RDDR, Yabloko 24 - 29.99%

Vote for Russia's Choice, RDDR, Yabloko > 30%

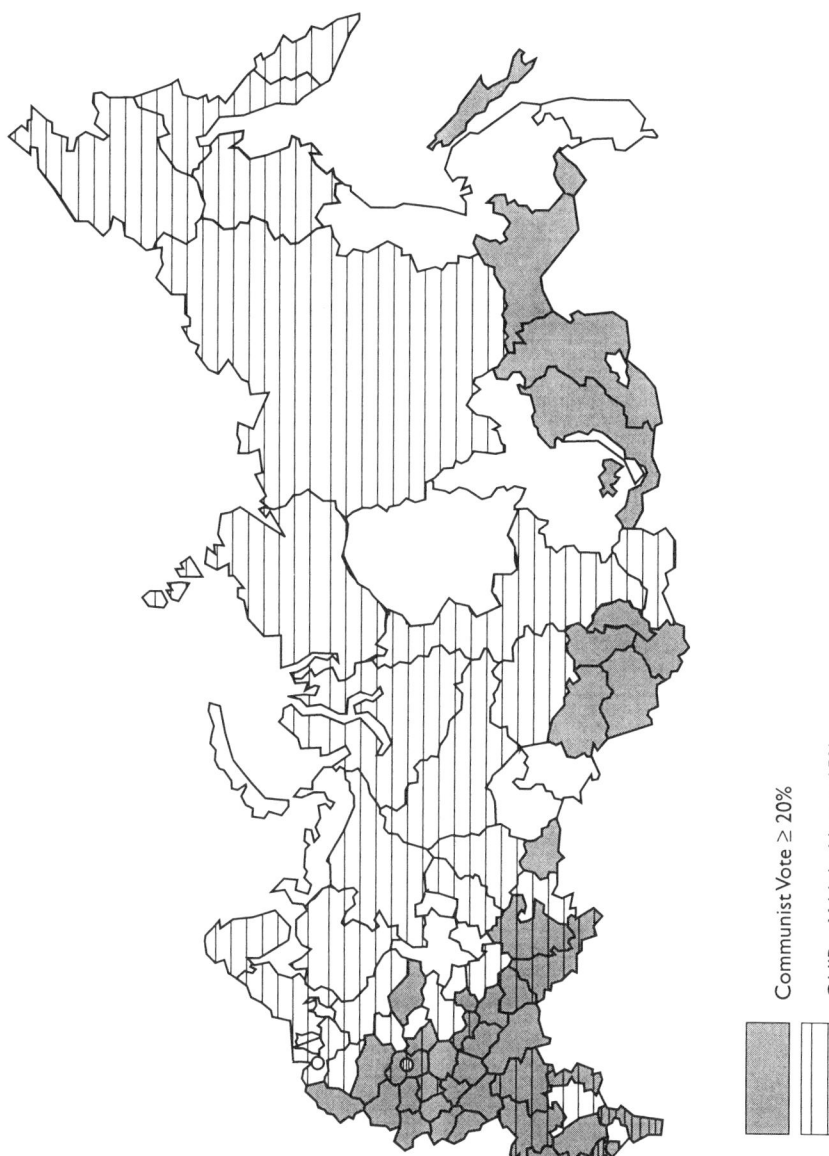

Fig. 4.5. Vote for major pro-reform blocs and for Communists, December 1995. (Data from *Transition*, Feb. 23, 1996.)

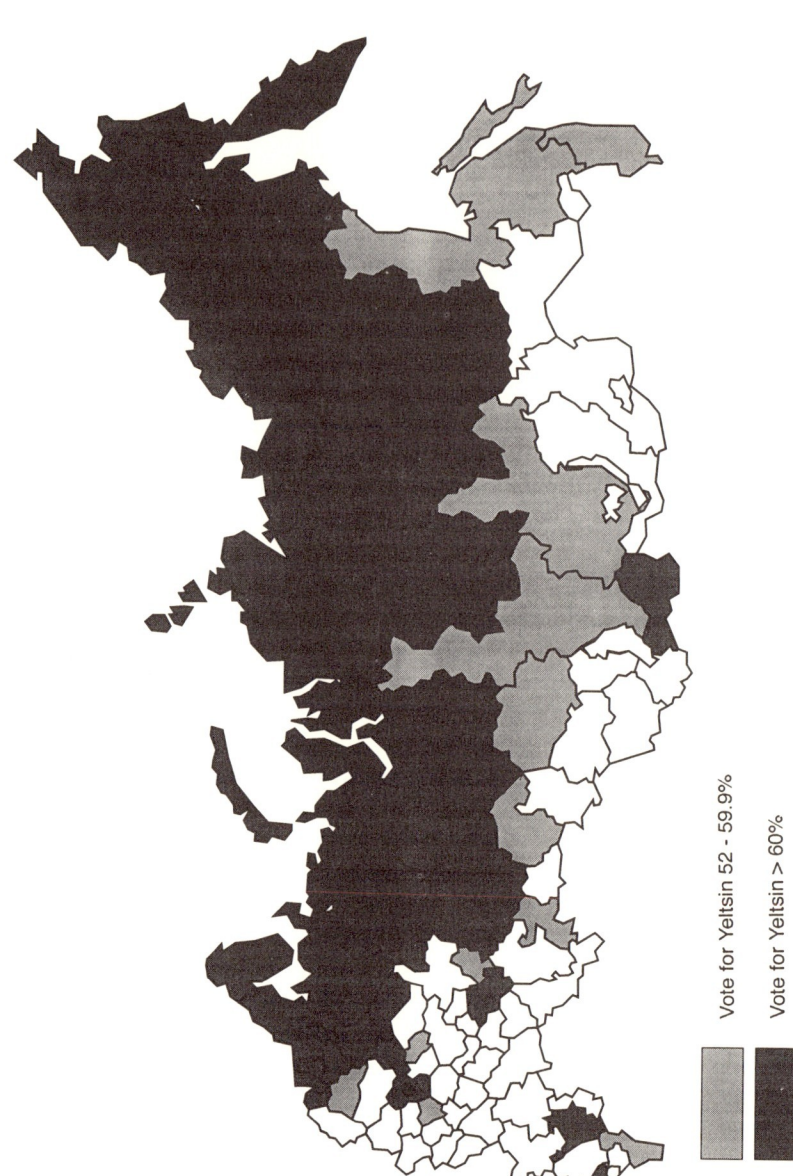

Fig. 4.6. Second-round vote for Yeltsin in 1996 presidential election. (Data from Central Electoral Commission, Moscow.)

cumbents at higher rates when spending is relatively high or increasing. This hypothesis is tested against a number of alternative theoretically plausible explanations for why different regions might exhibit different electoral preferences. Below I discuss what such explanations are.

Regional Economic Performance

Some theories of voting behavior in Western democracies suggest that election outcomes are heavily influenced by "retrospective" voting on economic issues (see Fiorina 1981; Lewis-Beck 1988; Kiewiet 1983; Key 1966). Voters reject incumbents and favor their opponents when they perceive macroeconomic conditions—either in society as a whole or as they impinge on the individual or subgroup—to be bad or deteriorating. Economic variables to which voters might respond include levels of or changes in unemployment, real income, and inflation (Lewis-Beck 1988; Kiewiet 1983).

The early 1990s witnessed depression, high inflation, and growing unemployment throughout Russia. However, performance did vary substantially from place to place. While officially recorded industrial output dropped 61 percent in Ust-Orda Autonomous Okrug between 1990 and 1993, in Ulyanovsk Oblast the drop was only 2 percent (Goskomstat Rossii 1994, 613–15). As of mid-1993, one in 14 enterprises in Moscow or Moscow Oblast was insolvent; in Chukotka, the figure was one in two. Inflation also varied: while nationwide, the consumer price index rose by 26 times between December 1991 and December 1992, the regional increase ranged from 12 times (in Volgogradskaya Oblast) to 53 times (in Magadan) (Goskomstat 1995). Finally, regions differed not just in the level of average wages and other incomes but in whether those wages were paid on time—and, if not, in the length of delay. As of June 1996, as voters went to the polls to elect a new president, workers in Karachaevo-Cherkessia were owed on average only about 25,000 rubles each. In Magadan, the average was 1.8 million rubles per worker.

Thus, a plausible first hypothesis is that levels of support for Yeltsin and his allies varied with regional economic performance. Where inflation, enterprise insolvency, unemployment, and wage delays were highest, and where real income growth was lowest, one might expect the drop in support for Yeltsin and the reformers to be greatest.

Regional Impact of Reform

However good or bad a region's macroeconomic performance, voters might be influenced by the degree to which economic reform had brought—or could be expected to bring—concrete benefits to them. A common assumption in discussions of postcommunist politics is that support for incumbent reformers tends to fall as voters experience the costs of reform. "Even when people do support the radical treatment at the outset . . . this support erodes, often drastically, as social costs are experienced" (Przeworski 1991, 167). Ambivalence about democratic and free-market institutions may increase over time as a result of social learning about the costs of reform (Whitefield and Evans 1994).

This might affect regional voting in two ways. First, it might interact with regional economic specialization. Over time, voters may realize that their region does not occupy a favored niche in the political economy of the future and may grow more reluctant to embrace free-market liberalism. Considerable evidence suggests that economic reform in Russia improved conditions for the raw materials sector, while exacerbating problems of agriculture.[5] Thus, more agricultural regions might be expected to vote against the reformers more frequently, and raw-materials-producing regions to vote for them. Another possibility, which unfortunately data were not available to test, is that regions concentrated on the defense industries might turn antireform as the sector lost state orders and hope for the future.

Second, particular reforms may proceed at a different pace and have a different impact in different regions. Where more enterprises and apartments are privatized, there may be more property-owners with a stake in the system.[6] Regions producing exportable goods will have more to gain from foreign trade liberalization. The level of support for central reformers may therefore be higher in regions where privatization is more advanced and where exports are sizable.

Social and Cultural Characteristics

A third possibility is that variation in regional voting reflects underlying variation in political culture, civic organization, and religious or ethnic traditions. Some have argued that voting behavior is determined largely by social identities, forged in the heat of particular historical conflicts and perpetuated by intergenerational and organizational mechanisms of socialization (Lipset and Rokkan 1967). According to Lazarsfeld, Berelson, and Gaudet, "a person thinks, politically, as he is, socially. Social characteristics determine political preference" (1968, 27). To Harrop and Miller, "a cross on the ballot is an implicit statement of social identity" (1987, 173).

Russian regions vary widely in their ethnic composition, religious heritage, and level of modernization. They also have histories of different patterns of social relations, dating from the imperial era to the late Soviet epoch, with which some scholars have associated distinctive subcultures. Divergent patterns of voting might mirror geographical divisions in the cultural attachments of voters, or the attitudinal consequences of different patterns of informal organization and socialization.[7] Such cleavages might take some time after the introduction of authentic elections to be fully expressed because of the lag necessary for public confidence to grow that anti-incumbent voting would no longer be punished.

What particular sociocultural divisions might shape political loyalties in Russia? Lipset and Rokkan, in a well-known article, suggested that the social identities that structure political competition emerged in epochs of revolutionary conflict. Cleavages between opposing subgroups of the population were created by the nation-building and industrial revolutions, and then preserved by the organizations, parties, and socialization mechanisms the competing subgroups created (Lipset and Rokkan 1967). Others suggest virtuous and vicious cycles that sustain "civic" or "uncivic" forms of social capital through long periods (Putnam 1993). According to Putnam, informal patterns of interaction, cooperative norms, and levels of social trust may be self-reinforcing even without any organized socialization mechanism and may survive for centuries despite macroinstitutional changes.

Unfortunately, neither Lipset and Rokkan nor Putnam explain why some historical conflicts yield lasting social identities in a specific context while others do not. Some parties, churches, traditions, and organizational forms die out, while others persist. Thus, any selection of hypotheses based on social and cultural identities, present and past, risks excluding important ones.

Some of Lipset and Rokkan's four cleavages, elaborated in the context of Western Europe, are clearly relevant to contemporary Russia. First, the country's imperial and Soviet history suggests the importance of the cleavage between the "central nation-building culture" and "ethnically, linguistically, or religiously distinct subject populations in the peripheries" (Lipset and Rokkan 1967). Ethnicity and religion are plausible causes of variation in political attitudes in Russia, a multinational state with three major faiths. Second, the division between agricultural and industrial interests that Lipset and Rokkan associate with the industrial revolution might be expected to be salient in a late-industrializing country such as Russia.[8]

A second source of political orientations of post-Soviet citizens is, of course, the experience of the Soviet era. Many scholars have described the efforts of successive Soviet regimes to inculcate a new set of values and beliefs in the population, while repressing social organizations that could support independent cultural orientations (e.g., Fitzpatrick 1978). But since the regime generally employed universalistic mobilization strategies, appealing to all Soviet citizens against hypothetical class enemies, it is not clear how this in itself could explain *regional* variations in citizens' political attitudes. Others have suggested that beneath the surface of Soviet society, social divisions were created by modernization (Lewin 1988; Hough 1990). Such cleavages might be reflected, again, in different patterns of voting among regions with different balances of agriculture and industry and with more and less educated populations. Finally, various scholars have suggested the importance of generational shifts in political attitudes, forged by the different historical experiences of each age cohort (Jennings and Niemi 1981; Bahry 1987b). The war and the Stalin era may have left a particular mark on generations then coming of age in Russia. Patterns of voting might, therefore, differ across regions depending on the age distribution of their populations.

To summarize, one might hypothesize a greater frequency of pro-reform voting in regions that were more industrialized and urbanized, and where the population was younger or better educated. One might expect to see different patterns of voting in peripheral regions with larger non-Russian or non-Christian populations, but the precise implications for voting are less clear.

Quality of Life

Political geographers suggest that, besides income, other more subtle determinants of the "quality of life" or "standard of living" in a region may affect how people vote. Such aspects of the quality of life often include measures of health, nutrition, education, work conditions, employment, consumption, transportation, housing, recreation, social security, and human freedom.[9] In Russia, one might expect a higher rate of anti-incumbent voting where environmental pollution or crime created greater hazards and where life expectancy had recently dropped sharply. In addition, voters in regions suffering a larger influx of refugees from other former Soviet republics or war zones might be less favorably inclined toward the central powers. Some scholars have suggested that the presence of refugees kindled support for the ultranationalistic Vladimir Zhirinovsky in parliamentary and presidential elections.

Public Spending and Special Benefits

Finally, as previously hypothesized, voters might make their choices based not so much on local economic performance, local costs and benefits of reform, social identity, cultural values, or quality of life, as on the perceived performance of the government. Are public services provided adequately, at rates increasing or at least not too sharply decreasing? Are roads built, hospitals and schools funded, pensions paid on time? Falling support for incumbent reformers might constitute a protest against the drop in real public spending associated with stabilization programs.

Unfortunately, data are not available about the regional breakdown of federal state spending. But by 1992, most of the government spending programs likely to affect voters directly were under the aegis of regional governments. While regional spending constituted more than 40 percent of total budget spending (rising to about 50 percent by 1996), the regional governments were responsible for 66 percent of spending on education and 89 percent of healthcare expenditures (see chap. 3).

Geographically, levels of per capita regional budget spending varied considerably. In 1991, expenditure ranged from 663 rubles per capita (in Checheno-Ingushetia) to 4,488 in Chukotka. The era of rapid economic reform saw these disparities widen. While in Magadan Oblast real per capita spending dropped 80 percent between 1991 and 1992, in Khanty-Mansiisky Autonomous Okrug it increased by an estimated 41 percent. The coefficient of variation for per capita regional spending increased from .50 in 1991 to more than .80 in 1992 (Le Houerou 1993, Annex 5, tables 1, 2). Since property was still not a source of income for most voters, and most government revenues came from taxes on industry, reluctance to pay tax was unlikely to constrain voters' demand for public services. And since the ability to fund such regional public services depended not just on the level of taxation in the region but also on the proportion of tax the region succeeded in retaining and on central fiscal transfers, regional spending varied with the region's ability to extract redistributive benefits from Moscow. As table 4.1 shows, regional spending levels were very closely associated with the tax revenue retained by the region and the level of central transfers in the early 1990s. In each year, between 85 and 100 percent of the variation in regional spending could be explained by these two variables. The estimated real change in direct federal transfers between 1993 and 1994

TABLE 4.1. Relationship between Central Transfers and Regional Budget Spending (OLS regression coefficients; dependent variable is per capita regional budget spending, 1,000 Rs per cap)

	1992	1993	1994	1995	1996
Tax revenues retained by region[a] (1,000 Rs per cap)	.91*** (.03)	1.19*** (.13)	1.01*** (.03)	.90*** (.06)	1.00*** (.02)
Total central transfers[b] (1,000 Rs per cap)	1.42*** (.06)	1.44*** (.04)	1.01*** (.03)	1.28*** (.08)	2.33*** (.07)
Constant	−.00 (.63)	−1.57 (22.47)	−124.07*** (23.69)	108.03 (112.99)	−311.39*** (75.22)
R^2	.944	.943	.973	.856	.974
Adjusted R^2	.942	.942	.972	.852	.974
N	87	87	85	86	86

Note: standard errors in parentheses. Total transfers do not include indirect transfers via additional tax breaks, since these are captured in the regional tax revenue figures.

[a]For 1992, total regional revenues.
[b]For 1992, subventions per capita.
*$p < .05$ **$p < .01$ ***$p < .001$

was significantly correlated with the change in estimated real regional spending between the two years (at $r = .66, p < .000$).

Helping to boost public spending in a region is not the only way that the central government might impress the region's voters and political elite that it has their interests at heart. Other techniques, used most notably during the 1996 presidential election campaign, include signing special agreements with the regional government or decrees promising additional economic aid. Bilateral power-sharing agreements were signed with more than 20 regions before the 1996 election, in almost all cases conferring some economic or other benefit.

Multiple regression offers a way to see how well each of these hypotheses fits the actual evidence of regional voting. Table 4.2 shows the results of regressing dependent variables measuring the regional vote for central incumbents and progovernment blocs on a range of indicators derived from the hypotheses discussed above. (For details of sources and operationalization, see appendix C.) The first two columns show regressions of the percentage of regional voters that voted "Yes" on the first question of the April 1993 referendum. (This question asked: Do you have confidence in the President of the Russian Federation Boris Yeltsin?) The next two columns show regressions of the regional vote for "Russia's Choice," the progovernment bloc headed by Yegor Gaidar, in December 1993.[10] The next regressions are of the regional vote for the "Our Home Is Russia" (OHIR) bloc of Prime Minister Viktor Chernomyrdin in the December 1995 parliamentary election. (Of the 43 blocs running this time, OHIR was the one most clearly associated with Yeltsin and his policies.) The final two columns show regressions of the first-round vote for Yeltsin (against nine other contenders) in the presidential election of 1996.

Each coefficient listed in the table estimates the size of a change in the pro-reform or pro-incumbent vote associated with a one-unit change in the given independent variable, holding constant all the other independent variables included in the regression.[11] A positive coefficient suggests that an increase in the independent variable is associated with an increase in the dependent variable—for example, a high pro-Yeltsin vote in the previous election was associated with a higher vote of trust in Yeltsin in April 1993. A negative coefficient suggests a negative relationship—for example, the greater the proportion of a region's population comprised of people under age 16, the lower was the vote of trust in Yeltsin in April 1993. Those with asterisks meet standards for statistical significance—that is, for those with two asterisks, we know that the probability that the true coefficient is actually zero is less than .05 or one in twenty.

In each case, column 1 gives the estimated coefficients when all theoretically relevant independent variables are included. Column 2 shows a reduced model, formed by excluding all independent variables that do not significantly improve the fit of the regression, as judged by an F-test significant at the .10 level.

TABLE 4.2. Voting for Yeltsin and Incumbent Pro-Reform Blocs

	April 1993 Referendum: Vote for Yeltsin, Q1		Dec. 1993 Vote for Russia's Choice		Dec. 1995 Vote for "OHIR"		Vote for Yeltsin 1996 (1st Round)	
	(1)	(2)	(1)	(2)	(1)	(2)	(1)	(2)
Public Spending								
Regional budget expenditure per capita	.02** (.01)	.01*** (.00)	.01** (.00)	.01*** (.00)	.01 (.01)	.02** (.01)	.01** (.00)	.01*** (.00)
Recent change in regional budget expenditure per capita	.20 (.25)		.21* (.10)	.11** (.04)	.008** (.004)	.005** (.002)	−.00 (.00)	
Bilateral power-sharing agreement signed	—		—		—		2.62 (1.58)	2.70** (1.20)
At least one presidential decree or govt. resolution passed in '96 on aid to region	—		—		—		.06 (1.42)	
Economic Performance								
Estimated regional output per capita	−.00 (.01)		.00 (.00)		.00 (.00)		−.00 (.00)	
Estimated recent real income change	−6.12 (5.12)		−3.95* (2.26)	−4.23** (1.59)	−.01 (.02)		.00 (.03)	
Unemployment	.81 (1.61)		−.32 (.66)		−.03 (.35)		−.33 (.43)	
Inflation	.03 (.32)		.14 (.14)		4.47** (2.20)		.26 (2.51)	
Proportion of enterprises insolvent	2.18 (6.83)		−.03 (.14)		.12 (.07)		.12 (.10)	

(continued)

TABLE 4.2.—Continued

	April 1993 Referendum: Vote for Yeltsin, Q1		Dec. 1993 Vote for Russia's Choice		Dec. 1995 Vote for "OHIR"		Vote for Yeltsin 1996 (1st Round)	
	(1)	(2)	(1)	(2)	(1)	(2)	(1)	(2)
Wage arrears	−3.64 (2.55)	−2.11** (.96)	−2.21* (1.17)	−1.39** (.65)	−4.36*** (1.54)	−3.63*** (1.06)	−.02*** (.01)	−.02*** (.00)
Regional Costs and Benefits of Economic Reform Program								
Sectoral								
Percent of work force in agriculture	−.75* (.40)	−1.15*** (.21)	−.39** (.18)	−.57*** (.07)	−.14 (.19)		.16 (.22)	
Region's share in RF raw materials output	.38 (.63)		.22 (.22)		.30 (.22)	.45** (.18)	.65*** (.25)	.64*** (.18)
Price and trade liberalization, privatization								
Exports per capita	−.04 (.12)		−.01 (.01)		−.00 (.00)		.00* (.00)	.004** (.002)
Value of enterprises privatized per capita	−.64 (.51)	−.26 (.43)	−.36 (.32)	−.30 (.18)	.07 (.06)		.04 (.08)	
Proportion of apartments privatized	.45 (.30)	.41* (.23)	−.01 (.14)		−.04 (.07)		−.05 (.08)	
Social and Cultural Cleavages								
Percent of population Russian	.15 (.22)		.06 (.08)		−.17** (.08)	−.09** (.03)	−.10 (.10)	
Region predominantly Christian	−8.51 (8.45)		−1.59 (3.01)		−4.72 (3.15)	−3.83** (1.81)	.29 (3.93)	

	(1)	(2)	(3)	(4)	(5)	(6)	(7)	(8)
Region an ethnically defined republic	−.48 (7.77)		1.21 (3.19)		−3.46 (3.16)		−2.37 (4.05)	
Percent of population above working age	−1.28 (.78)		−.34 (.36)		.20 (.41)		1.11** (.49)	.65* (.34)
Percent of population below age 16	−2.04 (1.31)		−.17 (.58)		.23 (.60)		1.96*** (.70)	1.95*** (.37)
Percent of population with higher education	−.60 (.46)	−.46 (.28)	.10 (.19)		−.06 (.22)		.30 (.28)	
Quality of Life								
Pollution	.01 (.01)		−.00 (.01)		.01 (.01)	−.00 (.00)	.01 (.01)	−.00* (.00)
Crime	.55 (.37)	.43* (.25)	−.00 (.15)		.00 (.00)		−.00 (.00)	
Recent change in life expectancy	1.16 (2.07)		−.83 (.85)		.57 (.79)		−1.52 (.94)	−1.27** (.68)
Refugees and forced migrants per capita	.18 (.79)		.34 (.34)	.20 (.23)	.18 (.19)		−.51** (.23)	−.37*** (.07)
Control Variable								
Pro-Yeltsin or pro-reform vote, previous time	.38** (.16)	.26** (.11)	.13* (.07)	.11** (.05)	.20 (.17)	.19* (.10)	.70*** (.09)	.63*** (.06)
Constant	110.53 (58.32)	51.36*** (11.35)	12.95 (24.35)	19.20*** (4.49)	.79 (27.43)	16.69*** (2.37)	−77.66** (34.26)	−63.35*** (17.65)
R^2	.70057	.63068	.74963	.70301	.61636	.49087	.85048	.81673
Adjusted R^2	.52091	.57974	.60657	.66274	.42453	.43687	.76596	.78523
N	64	66	66	67	72	73	72	75

Note: standard errors in parentheses. For sources of data and definition of variables, see appendix C.
*$p < .10$ **$p < .05$ ***$p < .01$

The figures in table 4.2 offer some clues about what was causing the increasing regional variation in support for Yeltsin and the pro-reform parties.[12] First, the results offer some strong confirmation of the hypothesis of this chapter. Higher and increasing government spending did appear to buy votes for central incumbents. In regions where regional government spending had been relatively high in the previous period, Yeltsin polled significantly higher in both 1993 and 1996, and the most progovernment blocs polled higher in the 1993 parliamentary election and probably also in the 1995 election. In regions where real regional spending had *increased* relatively more in the preceding period, Russia's Choice got a higher vote of support in 1993, as did OHIR in 1995 (note that these results already control for the regions' economic performance, sociocultural characteristics, costs and benefits of reform, and quality of life). Not only that, but regions with which Yeltsin had signed a bilateral power-sharing agreement also had significantly higher votes for him in 1996—the signing bonus appeared to amount to more than two additional percentage points of the vote. Whatever other factors were shaping the developing pattern of regional voting, they could be offset to some degree by federal allocations, agreements, and government spending.

What other factors were also significant? With one important exception, the regressions uncovered little impact of economic performance on regional voting. Regional output, recent real income changes, enterprise insolvency rates, and unemployment levels were not in general significantly related to votes for or against national incumbents. The prime minister's OHIR bloc seems actually to have polled better in regions where inflation the previous year had been particularly high (since inflation tended to be higher in more industrialized, urbanized regions, this may in fact have been picking up some other related factor). The one economic performance variable that does seem to have played an important part in all years was the extent of wage arrears in the region. Where workers were owed more back pay, the level of voting against the progovernment bloc or against Yeltsin was significantly higher.

The sectoral impact of reform does seem to have influenced voting in more or less the expected way. Agricultural regions were less likely to give Yeltsin a high vote of trust in the April 1993 referendum or to vote for Russia's Choice in 1993—right after witnessing the drastic deterioration of market conditions that economic reform brought them. In raw-materials-producing regions—big gainers from reform and political allies of the incumbents—voters were significantly more supportive of Chernomyrdin's OHIR in 1995 and of Yeltsin in the 1996 presidential election. Similarly, exporting regions gave Yeltsin a higher vote in 1996. Measures of the rate of privatization of enterprises and apartments were generally not significant.

Among sociocultural variables, the regressions detected a slightly greater readiness of regions with minority cultures or ethnicity to vote for the "party of power" at least in 1995. That year, regions with larger non-Russian populations and with non-Christian traditions voted with greater frequency for OHIR.[13] However, ethnicity and religion variables were not significant in any of the other years; and given ethnicity and religion, republic status did not make a significant independent contribution to regional voting behavior in any year. Nor did levels of higher education make a significant difference to the voting totals. In the 1996 presidential election, regions that contained larger concentrations of both the old and the young gave Yeltsin a higher vote. (One *cannot* deduce from this that the old were more likely to vote for the incumbent president—perhaps *other* voters in regions with relatively more elderly residents tended for some reason to be more pro-Yeltsin. Since the young population was below voting age, one obviously can not infer from this result how they would vote.)

Quality of life factors played almost no discernible role in the regional votes. The one significant finding is that, as might be expected, populations of regions with a particularly high rate of refugees and forced in-migrants tended to vote against Yeltsin in 1996, perhaps blaming him for the social dislocation in border regions.

In short, regional electorates seemed willing to punish Yeltsin and the reformers at the ballot box for the terms of trade shock against agriculture after price liberalization, and later on for the increasing problem of wage arrears and for the floods of refugees. Raw-materials-producing and exporting regions—some of the main beneficiaries of reforms—were increasingly ready to support the president and his allies. Sociocultural factors—ethnic and age composition, religion—may have played a small role in some elections, though the results are hard to interpret. But all these factors could be offset to some extent by fiscal and spending policy. Higher and more rapidly increasing levels of regional government spending seemed to buy votes for the president and incumbent central reformers. By increasing the resources regional governments had to spend on local programs, incumbents in Moscow appeared to be able to boost their own local popularity.[14]

How large were the effects? How many votes could the central incumbents "buy" by boosting regional spending or signing an aid decree? The imperfect data and techniques cannot give answers with precision. Nevertheless, the effects seem at times to be sizable. Controlling for other factors, the estimates in table 4.2 suggest that somewhere between 50 and 150 rubles per capita in additional 1991 regional spending could buy Yeltsin an extra percentage point of support in the 1993 referendum.[15] That year, the mean regional spending level was 1,338 rubles per capita, while individual regions ranged from 663 to 4,488. Had the median-spending region, Kirov Oblast (1,074 rubles per capita), spent as much as the highest-spending region, Chukotka (4,488 rubles per capita), the estimates suggest the vote of support for Yeltsin there would have been from 24 to 67 percentage points higher.

In 1992, the mean region suffered a drop in estimated real regional budget spending of about 20,000 1992 rubles per capita. The change in individual regions ranged from a drop of 168,000 in Chukotka (which had done so well the previous year) to a gain of 10,000 in Khanti-Mansiisky AO. Had the median region, Kursk Oblast, with an estimated drop of about 14,000 rubles per capita, sustained the spending performance of Khanti-Mansiisky AO, the estimates suggest that its vote for Russia's Choice in December 1993 would have been from 2.4 to 4.9 percentage points higher. (The mean regional vote for Russia's Choice in that election was about 14.5 percent.)

What about the 1996 presidential election? In 1994, the median region, Ryazan Oblast, had spent about 600,000 rubles per capita. Had it spent as much as Murmansk Oblast, 25 places above it in the rankings, the estimates suggest it would have given a first-round vote for Yeltsin 2.8 to 3.5 percentage points higher. How much was a bilateral agreement worth in votes of support for the president? The estimates suggest that, controlling for other factors, regions with which Yeltsin had signed a bilateral agreement on average gave him a 2.6 to 2.7 percentage point higher vote in June 1996. By the time of the presidential election's second round, Yeltsin had signed such agreements with 27 regions—apparently, an electorally useful move.

A more detailed analysis of the regional returns in the 1996 presidential election confirms these results and suggests additional insights. This election occurred in two rounds: the first pitted 10 candidates of different ideological positions against each other; since none received more than 50 percent, a runoff was held on July 3 between the two first-round leaders—Yeltsin and the Communist leader Gennady Zyuganov. The first-round regional vote for Yeltsin, as shown in table 4.2, can be interpreted as a measure of relatively strong support for him at this time; the second-round Yeltsin vote includes in addition many weak supporters who would have preferred one of the excluded candidates or who were motivated primarily by hostility toward Zyuganov. Thus, the second-round regional results suggest more directly which aspects of policy or regional characteristics made a region's wavering voters choose Yeltsin in the end.

These are analyzed in table 4.3. As in the first round, regions with large wage arrears or larger influxes of refugees tended to return smaller pro-Yeltsin votes, while raw-materials-producing and exporting regions voted more strongly for the incumbent president. Regions with large non-Russian populations also voted more strongly for Yeltsin, as, oddly enough, did regions that had recently experienced a bigger drop in life expectancy. Since drops in life expectancy were higher in more urbanized, industrialized, and northern regions—where support for Yeltsin tended to be strong—this relationship may well be spurious.

Particularly intriguing, though, are the results related to public spending and federal aid. As in the first round, regions that had relatively higher regional government spending also had higher votes for Yeltsin. Other central policies

TABLE 4.3. The 1996 Presidential Election: Voting for Yeltsin in Rounds 1 and 2

	1st Round		2nd Round	
	(1)	(2)	(1)	(2)
Public Spending				
Regional budget expenditure per capita	.01** (.00)	.01*** (.00)	.01 (.00)	.01*** (.00)
Recent changes in regional budget expenditure per capita	−.00 (.00)		.00 (.00)	
Bilateral power-sharing agreement signed	2.62 (1.58)	2.70** (1.20)	3.00* (1.76)	2.95* (1.57)
At least one presidential decree or government resolution passed in '96 on aid to region	.06 (1.42)		2.69* (1.59)	2.84** (1.39)
Economic Performance				
Estimated regional output per capita	−.00 (.00)		−.00 (.00)	
Estimated recent real income change	.00 (.03)		.01 (.03)	
Unemployment	−.33 (.43)		.50 (.48)	
Inflation	.26 (2.51)		1.43 (2.81)	
Proportion of enterprises insolvent	.12 (.10)		.17 (.11)	.14* (.08)
Wage arrears	−.02*** (.01)	−.02*** (.00)	−.02*** (.01)	−.02*** (.00)
Regional Costs and Benefits of Economic Reform Program				
Sectoral				
Percent of work force in agriculture	.16 (.22)		−.16 (.25)	
Region's share in RF raw materials output	.65** (.25)	.64*** (.18)	.42 (.28)	.49** (.21)
Price and trade liberalization, privatization				
Exports per capita	.00* (.00)	.004** (.002)	.01* (.00)	.01*** (.00)
Value of enterprises privatized per capita	.04 (.08)		.03 (.09)	

(continued)

TABLE 4.3.—*Continued*

	1st Round		2nd Round	
	(1)	(2)	(1)	(2)
Proportion of apartments privatized	−.05 (.08)		.02 (.09)	
Social and Cultural Cleavages				
Percent of population Russian	−.10 (.10)		−.20* (.11)	−.18*** (.04)
Region predominantly Christian	.29 (3.93)		−5.98 (4.40)	
Region an ethnically defined republic	−2.37 (4.05)		−7.94* (4.53)	
Percent of population above working age	1.11** (.49)	.65* (.34)	.34 (.54)	
Percent of population below age 16	1.96*** (.70)	1.95*** (.37)	.68 (.79)	
Percent of population with higher education	.30 (.28)		.27 (.31)	
Quality of Life				
Pollution	.01 (.01)		.01 (.01)	
Crime	−.00 (.00)	−.00* (.00)	−.00 (.00)	−.00 (.00)
Recent change in life expectancy	−1.52 (.94)	−1.27* (.68)	−2.45** (1.05)	−2.66*** (.76)
Refugees and forced migrants per capita	−.51** (.23)	−.37*** (.07)	−.37 (.26)	−.40*** (.08)
Control Variable				
Pro-Yeltsin or pro-reform vote, previous time	.70*** (.09)	.63*** (.06)	.63*** (.10)	.68*** (.07)
Constant	−77.66** (34.26)	−63.35*** (17.65)	−3.53 (38.36)	17.79*** (5.55)
R^2	.85048	.81673	.85491	.82210
Adjusted R^2	.76596	.78523	.77290	.78821
N	72	75	72	75

Note: standard errors in parentheses. For details of data sources and variable construction, see appendix C.
*$p < .10$ **$p < .05$ ***$p < .01$

allocating benefits to particular regions were also followed by a relatively higher Yeltsin vote. The regressions still suggest that regions with which Yeltsin had signed a bilateral agreement were more prone to support him—though the significance of this result falls to the .07 level (model 2). At the same time, in the second round another variable became significant. If a region had benefited from at least one presidential decree or government resolution promising aid to the region during the first six months of 1996, that region's voters rewarded the incumbent president at the polls, giving him nearly 3 percentage points more. Such largesse and benefits appear to have been more influential in boosting the less committed support for Yeltsin (in the second round) than in eliciting an absolute preference for him (in the first).

Besides considering regional voting for Yeltsin or for pro-reform central incumbents, it is interesting to examine the determinants of other parties' votes. Table 4.4 shows a more detailed analysis of the regional results from the December 1993 parliamentary election. As well as repeating the Russia's Choice results for comparison, it gives estimated coefficients for regressions of the total vote for the three extreme opposition blocs—the Communists, Agrarians, and Liberal Democratic Party—as well as of the Communist and LDP votes taken separately.

The pattern of opposition voting mirrors the pro-reform voting in various intuitively plausible ways. Both the Communists and LDP performed better in more agricultural regions and in those with lower economic output (significant, however, only at .09 for LDP in model 2). While Russia's Choice drew its strength from the industrialized regions, the extreme opposition did better in less developed parts. Both the LDP and Communist Party apparently also benefited from the protest vote in regions with relatively large wage arrears—regions where Russia's Choice polled significantly lower.[16]

At the same time, the results reveal interesting divergences between the regional bases of support for the Communists and Zhirinovsky's LDP. The regions where the protest vote took a particularly procommunist tinge seemed to be those most likely to be concerned with economic welfare and softening the pain of reform. Regions with larger dependent populations—of the young and old—were particularly supportive of the Communists, though not of the LDP.[17] In fact, the more children under 16, the lower the vote for Zhirinovsky. And the protest vote in regions where public spending was particularly low or dropping particularly fast went to the Communists but not at all to the LDP.[18] On the other hand, protest seems to have favored Zhirinovsky in regions suffering particular social dislocations. Where unemployment, the crime rate, or the inflow of refugees was higher, the LDP appeared to benefit. Crime and refugees were issues that Zhirinovsky exploited rhetorically in campaign speeches. (In high crime regions, the Communist vote was actually lower, suggesting perhaps a battle between the two parties for the extreme opposition vote.)

TABLE 4.4. Why Did Different Regions Support Different Political Blocs in the December 1993 Parliamentary Election? (OLS regression coefficients)

	Russia's Choice		3 Opposition Blocs[a]		Including Communists		Including LDP	
	(1)	(2)	(1)	(2)	(1)	(2)	(1)	(2)
Public Spending								
Regional budget expenditure per capita	.01** (.00)	.01*** (.00)	−.01** (.01)	−.01** (.00)	−.01** (.00)	−.01* (.00)	.00 (.00)	−.00* (.00)
Recent change in regional budget expenditure per capita	.21* (.10)	.11** (.04)	−.27 (.19)	−.23** (.09)	−.20 (.13)	−.22* (.11)	.08 (.11)	
Economic Performance								
Estimated regional output per capita	.00 (.00)		−.01* (.01)	−.01*** (.00)	−.00 (.00)	−.01*** (.00)	−.01* (.00)	
Estimated recent real income change	−3.95** (2.26)	−4.23** (1.59)	5.23 (4.03)		3.06 (2.89)		.48 (2.41)	
Unemployment	−.32 (.66)		2.28* (1.18)	2.52** (1.01)	.55 (.85)		1.35* (.70)	1.51*** (.55)
Inflation	.14 (.14)		−.18 (.26)		−.30 (.19)	−.36** (.16)	.13 (.15)	
Proportion of enterprises insolvent	−.03 (.14)		−.29 (.26)		−.16 (.19)		−.16 (.15)	
Wage arrears	−2.11** (.96)	−2.21* (1.17)	6.80*** (2.08)	5.30*** (1.40)	3.90** (1.50)	1.11 (1.02)	3.79*** (1.24)	4.58*** (.70)

Regional Costs and Benefits of Economic Reform Program

Sectoral

Percent of work force in agriculture	−1.15*** (.21)	−.39** (.18)	.96*** (.32)	.93*** (.16)	.22 (.23)	.36** (.14)	.44** (.19)	.39*** (.10)
Region's share in RF raw materials output	.22 (.22)		−.63 (.39)		−.49* (.28)		−.17 (.23)	

Price and trade liberalization, privatization

Exports per capita	−.01 (.01)		.03** (.01)	.04*** (.01)	.02 (.01)	.01* (.01)	.01 (.01)	.02** (.01)
Value of enterprises privatized per capita	−.26 (.43)	−.36 (.32)	.64 (.56)		.43 (.40)		−.17 (.34)	−.53** (.24)
Proportion of apartments privatized	−.01 (.14)		.01 (.24)		.01 (.18)		.13 (.15)	

Social and Cultural Cleavages

Percent of population Russian	.06 (.08)		−.17 (.14)		−.17* (.10)		.03 (.08)
Region predominantly Christian	−1.59 (3.01)		6.56 (5.37)		3.66 (3.85)		2.07 (3.21)
Region an ethnically defined republic	1.21 (3.19)		−7.07 (5.69)		−4.83 (4.09)		−1.02 (3.40)
Percent of population above working age	−.34 (.36)		1.12* (.64)	1.16*** (.27)	.87* (.46)		−.48 (.38)
Percent of population below age 16	−.17 (.58)		.27 (1.04)		1.64** (.75)	.57** (.28)	−2.29*** (.62)	−2.00*** (.20)
Percent of population with higher education	.10 (.19)		.30 (.34)		.46* (.24)		−.27 (.20)

(continued)

TABLE 4.4.—Continued

	Russia's Choice		3 Opposition Blocs[a]		Including			
					Communists		LDP	
	(1)	(2)	(1)	(2)	(1)	(2)	(1)	(2)
Quality of Life								
Pollution	−.00		.01		−.00		.00	
	(.01)		(.01)		(.00)		(.01)	
Crime	−.00		−.46*	−.51**	−.33	−.51***	.24	.38***
	(.15)		(.27)	(.21)	(.20)	(.16)	(.16)	(.12)
Recent change in life expectancy	−.83		−.17		−.26		.23	
	(.85)		(1.52)		(1.09)		(.91)	
Refugees and forced migrants per capita	.34	.20	−.08		−.31	−.27	.60*	.81**
	(.34)	(.23)	(.60)		(.43)	(.39)	(.36)	(.31)
Control Variable								
Pro-Yeltsin or pro-reform vote, previous time	.13*	.11**	−.21	.00	.04	.19***	−.16**	−.14**
	(.07)	(.05)	(.13)	(.09)	(.09)	(.07)	(.08)	(.05)
Constant	12.95	19.20***	33.95	23.67*	−27.46	10.79	81.30***	64.43***
	(24.35)	(4.49)	(43.47)	(12.44)	(31.22)	(9.99)	(25.96)	(6.52)
R^2	.74963	.70301	.80553	.76569	.70516	.60303	.81322	.76322
Adjusted R^2	.60657	.66274	.69441	.71966	.53668	.52506	.70650	.72239
N	66	67	66	67	66	67	66	68

Note: standard errors in parentheses. For details of variable construction and data sources, see appendix C.
[a] Agrarians, Communists, and LDP.
*$p < .10$ **$p < .05$ ***$p < .01$

Putting these various findings together, the emerging geographical variation in Russian voting seems to follow quite an intelligible logic—one that is largely economic, reactive, and reasonably flexible. Sociocultural markers—language, tradition, ethnicity—correlate at times with voting, but they explain only a small part of the pattern. More central are differences in regions' economic profiles. While exporting and raw-materials-producing regions apparently paid Yeltsin and his allies back in votes for the benefits that liberalization had brought them, agricultural regions punished the incumbents for the increasingly dismal prospects of one of their main economic sectors. More generally, regional populations severely affected by wage arrears and refugee flows took out their anger on those in power, while those with larger old and young populations seemed to prefer the social policies of the Communists. Yet, these sources of discontent could be offset, to a greater or lesser degree, by more generous state spending in the given region, or in 1996 by central concessions in the form of bilateral agreements or decrees.

None of the results discussed in this chapter reveals directly why *individual* voters chose to vote for one party or another. An association between older populations and Communist voting at the regional level, for example, does *not* necessarily imply that individuals who are old are more likely to vote Communist—to assume as much is to commit the "ecological fallacy." Such questions can be answered most directly by surveys of individual voters. The focus of the analysis here is what characteristics of *regions* correlate with particular patterns of voting.

Nevertheless, the region-level results do correspond in some ways to patterns other researchers have found in individual-level voting surveys. One nationally representative survey of 1,599 respondents taken right after the 1996 presidential election found that the rate of reported voting for Yeltsin was much higher among respondents with four or more children aged under 16—which would correspond to the higher pro-Yeltsin voting in regions with larger young populations (Rose 1996, 50).[19] Those that felt more unsafe going out on the streets were less likely to vote for Yeltsin, corresponding to the lower vote for him in high-crime regions. The propensity of more agricultural regions to vote against Yeltsin and Russia's Choice also had an analogue at the individual level: agricultural workers (in kolkhoz or sovkhoz) said they voted for the three opposition parties over the three most pro-reform blocs in 1993 by a ratio of almost six to one.[20]

Explaining the North-South Divide

If these factors explain voting variation across Russia's regions, which if any of them can account for the increasingly evident north-south divide? The latitude of a region's capital city can by itself predict about one-third of interregional variation in the vote of support for Yeltsin in April 1993, for Russia's Choice in December 1993, and for the Communists in both December 1993 and

December 1995. It can also explain about one-quarter of the variation in the second-round vote for Yeltsin in 1996. Are southern regions more anti-reform because of ethnicity, lower levels of modernization, poorer recent economic performance, lower public spending, or other variables?

For a factor to offer a plausible explanation for the north-south divide in regional voting, it must meet two criteria. First, it should itself be correlated with north-south location. In other words, to explain why southern voters are more conservative in Russia, one would have to point to some empirically demonstrable characteristic of the *south*. Second, controlling for this factor should dramatically reduce the estimated relationship between north-south location and the regional voting result. A natural place to look for such an explanatory factor is among the variables already discussed in the previous section, each of which might theoretically influence regional voting patterns.

Among the independent variables from the regressions previously presented, a number are correlated with north-south location. All those for which the correlation is at least .20 are shown in table 4.5. These suggest a number of hypotheses about the determinants of southern conservatism. The relatively lower per capita income or the apparently higher inflation in southern regions might be the cause. Alternatively, southern voters, located in an economy more dependent on agriculture and less able to export, might view their prospects as poor under a market system. Northern regions appeared quicker to privatize enterprises (or perhaps were endowed with more valuable enterprises to privatize), but considerably slower to privatize apartments—probably because fewer of the population wished to stay long-term in the less hospitable climatic zones. These factors seem unlikely to explain why voters in northern regions were more favorable toward reformers, however. So do the greater pollution and sharper drop in life expectancy of northern regions—apparently such concomitants of industrial development are outweighed by other positive aspects. Southern populations contained larger non-ethnic-Russian minorities, and more of the non-Christian regions lie in the south. The presence of larger numbers of refugees in the south might also have sparked a conservative counterreaction. In addition, southern regions tended to have more elderly populations. Finally, along with lower levels of economic development in the south went lower levels of regional budget spending: this might also explain the south's lower support for central incumbents.

I tried adding each of these factors individually (chosen for the appropriate time period) to regressions of the vote for Russia's Choice in December 1993 and for Yeltsin in the second round of the 1996 presidential election on regions' north-south location. In the regression for the Russia's Choice vote, the estimated coefficient on the region's latitude without any control variables included was .63 (significant at $p = .0000$). In other words, for every degree further north a region's capital was located, the vote for Russia's Choice was .63 percentage points higher. Only two of the latitude-correlated variables reduced

TABLE 4.5. Independent Variables Correlated with the (North-South) Latitude of Regions' Capital Cities

	Correlation with (North-South) Latitude of Region's Capital
Proportion of work force in agriculture	−.49
	(.00)
Estimated output per capita	.44
	(.00)
Inflation December 1992–December 1993	−.25
	(.02)
Value of exports per capita 1993	.24
	(.03)
Value of exports per capita 1994	.25
	(.03)
Charter capital of enterprises privatized in 1993	.23
	(.03)
Charter capital of enterprises privatized in 1993 and 1994	.26
	(.02)
Proportion of apartments privatized by 1992	−.53
	(.00)
Proportion of apartments privatized by 1995	−.59
	(.00)
Proportion of population Russian	.22
	(.05)
Region predominantly Christian	.33
	(.00)
Proportion of population above working age 1994	−.21
	(.05)
Refugees per 1,000 regional residents 1993	−.30
	(.01)
Refugees per 1,000 regional residents 1995	−.32
	(.00)
Change in life expectancy 1991–93	−.63
	(.00)
Pollution level 1994	.54
	(.00)
Regional budget spending 1991	.43
	(.00)
Regional budget spending 1993	.25
	(.02)

Note: All correlation coefficients greater than .20 shown. Significance level in two-tailed test in parentheses.

this coefficient estimate below .55. These were the change in life expectancy and the proportion working in agriculture. In the regression for the second-round Yeltsin vote in 1996, the coefficient on latitude started out at 1.07 (significant at $p = .0000$). When latitude-correlated control variables were added one by one, the same two variables lowered the latitude coefficient the most. The life-expectancy change variable lowered the latitude coefficient to .39, and agricultural employment lowered it to .32.

The most plausible interpretation of these results is that the north-south divide in Russian voting behavior is related primarily to the more agricultural economic profile of southern regions. The association of *lower* drops in life expectancy in the south and higher anti-Yeltsin voting is puzzling more than revealing at first glance. Yet, this may actually just be picking up the relationship with agricultural employment since the change in life expectancy was quite highly correlated with agricultural employment (at $r = .68$, significant at $p = .000$). More agricultural regions suffered a smaller drop in life expectancy in the early 1990s. When the two variables were added to the regression together, agricultural employment was highly significant, but the change in life expectancy was not. (The same was true for the Russia's Choice regression.)

Such a conclusion coincides with evidence from some local participants in the political life of the south. In the summer of 1996, I posed the question of the south's conservatism to political leaders in Tambov Oblast, an agricultural region to the south of Moscow with perhaps the most distinct claim to be part of the "Red Belt." In the 1995 parliamentary election, the regional vote for the Communists—40 percent—had been nearly double the party's unexpectedly high national average. In December 1995, the region defiantly elected as its head of administration a career Communist leader, Aleksandr Ryabov, who had supported the August 1991 attempted coup.

I asked Ryabov's deputy, Yuri Blokhin, whether it was political tradition or a particular set of local attitudes that explained the region's preference for the Communists. He answered that if anything Tambov Oblast's historical traditions pulled in the opposite direction. The main historical reference for Tambovites was the uprising of peasants under Aleksandr Antonov in 1920 *against* Bolshevik rule, a violent anticommunist jacquerie that established a tradition of resistance by guerrilla tactics. In Blokhin's view, anti-Yeltsin voting had more to do with the deteriorating economic condition of agriculture in the period of reform.

> A trader in Moscow earns half a million rubles a month. A farmer who raises cows here earns 170,000. He watches television shows where everyone is smiling. And then he looks at his wife, who has no teeth. And there's no money to buy any.[21]

Valery Koval, the mayor of Tambov, widely considered to come from the democratic reform side of the spectrum, also saw in the south's Communist voting a reaction against current economic conditions in the countryside: "Those who vote for Zyuganov are not voting for communism as an idea, or for a return to the past." In the old days, according to Koval, Communists were "hated in the countryside more than in the cities," as the dependence of ordinary farm workers on the often corrupt kolkhoz directors bred resentment. The Communists' newfound popularity, he argued, was a direct reflection of discontent with local economic decline.

> In the countryside, trains don't go to some towns anymore. Buses don't go to some villages. In some, they don't bring in bread regularly; electricity is often shut off. In the old days, musical groups used occasionally to go out on tours. Now they don't.[22]

According to the chairman of the Lenin Kolkhoz, just outside Tambov city, the reason agricultural workers tended to vote against Yeltsin was not just that current conditions were bad, but that they saw absolutely no hope for the future. Foreign food goods were cheaper than those domestic farms could produce, given prevailing energy prices. Fields had not been fertilized for four years, and not surprisingly, yields were declining. Both Koval and Blokhin pointed to the sharp rises in regional support for Yeltsin during his 1996 election campaign, after he began to address the sources of southern discontent, paying wage arrears and increasing pensions. Political opinion seemed both to be quite fluid and to be susceptible to economic policy initiatives.

Similar views are often expressed by other southern politicians. When asked about the procommunist voting of his province, Yegor Stroyev, the governor of Orel, explained it as follows.

> Today only 3 percent of the villages here have natural gas; meanwhile gas is carried through the region by pipeline to the whole of Europe. They have never built any roads here. They have never provided enough fertilizer. And you wonder why people here think like they do? (Medvedev 1996, 16–18)

Voting for Regional Politicians

The preceding analysis found that higher levels of and increases in regional public spending were associated with higher subsequent levels of regional support for central incumbents. The implication was that central officials, by increasing regions' ability to finance public services, could buy themselves local support. For regional spending to occur, however, regional administrations have to authorize it. It is easy to imagine why governors ideologically and politically sympathetic to Yeltsin might wish to do so. But various governors in the early 1990s vociferously opposed him. Would such regional leaders use aid from Moscow in a way that would boost local support for their political opponents in the capital?

A second puzzle complicates the picture still further. The analysis of chapter 3 found that a relatively *low* level of electoral support for Yeltsin was associated with *higher* subsequent net central transfers. Strategically, therefore, a governor concerned to extract more central benefits should nurse public hostility toward the center in his region as a source of leverage. Would it not be irrational for such a governor to undermine his own bargaining position by boosting public spending?

To answer these questions requires an analysis of the relations between regional governors and their constituents. It turns out, when such an analysis is conducted, that increases in public spending in a region do not just improve the electoral chances of central politicians—they also raise support for the regional governor. So, in order to buy votes for themselves, it makes sense for regional governors—even those ideologically opposed to Yeltsin and the central reformers—to increase public spending in their region. Such a policy may increase the popularity of their central rivals and reduce their leverage in future bargaining with the center. But in the short run, the benefit of the additional support from constituents may outweigh such costs. The rest of this section presents the evidence on which this argument is based.

What determined whether regional electorates supported or opposed their regional political leadership in the early 1990s? Two measures of this were constructed from electoral results. Between the beginning of 1993 and mid-1996, 33 regions held elections for regional governor (see chap. 2). In all but one of these (Kalmykia in April 1993), the incumbent was running for reelection. In another three cases (Ingushetia in February 1993, Karelia in April 1994, and Kalmykia in October 1995), he was running unopposed. In the remaining 29 cases, the incumbent won in 17 and another candidate defeated him in 12.

The factors that might plausibly explain the electoral success or failure of incumbent regional officials are mostly similar to those that would explain support for central incumbents. Relatively strong economic performance in the region might predispose voters more favorably toward the incumbent. A rapid pursuit of economic reform could either create a constituency supportive of the incumbent's policies or create short-run dislocations costly to his popularity. Different age, ethnic, and educational structures of the regional population might lead to different degrees of loyalty or readiness to question incumbents. A higher local "quality of life" might boost the governor's support, as might higher or increasing rates of public spending. A final, additional factor is necessary to try to detect the impact of manipulation or even fraud in the regional election results. A governor with background and connections in the regional party or state apparatus would have greater experience and resources to accomplish such manipulation or distortion of the results.

Table 4.6 shows the results when a dummy variable taking the value 1 if the incumbent was reelected and 0 if he was not is regressed with logistic regression on a range of such independent variables. The analysis includes all gubernatorial elections between January 1, 1993, and July 1, 1996, in which the incumbent governor or president ran and in which there was at least one other candidate. Logistic regression is a technique analogous to the more common ordinary least squares type but which is appropriate when the dependent variable is dichotomous. Column one shows the estimates when a full range of theoretically plausible independent variables are included. Column two shows a shortened regression, from which each of the variables from column one has been excluded if doing so increased the significance of the regression, as judged by its chi-square.

With relatively few cases available, it was necessary to economize on independent variables in order for the logistic regressions to yield results. Sectoral cleavage variables—agricultural employment and raw materials production—were left out since, while inhabitants of different regions may certainly have different expectations about how their region will fare in the free market, there is no plausible reason why they would hold *regional* officials responsible for this. As an additional check, however, each of these was added to the final form regression to see whether it was in fact significant and whether it substantially changed the significant results. In each case, the added variable was highly insignificant, reduced the significance of the regression's chi square, and while somewhat reducing the significance of the other estimates did not lead to major changes in their values.[23]

In each case, the independent variable for the most appropriate time period was chosen from available sources (for example, the insolvent enterprise variable for January through May 1993 was used for the Orel Oblast election held in April 1993; the variable for January through August 1993 was used for the Bashkortostan election held in December 1993; and the 1995 version of the variable was used for the Moscow Oblast election held in December 1995). To make nominal variables comparable across years, each was expressed as a proportion of its mean in that time period, and variables measuring change across years were expressed as percentage changes in real terms.

A second attempt to gauge regional support for incumbent governors employed the results of the December 1993 election to the upper house of the Federal Assembly, the Federation Council. In this election, the almost universal practice was for members of the high regional leadership—the president or head of administration, chairman of the regional legislature, their deputies, other executive and legislative officials—to run for each region's two seats. The top executive official (head of administration or republic president) was elected in two-thirds of all regions.

TABLE 4.6. Logistic Regression of Whether the Incumbent Governor Was Reelected if Regional Election Held (1993 through mid-1996)

	(1)	(2)
Public Spending		
Regional budget expenditure per capita	9.66 (14.43)	
Change in real regional budget expenditure per capita	.16* (.09)	.11** (.05)
Economic Performance		
Estimated economic output per capita 1993	2.86 (2.85)	4.52** (2.22)
Estimated change in average real income	−2.81 (4.34)	
Proportion of enterprises insolvent	4.54 (6.09)	5.37* (3.14)
Regional Costs and Benefits of Economic Reform Program		
Book value of enterprises privatized	−.05 (.62)	
Percent of apartments privatized	.44 (2.08)	
Social and Cultural Cleavages		
Percent of population Russian	−4.81 (13.71)	
Percent of population above working age	1.65 (9.70)	
Region an ethnically defined republic	−23.11 (17.60)	−12.78** (6.33)
Percent of work force with higher education	−3.66 (4.77)	
Manipulation or Elite Support		
Head of region a former state or party apparatus worker	−5.16 (3.16)	−3.95* (2.37)
Quality of Life		
Refugees or forced migrants per 1,000 residents	3.15 (2.15)	2.31 (1.67)
Constant	−.35 (17.12)	−6.66** (3.28)
Model χ^2	19.84 (Sig at $p = .10$)	19.61 (Sig at $p = .004$)
N	26	27

Note: standard errors in parentheses.
*$p < .10$ **$p < .05$ ***$p < .01$

Table 4.7 shows the results when a dummy taking the value 1 if the highest regional executive official running for the election was elected to the Federation Council and 0 if he was not is regressed by logistic regression on similar independent variables, as before measuring economic performance, reform-related interests, regional government spending, and sociocultural characteristics of the region's population.[24]

Two factors were significant at the .05 level in both regressions. In regions with higher economic output per capita, the incumbent governor was more likely to be reelected and the highest executive official running was likely to win election to the Federation Council. More developed regions, thus, seem more likely to support their incumbents. This runs counter to the expectation that in more rural, traditional regions, voter loyalty or manipulation would be greater.[25] In less developed regions, unusually high proportions of voters actually opposed those in power. (This may in fact reflect a greater loyalty or capacity for manipulation of the *previous* leadership. Regional governors appointed by Yeltsin often replaced locally entrenched bosses—such as Ryabov in Tambov—and the elections may have given such bosses the opportunity to return to power.)

Second, regions where real spending had increased more in the preceding period (or fallen less) were significantly more likely to vote for the incumbent. This has an important implication in light of the results presented earlier in this chapter. At first glance, it seemed paradoxical that governors philosophically or personally opposed to Yeltsin would use central transfers in ways that would boost local support for the center. Strategically, such a policy also seemed unwise, since local discontent was an effective lever to pry further aid from the center. The regressions suggest an explanation. Increased regional spending appears to increase the electoral appeal of *both* central and regional incumbents. In this way, their political fate is linked, whether or not they share political views or loyalties. Voters apparently assign credit for more generous provision of public services to both levels of government. Thus, while regional leaders might prefer to encourage anti-Yeltsin voting, they seem unable to buy support for themselves without also buying support for him. In this way, central redistribution turns institutional adversaries into, if not friends, at least somewhat improbable political partners.[26]

Conclusion

Russia's postcommunist political development depended in part on what was causing the increased polarization of opinion and political loyalties across the country's regions. This would determine what constitutional arrangements linking center and periphery were feasible, what central political strategies were likely to be effective, and ultimately how great the danger of national disinte-

TABLE 4.7. Logistic Regression of Whether the Most Senior Regional Executive Official Running in December 1993 Federation Council Was Elected

	(1)	(2)
Public Spending		
Regional per capita budget expenditure 1991	.001 (.003)	
Change in real per capita regional budget expenditure 1991–92	.14** (.07)	.11** (.04)
Economic Performance		
Estimated economic output per capita 1993	.01* (.00)	.006** (.003)
Change in average real income (June 92–June 93)	.81 (2.11)	
Unemployment August 1993	2.46* (1.40)	1.58* (.95)
Proportion of enterprises insolvent (Jan.–Aug. 1993)	−.18 (.19)	
Regional Costs and Benefits of Economic Reform Program		
Book value of enterprises privatized in 1993	-.08 (.40)	
Percent of apartments privatized	.32* (.18)	.30** (.14)
Social and Cultural Cleavages		
Percent of population Russian	.30* (.17)	.13 (.09)
Percent of population above working age	−.66* (.40)	−.23 (.15)
Region an ethnically defined republic	15.63 (9.72)	5.73 (4.50)
Percent of work force with higher education	.06 (.18)	
Manipulation or Elite Support		
Head of region a former state or party apparatus worker	4.36* (2.53)	2.54* (1.50)
Quality of Life		
Refugees or forced migrants per 1,000 residents	.62 (.42)	
Constant	−22.80 (15.79)	−12.28 (7.81)
Model χ^2	26.19 (Sig at $p = .03$)	23.53 (Sig at $p = .003$)
N	58	61

Note: standard errors in parentheses.
*$p < .10$ **$p < .05$ ***$p < .01$

gration would prove to be. How entrenched or changeable were regional voting patterns? Did emerging regional differences represent the inexorable legacy of history or responses to more transitory phenomena? In Western Europe, Lipset and Rokkan argued, contemporary political cleavages reflect the impact of revolutions several centuries past. In Italy, Putnam traced current regional differences in political culture as far back as the thirteenth century. If Russia's regional polarization had similarly entrenched cultural or historical roots, the chances and political strategies for integration in a democratic state seemed open to question.

The evidence previously presented does confirm the continuing influence of cultural cleavages. Ethnic and religious differences between regions did correlate with voting differences. But ethnic minority and non-Christian republics did not, as some had feared, turn out to be bastions of conservatism. In fact, the votes for Yeltsin in July 1996 and Chernomyrdin's Our Home Is Russia bloc in December 1995 were *higher* in regions with larger non-Russian populations. Non-Christian regions also supported OHIR at higher rates. Other things being equal, it was the predominantly Russian oblasts and krais that voted most insistently against the powerholders at the center.

Sociocultural differences, however, explained only part of the puzzle. Equally important were a region's economic profile and its recent gains and losses from the policies enacted by the Moscow incumbents, including the introduction of pro-market economic reforms. Where wages were not paid for months on end or where streams of refugees flowed into the region, relatively more voters expressed discontent with reformers in Moscow. Regions with a particularly large dependent population—those below or above working age—tended to vote in December 1993 against the Moscow incumbents, who had cut social provision, and in favor of the Communists, who had promised to restore it. Such demographic effects are easier to read as responses to state policy than as indicators of different political values among different age groups. Regions with larger young populations reversed themselves to vote particularly strongly *for* Yeltsin in the first round of 1996, after he had promised to end universal conscription and to increase student stipends and family benefits.

Those regions with raw-materials-producing industries and export potential apparently rewarded the reformers for the new opportunities opened up by liberalization. Those with strong agricultural sectors seemed to take revenge at the ballot box for the sharp shift in terms of trade against the farm sector. The agricultural character of the south offered the most plausible explanation for the increasingly pro-opposition voting of southern regions. Since dramatic reform of agriculture and its partial replacement by small business and service industries was not likely to occur overnight, these geographical divisions appeared likely to reappear in voting tallies for some time to come.

Yet, to the extent that the central government could collect and reallocate revenue, it retained considerable leverage to offset and control the hostility of economically disadvantaged regions. The most obvious instruments were those of public spending, bilateral negotiation, and economic concessions. While each 50,000 rubles owed in wage delays to the average worker as of June 1996 cost Yeltsin about 1 percentage point of the second-round vote, more generous public spending in the region in previous years buffered the population against such responses. For each additional 100,000 rubles per capita that the regional government had spent in 1994, the second-round vote for Yeltsin was on average 1 percentage point higher.[27] If the estimates in table 4.3 are right, either a bilateral power-sharing agreement signed between Yeltsin and the given region or at least one decree passed that year promising aid earned him a boost in his second-round vote of almost 3 percentage points.

This view is not just supported by cross-regional statistical analysis, it echoes a theme common in the explanations of Russian politics offered by its experienced practitioners. Even in ideologically communist Tambov, the deputy governor, an experienced Party worker, insisted that more generous central aid or social policy could boost local support for Yeltsin. "Just in the last three months, when he started paying pensions and wages, Yeltsin's rating in the oblast rose from 8 percent in January to about 21 percent in the [first round of the presidential] election," he said, in June 1996. The president's vote rose precisely because Yeltsin "defined the direction of social programs."[28] In Karelia, Yeltsin's vote in the 1996 election was high despite a governor who refused publicly to endorse the sitting president. When I asked him why, despite economic problems in the region, support for Yeltsin was so high, he pointed to three central initiatives: a decree of 1991 that declared an economic experiment in Karelia, providing it with various privileges; another decree in August 1993 broadening the economic autonomy of the republic; and generous aid to the northern territories of Russia—for instance, the granting of pensions five years earlier than in the rest of the country. "All this created a context in which, despite all the economic difficulties, despite all the political conflict, people expressed gratitude toward the president."[29]

Such federal strategies are, of course, constrained by the center's limited resources and by the economically rational desire to reduce redistribution in the interest of efficiency. The recurrent dilemma for reformist politicians in similar conditions, however, is how they should balance the efficiency goals of economic reform against the political requirements of maintaining public support and preventing state disintegration. Governments that have to worry about reelection—even if just to preserve the gains of economic reform—may have to continue to redistribute in economically undesirable ways.

Lest it seem strange that regional politicians would help central incumbents restore their local support by authorizing more generous local spending and benefits, this chapter uncovered a source of shared interest between executives at the two levels. Increased regional spending is not only an effective strategy for reducing voter hostility toward central incumbents, it is also perhaps the best way for regional leaders to boost support for themselves. Whether or not they shared philosophical convictions, personal sympathies, or political networks, Yeltsin and his governors shared an interest in nurturing support with which to face future elections. And voters, by apparently holding incumbents at both levels responsible for declining state services, made it difficult for one to achieve his aim without also assisting the other. This may have helped to offset the incentives for division and confrontation already discussed in chapter 3.

Regional governors faced a strategic dilemma. They apparently could not win local support for themselves via increased spending without simultaneously alleviating local resentment of the center. But a regional public *hostile* to the center was, as chapter 3 showed, a valuable asset in bargaining for central transfers. The choice they faced was thus whether to exacerbate local discontent by cutting spending sharply and blaming Moscow, in the hope of exploiting public protest to pry greater concessions from the center—or whether to try to spend their way to local popularity, within the limits of their resources, even at the cost of undermining their bargaining power vis-à-vis the center. The following chapter considers how different regional leaders made this trade-off.

CHAPTER 5

Political Strategies of Regional Governors

Under all regimes, an element of conflict exists between political leaders of the periphery and those at the center. But in Russia in the 1990s tensions seemed unusually great. An embattled President Yeltsin accused his local counterparts in 1992 of using "guerrilla tactics" against the central authorities. They, in turn, cast their relations with Moscow as a struggle for liberation and dignity. "Who are we?" Boris Nemtsov of Nizhny Novgorod demanded of his fellow regional leaders in September 1992. "Are we genuine governors, who answer for millions of people living in the region, or beggars who appeal to the government and beg for what we should have been given long ago?"[1]

Confrontation appeared to be the order of the day. As described in chapters 1 and 2, regional leaders employed a repertoire of obstructive measures. Some declared their provinces autonomous, sovereign, or even independent, refused to remit tax, claimed local natural resources, sued federal institutions in court, withheld grain supplies, or refused to send conscripts to serve in the army (Pashkov 1993). Others threatened to halt implementation of central reform programs such as privatization, to withhold support in national referenda, or to declare a local state of emergency if their demands were not met. Governors warned of hunger in their regions, mass bankruptcies, and civil unrest. Though the ethnic republics led the assault, they were soon followed and even rivaled by ordinary oblasts and krais. By 1993, regions from Sverdlovsk to Vologda were declaring themselves republics with all the rights of their ethnic counterparts (Smirnov and Kotelnikova 1993; Petrovsky 1993). One region, Krasnoyarsk, set up a customs post at its border (Fedorchenko 1994), and deputies from the Far Eastern island of Sakhalin threatened to appeal for help to Japan and other Asian countries if Moscow did not send aid (Reznik 1995). In turn, the center delivered ultimatums, threatened embargoes, and, in the case of Chechnya, invaded with brutal military force.

What kept these individual challenges from linking up into a nationwide rebellion? As argued in chapter 1, individual cases of defiance reduce the deterrent power of the center, drain it of resources for enforcement and for providing public goods, and can initiate spirals of "opting out" of increasingly expensive and ineffective central arrangements. Yet in Russia, the rush to regional defiance did not pass a certain point. Even as it became increasingly obvious that the center rewarded challenges with fiscal concessions, some of the early protesters were in fact becoming relatively more moderate in their demands. A dynamic of calming competed with the dynamic of escalation.

In the hope of explaining this puzzle, the present chapter examines what determined whether a given regional leader challenged Yeltsin's authority or supported him at key moments of constitutional crisis. The appearance of continual conflict actually hid a more complex reality. Not all regions were equally assertive; in fact, there was remarkable variation in the degree to which the leaders of different provinces challenged the center. While some, like Chechnya's Dzhokhar Dudaev, pressed maximalist demands, others, like his neighbor, Dagestan's Magomed-Ali Magomedov, preserved a deliberate silence. Yet other leaders—Kalmykia's Kirsan Ilyumzhinov—slipped back and forth from the role of sovereignty-seeking, anti-Yeltsin gadfly to that of self-sacrificing champion of Russian national integrity, changing their tack by 180 degrees within a matter of weeks. Moreover, regional activism fluctuated in observable cycles. The assertiveness of both regions and the center waxed and waned, with the center often temporarily clawing back past concessions in moments of victory (for instance, after the August 1991 failed coup and the October 1993 storming of the parliament).

Though ethnic identity or nationalist sentiment might explain a part of this variation, such factors do not operate in any obvious way. Among both autonomous republics and ordinary oblasts and krais, some regions marked themselves out as risk-seeking, confrontational practitioners of the politics of brinkmanship while others adopted docile postures, joining regional protests against the center only after all others had, if then. If ethnic identity were the key, one might have expected the eastern, Buddhist republic of Tyva—where 64 percent of inhabitants were Tyvans, 99 percent of these spoke Tyvan as their mother tongue, 60 percent of public school students studied in the Tyvan language, and where ethnic consciousness was catalyzed by violent clashes between Tyvans and Russians in 1990—to have led the pack of separatists. In fact, it was far less assertive than Komi, a Christianized republic, where fewer than a quarter of inhabitants were Komis, nearly one-third of these no longer spoke Komi as their mother tongue, and where all schooling in 1993 was in the Russian language (Treisman 1997). Among the ethnic republics, there was no relationship between the concentration of the titular nationality and the separatist activism of its leader. Indeed, the more *Russians* there were in a republic's population, the faster it declared sovereignty in the 1990 sovereignty drive (Treisman 1997).

Why did leaders of different regions within the same system, with similar levels of ethnic or geographical remoteness from the center, adopt such different strategies? Why did some leaders choose tactics of high-stakes blackmail, while others consistently supported President Yeltsin? What rendered one governor a rebel, another an obedient follower? The statistical analyses presented in this chapter suggest an answer. While the leaders of ethnic republics were more likely to oppose Yeltsin than those of administratively lower units were, the leaders of all regions appeared to be sensitive to the trend in political opinion within their own electorate. Governors were less likely to challenge Yeltsin's authority at moments of crisis if the level of public support for Yeltsin and his reformist allies in their region, as judged by votes in national elections, had recently been rising. By contrast, where regional voters were deserting the president, the chance of the governor publicly defying Yeltsin at moments of crisis was considerably higher.

This finding has an additional significance when combined with the results of chapters 3 and 4. Chapter 4 found that the level of regional support for Yeltsin and the reformers was itself related to recent changes in the level of regional government spending (which was increased by larger central fiscal transfers) and by other central financial aid. Such transfers were, in turn, disproportionately channeled to regions that had earlier staged protests—declaring sovereignty, staging strikes, and voting against Yeltsin. Thus, the outline of a stabilizing feedback emerges: regions that protested were appeased with greater fiscal transfers from the center; this increased the level of regional spending; and this, in turn, both increased voter support for the central incumbents and, indirectly, reduced the incentive for the regional political elite to protest.

Governors and President: Support or Opposition?

What might determine whether a regional governor would support or oppose the central government at crucial moments? Western scholarship on political action and center-periphery relations suggests several possibilities, some of which recall the theories of integration discussed in chapter 1. First, the *personal backgrounds* of regional politicians are likely to color their attitudes and influence the political positions they take. Officials may have been conditioned through past participation in political and social organizations, by past employment, and by their social circles (Rosenberg 1989). Leaders who have made a career in the party or state apparatus might be less eager to see the powers of the bureaucracy reduced through democratic and market reform and more likely to oppose President Yeltsin, the central advocate of such reforms. Similarly, regional leaders' political beliefs, values, and loyalties may be shaped by ethnic identities. Politicians of non-Russian ethnicity may be less likely to be swayed by Yeltsin's appeals for support in the name of Russian nationalism.

Second, regional leaders may select their strategies based on their current place in the system of *political institutions,* and the nature of their *political resources.* While national parties and state hierarchies are weak, they may play some role in shaping loyalties. In 1992–93, politics in Russia was in large part structured by a competition between the executive and legislative branches. Parliamentarians at different levels of the state tended to view each other as allies with shared institutional interests, and executive branch officials tended to side with other executives. In such a context, one might expect executives who were *also* in the legislature to be somewhat less dependent on support from Yeltsin—and therefore less loyal to him. Thirty-one of the 89 heads of administration and republic presidents had been elected to the national Congress of People's Deputies in 1990. If institutional position was important in determining policy, such executives should be more likely to oppose Yeltsin than their counterparts.

Similarly, a regional governor's likelihood of challenging Yeltsin might be influenced by the *manner of his appointment.* All heads of administration were initially appointed by President Yeltsin, usually from a shortlist provided by the regional soviet. However, in many regions Yeltsin merely reappointed the former head of the regional soviet's executive committee, who had been elected to the regional legislature in 1990 and then chosen to be chairman by his fellow parliamentarians. Such politicians might be expected to be more confident about their local base of support—both among the regional electorate and elite. And in 22 regions, elections were held for chief executive between 1991 and 1993, reducing even more greatly the Russian president's leverage.

Regional elections may have another effect. Where regional politicians are subject to elections, their positions in national debates are likely to be influenced by the *views of voters* in their constituencies (Miller and Stokes 1963; Page and Shapiro 1983). Some may see their role as primarily to express the views and demands of those they represent and may expect to be rewarded or punished at the polls on the basis of how faithfully they perform this function. A regional electorate hostile to the president may produce a governor and parliamentary delegation hostile to him; a shift in constituency support to or from the president may induce a parallel shift among the region's politicians. In such a view, regional politicians will at times be constrained from instrumental protests against central policies if attitudes towards central incumbents among their constituents are too positive. Such attitudes may make it easier for the center to respond to such protests by removing the governor, since his constituents would be less likely to rally behind him.

Fifth, the positions taken by provincial leaders in national politics might depend on *characteristics of their region.* In those regions most dependent on central financial support to fund public services, leaders might be more cautious about antagonizing either the president or the central parliament, both of whom participate in the allocation of central transfers (see chap. 3). On the other hand, in provinces that fund public services largely or entirely through domestic tax revenue, leaders might be less cautious. Fiscally self-sufficient regions might be less restrained in their criticism of the center than those provinces that relied on central transfers and were vulnerable to retaliatory cutbacks in central funding.

Finally, the *administrative status* of the region might affect both the governor's political resources in confronting the center and the preferences of the domestic political elite. Various authors have commented on the way nationalism was institutionalized territorially in the Soviet system through the creation of Union and autonomous republics (Brubaker 1994; Roeder 1991; Zaslavsky 1992a). Indigenous cadres were recruited and ethnic identities woven into the formal administrative architecture, as a way of coopting and defusing the threat of independent nationalist mobilization. The political elites in autonomous republics have experience of higher administrative authority, as well as a potentially mobilizable set of political resources, largely created by the center but which could be used against it. This might make the leaders of autonomous republics—regardless of their ethnicity—more likely than those of oblasts or krais to oppose Yeltsin.

Two moments of defining clarity in Russian politics came in December 1992 and September 1993. At both of these times, all regional governors came under pressure to explain their position with regard to ongoing struggles in Moscow between the president and parliament. In December 1992, the Seventh Congress of People's Deputies met at the height of a season of escalating parliamentary attacks on the reformist government. On December 10, Yeltsin demanded the holding of a national referendum in which citizens would declare whether they had confidence in the president or the parliament. At the Congress, Yeltsin was forced to surrender his prime minister, Yegor Gaidar, replacing him with the centrist industrialist, Viktor Chernomyrdin. Almost all regional leaders around this time made statements in the press, offering different degrees of support for each side. While 39 chief executives publicly declared support for Yeltsin or his government, 40 did not. Of these, seven went on record as positively critical of Yeltsin or the government (information was not available about the remaining nine).[2]

The second moment came in September 1993 when Yeltsin declared a state of emergency, dissolved the Parliament, and announced that new elections would be held in December. A rump of parliamentary deputies continued to meet, barricaded inside the White House, by candlelight after the electricity was turned off. At this time, while most regional governors supported the national head of the executive or remained publicly silent, some came out publicly in support of the parliament. Sixty-three sided with Yeltsin or were ambiguous, while 15 overtly opposed him or sided with the Parliament (information was missing for the remaining ten).[3]

This latter crisis quickly broadened from a mere competition for power between central elites to entangle the question of federal stability. Some acts of regional opposition to Yeltsin took on a distinctly separatist tone. For instance, parliamentary leaders from 15 Siberian regions met in Novosibirsk on September 30 at the invitation of the oblast's governor, Vitali Mukha. The assembled leaders threatened to create a Siberian republic, to withhold all taxes from Moscow, and to cut communications along the Trans-Siberian Railway if the president did not rescind his decree dissolving parliament (see chap. 2). Had the crisis not been resolved when it was, such disintegrative tendencies might have spread.

Both cases were of great importance for the development of the Russian political system. One brought to an end the faltering experiment with "shock therapy" and introduced a period of intense confrontation between president and parliament over the proposed referendum. The other led to the military storming of the parliament building and the arrest of its leaders. Thus, the positions taken by the regional leaders are important in their own right. However, they also provide a way to assess which characteristics of regional governors and their constituencies made them more or less likely to side with the president at moments of crisis. Thus, analysis of these cases provides evidence about the basis of integration or disintegration in relations between central and peripheral elites.

Dichotomous dummy variables were constructed based on the responses of regional governors in each of these two conflicts. In both cases, the variable took the value 1 if the regional head of executive (president or chair of Council of Ministers in the republics; head of administration in the oblasts and krais) publicly opposed President Yeltsin or his government, and zero if he publicly supported the president, made a neutral or unclear statement, said nothing, or if no information was available. Thus, it is a measure of quite active opposition to the president. These two dependent variables were regressed by logistic regression on a set of independent variables designed to reflect the hypotheses previously outlined (for sources and explanations of the variables, see appendix D). The results are shown in table 5.1. Column 1, in each case, lists the coefficient estimates from the full model when all variables are included. Column 2 contains the coefficient estimates for the variables that remain once all variables that do not increase the significance of the model's chi-square are excluded. The results identify who the "spoilers" were in center-region relations—what kinds of regional governors were more likely to side with President Yeltsin or remain neutral in a crisis and which were more likely to oppose him.[4]

One of the most intriguing results in table 5.1 is the picture it offers of electoral influences taking root in Russia. By September 1993, the evidence suggests that regional leaders were beginning to take note of local opinion and voting patterns, and to act accordingly. In regions where the vote for Yeltsin was higher in the April 1993 referendum than in the 1991 election, the governor was much less likely to oppose the president publicly during his showdown with the

TABLE 5.1. Which Regional Chief Executives Opposed Yeltsin at Moments of Constitutional Crisis? (Logistic regression coefficients. Dependent variable is: Regional executive opposition to Yeltsin in December 1992 and September 1993)

	Opposed Yeltsin December 1992		Opposed Yeltsin September 1993	
	(1)	(2)	(1)	(2)
Regional Public Opinion				
Vote for Yeltsin	.08	.07	−.07	
June 1991	(.06)	(.04)	(.05)	
Pro-Yeltsin vote *rose*			−3.58*	−2.43*
June 1991–April 1993			(1.56)	(1.16)
Background of Governor				
Former state or	1.29		1.97	
party official	(1.21)		(1.31)	
Russian nationality	1.34		5.22*	4.07*
	(1.59)		(2.21)	(1.73)
Governor's Institutional History				
Elected to Russian	2.14	2.06*	2.57	2.70*
legislature 1990	(1.16)	(.94)	(1.39)	(1.22)
Chairman of regional	.27		−1.41	
executive committee before	(1.26)		(1.39)	
Yeltsin appointed him				
Popularly elected	.87		3.54*	3.17*
regional chief executive	(1.54)		(1.49)	(1.29)
Region's Dependence on Central Subsidies				
Central subventions as	−.02		.003	
percentage of regional	(.04)		(.03)	
tax revenue, 1992				
Republic Status	−.71		4.93*	4.58**
	(1.63)		(1.95)	(1.59)
Constant	−9.86*	−7.56**	−5.42	−7.88**
	(4.53)	(2.74)	(4.22)	(2.61)
Model χ^2	10.30	7.72	31.17	26.24
	(Sig at .25)	(Sig at .03)	(Sig at .0003)	(Sig at .0001)
N	65	88	65	65

Note: standard errors in parentheses.
*$p < .05$ **$p < .01$

Supreme Soviet that fall. Indeed, the logistic regression estimates imply that the difference was huge. Where public support for Yeltsin had dropped, the regional leader was about 12 times more likely to voice criticism of him or throw in his lot with the besieged parliamentarians.[5] Electoral outcomes appear to have had a very marked effect on strategies of the regional political elite.[6] This conclusion is supported by some evidence from regional leaders' own public statements. The leaders of Khanty-Mansiisky Autonomous Okrug, for instance, declining to join the higher level Tyumen Oblast soviet in open condemnation of Yeltsin's September decree, pointed out that "they could not ignore the fact that 84 percent of people in the okrug who had voted in the April referendum had expressed confidence in Yeltsin" (Teague 1993, 21). One recent survey of public opinion in four regions also concluded that in making demands for greater autonomy, regional elites "may, in fact, have been representing the views of the majority of their constituents" (Andrews and Stoner-Weiss 1995, 404).

Journalists and observers have often deplored authoritarian aspects of the Russian state and insensitivity of leaders to voters' opinions, and associated this with voters' sense of apathy and powerlessness. But, if these results are correct, they suggest that the ineffectiveness and internal conflicts of Russian government may not always reflect weak incentives to listen to the electorate and a shielding of the elite from genuine democratic pressures. They may result, rather, from the way electoral pressures at different levels create conflicts, or from the incentives toward populist, disconnected, and ineffective responses to contradictory voter demands.

More evidence for such a view is offered by another aspect of the results. Those regional leaders who had been popularly elected in their region, rather than appointed by Yeltsin, were significantly more likely to oppose him in September 1993. Indeed, a regional leader who was elected had odds more than 20 times higher than an appointed counterpart of publicly criticizing the president during the September crisis.[7] Regional elections seem to give local leaders courage to stand out vigorously against the authorities at the center.[8] According to the Federation Council chairman, Yegor Stroyev, himself the elected governor of Orel Oblast: "elected regional governors have more confidence and freedom in their actions and statements. An appointed representative, though, has to watch his every word" (Medvedev 1996).[9] Thus, local democratization appears to have influenced relations between central and regional political leaders in two significant ways. Electoral legitimacy reduced regional leaders' personal dependence on Moscow and left them freer to try to build local support coalitions through the politics of confrontation. At the same time, most regional leaders were visibly tailoring their stance in relations with the center to be consistent with the trend in local voting.

Leaders of republics were more likely to oppose the president in September 1993 than those of oblasts or krais—the estimates imply odds nearly 100 times higher.[10] And this result already controls for the level of and recent change in local support for Yeltsin. Even in a republic where the electorate was increasingly supportive of the president, the leader would be more likely to oppose him than the leader of a similar oblast. Oddly enough, regional leaders who were Russian were much more likely to be spoilers than those of minority ethnicity. This may reflect a greater need of Russian heads of government in non-Russian republics to prove their local loyalty to their own voters. But it suggests that anticenter activism may have more to do with the opportunities created by republic status than with ethnicity per se.

Besides electoral interests and the opportunities associated with republic status, aspects of the leader's personal situation at times also influenced his strategy. Those previously employed in the state or party administration—the career apparatchiks—may have been somewhat more inclined to resist the president, but this is not significant. And having been the leader of the region's government under communist rule made no noticeable difference. But, exactly as one might expect, those governors who were themselves members of the national parliament were more likely than others to take its side against President Yeltsin during both the December 1992 and September 1993 crises. Institutional position thus did seem to affect political action: where governors stood was related to where they sat. When the institutions of government at the center are divided among themselves, integrating regional politicians into them through multiple officeholding risks merely extending the central split into the regions. Finally, there is no evidence either in December 1992 or September 1993 that regions more dependent on central subsidies were any less likely to oppose Yeltsin.

In brief, the strategies of regional leaders in dealing with the central government at moments of crisis seem to have been fundamentally shaped by their perception of the institutional context of center-region politics and their own place and interests within it. Elections appeared to have found an important place in the strategic calculus. They did so in two ways. First, those governors who were elected rather than appointed felt freer to criticize the president publicly—and governors who were also elected members of the central parliament were more likely to side with it against Yeltsin. In this sense, the extension of elections to regions acted as a catalyst for conflict. Yet, at the same time, *how* regional electorates voted could restrain the impetus for confrontation. Whether a governor was elected or appointed, he appeared to take stock of how his electorate voted in national elections. Where regional populations had soured on Yeltsin particularly fast, the governor was far less likely to defer to the head of state. But where the benefits of reform or higher regional spending had bought Yeltsin a more supportive electorate, the governor tended to remain loyal. These results suggest that those who associate a confrontational style of government with the lack of genuine electoral institutions in Russia may be mistaken; in fact, such problems seemed to result from *responsive* leaders in a structure that provided incentives for conflict between *different* elected institutions—the regional governments, presidency, and national parliament.

Another way to gauge variation in regional governors' strategies is to examine which chose to support President Yeltsin during the 1996 presidential election campaign. Information on this was compiled by Robert Orttung of the Open Media Research Institute from a variety of sources. According to this listing, while 77 regional leaders eventually supported Yeltsin's campaign, 12 did not. Table 5.2 shows the results when a dummy variable based on this listing is regressed on a range of plausible independent variables with logistic regression. Besides the governor's background and institutional position, regional public opinion, dependence on central aid, and republic status, a number of variables are included to measure particular aid to or campaigning in the region, on the assumption that governors favored by recent Yeltsin initiatives might prove more loyal at election time. Because of the sparse information available on some of the governors, including the personal background variables in the regression leads to a substantial drop in the number of valid cases. Regressions are therefore shown both with the background variables and without (when included, these were not at all significant). Data sources and variable descriptions are provided in appendix D.

As in the previous period, a recent relative increase in pro-reform voting seemed to increase the governor's propensity to support the Yeltsin campaign. This reflected recent changes rather than a traditional pro- or anti-Yeltsin orientation in the region. A control variable measuring the rate of support for Yeltsin in the April 1993 referendum was not significant. As in September 1993, republics were more likely than oblasts or krais to oppose Yeltsin, suggesting their greater institutional independence. Interestingly, regions with which Yeltsin had signed a bilateral power-sharing agreement also generally had a more pro-Yeltsin governor, though a separate analysis would be necessary to determine whether pro-Yeltsin governors tended to receive agreements or whether those that received agreements subsequently became pro-Yeltsin. The size of this effect exceeded the republic status effect, such that the head of a republic that received a bilateral agreement would be more likely to support Yeltsin than the governor of an oblast without an agreement.

Again, these results suggest the influence of trends in regional voting on the governor's choice of political strategy and alliances. Where voting for pro-reform parties increased or stayed relatively stable between 1993 and 1995, the governor was more likely to support Yeltsin's campaign. The background of regional leaders—even whether they were elected or appointed—did not significantly influence their stance toward Yeltsin this time around. Republic leaders apparently had greater institutional resources or incentives than oblasts or krais to play "hard to get." But those treated to a bilateral power-sharing agreement could in general be brought on board.

The implication of these results is surprising. To the extent that regional politicians in Russia are obstructionist, confrontational, and parochial this would seem to reflect less the prejudices or concerns of antidemocratic and in-

TABLE 5.2. Which Regional Chief Executives Supported Yeltsin During 1996 Presidential Election Campaign? (Logistic regression coefficients. Dependent variable is: Regional executive was pro-Yeltsin.)

	A		B	
	(1)	(2)	(1)	(2)
Regional Public Opinion				
Vote for Yeltsin April 1993	.07 (.06)		.06 (.04)	
Above average rise (below average fall) in vote for reform parties in 1993–95 parliamentary elections[a]	3.45** (1.56)	1.73* (.94)	3.03*** (1.14)	2.33*** (.90)
Background of Governor				
Former state or party official	−10.05 (72.43)	−9.06 (50.64)		
Russian nationality	−.59 (1.56)			
Governor's Institutional History				
Popularly elected regional chief executive	−2.38 (1.62)		−.81 (1.02)	
Region's Dependence on Central Subsidies				
Central budget transfers as percentage of regional tax revenue, 1995	.46 (.87)		1.00 (.72)	
Republic Status	−1.33 (1.76)	−1.98** (1.00)	−3.66** (1.52)	−2.60*** (.95)
Presidential Aid and Campaigning				
Yeltsin visited region in 1996	2.58 (2.86)		.60 (1.72)	
Bilateral power-sharing treaty signed	15.03 (74.52)	11.00 (52.22)	5.38*** (2.03)	3.35** (1.34)
Yeltsin decree or government resolution giving region aid in 1996 (Jan. 1–June 15)	−1.94 (2.29)		−1.13 (1.22)	
Constant	7.45 (72.51)	9.57 (50.65)	−2.48 (2.45)	.91 (.58)
Model χ^2	30.57 (Sig at .0007)	25.66 (Sig at .0000)	27.47 (Sig at .0006)	21.23 (Sig at .0001)
N	64	67	77	77

Note: standard errors in parentheses. A regressions include governors' background variables, leading to a drop in the number of available cases by at least 10; B regressions exclude these two variable in order to increase the number of cases.

[a]Classification of parties from Clem and Craumer (1995b). Reform parties in 1993: Russia's Choice, Russian Movement for Democratic Reform (RDDR), Party of Russian Unity and Accord (PRES), Yabloko; Reform parties in 1995: Russia's Democratic Choice, RDDR, PRES, Yabloko, Our Home Is Russia, Worker's Self-Government, Pamfilova et al., Forward Russia, Common Cause, CD Union.

*$p < .10$ **$p < .05$ ***$p < .01$

sulated regional elites than the cues they are taking from regional voters. Confrontation was not caused by too little democracy but by the incentives embedded in the particular democratic institutions that had evolved in Russia's federal system.[11]

Conclusion

While what struck most observers about intergovernmental politics in Russia in the early 1990s was the open confrontation, protest, and threats, in fact the degree and types of conflict between Moscow and the regions were highly varied. Not all governors responded to the apparent fiscal incentives for disruptive action. Of course, in any interaction with the center there is a danger that its strategy will change from one of offering carrots to using sticks—in the Russian expression, from the "spice cake" to the "whip." But clearly some factors must account for the regions' different evaluations of this danger, their different degree of risk aversion, and their different sense of vulnerability to potential central pressure.

The analysis in this chapter suggested several answers. Some of the constraints on centrifugal activism appear to have been linked to the ways in which specific regional leaders were institutionally integrated into national politics. A governor who was a member of the national parliament would take its side against the president more often than one who was not; but a region's parliamentary delegation that contained the region's governor would take the president's side more frequently (see appendix D). In part, regional elections, at least in off years in between national elections, seemed to give regional politicians greater confidence in opposing the center. Those who had local electoral legitimacy were less manageable than those who owed their position to central appointment.

Yet, at the same time, one of the *constraints* on regional leaders' strategies appeared itself to issue from the new logic of electoral politics. Regional leaders responded to recent voting by their constituents. Where the regional electorate was growing more favorable toward the president—or at least turning against him more slowly—the governor was more likely to support him in political struggles. While electoral institutions can create conflicts when voters express themselves inconsistently at the national and local levels, they could also constrain instrumental transfer-seeking confrontations by rendering regional leaders' threats less credible or by making them fear for their local political positions. Greater fiscal vulnerability may have played some role, but the results were not clear.[12]

These constraints appear to have been less binding on the leaders of Russia's autonomous republics. This chapter found evidence that higher past administrative status provided regions with resources for anticenter mobilization.

The evidence suggests, however, that the *motivation* for such mobilization was not, as one might assume, primarily rooted in primordial nationalist identities, cultural division, or ethnic conflict. Such mobilization looked far more like a rationally calculated means by which often ethnically Russian regional leaders applied pressure in the tense game of bargaining and threats that characterized Russia's politics.

The apparent responsiveness of regional leaders to their constituents' voting patterns acquires particular significance when linked to the results of the previous chapters. Chapter 3 showed that the central state in Russia in the early 1990s practiced a policy of fiscal appeasement, rewarding with greater net transfers those provinces that posed a threat to stability by their anti-Yeltsin voting or by their leaders' mobilization of discontent. Chapter 4 suggested that, when the beneficiaries of greater net transfers spent them in their region—as was generally the case—this, in turn, led to higher local votes of support for Yeltsin and the central incumbents. With the results of this chapter, the feedback is complete. By increasing the regional vote for Yeltsin, the center with its policy of targeted fiscal redistribution seemed able sharply to reduce the chances that that region's leader would publicly criticize Yeltsin and side with his opposition—even though such a strategy of confrontation might elicit additional financial concessions from Moscow.[13]

This logic is evident in the contrasting political history of several regions. The republic of Kabardino-Balkaria, in the North Caucasus mountains, shows one trajectory (see table 5.3). While Yeltsin started out here popular, with 64 percent of the vote in 1991, his rating dropped precipitously as conditions in the republic deteriorated. In 1992–93, the proportion of enterprises making a loss shot up from 6 to 22 percent, a rise 50 percent higher than the average. A small positive net transfer from the center in 1992 (2,700 rubles per capita) was not enough to prevent a sharp drop in real regional spending—by nearly 60 percent, compared to an average regional drop of 44 percent. By the April referendum, Yeltsin's support had slipped 28 percentage points. The republic's elected president, Valery Kokov, also took the risk of openly opposing Yeltsin during the September crisis, accusing the president of trying to "provoke a crisis of dual power" and equivocating when asked whether he would obey the orders of Yeltsin or of the vice president and rebel leader, Alexander Rutskoi (Teague 1993, 17).

Then, however, came the center's attempt at appeasement. Moscow reached into its pockets. In 1994, real direct transfers to the region grew by 124,000 rubles per capita, nearly six times the average increase, and the region was permitted to retain an additional 13 percent of the tax revenue it collected. While real spending in the average region dropped 116,000 rubles (10 percent), it *rose* in Kabardino-Balkaria by 34,000 (7 percent). A bilateral power-sharing agreement was signed with the republic that same year, and it was given the sta-

TABLE 5.3. Aid, Voting, and Governors' Strategies in Three Russian Regions

Region	1991 Yeltsin Vote (%)	Net Transfers 1992 (t.R.pc)	Real Spending Change 1991–92 (%)	Change in Yeltsin Vote 1991–Apr. 1993 (%)	Governor Opposed Yeltsin Sept. 93	Change in Real Transfers 93–94 (t.R.pc)	Change in Reg. Tax Share 93–94 (%)	Real Spending Change 93–94 (%)	OHIR Vote 95–RC Vote 93 (%)	Aid Decree 96	Change in Yeltsin Vote 1993–96
Kabardino-Balkaria	63.9	+2.7	−57	−28.1	YES	+123.8	+12.7	+7	+18.4	YES	+27.8
Yaroslavl	54.8	−18.1	−.02	+14.0	NO	+16.0	−3.6	−22	−13.6	YES	−8.3
Sakha	44.9	+7.5	−26	+23.2	NO	+20.8	+0.2	+19	+0.4	YES	−3.5
Average	52.3	−3.1	−44	+4.2		+21.9	+3.7	−10	−5.2		−3.9

Source: see appendixes to chapters 3, 4, and 5.

tus of a free economic zone. Votes followed the money. In December 1995, in the average region Chernomyrdin's Our Home Is Russia polled 5.2 percentage points below the total for its 1993 predecessor as the "party of power," Russia's Choice. But in Kabardino-Balkaria, OHIR's vote was 18 percentage points higher than its predecessor. Kokov, who had opposed Yeltsin in 1993, now became his political ally, endorsing his presidential election campaign. On April 3, 1996, the federal government signed a decree providing assistance to the republic. By the July election, Yeltsin's vote had rebounded upward, regaining the 28 percentage points it had dropped in 1993.

An opposite trajectory can be seen in the central Russian oblast of Yaroslavl. There, voters had started out in 1991 relatively unimpressed with Yeltsin, giving him about 55 percent, less than his nationwide total (though slightly more than the unweighted average across regions). Despite paying more in tax to Moscow than it received in transfers, the oblast was nevertheless allowed to keep sufficient revenues to be able to shield itself from the 1992 spending cuts and keep real regional budget spending more or less constant— at a time when in the average region it fell by 44 percent. While in its neighbors, large wage arrears backed up, in Yaroslavl, wages were paid on time. In 1992, the oblast had the lowest wage arrears of any region in Russia. This relatively enviable performance was followed by a jump in Yeltsin's support in April 1993 by more than three times that in the average region. And the governor did not challenge Yeltsin during the crisis later that year.

Quiescence, however, was not rewarded. Real federal transfers increased only about 16 percent in 1994, compared to a 22 percent rise in the average region. And while the average region got to keep about 3.7 percentage points more of its total tax revenue that year, Yaroslavl was required to give up an additional 3.6 percentage points. That year the region, along with neighboring Tverskaya Oblast, had the dubious distinction of paying a higher proportion of its tax revenue to Moscow than any other. In the face of this, the region could not maintain its spending levels, and real regional expenditures dropped more than twice the national average.[14] Voters responded in kind. OHIR in 1995 polled more than 13 percentage points lower than Russia's Choice had two years earlier—compared to a difference of 5 percentage points in the average region. While the administration signed a decree in aid of the region in 1996 and its governor, a Yeltsin appointee, publicly supported the president's reelection campaign, this only slowed the flow of deserting voters. Yeltsin's total in July was more than 8 percentage points lower than the level of regional support for him in April 1993.

The most effective regional strategy, where it could be sustained, combined credible challenges with a readiness to negotiate. In some of the richer ethnic republics, presidents managed to keep up the pressure and the implicit threat despite a voting trend toward support for Yeltsin. A good example is the diamond-rich, remote, eastern republic of Sakha. The republic's population started out in 1991 with an unusually low vote for Yeltsin—45 percent—and a particularly high rate of support for the main Communist contender, Nikolai Ryzhkov. The next year, however, Sakha managed to get away with paying only about 1 percent of total tax revenues to Moscow. This huge reduction in remittances helped to cushion the region from the shocks of liberalization. While spending in the average region dropped 44 percent in real terms in 1992, in Sakha it fell only 26 percent. Apparently rewarding Yeltsin for his connivance at the republic's tax withholding, voters boosted their level of support for him by 23 percentage points in the April 1993 referendum. And, unlike some of his colleagues, the republic's president, Mikhail Nikolaev, took Yeltsin's side in the dispute with the parliament later that year.

Despite the surge in support for Yeltsin, Sakha's political elite was able to continue dramatizing a threat to central control. While Nikolaev, negotiating with Moscow, could cast himself as reasonable and open to compromise, his hand was strengthened by an assertive republic legislature. Sakha's Supreme Soviet in 1993 adopted its own laws on mineral resources and on citizenship, which were believed by many to violate the Russian Constitution. It considered a law on declaring economic states of emergency under which Sakha could suspend shipments of diamonds and precious metals to Moscow, or even stop the independent sale of these (Kempton 1996, 597). At the same time, Nikolaev could also point to pressures from the nationalist organization Sakha Omuk (Khazanov 1995, 182–83).

Against this drumbeat, Moscow continued to compromise. The republic's ability to increase its share of retained tax revenue was limited by mathematics—it was already in 1993 retaining 99.83 percent. But the center did enter into negotiations to regularize this arrangement. A bilateral power-sharing agreement was signed in June 1995, along with a secret decree that raised the republic's gold mining quota from 12 to 15 percent and its quota for gem-quality diamonds from 20 to 25 percent. According to the newspaper *Segodnya,* this would give Sakha an additional $50 million in 1995.[15] Meanwhile, in 1994, real regional budget spending still managed to grow by 19 percent, at a time when it was falling in most regions. In addition, on the eve of the parliamentary election in November 1995, Chernomyrdin signed a generous decree promising the republic aid for its socioeconomic development and money to finance road building and a hydroelectric plant.[16] OHIR's vote that December was actually higher than that of Russia's Choice two years before—a feat the bloc achieved in only 11 of the country's regions. In the second round of the next year's presidential election, Yeltsin's level of support, already high in April 1993, fell less than the average drop.[17]

In brief, the way regions voted and the way regional leaders chose their strategies was related to the center's fiscal policy and the way regional spending levels changed during the period of painful adjustment. Crises could, at times, be alleviated by fiscal concessions, and regional leaders could be brought on board the president's electoral alliance. By contrast, fiscal neglect of regions often led to growing discontent with central incumbents. While various other factors also shaped the patterns of voting and regional assertiveness, central politicians were not resourceless in the face of these developments. The particular central redistributive strategy adopted, while balancing on the edge of fiscal solvency, appears to have stabilized the nationwide dynamic of regional crises.

CHAPTER 6

Yugoslavia, the USSR, Czechoslovakia—and Russia

Previous chapters have argued that an important contributor to national integration in Russia in the 1990s was the central authorities' use of fiscal transfers and tax breaks to appease many of the government's most vocal regional critics. Chapters 3 through 5 presented evidence that such a pattern of redistribution did in fact occur and showed how it could slow the formation of bandwagons of regional protest. The logic of the argument of chapter 1 is formalized in a simple political economy model in appendix A.

This chapter places Russia's experience in comparative context. Alarm over Russia's cohesion in the early 1990s was fueled in part by comparisons to the three other communist federations that had existed in the late 1980s. In the Soviet Union, Czechoslovakia, and Yugoslavia, communist leaders had adopted pseudo-federal structures in the hope of preventing or co-opting potential nationalist challenges from minority ethnicities. Yet as the party's control weakened and governments attempted economic and political reforms, ethnically defined subunits became a focus of conflict with the central authorities. In Yugoslavia and the Soviet Union, challenges spiraled until even initially reluctant separatists began to join in. The result was a central fiscal crisis as more and more regions refused to remit tax revenues.

To some observers, the collapse of reforming communist federations seemed inevitable. Economic crisis and ethno-federal structure appeared to be a particularly explosive combination.[1] Yet Russia had both these features. Indeed, its economic crisis in 1992–93 appeared in many ways more severe than that faced by any of the other three prior to dissolution.[2] Unilateral tax withholding had spread to more than 30 of the country's 89 regions by late 1993.

If, as argued in this book, central fiscal appeasement helped to contain such pressures in Russia, did it fail in these other three cases? This chapter examines the fiscal crises and central responses in pre-dissolution Yugoslavia, Czechoslovakia, and the Soviet Union. It finds that, in fact, in no other case was a similar policy attempted. In none of the three did the central regime direct resources disproportionately toward the most credible separatist regions. In part, strategies of central economic or fiscal accommodation were not attempted because those controlling central policy did not place a sufficient priority on national integration.[3] But in part, appeasement was passed up because

137

central politicians mistakenly chose other policies that actually exacerbated centrifugal splits.

This chapter does *not* pretend to offer a full analysis of all the reasons for disintegration in each country or to assess whether fiscal appeasement could have overcome them. Each of the cases differed from the others and from Russia in significant ways, and fiscal policy was only one element in a complex mix of historical factors and strategic choices.[4] Obviously, a strategy of selective fiscal appeasement can only work within certain boundary conditions—if divisions are too great or central resources too meager, such a policy will not be enough to prevent secession. Another book would be required to examine adequately whether a feasible central policy existed in Yugoslavia, Czechoslovakia, or the USSR that could have forestalled the split. The goal here is much more limited. If fiscal appeasement is to be a convincing explanation of Russia's fate, the argument must be at least consistent with the course of events in these three other countries. If a similar strategy of fiscal appeasement *was* attempted in any of these and *exacerbated* rather than alleviated the centrifugal dynamic, this would cast doubt on the story told.

To calculate accurately the aggregate balance of fiscal flows in any one of these countries would pose formidable challenges. No definitive accounting is available, and the pattern of fiscal favoritism in each is debated. The analysis offered in this chapter is no more than a rough attempt to estimate the approximate scale and direction of visible redistribution. No claims of precision can be made. However, considerable information and statistical data about each country's last years are available; and so, exercising due caution, I believe some tentative conclusions can nevertheless be reached.

Fiscal Crises in Four Countries

The political crises that preceded the collapse of Yugoslavia, the USSR, and Czechoslovakia varied in many ways. But each had a clear fiscal element. In Yugoslavia, republic leaders had been arguing about the level of fiscal transfers since at least the mid-1980s, and by late 1990 both Serbia and Slovenia had simply stopped remitting part of their federal tax (Mencinger 1993, 84; Zizmond 1992, 110). A similar scenario occurred in the Soviet Union in late 1991, as an increasing number of republics combined political defiance of the Union government with fiscal withholding, starving central agencies of funds. In Slovakia, resentment at a perceived failure of the Prague government to respond adequately to the republic's relatively more severe economic crisis helped fuel support for politicians advocating independence.

Yet, this did not distinguish these cases from the experience of Russia. In fact, the fiscal crisis Russia faced in the early 1990s was in many ways as severe—and its fiscal system as vulnerable—as those in the three communist federations that disintegrated. This section examines the similarities and differences in the crises that rocked the budgetary systems of these four countries and in the structure of their fiscal institutions.

One feature common to all four was a central government with relatively meager revenues. In Yugoslavia, Czechoslovakia, and the Soviet Union, the federal budget's own revenues in the year before disintegration came to less than 12 percent of GDP (see table 6.1). In Russia, federal own revenues dipped below this level in 1993 and approached it again in 1996, when federal revenues came to 12.5 percent of GDP, or about 10.7 percent if sales of foreign exchange are excluded.[5] By comparison, central government revenues in the early 1990s came to about 40 percent of GDP in Italy, 36 percent in Austria, 19 percent in the United States, and 17 percent in Belgium and South Korea.[6]

However, if all four central governments had anemic revenues, the history behind this differed. In Yugoslavia, extreme decentralization had been the norm since the constitutional reforms of the early 1970s. By 1985, the federal government in Belgrade collected less than 5 percent of gross social product (GSP) in revenue, and it spent this mostly on supporting the Yugoslav National Army, paying military pensions, financing central administration, and supplying a Federal Development Fund that redistributed investment resources from the richer northern republics to the less developed southern ones. The vast majority of public services and infrastructure projects were financed by associations of consumers and providers known as "self-governing communities of interest", at the local or republic level. In fact, in 1989-90, the federal government of Ante Markovic was attempting to *recentralize* budget revenues somewhat as part of the IMF-monitored stabilization program, bringing previously off-budget items on budget and increasing sales tax to pay for social safety net spending and rehabilitation of the banking system. Both revenues and expenditure increased as a percentage of GSP in 1990, though both still remained under 10 percent (Mihaljek 1993; OECD 1990).[7]

By contrast, Czechoslovakia and the USSR were both undergoing a decentralization of revenue and spending to the republic governments in their final years—in the former by design, in the latter largely by default. Before 1990, Czechoslovakia had been highly centralized, with the federal government collecting nearly 50 percent of revenues, compared to 28 percent for the republics. Most of this federal revenue, however, had been transferred down to the republics to spend. In the early 1990s, the system was reformed to give the republics their own revenue sources in line with expenditures and to reduce the need for federal transfers. As a result, by 1992 the breakdown of revenues had been reversed, with the federal government collecting 22 percent and the republics raising 65 percent. Republic revenues and spending both increased between 1989 and 1992 as a share of GDP, though federal spending levels remained relatively constant (see table 6.2). The Soviet system suffered a drastic

TABLE 6.1. Federal Own Revenue in Three Reforming Communist Federations and Russia

	\multicolumn{10}{c}{Federal Own Revenue}									
	1985	1987	1988	1989	1990	1991	1992	1993	1994	1995	1996
Yugoslavia[a] (% GSP)	3.5	4.9	4.6	4.4	9.7	—					
(% cons. bud. rev.)		45.0			45.5						
USSR (% GDP)				21.3	23.9	2.9[b]					
(% cons. bud. rev.)				52.0	59.5	11.4	—				
Czechoslovakia (% GDP)				26.2	18.8	12.7	11.7				
(% cons. bud. rev.)				47.8	32.9	24.8	22.2				
Russia (% GDP)							15.9	11.8	13.3	13.7	12.5
(% cons. bud. rev.)							55.4	44.0	47.7	52.5	50.4

Source: Czechoslovakia: *Statistická Rocenka Ceské Republiky 1993* (Prague: Cesky Statisticky Urad, 1993, 119), *Statistická Rocenka Ceské a Slovenské Federativni Republiky 1991* (Prague: Federalni Statisticky Urad, 1991,151). USSR: IMF, *The Economy of the Former USSR in 1991* (Washington, DC: IMF, April 1992, 67–68). Yugoslavia: Mihaljek (1993, 190.) Russia: Working data of World Bank, April 1997; 1994 without Chechen republic; cash not commitment basis.
[a]Ministry of Finance estimate.
[b]1991 January–October.

TABLE 6.2. Federal Expenditures in Three Reforming Communist Federations and Russia

	Federal Expenditures (excluding grants to republics)									
	1987	1988	1989	1990	1991	1992	1993	1994	1995	1996
Yugoslavia (% GSP)	5.7	5.1	5.1	9.8	—					
USSR (% GDP)			24.3	30.6	9.8[a]					
Czechoslovakia (% GDP)			9.3	10.8	12.0	11.4	—			
Russia (% GDP)						23.4	17.2	18.6	15.7	12.3

Source: Czechoslovakia: *Statistická Rocenka Ceské Republiky 1993* (Prague: Cesky Statisticky Urad, 1993, 119), *Statistická Rocenka Ceské a Slovenské Federativní Republiky 1991* (Prague: Federalni Statisticky Urad, 1991,151). USSR: IMF, *The Economy of the Former USSR in 1991* (Washington, DC: IMF, April 1992, 67–68). Yugoslavia: Expenditures 1987–89 from OECD 1990, 1990 calculated from Mihaljek 1993. Russia: 1992–94: Le Houerou 1995, tables 1.1, A1–3; 1996: from Institute for the Economy in Transition, *Economic Trends and Perspectives* (February 1997). Expenditures exclude intergovernmental transfers; 1994 without Chechen republic; cash not commitment basis. 1995: *Russian Economic Trends* (1996, 5, 2, calculated from 11, 12, 22, 28–29). Figures have been adjusted where appropriate to exclude intergovernmental transfers, using data from Lavrov (1996, table 2). 1996: *Russian Economic Trends* (1996, 5, 2, 11), expenditures adjusted for center-region transfers (these estimated at 1.5% of GDP = average for I and II quarters, from *Russian Economic Trends* (1996, 5, 2, 11, 27).)

[a]1991 January–October.

hemorrhage of revenue from the center to the republics in 1990–91, as the republics—often unilaterally—halted tax payments. The federal budget's estimated own revenues dropped from about 24 percent of GDP in 1990 to less than 3 percent in the first 10 months of 1991.

As in the Soviet Union and Czechoslovakia, Russia's federal revenues showed a distinct downward trend, though the decline was at a more moderate pace—from 15.9 percent of GDP in 1992 to 12.5 percent in 1996. Thus, if meager federal budget revenues are a risk factor in reforming federations, Russia was nearly as badly off as Czechoslovakia or Yugoslavia.

The federal budget's problems in these countries do not seem to have been shared to the same extent by other levels of the state. In all four cases, lower levels' revenues either *increased* as a percentage of GDP or at least fell less than federal revenues. These fiscal crises did not represent a growing failure of the state at all levels to collect taxes, except in Russia in 1995–96 when both federal and regional/local budget revenues were falling. To a considerable extent, the center's fiscal troubles seem to have reflected a redistribution of revenue to lower level budgets.

The USSR suffered the most marked drop in consolidated budget revenues. But the estimated fall in Soviet consolidated budget revenues—from about 40 percent of GDP in 1990 to about 26 percent in 1991—was much smaller than the fall in federal revenues—from 24 to 3 percent (see table 6.3). About one-third of the center's losses were actually offset by increases in republic level and local budgets. If revenues from off-budget funds are included, the actual drop is even less extreme, from about 45 percent in 1990 to 35 percent in 1991.[8] In Czechoslovakia, consolidated budget revenues hardly fell at all between 1989 and 1992: the drop in federal revenues was almost completely compensated by increases in republic and lower level budgets. (However, revenues of off-budget funds apparently did drop sharply during this period.)[9] As already mentioned, both federal and republic revenues increased in Yugoslavia—consolidated revenues almost doubled between 1987 and 1990.

In Russia, regional and local budget revenues increased during the first period of the center's fiscal crisis, rising from 12.8 to 15.0 percent of GDP between 1992 and 1993, as federal budget revenues fell from 15.9 to 11.8 percent (see table 3.1 in chap. 3). However, regional revenues subsequently fell while federal revenues recovered, only to drop again in 1996. Russia's consolidated state budget gathered 28.7 percent of GDP in 1992 and 24.8 percent in 1996 in revenues. (The drop is somewhat larger if off-budget fund revenues are included—from 46.1 percent of GDP in 1992 to 33.9 in 1995—a larger fall than the USSR experienced in its disastrous final year.) Thus, the nature of the fiscal crises in these countries usually had more to do with a reallocation of revenues between levels than a collapse of tax collecting capacity per se. Yugoslavia, Czechoslovakia, and the USSR evidently did not collapse because of

TABLE 6.3. Consolidated Budget Revenues in Three Reforming Communist Federations and Russia

	\multicolumn{10}{c}{Consolidated Budget Revenues}									
	1987	1988	1989	1990	1991	1992	1993	1994	1995	1996
Yugoslavia (% GSP)	10.9			21.3	—					
USSR (% GDP)			41.0	40.2	25.5	—				
Czechoslovakia (% GDP)			54.8	57.1	51.2	52.7	—			
Russia (% GDP)					33.7[a]	28.7	26.8	27.9	26.1	24.8

Source: Russia: 1991, from Aleksashenko (1992). Other years, working data of World Bank, April 1997. Czechoslovakia: *Statistická Rocenka Ceské Republiky 1993* (Prague: Cesky Statisticky Urad, 1993, 119), *Statistická Rocenka Ceské a Slovenské Federativní Republiky 1991* (Prague: Federalni Statisticky Urad, 1991, 151). Yugoslavia: calculated from Mihaljek (1993). USSR: from Aleksashenko (1992, 446). Fischer (1992, 89), for 1989.

[a] Estimates of Sergei Aleksashenko. IMF estimates (IMF Economic Reviews *Russian Federation,* April 1992, 70) of "enlarged actual Russian budget (with takeover)" for 1991 differ from these estimates. The Fund estimates this at 287.6 bn Rs, or 25.5% of GNP.

atrophy of the tax collection agencies or greater resistance of citizens to paying taxes, and Russia did not survive because of an unusually effective tax service.

Large federal budget deficits are often viewed as signs of particularly severe fiscal crises. Yet, such problems do not explain the collapse of these postcommunist federations. Both Czechoslovakia and Yugoslavia had no significant central deficit, and despite dwindling republic contributions the Belgrade government appeared quite able to finance its spending from its share of sales tax and customs duties (see table 6.4). By the end of 1991, the Soviet Union did have a sizable deficit of the Union budget—5.8 percent of GDP before taking into account extrabudgetary funds, debt write-offs, and compensation to savings deposits, which would have boosted the deficit to about 17 percent. Russia, the one survivor in the group, had even higher federal deficits, reaching 9.0 percent of GDP in 1992 and 8.0 percent of GDP in 1993. If off-budget funds are included in the accounting, the Russian federal deficit in 1992 was actually around 20 percent.

One feature common to all was an element of tax sharing between federal and republic or regional levels. In Czechoslovakia in 1992, turnover and profit taxes were collected by the federation but then divided between the federation and republics in predetermined proportions. In the other three federations such tax sharing was the subject of considerable ongoing negotiation. While the Yugoslav federal budget received all the revenue from tariffs, it shared with the republics proceeds from the federal sales tax and received additional contributions from the republic budgets. The shares and contributions were negotiated annually between the two sides. In Russia, the tax service is formally subordinated to the central government, but in practice its regional branches rely on and cooperate with the local authorities. VAT and corporate profit tax were shared in the mid-1990s at rates established in annual budget laws. In the USSR after 1988, profit taxes from Union enterprises were shared with the republics.

One feature of fiscal practice that may set Russia apart from the other postcommunist federations is recent change in the level of intergovernmental fiscal transfers. While transfers between different level budgets constitute only one in a range of channels of fiscal and financial redistribution, they may affect both elite and public perceptions of mutual dependency or regional interest. In Czechoslovakia and Yugoslavia, the volume of transfers between federal and republic governments fell practically to zero in the years before federal collapse (see tables 6.5 and 6.6). Interestingly, the balance of such flows had been going in opposite directions in the two countries. In Czechoslovakia, the center had been making large transfers to the republics. These were deliberately reduced by the central reformers, who instead increased the republics' own revenue sources. Federal transfers to lower levels fell from 17 percent of GDP in 1989 to 0.5 percent in 1992. In Yugoslavia, in the past the republics had been making contributions to the center to help finance federal programs. These con-

TABLE 6.4. Federal Budget Balance in Three Reforming Communist Federations and Russia

Federal Budget Balance

	1987	1988	1989	1990	1991	1992	1993	1994	1995	1996
Yugoslavia (% GSP)	0.0	0.0	0.6	0.1	—					
USSR (% GDP; 1991 Jan.–Oct.)			−3.1	−6.3	−5.8[a]					
Czechoslovakia (% GDP)			−0.6	0.5	0.6	−0.7				
Russia (% GDP)					−9.6	−9.0[b]	−8.0	−9.4	−3.0	−3.3

MEMO: GDP (Yugoslavia, GSP; USSR, GNP; Russia, GNP (91), GDP (92–6))

	1985	1987	1988	1989	1990	1991	1992	1993	1994	1995	1996
Yugoslavia (bn new Ds)	1.1	4.9	14.9	221.9	944.3[c]						
USSR (bn Rs)				943	1000	1892.4					
Czechoslovakia (bn Kcs)				758.7	811.3	977.8	1,057				
Russia (trn Rs)						1.13	18.1	162.3	630.0	1,630	2,256

Sources (Budget Balance): Czechoslovakia: *Statistická Rocenka Ceské Republiky 1993* (Prague: Cesky Statisticky Urad, 1993, 119, *Staststická Rocenka Ceské a Slovenské Federativní Republiky 1991* (Prague: Federalni Statisticky Urad, 1991, 151). USSR: IMF, *The Economy of the Former USSR in 1991* (Washington, DC: IMF, April 1992, 67–68). Yugoslavia: balance from OECD (1990, 62 for 87–89); for 1990, calculated from Mihaljek (1993). Russia: 1991: M. I. Khodorovich, "Problemy Fiskalnogo Federalizma v Rossiiskoi Federatsii," *Finansy* (1992, 12, 12). 1992–94: Le Houerou (1995, table 1.1); 1995–96: *Russian Economic Trends* (1997, 3, 12).

[a] If stabilization fund and pension fund deficits, deposit compensation and debt writeoffs are included, broader central budget deficit came to 16.8% (calculated from IMF, *The Economy of the Former USSR in 1991* (Washington, DC: IMF, April 1992, 67–68).) The actual budget deficit may have been even higher (see Bahry 1991, 247).

[b] If deficit of off-budget funds included, federal deficit in 1992 was actually about 20 percent.

[c] GMP in 1990. GSP was not available, but GMP as reported by the *Europa World Yearbook* was equal to GSP for each of the four previous years.

tributions dropped from 37 percent of federal revenue in 1985 to 6 percent in 1990.

Comprehensive data are not available to evaluate the overall trend in such transfers during the last years of Soviet rule (I was unable to locate important figures for Russia, Belarus, and Tajikistan). Among the other republics, the absolute value of net transfers to or from the center in the state's final year (1990–91) dropped for some (Estonia, Latvia, Lithuania, Ukraine, Moldova, Georgia, and Kazakhstan) while increasing for others (Armenia, Azerbaijan, Kirghizia, Turkmenistan, and Uzbekistan). Where center-republic flows dropped, this reflected either deliberate attempts of central reformers to devolve self-financing and fiscal responsibility or unilateral refusals of republics to pay net taxes to the center. Where net center-republic transfers increased, this was caused by central policymakers' attempts to alleviate fiscal problems in those regions through greater subsidies. In post-Soviet Russia, however, the volume of direct federal budget transfers to the regional governments *rose* from 1.5 percent of GDP in 1992 to 3.4 percent in 1994. However, the levels later fell again in 1994 through 1996. And in 1992 through 1994, the very large drop in quasi-fiscal transfers such as credit subsidies almost definitely exceeded the increase in budget transfers.

In short, the nature of the fiscal crises in the three failing communist federations varied. But each had a federal government with weak revenue powers by the end, and in at least two of the three cases the level of fiscal flows between center and regions was falling. However, Russia, the one surviving postcommunist federation, *also* had a central government with limited (and falling) revenues by 1996 and falling levels of center-region fiscal flows (in 1994–96). In some ways, the crisis Russia faced in the early 1990s seemed more severe than in the other three cases. The Russian central budget deficit was probably larger than in any of the others at its highest point, and the drop in revenues of the consolidated budget plus off-budget funds in 1992 through 1995 was particularly great. The relative severity of fiscal strains thus does *not* explain why Russia remained intact while the others disintegrated.

TABLE 6.5. Grants from Federation to Czech and Slovak Governments, in Percent of Czechoslovakia GDP

	To Czech Republic	To Slovak Republic
1989	9.9	7.1
1990	4.6	2.9
1991	0	0
1992	0.3	0.2

Source: *Statistická Rocenka České Republiky* 1993.

TABLE 6.6. Yugoslavia, Financing the Federation

	Total Federal Revenue (mn dinars)	Contributions as % of Total Revenue	Customs Duties as % of Total Revenue	Federal Sales Tax as % of Total Revenue	Nat Bank Credit to Fed, as % of Total Revenue
1982	19.9	40.2	14.1	42.7	41.7
1985	68.6	36.6	21.9	38.5	14.9
1987	300.9	20.7	26.2	51.1	23.9
1988	813.1	15.4	29.5	52.5	10.7
1989	11,376.0	13.8	28.5	54.9	10.3
1990	97,542.0	6.1	35.0	56.3	—

Source: Mihaljek 1993, 190.

Central Fiscal Policy in the Final Years

If the nature of the fiscal crisis in Russia was as serious and its fiscal system as vulnerable as in the other three countries, it makes sense to consider what role particular fiscal policies played in its more successful struggle to survive. Were policies of accommodating the most credible separatists with fiscal concessions attempted anywhere other than in Russia?

In Czechoslovakia, Yugoslavia, and the USSR, the most adamant early demands for greater independence came from, respectively, Slovakia; Slovenia and Croatia; and the Baltic republics, particularly Lithuania. So it is important to examine whether these republics were favored or disfavored by fiscal and financial arrangements in the federation. Most significantly, one needs to assess how the terms of such arrangements were *changing* in the years that preceded the federation's collapse.

Once again, a major caveat is in order. To attempt to identify the "winners" and "losers" from aggregate redistribution in each of these countries is highly problematic. Data are not available to do so in a thorough and exhaustive way. As before, the following estimates must be taken as very rough attempts to judge the magnitudes involved and the directions of change. Nevertheless, a fairly consistent picture seems to emerge.

Czechoslovakia

In Czechoslovakia, published figures suggest federal fiscal transfers to both republics decreased in the early 1990s to around zero (see table 6.5).[10] But the impact on Slovakia might be expected to have been greater since it was more dependent on such transfers to fund republic expenditures. In 1989, federal grants to the Slovak Republic came to 1.43 times the republic's own revenues; such grants to the Czech Republic were equivalent to only 96 percent of own revenues. Real republic budget expenditure fell more sharply in Slovakia during this period than in the Czech Republic (see table 6.7).[11]

Such a reduction in federal grants coincided with an economic crisis that was more severe in the Slovak than in the Czech Republic. While Czech unemployment in 1992 remained only about 2 percent, in Slovakia the rate rose above 10 percent. However, federal government spending priorities appeared in various ways to focus more on Czech than Slovak needs. Unemployment benefits had been made a federal rather than republican responsibility in 1992, in large part because Slovakia was having difficulty financing its large required benefit payout from its budget revenues. But the proportion of total state budget spending going toward social security benefits dropped between 1989 and 1992, at a time when Slovakia's relative need for them was increasing (see table 6.8). (In Slovakia, during the same three-year period, the share of spending on

TABLE 6.7. Republic Budget Expenditure per Capita in Czechoslovakia 1989 and 1992 (includes grants to local government)

	1989 (CSK per Capita)	1992	Nominal Change 1989–92 (%)	Real Change 1989–92 (%)	1992 Estimated per Capita Spending When Federal Spending Is Included[a] (CSK per Capita)
Czech Republic	15,068	21,288	+41.3	−26.4	32,234
Slovak Republic	17,507	23,360	+33.4	−30.5	32,038

Source: Calculated from *Statistická Rocenka Slovenskej Republiky 1993* (Bratislava: Statisticky Urad Slovenskej Republiky, 1993, 97); *Statistická Rocenka Ceské a Slovenské Federativni Republiky 1991* (Prague: Federalni Statisticky Urad, 1991, 151); *Statistická Rocenka Ceské Republiky 1993* (Prague: Cesky Statisticky Urad, 1993, 119).

[a]Estimates of OECD (from *OECD Economic Surveys: The Czech and Slovak Republics 1994* (OECD 1994, 55).) Note: CPI rose ca. 92 percent between 1989 and 1992.

social services and activities rose from 39.8 to 71.9 percent of total republic spending, and around this time Slovak demonstrators began to call for compensation for the particularly harsh consequences of the transition in their republic [Cox and Frankland 1995, 83].) At the same time, the share of spending on federal administration rose from 2.9 percent of total federal expenditure in 1991 to 3.7 percent in 1992. Since the federal government was in Prague, such spending would have had fewer indirect benefits for Slovaks.

Two other aspects of interrepublic resource flows are harder to assess. Some have argued that in the past distorted administrative prices transferred wealth from one republic to the other (see OECD 1994, 56–57). As prices liberalized in 1991–92, the transfers associated with such distortions might be expected to decrease. The net interrepublic effect of this is unclear. The situation with regard to credit and currency emission is complex. M1 grew more than twice as fast proportionately in the Czech Republic in 1991–92 as in Slovakia, and domestic credit grew faster in the Czech Republic in 1992 (whether growth is measured as a percentage of the previous credit stock, in per capita terms, or

TABLE 6.8. Expenditures of State (Federal + Republic) Budgets on Social Security Benefits, Czechoslovakia

	1985	1989	1990	1991	1992
SSB as % of total state spending	34.6	34.9	32.6	29.9	28.5

Source: Statistická Rocenka Ceské Republiky (1993, 122).

TABLE 6.9. Growth of M1 in Czech and Slovak Republics, 1991–92

	Czech Republic	Slovak Republic
M1, 1991	256.0	113.2
M1, 1992	306.9	124.0
Growth	19.9%	9.5%

Source: Polish, Czech, Slovak, and Hungarian Statistical Agencies, *Statistical Bulletin*, 1994/1 (Budapest, 1994, tables 3.6, 3.7).

as a percentage of total Czechoslovak GDP; see table 6.9 and 6.10). But it is not clear how much of credit increases issued by Czech banks might in fact have gone to Slovak borrowers. Slovak commercial banks received considerably more in refinancing loans from the State Bank of Czechoslovakia (by the end of 1992, 9.3 billion Koruny compared to 7.6 billion Koruny for Czech banks). In part, this was due to a lower demand for such loans on the part of Czech banks, which had an easier time raising finance through deposits.

In summary, there is little evidence that the federal government attempted to increase fiscal or financial redistribution to Slovakia to appease those resentful of the center, and there is some evidence that Slovakia's position even worsened, while the Czech Republic's improved. Fiscal reforms of the early 1990s reduced Slovakia's fiscal dependence on the center, while simultaneously reducing the center's ability to adjust fiscal flows to alleviate political crises. At the center, not only was the ability to intervene reduced; so was the will to do so. While Slovakia in general suffered greater pain and uncertainty associated with liberalizing reforms, the central state was committed to reducing its redistributive interventions that might offset such temporary costs. The federal finance minister, Václav Klaus, refused on principle to make exceptions and soften the impact of liberalization. When this alienated the Slovak leader-

TABLE 6.10. Domestic Credit Growth in Czech and Slovak Republics, 1991–92

	Czech Republic			Slovak Republic		
	bn Kcs	as % of CSFR GDP	bn Kcs per cap	bn Kcs	as % of CSFR GDP	bn Kcs per cap
1991 outstanding credit, end of period	495.4	50.6	48.0	207.1	21.2	39.1
1992 outstanding credit, end of period	578.6	54.8	56.2	236.0	22.3	44.5
Increase 1991–92	+17.2%	+8.3%	+8.2 bn Kcs	+14.0%	+5.2%	+5.4 bn Kcs

Source: Polish, Czech, Slovak and Hungarian Statistical Agencies, *Statistical Bulletin*, 1994/1 (Budapest, 1994, table 3.8).

ship, "Klaus argued that if the Slovaks could not accept the sacrifices needed for the establishment of a capitalist market, they should be encouraged to quit the union" (Cox and Frankland 1995, 84).[12]

It is easy to see how this could predispose Slovakia's new electoral politicians to favor strategies of populist nationalism and of mobilizing Slovak anticenter resentment rather than strategies of attempting to buy local support by channeling (reduced) central largesse. Such changes at the center also helped create an atmosphere in which Valdimir Meciar's type of appeal—attributing the economic hardships of Slovaks to the "Prague intellectual ghetto" and calling for negotiated secession—could be electorally powerful (Cox and Frankland 1995, 83). Meciar's victory in the June 1992 elections led directly to separation, even though a majority of Slovaks consistently said in polls that this was not what they wanted. As recently as April 1992, only 17 percent had said that they supported outright independence, while the majority favored a looser relationship within the federation (Cox and Frankland 1995, 84).

Yugoslavia

By the early 1970s, Yugoslavia had become a particularly decentralized federation, held together largely by the party (the League of Communists of Yugoslavia). Even the military was highly decentralized, with the central Yugoslav National Army complemented by developed militias in the republics, equipped with arms stores and trained in mounting defensive guerrilla operations (Woodward 1995, 26–27). Interrepublican fiscal and financial relations had been growing more and more contentious in the 1980s, as income disparities between parts of the federation widened. An attempt to recentralize economic management and control over foreign exchange in order to meet conditions for a three-year IMF standby loan in the mid-1980s aroused Slovenian animosity.

The growing economic antagonism between Slovenia and the federal government had particularly serious implications because stability in Yugoslavia traditionally depended on peaceful relations between Serbia and Slovenia.

> Although outsiders wishing to emphasize the historical character of contemporary Yugoslav politics insist on a long-standing Serb-Croat conflict, the far more important relationship in Yugoslavia was between Slovenia and Serbia. Political alliances between Slovenia and Serbia had been essential to stability in the first Yugoslavia, and it was generally believed that Slovenia acted as a brake on autonomist forces in Croatia (which periodically appeared, most recently in 1967–71) in the interests of political stability in the second Yugoslavia. The absence of confrontation between Slovenia and Serbia was far more crucial than the presence of conflict between Serbia and Croatia. (Woodward 1995, 63)

During the last years of its existence, fiscal and financial resources were redistributed among Yugoslavia's republics and autonomous provinces by several mechanisms (Mihaljek 1993; Kraft and Vodopivec 1992; Kraft 1992; Dubravcic 1993). Kraft and Vodopivec analyzed the size of such flows for data from 1986 (see table 6.11). Among channels of redistribution, the main ones included formal taxes and formal subsidies, the extension of credits at negative real interest rates or without the expectation of repayment, grants from investment funds, gains and losses on monetary assets due to high inflation, and implicit taxation through price regulation. They found that in 1986 manufacturing enterprises paid on average 14 percent of net value added in taxes, received 1 percent in formal subsidies, but received 44 percent in net "gains on money" as the value of their debt was eroded by inflation. When all the channels are added up and expressed in per capita terms, they find that Slovenia was by far the largest loser from redistribution, and Montenegro and Kosovo the biggest winners. Croatia and Serbia both came out about even.

Did Slovenia's position improve in the late 1980s? I know of no comprehensive analysis, but it is possible to assess change in many of the streams. The balance of federal tax revenue shifted increasingly from republic contributions to sales tax and customs duties during these years, but it is not clear that this would have had either a positive or a negative impact on Slovenia.[13] One overt channel of redistribution of investment finance from the developed to less developed republics was the Federal Development Fund. Between 1984 and 1989, contributions to the Fund dropped sharply. But Slovenia's proportionate share in financing the Fund increased from 15.8 percent to 23.8 percent (see table 6.12). Eventually, in the summer of 1990, Slovenia withdrew its support from the Fund in protest.

Probably the most significant redistributive flow in the late 1980s, however, consisted of concessionary loans from the central bank. The institutional structure of the National Bank of Yugoslavia paralleled that of the federal government. Each of the eight governors of the central banks of the republics and autonomous provinces were members of the NBY's board, along with the NBY's governor, who was selected by the Federal Assembly (Cvikl, Kraft, and Vodopivec 1993, 306; OECD 1990, 44). Among the Yugoslav republics, however, there was a sharp difference of interest over monetary policy. The less-developed republics and provinces and Serbia favored expansionary credit policy and had a majority, while Slovenia and Croatia favored tighter controls. Decisionmaking on the NBY's board shifted from a unanimity rule to a majority rule in the 1980s, leaving Slovenia and Croatia less and less able to affect central monetary policy. Big increases in cheap credit in the late 1980s resulted in hyperinflation.

Concessionary loans issued by the NBY went largely to support agriculture and exports. However, despite Slovenia's and Croatia's leading roles as ex-

TABLE 6.11. Estimated Interrepublican Redistribution in Yugoslavia, 1986 (All figures represent percent of Yugoslav GSP except for last column, which represents percent of Yugoslav GSP per 10 mn residents.)

	(1) Disbursements from the Federal Fund[a]	(2) Net Subsidies Inc. Gains/ Losses on Money	(3) Estimated Loss Due to Admin. Pricing		Total Transfers (1 + 2 + 3)	Total Transfers per 10 Million Residents (% Yugoslav GSP per 10 Million Residents)
			p1	p2		
Bosnia	0.4	2.3	−0.5	−0.3	2.2 to 2.4	4.9 to 5.4
Montenegro	0.1	0.7	−0.2	−0.1	.6 to .7	9.4 to 11.0
Macedonia	0.2	0.8	−0.6	−0.4	.4 to .6	1.9 to 2.8
Kosovo	0.6	1.2	−0.3	−0.2	1.5 to 1.6	7.7 to 8.3
Slovenia		−0.9	−0.9	−0.3	−1.8 to −1.2	−9.2 to −6.2
Croatia		1.1	−1.3	−0.5	−.2 to .6	−0.4 to +1.3
Serbia (incl. Vojv.)		1.2	−1.6	−1.7	−.4 to −.5	−0.5 to −0.6
Yugoslav Total	1.2	6.8	−5.4	−2.4	2.6 to 5.6	1.1 to 2.4
Memo: republic GSP as	Bos	Mn	Ma	Ko	Slov	Cro	Serb	S+V
% of Yugoslav GSP, 1986	13.5	2.0	5.7	2.3	18.1	24.7	23.4	33.7

Source: Kraft (1992); Kraft and Vodopivec (1992); Yugoslav Federal Statistical Agency, *Statisticki Godisnjak Jugoslavije 1988* (Belgrade: 1988, 469); Yugoslav Federal Statistical Agency, *Statisticki Godisnjak Jugoslavije, 1990* (Belgrade: 1990, 496).

Note: p1 and p2 represent two different assumptions about the degree of price distortion.

[a]Federal Fund for the Crediting of the Development of the Less-Developed Regions.

TABLE 6.12. Operations of the Yugoslav Federal Development Fund in the Late 1980s

	1984	1986	1988	1989
Total Contributions as % of Yugoslav GDP (disbursements roughly similar)	1.3	1.2	1.1	0.3
Slovenia's Contributions as % of Yugoslav GDP	0.20	0.21	0.23	0.07
Slovenia's Contributions as % of Total	15.8	18.0	20.1	23.8

Source: Yugoslav Federal Statistical Agency, *Statisticki Godisnjak Jugoslavije 1990* (Belgrade: 1990, 496).

porters, they got far smaller shares of these central loans in the late 1980s than their share in GNP (see table 6.13). Serbia, which under Milosevic tightened its political control over Kosovo, Vojvodina, and Montenegro, was able to benefit much more.

The result was an inflationary monetary system in which Slovenia did not even receive its share of inflationary credits, and in which it was asked to pay an increasing share of investment funding to finance development of the less developed regions (a policy that had already been attempted for decades with meager success). Thus, far from appeasing Slovenia with more generous fiscal and financial policy, the center appeared to be doing the opposite.

During 1990–91, Serbia's increasingly open ability to exploit the federal government for its own purposes combined with a central economic policy of IMF-inspired austerity to exacerbate relations with Slovenia still further. Slovenia had supported the federal stabilization program initially. But it turned against it in the summer of 1990, "when the federal government started an incompre-

TABLE 6.13. Access to Concessionary Loans and Money Creation of Three Yugoslav Republics, 1987

	Croatia	Slovenia	Serbia
% of increase in concessionary loans for agriculture	23.6	6.1	57.0
% of increase in concessionary loans for exports	33.5	17.9	29.0
Share in total money creation	19.7	7.5	38.8
Share in GNP	25.3	16.8	37.3

Source: Dubravcic (1993, 266).

hensible series of exceptions (corrections to the exchange rate) and measures (pay rises for federal administration, selective loans to agriculture)" apparently to benefit Serbia (Mencinger 1993). Serbia had already in March 1989 introduced economic sanctions against Slovenia, and in his inaugural speech after his reelection in December 1989, Milosevic reiterated that the break in economic relations with Slovenia would last until "the powers of conservatism and violence" were removed from the republic (Necak 1993, 182). In late 1990, Serbia failed to transfer sales tax to the federal budget and imposed special tariffs on Slovenian and Croatian products. Around the same time, the Serbian National Bank exceeded its credit expansion limits set by the central bank.

A competition erupted between the different republics to withhold tax revenue and to exceed their credit limits. Slovenia began withholding payments to the federal budget and subsidizing exports through issue of Slovenian government bonds, and it announced it would reduce its contribution to the army in 1991 from 15 to 3 billion dinars (Mencinger 1993, 84; Ramet 1992, 45–46). As a result of such steps, the federal government by December 1990 was operating "at a level 15 percent below its basic budgetary needs" and had to lay off 2,700 central officials (Ramet 1992, 45–46). In February 1991, the Federal Executive was forced to take out a loan from the central bank to finance the army. In turn, the center's inability to meet its commitments to the republics set off additional revolts. In March 1991, Bosnia threatened to cease all payments to the central budget unless the federation settled its debt to the republic within a week. Montenegro and Macedonia also complained of unmet central commitments. The political impact of such developments was felt in December 1990, when 88 percent of Slovenian voters in a plebiscite voted for independence (Necak 1993, 184).

Thus, in Yugoslavia in the late 1980s and early 1990s, a weak federal government starting from a low fiscal base and attempting to impose an anti-inflationary fiscal policy, while controlled more and more tightly by Serbia, increasingly ignored the demands of republics where threats of secession were most credible. In doing so, it undercut the central bargains of Yugoslav federal politics. Federal economic policymakers failed to recognize and accommodate the "socially polarizing and politically disintegrating consequences" of the IMF program (Woodward 1995, 383). Monetary expansion by the NBY, rather than being used to redistribute income to the separatist regions, came largely at the expense of Slovenia and Croatia, which received small shares of cheap central credits but suffered the losses of resulting inflation. Again, the situation stands in sharp contrast to that of Russia.

The USSR

The Soviet case shows interesting similarities to the Yugoslav pattern of events. In the late 1980s, central fiscal policy appears to have increasingly redistributed income *away* from the richest and most Europeanized republics—the most plausible separatists—to the less developed regions of Central Asia and Azerbaijan. Between 1986 and 1989, net transfers from each of the Baltic republics to the center increased (by 7 percent for Estonia, by 25 percent for Latvia, and by 81 percent for Lithuania).[14] Meanwhile, net transfers to Azerbaijan rose between 1987 and 1989 by 58 percent; those to Uzbekistan rose by 53 percent; and those to Kazakhstan by 121 percent (see table 6.14).

These were, of course, the years of early nationalist mobilization in the Baltic states, a process that set the pattern for other more quiescent regions to follow. Gorbachev, in his memoirs, links the growth of nationalist opinion in the Baltic republics to perceptions of economic exploitation. While the history of Soviet invasion provided the focus for grievances, "the main motive, finding broad response even among part of the nonnative population, was the conviction that the Baltics were being 'cleaned out' by the Union and in freedom would live much better" (Gorbachev 1995, vol. 1, 511). He blamed nationalist activists for spreading this—to his mind, erroneous—idea. "If they assure people day in, day out from the television screen that, once separated, they will live several times better, after a certain time this becomes the *idée fixe* of the entire population" (vol. 2, 498). Not believing such claims to be true, Gorbachev showed little inclination to indulge them.

TABLE 6.14. Net Budget Transfers from the Union (rubles per capita)

	1986	1987	1988	1989	1990	1991
Estonia	165	147	126	153	165	0
Latvia	−323	−414	−390	−405	189	0
Lithuania	−141	−142	−141	−254	−140	0
Russia	n.a.	n.a.	n.a.	n.a.	n.a.	n.a.
Belarus	n.a.	n.a.	n.a.	n.a.	150	n.a.
Ukraine	n.a.	n.a.	n.a.	−196	−155	−140
Moldova	79	60	12	67	93	−49
Georgia	n.a.	n.a.	n.a.	52	139	0
Armenia	n.a.	n.a.	n.a.	692	187	206
Azerbaijan	n.a.	40	17	64	91	518
Kazakhstan	n.a.	113	195	250	307	253
Kyrgyzstan	n.a.	92	146	127	214	453
Tajikistan	n.a.	n.a.	n.a.	n.a.	n.a.	499
Turkmenia	n.a.	n.a.	n.a.	142	207	400
Uzbekistan	n.a.	101	122	154	335	638

Source: IMF *Economic Reviews* (Washington, DC: IMF). Armenia, Belarus, Estonia, Ukraine: April 1992; Georgia, Kazakhstan, Kyrgyzstan, Tajikistan, Uzbekistan: May 1992; Lithuania: April 1992 and 1993, Kazakhstan: also Shome 1993, 310.

He did offer the Baltic republics a major concession in November 1989, when the center passed a law that gave them the right to form their own budgets and control their own banking systems. They were also assigned advantageous rates of tax retention, and Estonia got the right to establish a "one-channel" revenue system (Khodorovich 1991, 8; Bahry 1991, 238). However, the new policy did not last long enough to be implemented. In March 1990 the newly elected Lithuanian parliament voted to secede. Moscow responded with a combination of military and economic pressure. Troops were dispatched to occupy Communist Party buildings in Vilnius and round up Lithuanian army conscripts who had deserted from the Soviet Army. In a speech around this time, Gorbachev referred to Lithuania as "the sea frontiers to which Russia has marched for centuries."[15] Far from appeasing the separatists economically, the center imposed an embargo and blockade. The blockade, which lasted until the end of June, caused gasoline rationing and shortages of hot water and heat. Though the embargo was formally suspended in June, supplies of gas, coal, and other goods to Lithuania and the other Baltic republics were often interrupted during the rest of the year (Diuk and Karatnycky 1993, 133–36).

Such interruptions of the established order of interrepublican deliveries had profound implications for the Baltic economies. Probably the most significant mechanism of interrepublican redistribution in the late Soviet era was the system of administrative pricing, which resulted in trade of products and raw materials between republics at rates far below or above world market prices. The greatest losers from internal Soviet trade were producers of fuels and minerals, the greatest beneficiaries exporters of overpriced manufactured goods. The gains and losses from such pricing have been estimated by Orlowski (1993).[16] They are shown in table 6.15. As can be seen, the Baltic republics received large net implicit transfers due to their purchases of oil and gas at a fraction of world prices. Latvia, Estonia, and Lithuania received implicit subsidies through such trade estimated at 10, 12, and 17 percent of republic GDP respectively even in 1990, the year of the embargo. Sharp cuts in such implicit transfers, and the economic dislocation they caused, would have reduced the opportunities for moderates in the republican leadership to secure public support through distribution of material benefits and would have increased the potential appeal of nationalist, anti-Moscow mobilizational strategies. Such a view coincides with the empirical analysis of one scholar, who found that the level of support in different republics for preserving the integrity of the USSR in the referendum of March 1991 was positively related to the level of implicit subsidies received by that republic via administrative pricing (Austin 1996).

In his memoirs, Gorbachev sees things differently. In his view, central economic pressure was in late 1990 fostering a softening of the Baltic position, which would have continued had Russia not joined the movement for sovereignty. Yet he also notes how in January 1991 economic discontent actually produced demonstrations in favor of presidential rule in Lithuania, which Landsbergis was able to exploit. "The struggle shifted from a constitutional framework to a framework of open confrontation" (1995, vol. 2, 505). How central economic pressures could simultaneously induce moderation and create incentives for radicalization of the nationalist movement is left intriguingly unexplained.[17]

As in the Yugoslav case, a weak center appeared to be reducing redistributive benefits to—or placing a greater part of the burden on—the richer, northern republics that had the greatest hope of integration into Europe. This played into an atmosphere in which when the first competitive elections were held in these regions, separatist nationalists won a strong mandate. Declarations of independence followed. These were punished by the center with military pressures and economic sanctions, which actually accelerated the republics' drive toward economic autonomy and European reintegration. The significant difference from the Yugoslav scenario appears to have been that in the Soviet case the largest republic disagreed with the center about the appropriate response to the separatist threat. Had Yeltsin turned out to be a Russian Milosevic, the results might have been quite different.

The Soviet budget discussions for 1991, in which the Baltic republics did not participate, led to agreement on a sharp devolution of budgetary power to

TABLE 6.15. Estimated Net Indirect Transfers to Republics as Result of Underpriced Exports/Imports of Oil and Gas, and Overpriced Exports/Imports of Non–Oil-and-Gas Goods, 1990

	Transfer as Percent of 1990 GDP
Armenia	9.2
Azerbaijan	10.1
Belarus	8.9
Estonia	12.1
Georgia	16.0
Kazakhstan	0.5
Kirghizia	2.7
Latvia	10.4
Lithuania	17.1
Moldova	24.1
Russia	−3.7
Tajikistan	6.1
Turkmenia	−10.8
Ukraine	3.6
Uzbekistan	1.3

Source: Orlowski 1993, 1006.

the republics. The republics increased their share of revenues by nearly one-third. In return, they agreed to provide the center with an additional 42 billion rubles in contributions to fund central programs (Khodorovich 1991). Almost none of these contributions materialized. According to the finance minister, as of the middle of the year, besides the Baltics, Uzbekistan and Kazakhstan had not paid anything; Ukraine, Georgia, and Moldova had not paid their agreed contributions; and Russia had not remitted its agreed share of the profit tax (Orlov 1991). While the center tried to continue the large subsidies to the Central Asian republics and Azerbaijan—and in some cases to expand them sharply[18]—the subsidizing republics increasingly refused to provide the finance and even refused to compensate other republics for their gains from the price reforms of April 1991 (Orlov 1991).

Conclusion

The fiscal crisis that Russia faced in the early 1990s was in most ways at least as severe as those that accompanied the disintegration of the other three reforming communist federal states—Czechoslovakia, Yugoslavia, and the Soviet Union. All four experienced a marked decentralization of tax revenue and spending during the previous decades or years. All four had relatively meager federal budget revenues at the end—in each case, below 13 percent of GDP. Each had a system in which some taxes were shared between different levels, often at rates determined by ongoing bargaining, and each suffered from threatened or actual tax revolts by discontented members.

Russia, however, managed to contain the impact of such revolts, which at times seemed to challenge the state's continued integrity. It did so largely through a policy of central fiscal appeasement of most of the more separatist regions. Against the advice of most economists and politicians, Yeltsin generally sought to accommodate his loudest regional opponents, while firing disobedient regional officials when they did not have local support. This prevented bandwagons of protest against Moscow from gathering speed and thus helped to sustain the ability of the center to deter additional acts of insubordination.

This chapter has argued that in none of the other three cases was a similar policy of fiscal appeasement seriously attempted. In all three, not only do intergovernmental transfers seem to have been reduced as a percentage of GDP,[19] but as far as can be made out they were targeted increasingly *away* from the most assertive, would-be separatist members of the federation. The causes of this were different in the different cases. In Czechoslovakia, it resulted mostly from a central commitment to economic liberalization, which affected the more economically vulnerable, heavily industrialized, and unprofitable republic of Slovakia more harshly than its more economically healthy neighbor. In Yugoslavia, it resulted from the increasing control of federal institutions, among them the central bank, by a coalition of members with an interest in expansionary monetary policy and extracting subsidized loans. In the Soviet Union, it resulted in part from the shrinking ability of the center to enforce fiscal agreements, but also from an attempt by the center to discourage separatism through dishing out economic punishment. In each case, this contributed to a political context in which antifederal populist appeals offered ambitious regional politicians the best hope of self-advancement and power consolidation, and in which the leaders of key republics had less and less interest in remaining in the federation.

This, of course, is not to argue that a strategy of central fiscal appeasement if tried would have been sufficient to preserve any of these failed federations. No mechanism of integration is proof against all centrifugal pressures. Fiscal appeasement can only complement and conserve the threat and use of force when the historically conditioned hostility of regional publics toward central political leaders is not excessive. Not all supporters of nationalist goals can be bought off with a combination of threats and concessions. The contribution of the argument in this book is to show that concessions can at times work in ways that are quite counterintuitive and that concessions should often be made to the most vehement protesters, not to those seemingly easiest to buy off.

The use of force is extremely expensive. Whether a regime survives may depend on how cost-effectively it can conserve its deterrent. In the Russian case, a feedback of fiscal redistribution and political opinion made it possible to substitute appeasement at times for force, without encouraging others or promoting escalating spirals of demands. Had force alone been tried, it would probably have accelerated disintegration by reducing the credibility of the deterrent. Had the invasion of Chechnya come at a moment of high mobilization of all the ethnic republics, the consequences would have been much harder to localize.

Some have argued that the collapse of the Soviet Union was actually brought about by a failure of will at the center and that "only repression could have succeeded" (Laqueur 1994, 161). What such arguments underestimate is how limited the repressive resources of even the Soviet state were by 1991. Too great a reliance on threats of force at a time of general anticenter mobilization leads to a collapse in the credibility of the threat, as coercive bodies show themselves reluctant or poorly equipped to act in several arenas at once, while the protesters expand into multiple arenas. Sometimes, in the politics of fragile, divided protodemocracies, appeasement is simply more effective.

CHAPTER 7
Conclusion: Democratization and Political Integration

Democratization subjects states to an unusual degree of uncertainty and potential instability. Democracy—an order in which elections are regularly lost by incumbents—has itself been called a system of "organized uncertainty" (Przeworski 1991). Attempts to introduce it are no less unpredictable. Whatever sources of social and geographical cohesion held the state together under authoritarian rule may weaken or disappear completely.

In multiethnic or regionally divided states, such uncertainty is particularly destabilizing. It can lead rapidly to cycles of group insecurity, competitive mobilization, and the reactive formation of exclusive laagers (Fearon 1993; Posen 1993). In decentralized states and federations, leaders of local administrative units often have resources to mobilize their populations in pursuit of parochial interests. Democratic elections, if introduced at the regional level, catalyze the expression of divisive demands (Linz and Stepan 1992). If, in addition, the state has a tradition of central redistribution of resources, local democratization may exacerbate interregional and interethnic competition for central spoils.[1] Finally, if electoral institutions are introduced in the midst of economic crisis, short-term economic problems can complicate the task for incumbent regimes of consolidating their support. When economic conditions—or the costs of reform—are spread unevenly across regions, geographical patterns of protest may threaten the state's cohesion.

So it is not surprising that the multiethnic federations of the postcommunist world experienced particular difficulties of democratic consolidation. Yugoslavia, the Soviet Union, and Czechoslovakia all disintegrated within three years of holding their first competitive elections. By 1993, the only former communist, democratizing state with a formally federal structure still in existence was Russia. To the surprise of certain observers and participants, it has managed to contain the processes of fragmentation—political, economic, and geographical—that seemed at first to be undermining its integrity, even while continuing and extending the scope of electoral choice. Despite a politics of intermittent conflict, center-region relations in the Russian Federation seemed by the late 1990s to be stabilizing.

Russia's experience is particularly puzzling when contrasted to that of the Soviet Union. Almost all explanations suggested for the USSR's rapid demise seem to predict a similar fate for Russia. Some writers have argued that the Soviet order succumbed to an ideological crisis. "In Yugoslavia and the Soviet Union, communist ideology provided the ideological legitimacy for multinational states. If the ideology were rejected, the basis for the state would disappear and each nationality could legitimately claim its own state" (Huntington 1991, quoted in Milanovic 1994, 61). Yet, if the ideological glue that held the communist USSR together came unstuck, there was little ideological legitimacy—in an age of postimperialism—upon which the Russian multinational state could fall back.

Others saw Soviet disintegration as the result of a weakening of central repression or a loss of nerve at the center to use force (Laqueur 1994).[2] If the USSR's ability and resolve to use repression against separatist regions had weakened, so too had that of Russia. Between 1989 and 1991, Soviet forces did attempt militarily to intimidate separatist populations in Georgia and Lithuania. Yet in 1992–93, the height of anti-Moscow mobilization in Russia, the center made no attempt to use force against regional challengers. It was only *after* the wave of separatist demands had already been brought under control, and major concessions made to various republics in a series of formal agreements, that Moscow embarked on the campaign to overthrow the Dudaev regime in Chechnya. As Nationalities Minister Nikolai Yegorov acknowledged in March 1995, Moscow recognized that it could not have used force against the Chechens earlier without sparking a broader rebellion (see chap. 2).

Still other scholars have related Soviet disintegration to the failure of central monitoring and enforcement capacity as economic power was devolved from principals in Moscow to agents in enterprises and regional governments (Solnick 1996). Such an argument could apply equally well to Russia, which underwent an equal or greater devolution of power to enterprises and regional governments. Milanovic suggests that the instability of communist federations was caused by the combination of economic failure and a state structure into which nationality had been institutionally incorporated as a means of coopting local elites (Milanovic 1994). Such factors existed also in the Russian Federation.

The country's recent experience indicates that existing theories are incomplete. This book has suggested an additional piece of the puzzle, which helps to account for Russia's survival as a multiethnic, decentralized, democratizing state. Beneath the surface of apparently chaotic and confrontational center-region politics, a poorly understood mechanism of integration was evolving in the early 1990s—and it was evolving precisely *out of* the threats, brinkmanship, and bargaining that appeared so often to endanger the state's survival. Paradoxically, many, though not all, of the sharp confrontations so often interpreted as symptoms of a rapid decline of political cohesion were themselves vital elements of this integrating mechanism. Dramatic regional protests provided information to the center that could not be credibly transmitted in any other way. This information made it possible for the central regime to use its limited powers of fiscal redistribution strategically, buying off most of the most determined regional malcontents with larger fiscal transfers and tax exemptions, and thus preventing them from undermining its much weakened deterrent. Bandwagons of protest were kept from gathering speed. This crude feedback of protest, targeted fiscal transfers, and voting made up at least temporarily for the absence of vertical integrating institutions such as national parties and disciplined hierarchical bureaucracies, and helped to keep Russia intact.

The Politics of Appeasement

This argument is counterintuitive for several reasons. Appeasement has generally been considered not only ethically dubious but technically irrational. One dictionary of political terms and phrases defines it as "a policy of acceding to the demands of aggressors, which often leads to more demands and greater concessions" (Safire 1993, 22). Churchill memorably described appeasement as the strategy of "one who feeds a crocodile, hoping it will eat him last" (Comfort 1993, 20). Perhaps the most common view is that demonstrating a willingness to concede merely creates incentives for challengers to make additional claims.

The dangers of appeasement appear particularly grave for a central government with limited resources whose survival depends on deterring challenges from a large number of regional officials, allied states, or colonies. Giving in to the claims of one can demonstrate weakness to others, inducing a rapid, multilateral spiral of rebellion.[3] The argument is as old as the Athenians' ultimatum to the councillors of Melos, which demanded nothing less than total Melian submission out of fear that any hint of leniency might encourage revolt in other vulnerable spots within the Athenian empire (Thucydides 1972, 400–408).

Such a calculus has often justified a strategy of deterrence through horrific example: the fewer are the center's resources to fight simultaneous rebellions, the more terrible must be the costs it imposes against even minor challenges.[4] According to Robert Axelrod, "the key to maintaining compliant behavior from the citizenry is that the government remains able and willing to devote resources far out of proportion to the stakes of the current issue in order to maintain its reputation for toughness" (1984, 155).[5] In the terms of expected utility theory, the smaller are the chances of actual punishment, the greater must be the pain inflicted if it does occur to create the same deterrent effect. Concessions to challengers will reduce the credibility of the center's deterrent. As one analyst warned, considering the situation in Russia: "It is likely that some regional actors would interpret any concessions by Moscow on issues of federalist distribution of power as an invitation to mount additional pressures against central authority in order to wrest further concessions" (Shoumikhin 1996, 5).

The argument of this book is not that central governments can safely fail to carry out their past threats of punishment—on the contrary, they must invest in the credibility of their deterrent. It is that they should sometimes *both* punish and then appease in future rounds. By rebelling even in the face of a credible deterrent, the leader of the challenging region signals that he has more to gain from a challenge than from obedience, even if the punishment is carried out. This might seem paradoxical, but sometimes conflict can mobilize support for a local leader far better than peaceful relations—even if the conflict imposes heavy costs on the region. Support for Dzhokhar Dudaev in Chechnya appeared to increase markedly after the Russian military invasion began.

While carrying out a threatened punishment is essential to keep the center's threats credible to other regions, it will not necessarily be enough to demobilize a revolt in progress. Yet lowering central demands or increasing central benefits to the region can undermine the local base of support for rebellion by reducing the discontent of regional constituents and giving them more to lose from an interruption of center-region relations. Furthermore, publicizing such appeasement may be rational for the center—even though this might seem likely to encourage other regions to press demands. The reason is that such appeasement—if it succeeds in demobilizing the first rebel—will free up central enforcement resources in future periods, thus increasing the center's capacity to punish other challengers. The center can thus unhitch a bandwagon before it gains speed. Strategies of appeasement can sometimes actually *enhance* the power of the center's deterrent.[6]

There may be some separatists so devoted to the cause that appeasement will never work. If the leadership and population of a region are completely and irrevocably committed to pursuing nothing less than complete independence no matter what the cost, then such attempts will obviously fail. (Presumably, so will attempts to deter them, though perhaps containment might succeed.) There is little point trying to conciliate a "romantic nationalist" who "thinks in terms of the spirit and culture of his people, not in terms of bargains and calculations" and who "will fight for his cause despite any number of rational arguments showing it to be unjustified" (Birch 1989, 67).

Yet, situations in which "romantic nationalists" have complete control over a region's policy are rare.

> Romantic nationalists may not be impressed by the arguments, but romantic nationalists are few in number. They can create minority nationalist movements and keep them alive, but they cannot win widespread support in their community unless they can point to broken promises, material disadvantages suffered, or the prospect of tangible gain. Poetry may inspire the few, but the masses need to be persuaded of actual losses and potential benefits. To explain why minority nationalist movements wax and

wane, we need to examine the material factors that lead to their growth and decline. (Birch 1989, 67)

While all individuals feel some loyalty to local (or ethnic) communities when their interests conflict with those of the center, it is unusual for individuals to give unlimited support to maximalist demands regardless of what the center may offer or threaten in response. Even if a given community contains some unconditional supporters of independence, even if the community's political leader is himself a "romantic nationalist," others will temper such goals with consideration of other values and objectives. To the extent that regional leaders need to take into account the preferences of members of their community, mass or elite, this will open a channel by which central policies of appeasement may constrain the leaders' separatist actions.

In practice, it is extremely difficult to tell whether a particular regional leader is a "romantic" or a "pragmatic" nationalist; most surely have features of both and the potential to change from one to the other. After the fact, it is easy to think of reasons why one leader, region, or ethnic group turned out to be especially separatist (e.g., why the Chechens rebelled, not the Tyvans). But our frequent mistakes in predicting which national groups will prove most assertive before the fact based on existing knowledge of their culture and history suggest reason to be cautious in evaluating how precisely we understand how these factors work. I am not arguing that the prevalence and intensity of "romantic nationalism" do not vary between ethnic groups and regions, but rather that this variation is not the only explanation for different outcomes. What is crucial is not just the characteristics that predispose members of one community to be more "romantic" in their approach to national or ethnic loyalty but also how these factors interact with, among other things, central policy.

If one accepts that irreconcilable, self-sacrificing separatist individuals are rare and that irreconcilable, self-sacrificing separatist communities are even rarer, then there may often be a role for appeasement. And, in cases like the one examined in this book, it may make sense for the center to appease not the most moderate, status-quo-respecting challengers, but precisely those that are most subject to romantic nationalism. In a region predisposed to romantic nationalism, military threats or force may fail to the stanch the challenge, instead *increasing* the incentive for local leaders to exploit local fear and resentment of the center as a strategy for personal political advancement. On the other hand, conciliatory financial strategies may give more moderate members of the community a greater stake in avoiding conflict and tip the local political balance against confrontation. Because even a few overt acts of regional defiance have such a large external effect, lowering the risk for other regions of pressing their own grievances against the center, it may be worthwhile to the center to invest a large amount of fiscal resources in appeasing the more trigger-happy region, even if this requires extracting somewhat higher revenues from more docile parts of the country or investing less in enforcement capacity. Since the center will in practice have no way to distinguish the (many) challengers that are appeasable at some non-infinite cost from the (extremely rare or nonexistent) challengers that are unshakably dedicated to their cause, it will often be optimal as a matter of policy to appease the most assertive challengers.

Historical Parallels

This view of the inner logic of Russian politics suggests new perspectives on—and questions that might be raised about—other historical periods and political systems.[7] On various occasions, leaders have combined deterrence with appeasement in the attempt to stabilize or slow the decline of their states or empires. The Athenians' strategy against the Melians was not unique in the ancient world. During the last centuries of the Roman Empire in the West, Rome enlisted the support of barbarian tribes on the periphery by paying their leaders subsidies, settling them in territory within the empire, and giving them tax rights over the local populations (Goffart 1980; Jones 1966, 215; see also Barnwell 1992, esp. 170–75). Such barbarian associates, which could be used as military auxiliaries, were known as *foederati*—the first "federates." "In the latter period of the Roman Empire the barbarians could extract huge sums of gold from the Romans simply by threatening invasion" (North 1981, 114). While such arrangements certainly did not reverse the gradual ebbing of Roman power, they may have prolonged and smoothed it out. One scholar credits this administrative innovation with turning the empire's decline into a process of creative transformation and notes that "there does not appear to have been a sense of the imminent disintegration of the Roman world amongst contemporaries" (Barnwell 1992, 174). According to Goffart, "the fifth century is less memorable for invasions than for the incorporation of barbarian protectors into the fabric of the West" (Goffart 1980, 230).[8]

Much later, the rulers of the Ottoman Empire bought the acquiescence of bandit leaders in their provinces rather than attempting simply to repress them. "The Ottoman sultans saw such innovative challenges . . . as opportunities for bargaining, initially reaching into the state's revenues, distributing patronage to buy off or channel newly emerging opposition. Only later did the sultans resort to force" (Barkey 1994, 2). The Ottoman regime became "the state as bargainer par excellence—bargaining to coopt and to incorporate, embodying within itself potential forces of contention. This strategy whereby inclusion into the state became the singly desirable reward worked to enhance the state's control over its vast territory" (241).

A similar process of negotiating with local powerholders characterized the method of state building through which some of the great European empires

Conclusion

were created. The rise of absolutism in France was one of the foremost successes of such a strategy (Root 1987, 1994). Central monarchs struck individual bargains with regional communities, taxing each specifically and trading local monopoly rights to the guilds in return for revenue (North 1981, 149). "As the state expanded it was confronted by a highly developed and intractable regionalism institutionalized in the form of local law and regional assemblies and sustained by powerful local notables. It could only *superimpose* its control on a number of entrenched and thriving institutions" (Brewer 1989, 6). Paris negotiated taxes with the regional estates in the *pays d'états*—Burgundy, Dauphiné, Provence, Languedoc, Guyenne, and Normandy—while they were collected directly by royal officers in the *pays d'élections* (7). "After the Fronde (1652), the provincial estates, the most vigorous upholders of local autonomy in France, were mostly paid off or subdued" (Root 1994, 19). The central state even encouraged the development of peasant assemblies and integrated them into national politics (Root 1987).

The findings of this book also suggest new questions that might be raised about the Habsburg Empire's late years. At that time, "Vienna's classic answer to . . . particularist grievances was to smother them with committees, with new jobs, tax concessions, additional railway branch lines, and so on" (Kennedy 1987, 217). Nationality considerations informed economic policy. "If, for instance, certain German communities in Bohemia stood to benefit primarily from road construction in a particular district, the government would at the same time propose similar road construction, whether necessary or not in a chiefly Czech section of that district" (217)[9] Such policies are often viewed as having added to the bureaucratic complexity and shortage of finance that contributed to the empire's demise. "Taxes took three volumes, each of six hundred closely printed pages, to explain. There were, in 1914, well over 3,000,000 civil servants, running things as diverse as schools, hospitals, welfare, taxation, railways, posts etc." (Stone 1984, 316). Yet, appeasing separatist and nationalist claims may actually have slowed the process of disintegration. Some historians have seen things in this light. Alan Sked has pointed to a surprising revival after the 1848 uprisings were defeated. "What happened was that in 1848 the Monarchy almost fell apart but thereafter recovered and in many ways *rose* rather than *declined* before 1914. It can even be argued that there was no domestic or even foreign threat to its integrity until 1918" (Sked 1989, 6).

Such parallels, however, also expose interesting differences. The type of central appeasement in both the Roman and Ottoman empires contrasts with that in the Russian Federation in one crucial way. The Russian strategy demobilized regional leaders by buying off their constituencies. The Roman and Ottoman strategies, by contrast, incorporated leaders of potentially aggressive bands directly into the system of incentives of the centralized administrative hierarchy. The Ottomans and Romans bought off bandit or barbarian leaders in order to demobilize their constituencies.

Both methods sometimes fail. Coopting the leaders of potentially troublesome groups risks merely creating incentives for new uncoopted leaders to emerge. The rank-and-file mercenaries under a bandit chief would not always follow their leader into state service. Such bandit troops "were less susceptible to the temptations afforded by legitimate roles and often returned to a life of depredation after one infraction; looting rather than collecting taxes proved to be a difficult habit to break" (Barkey 1994, 200). Conversely, buying off regional leaders through their constituents depends upon the nature of the relationship between leaders and their support base. If this changes—if local leaders consolidate their power—they may be less responsive to central bribes sent via their constituents.

All four of these examples suggest the limitations of such policies, which did not ultimately prevent the collapse of each of these regimes. Still, they may have been superior to any available alternatives and slowed the progress of decline. Historians have sometimes argued that by the seventeenth century, the Ottoman Empire was "weak and vacillating" and had "lost control of the provinces and its different classes" (Barkey 1994, 233). Yet it lasted for another 300 years.[10] The Habsburg Empire's nationality policies seemed at times to be the height of economic irrationality, but except for 1848 it managed to avoid social revolution in an ethnically diverse, modernizing state. According to Sked, between 1867 and 1914, the peak period of central accommodation, "almost nobody inside the Monarchy was working for a republic . . . and practically no one wanted to see the monarchy break up" (Sked 1989, 187). *Ancien régime* France's attempt to gain temporary increases in revenue by selling offices was counterproductive in the long run—as officials undoubtedly recognized at the time. But the Crown may not have had a more rational revenue-raising option (Brewer 1989, 19–20). As Talleyrand wrote:

> France seemed to be made up of a certain number of societies with which the government bargained. In this way, it kept each one under control using the credit that it had. Then the government turned to another, dealing with it in the same way. How could such a state of things continue?[11]

Nevertheless, continue it had for several hundred years.

More recent cases of fiscal appeasement are also easy to find. When Western Australia voted by a two-thirds majority to secede from the federation in 1933, the Commonwealth Grants Commission recommended increasing federal grants to Western Australia as well as to two other poorer states. This "led Western Australia to drop its attempt to secede, and since 1935 no more has been heard of this proposal" (Birch 1989, 188). Redistributive policies have been used to bolster central power in certain parts of Africa. In Zambia in the late 1960s and early 1970s, President Kaunda strategically targeted development aid to regions where support for the ruling party, UNIP, was relatively low. According to one scholar writing in the early 1980s: "While Zambia is still prone to ethnic conflict, redistributive policies have no doubt significantly lessened the potential for intensely divisive conflict" (Keller 1983, 264).

Various scholars have sought to explain the survival of Indian federal democracy since 1947, despite an ethnically, linguistically, and religiously divided population. Some have noted there a comparable process of regional protest and central accommodation. Though he does not analyze flows of fiscal resources, Subrata Mitra has described the complex repertoires of protest actions that local elites use to press their demands on the government in Delhi. He argues that the federal state draws strength from responding to such protests, conceding to some of the demands, and recruiting protesters into the political arena (Mitra 1992). This "blend of institutional participation and collective protest," he writes, is "an important explanation for the resilience of Indian democracy." Robert Hardgrave concurs.

> Historically, problems of ethnic and religious conflict in India have eased when political and group leaders have sought to deal with them through accommodation, bargaining, and the political process, and particularly when the center has sought accommodation with minority groups. Problems tend to get worse when the center intervenes directly to impose an outcome on a group or region asserting its independent interests and identity. Force alone has been unable to overcome separatist tendencies; if it is to be successfully applied, it must be accompanied by political dialogue and accommodation. (1993, 67)[12]

As long ago as the 1970s, Sidney Tarrow wondered at the surprising ability of the Italian government to defuse a violent separatist movement in the Alto Adige with financial concessions to the region, while France, with a more Jacobin and *dirigiste* approach, seemed far less successful at containing its regional autonomy movements in Brittany, the Basque country, the Midi, and Corsica. His tentative explanation:

> Perhaps the reason for the Italian success in this area lies with its more general failures. The Italian state is so riddled with clientelism that it responds to the threat of regional separatism as it does to every other problem in its troubled postwar history—with financial credits and political payoffs. (Tarrow 1977, 2)

Tarrow did not explain why these "financial credits and political payoffs" would actually work to contain discontent, or why such an apparently feeble central response might not encourage a destabilizing cycle of escalating demands. The logic of the argument made about Russia suggests one possible answer.

Within France, the separatist activism of Brittany and Corsica contrasts with the postwar moderation of Alsace. What accounts for the Alsatians' quiescence? According to Solange Gras, central policy played an important part. "Distrusted after 1918, Alsace has regained a privileged place in France. Presidents and ministers continually make conspicuous visits to the province, accompanied by subsidies and the tricolour: historic antagonisms are to be laid to rest" (Gras 1982, 310). President Giscard d'Estaing "contrasted subsidies for 'good Alsatians' with the criminal courts for 'bad' Corsicans and Bretons" (348). The former apparently succeeded better than the latter.[13]

Protest and Stability

A second counterintuitive aspect of the argument concerns the relationship between protest and political stability. A distinguished tradition of theoretical and empirical scholarship has argued that protest, noncivic forms of engagement, and excessive mobilization are dangerous for political order. In Huntington's well-known analysis, instability results when newly mobilized groups, frustrated by the lack of opportunities for social and economic mobility, press their demands in the political sphere, overloading fragile, underdeveloped political institutions (Huntington 1968). According to Crozier, the crises of the 1970s in Western Europe and America stemmed from governments' vulnerability to domestic social pressures: "The modern European state's basic weakness is its liability to blackmailing tactics" (Crozier 1977, 6).

This work suggests, on the contrary, that protests of different kinds can at times play an informational role that not only is not destabilizing but in fact is vital to the integration of a state with its society. And this role is crucial *precisely* in countries where other integrating institutions are underdeveloped. Protests do not just *overload* official institutions—they can create informal ones. In Russia, out of the mutual challenges, threats, and pacts of central and regional politicians, institutions have been taking shape.

Theorists of social movements have, in a similar vein, suggested the normality of "abnormal" political tactics. In Britain, protests "far from being the occasional outbursts of a hopelessly alienated minority" constitute "a legitimate pathway of political redress by widely differing sections of the community" (A. Marsh, quoted in Mitra 1991, 9). In France, Charles Tilly has noted that "instead of constituting a sharp break from 'normal' political life, violent protests tend to accompany, complement, and extend organized peaceful attempts by the same people to accomplish their objectives" (Tilly 1969, 10, quoted in Tarrow 1991, 9). Such conflicts, while seeming to indicate political instability, may in fact stabilize the regime by expressing social demands that can then be met and by indicating the location of rebellious groups that can then be incorporated into politics. Russia's success in outlasting the other postcommunist federations suggests that such cycles of protest and response can yield an albeit fragile equilibrium. While it may not serve purposes of social justice or economic efficiency, the politics of protest and fiscal redistribution may at times constitute a solution to—not a cause of—political instability.

This view of Russia's recent experience recalls a tradition of political thought that, in contrast to the more frequent emphasis on consensus, shared interests, and community spirit, views social conflict and the responses it prompts as the source of social integration.[14] According to Bernard Crick, writing in 1962:

> It is often thought that for [politics] to function, there must be already in existence some shared idea of a 'common good,' some 'consensus' or *consensus juris*. But this common good is itself the process of practical reconciliation of the interests of the various . . . aggregates, or groups which compose a state; it is not some external and intangible spiritual adhesive. . . . Diverse groups hold together because they practice politics—not because they agree about the 'fundamentals,' or some such concept too vague, too personal, or too divine ever to do the job of politics for it. The moral consensus of a free state is not something mysteriously prior to or above politics: it is the activity (the civilizing activity) of politics itself. (Crick 1962, quoted in Hirschman 1995, 238–39)

The kind of institutions that stabilize divided societies are neither given from on high nor chosen from below. They evolve out of the often conflictual interaction of social forces. As Dankwart Rustow argued in 1970, the institutions of stable democracy are built up out of compromise pacts in the midst of intense and long-lived social conflicts (Rustow 1970).

Decentralization, Regional Elections, and Stability

A third counterintuitive, and somewhat unsettling, implication of the book's argument is that democratization at the regional level—when it replaces a centrally appointed official with a regionally elected politician—can create particular problems for state integration and for efficiency-enhancing economic reforms. Regional democratization increases the incentive for regional leaders to seek confrontation with the center. The reasons are threefold.

First, subnational leaders who are elected may be under greater pressure to maximize the flow of resources to their region than appointees, who depend more directly on central power-holders. While central politicians must extract and redistribute resources in such a way as to win the support of a sufficiently powerful *national* coalition of political resource holders, regional politicians need only to construct a *locally* dominant supporting coalition. Each elected regional leader will therefore have a greater interest than her central counterparts in steering resources to her locality.

Second, high levels of redistribution will often reduce growth rates because of inefficient allocation of resources and the incentives created for rent-seeking. Since voters judge politicians on the basis of both public spending and economic performance, to maximize their support the politicians will need to find the optimal balance of growth and redistribution. But only the center has an *encompassing* interest in economic growth. Each regional leader would rationally prefer an increase in spending in his region, even at high cost in nationwide inflation and inefficiency. So the regional and central leaders will seek different points on the trade-off between redistribution and growth.[15]

Third, besides seeking local support through material appeals, regional politicians may seek to create artificial confrontations with the center as a means of mobilizing the population behind them. Elections at the local level create incentives for political entrepreneurs to politicize formerly repressed or dormant ethnic and regional cleavages and to exploit the politics of grievance (Linz and Stepan 1992; Horowitz 1993). By contrast, in a system with electoral institutions at the center but appointees in the regions, the regional officials will usually have greater incentives to place priority on loyalty to the center. In Russia this logic was demonstrated empirically: in regions where the head of administration had been elected he was much less likely to support Yeltsin than in regions where he had been appointed.

This argument runs counter to the tradition of thought that casts local self-governing institutions as a critical element of civil society, conducive to democratic stability and economic incentives (Diamond 1994, 8–9; Putnam 1993). Tocqueville saw provincial institutions as a particularly important check against tyranny of the national majority (1969, 96). Hayek argued that federalism could restrain state interventions and protect economic freedom (1948), and a tradition of political economy has argued that competition between self-governing subnational jurisdictions can also enhance economic efficiency and growth (Tiebout 1956; Weingast 1995).

Regional representative institutions "tie the King's hands" in much the way that a national parliament does, enhancing his ability to commit himself to respect property rights and market freedoms (Root 1994). Weingast has argued for the advantages of federal structure in preserving markets and constraining the center from imposing protectionist regulations or enforcing monopolies (Weingast 1995). Regions may cooperate to deter the central state from violating local liberties. This may help account for the economic successes of England in the eighteenth century (North and Weingast 1989).

More recently, various scholars have argued the benefits of regional democratization in states in transition from communist or authoritarian rule (Coulson 1995). According to one recent study, "decentralization of government and renewal of local democracy are vital elements of transformation in East-Central Europe" (Baldersheim and Illner 1996, 7). In Mexico, some have argued that decentralization of economic resources and powers to regional bosses should be combined with regional democratization to increase accountability.

> Ironically, if Zedillo carries out his promise to give state and local governments more powers and financial resources, allowing them to raise more revenues locally, he could also increase the resources and autonomy of the local bosses and *caciques*. Any moves toward decentralization must therefore be accompanied by democratization. There is a danger that decentralization will not help political reform if local governments cannot be held accountable. (Lustig 1996, 6)

The argument made in this book suggests, however, that while increasing electoral responsibility at the very local level may be unequivocally beneficial, more representative institutions at the *regional* level may increase pressure on the center to redistribute. Such institutions do not just tie the King's hands, they may pull at him from all sides, in a way that may reduce the economic rationality of central policy. While regional elections may increase the accountability of regional leaders to their electorates, they may also increase the pressure of regional lobbying for central aid and shift the pattern of interregional redistribution in favor of the most credibly separatist or militant regions (which have the greatest blackmail potential). The beneficial economic consequences of a decentralized division of power depend on a precarious balance in which the center is strong enough (to resist regional pressures) but not too strong (able to violate regional rights)—a balance that cannot itself be guaranteed by the institutional configuration. As Weingast points out, it is not federal structure per se that leads to economically beneficial kinds of credible commitment, but a particular kind he terms "market-preserving federalism" (1995).

Introducing electoral accountability at the municipal rather than regional level may create fewer pressures for central redistribution, since when there is a large number of small claimants each has far less power to threaten central priorities and thus extract privileges. Poland's pattern of elected municipalities but appointed provincial officials (at voivodship level) may offer a superior compromise between accountability and efficiency. An alternative interpretation of English history to that of North and Weingast attributes the relative economic liberalism of the eighteenth century not so much to the vibrancy of regional institutions as to their small territorial jurisdiction and limited role. "The local unit of the county, into which England was divided during the Anglo-

Saxon period, proved too small to sustain a local assembly or produce powerful regional loyalties" (Brewer 1989, 3). In England, unlike pre-Revolution France with its stronger regional estates, a "comparatively uniform and centralized administration of public monies through the Treasury and Exchequer was possible because of the existence of national institutions and the absence of institutionalized regionalism" (22). Root makes the point directly: "In the absence of independent regional governments that offered local leaders an alternative source of legitimacy, the local elites appointed to represent their communities did not have to be bought off by the English Crown" (1994, 16). Meanwhile, the central state was able to develop the most modern, efficient tax collection agency in Europe, with personnel appointed by the central government. "The lack of locally entrenched representative institutions made resistance to central government extremely difficult, while the presence of a centrally appointed administration made collection expeditious as well as discrete" (Brewer 1989, 132).

While in France the central state was forced to negotiate with village assemblies, guilds, and towns, and to collect taxes via private "farmers," in England the central government could send its own tax collectors into the localities. The legal system was implemented and enforced in the regions by justices of the peace, who like the commercial and agricultural interests in parliament showed an interest in increasing economic efficiency at the expense of local communal rights and in helping the state to gather taxes from less privileged social groups. They were not interested in enforcing guild restrictions at the expense of local prosperity (Weingast 1995, 7). What made for English success may not have been limitation of the power of the executive by the legislature and of the center by the regions so much as domination of the state—at both central and local levels—by narrow elites with an interest in increasing economic efficiency, private profit, and state solvency at the expense of the mass of the population, and the lack of an institutional support for the opponents of liberalization—peasants losing access to common lands and consumers paying ever higher excises.

If this line of argument is correct, it suggests a rather different view of the dilemmas of reform in China, which experienced a very sharp increase in economic growth in the 1980s and 1990s without the introduction of credibility-enhancing representative institutions. What leads to such growth may not be the introduction of representative institutions—and, in particular, autonomous institutions at the regional level—but the ability of narrow economic elites interested in rapid growth to negotiate among themselves while excluding the vast majority of the population from politics. The electorate of eighteenth-century Britain was only a slightly larger proportion of the population than the Communist Party nomenklatura is in China today.[16] The forums of the top party leadership may provide space for the leaders of different elite interests to reach compromises. Nomenklatura entrepreneurship in China and Russia is in some ways similar to the privatization of common lands by enclosure—officially sanctioned or otherwise—in seventeenth- and eighteenth-century England.

In brief, there may often be a trade-off between full representation of regional constituencies and the ability of a central government to introduce efficiency-enhancing reforms that shift the distribution of income. The more effectively regional constituencies are organized to bargain with the center—and the more able they are to threaten it with disruption—the more they will be able to secure a pattern of central redistribution that differs from the one that reform-oriented constituencies at the center might prefer. Increasing the representativeness of regional institutions, while desirable from the standpoint of democratization, may have costs in economic efficiency.[17]

The Ethnic Revival

One of the most unexpected features of the fall of Soviet power has been the dramatic revival of ethnonationalisms across Eastern Europe and Eurasia. Scholars disagree about the fundamental causes of this. The sudden invigoration of ethnic claims might reflect a retreat to premodern forms of solidarity, caused ultimately by the communist order's very success in eradicating traces of civil society around which newer definitions of identity could have crystallized. Nationalist ideologies, "frozen" for decades, return to fill a "vacuum" (Kolakowski 1992, 51; see also Rupnik 1994, 95); ethnic identities resurface because they are all that is left (see, e.g., Schöpflin 1994, 137–38). In such a view, national identities tend to be historically determined, slowly changing, often irrational, and nonnegotiable. "While one may readily give away material interests in the expectation of gaining something else, identity is not open to compromise" (Schöpflin 1994, 137–38).

The postcommunist "ethnic revival" might, by contrast, be explained by an essentially instrumental logic, in which ethnic forms of mobilization hold particular advantages for actors within the distinctive set of institutions evolving out of reforming communist orders. Ethnic identities resurface because they are effective tools. In this view, ethnicity is a resource that can be used rationally by entrepreneurs in the competition for political power or state-allocated material benefits. Central state redistribution provides an incentive to organize nationalist and separatist movements to compete for material and other benefits (Zaslavsky 1992b, 114). As one philosopher interpreted Soviet developments in the late 1980s, "Nationalities have turned into political parties" (Grigorii Pomerants, quoted in Zaslavsky 1992b, 107).

This study provides some support for the instrumental view. At least within Russia, social identifications such as minority nationality that could facilitate anticenter protests were useful for extracting benefits from the center. Chapter 3 established that mobilization around a national issue—sovereignty—was extremely effective in extracting fiscal benefits from the central government. There is also some evidence that leaders of ethnic republics considered the potential costs and benefits when deciding how hard to press separatist demands (Treisman 1997).

An implication of this is that the nationalist conflicts simmering in different parts of Russia may be less intractable and revolutionary than in some other parts of the world or other historical eras. Often, they will be subject to strategic constraints, and they may be affected by the distribution of material benefits.

Economic Reform in Divided States

Russia's experience suggests an important lesson about the way economic and political reforms can interact with stability in a transitional regime. During the 1980s and 1990s, not only the former communist states but many other developing and semideveloped countries faced a task of economic self-reinvention—from centrally planned or highly protected economies to free-market systems. Explaining the variation in results of different countries attempting such reforms became the focus of much of the political science profession.

Why did some countries achieve remarkable successes at the task of economic transformation, while others failed to implement needed reforms? If one can conclude anything with confidence from the analyses and intellectual debates of the 1990s, it is that there are no general and simple answers (Hirschman 1994, 343; Remmer 1995). An early suggestion that authoritarian regimes might be better able than democracies to implement temporarily painful economic reforms (O'Donnell 1988) ran into both theoretical and empirical problems (Remmer 1995, 105; Geddes 1995; Maravall 1995; Bates and Krueger 1993, 459; Nelson 1990). The failure to find consistent, general relationships between regime types and successful reform prompted a more detailed examination of the distinctive institutions of particular democratic and authoritarian orders.[18] Here too, the confusion continued. Some scholars argued that cohesive party systems, strong executives, and insulated economics ministries and central banks make economic reforms easier to implement (Haggard and Kaufman 1995). Others contended, based on the empirical experience of Eastern Europe, that, on the contrary, coalition governments, fragmented party systems, and responsive political institutions have been associated with greater success.[19]

The analysis of this book suggests the potential importance of another set of institutional and contextual variables. The way that attempts at economic reform interact with political factors in both democratic and authoritarian states is likely to depend in part on the degree of constitutional decentralization of the state and on the depth and pattern of ethnic, cultural, religious, and linguistic cleavages. In a constitutionally decentralized state, regional political leaders will have a greater capacity to impede implementation of central reforms or to bargain for benefits. Ethnic or cultural divisions will affect the ability of central leaders to build coalitions for reform, and the best strategy to do so. When ethnic divisions coincide with constitutional decentralization, the threat of secession usually lurks in the background.

While various scholars have suggested the importance of sociocultural cleavages and constitutional decentralization for strategies and outcomes of reforms (Przeworski et al. 1995; Horowitz 1993), little is known about precisely what difference they make. Most formal models of the politics of reform tend to assume a unitary state, albeit containing different interest groups or classes (Alesina and Drazen 1991; Fernandez and Rodrik 1991; Dewatripont and Roland 1991). The analysis of Russia presented in this book suggests more specifically how these factors may constrain reforms. In multitiered states without other strong forms of national integration, politicized central redistribution may sometimes be essential to keep the country intact. Economic reforms that require sharp cuts in central subsidies and in tax breaks may be impossible to implement in regionally divided, fragile democracies without prompting a spiral of regional separatism and a collapse of central authority. Some degree of politicized central redistribution may actually be vital to preserve the power of the state to accomplish more modest economic and political reforms.

This is surprising, because it runs against the advice leaders of such regimes have typically been given by macroeconomists, for whom politicized state redistribution is definitely a *problem* not a *solution*.[20] The standard recommendation is that one should simultaneously liberalize the economy and reduce the role of state redistribution. What little redistribution remains should be thoroughly depoliticized, with transfers targeted only at those individuals and regions with demonstrated need.

Yeltsin, to his discomfort, seemed intellectually to have accepted this argument. He spoke with great embarrassment of his ad hoc handouts of aid. In an interview in August 1994, he admitted:

> I have repeatedly heard rebukes along the lines that the president takes a bag of money with him on his trips and certain lucky enterprises receive support. I admit that I don't like that idea either. The president is not an ambulance. You can't salvage the situation or cure the country like that. You can't visit everyone who's in a bad way. (*Trud* 1994)

But, out of political instinct, guiltily, he did continue to respond to such pressures, signing special decrees to yield where he felt it most politically expedient. The analysis in this book suggests a political rationality behind his apparent intuition.

If implementing economic reforms is particularly hard in decentralized, ethnically divided states, implementing economic reform and regional democratization simultaneously in such states may be doubly difficult. The simultaneous introduction of elections at regional and central levels creates incentives for interlevel political conflict. Such conflict can easily escalate into spirals of confrontation—and ultimately state disintegration. To prevent this, a weakened central state must often conserve its capacity for repression by buying off regions that can be appeased with fiscal benefits. In such societies, rapid democratization at the regional level cannot be combined stably with too rapid a reduction in the economic role of the central state.

The analysis suggests a set of hypotheses about the relationship between institutional structure and reform. Economic reforms that include sharp reductions in or reorientations of central redistribution should be easiest to carry out in a unitary state—whether democratic or authoritarian (Poland after 1990 or Chile after 1973); next in a decentralized authoritarian state (China); then in a federal democratic state with a sound initial fiscal balance and strong tax collection capacity (perhaps Canada before 1975); and hardest of all in a federal, democratic state with an unsound fiscal balance and weak tax collection capacity (Russia). This might help to explain why no generally valid relationship has been found empirically between the degree of democratization and economic reform.

Postcommunist democratizing governments have a particularly poor record of consolidating themselves in power. Subsequent elections have tended to see voters desert them for rehabilitated communists or populist nationalists. Various factors explain why the popularity of incumbent reformers might fall over time—the transitional economic costs of reform, for instance, or the arrogance and mistakes of the new officeholders. But in countries with strains between center and periphery, and where the leadership places a priority on preserving state integrity, the honeymoon of the new regime is virtually doomed to be short. The democratic leadership in power *has* to disappoint its previous supporters, to take from the loyal to give to the disloyal, and this will leave it scrambling to reestablish a support coalition when the second elections come around. This is the dilemma that Yeltsin and other central politicians faced in the early 1990s—and which, to the surprise of most observers, he managed in 1996 to surmount.

The New Russian Politics

Russia's experience is rich in material to illuminate political and economic questions in other countries. But, as the Yeltsin era ends, its own future remains opaque. What has emerged from the transitional blur is a clear picture of the contradictory challenges that central politicians face. Theirs is a double task—not so much to play on two chessboards simultaneously as to play two games simultaneously *on the same chessboard.* First, they must construct and sustain a national coalition of voters that can win elections. Second, they need to divide and cajole individual regional leaders and their constituencies, integrating them into the federal equilibrium with a combination of threats and inducements.

Yeltsin's distinctiveness—and the reason for his political longevity—lay in his ability to play both games skillfully, though not without blunders. He was the first Russian politician to master the techniques and strategy of electoral campaigns. For the most part, he combined this with an intuitive feel for the modulations of carrot and stick, the husbanding of resources, and the selective deal-making necessary to divide and integrate regional leaders and their constituencies. "Imagine," he explained in late 1990, as Gorbachev struggled with the rise of Baltic nationalism, "that if you resist the people, then the people will further intensify their counterpressure.... Those [ethno-national] events would have passed off more easily, significantly more easily, if there had been no resistance."[21] While Yeltsin was only one of the central Russian players groping for this strategy, from his preeminent position he set the tone.

His successors will face the same double challenge. Failure on one dimension could mean policy ineffectiveness, dwindling national support, and—potentially—a reemergence of institutional struggle between parliament and president. Failure on the other could lead to a re-inflaming of separatist threats and regionalist passions. Several developments could change the logic. The emergence of genuinely nationwide parties could integrate the interests of politicians at the different levels at which elections are held in a more formal and durable way than the mere common objective of winning votes through public spending. Bargains in the Russian political world of the 1990s—those between politicians and voters, governors and president—lacked credibility. Political parties, by acting as independent enforcers, can make possible a more complex and effective structure of political exchanges. Second, an invigoration of municipal and local government might balance the powers of regional governors and buy the center a little breathing space to rebuild the capacity of central enforcement bureaucracies. But in the meantime, integration relies to a considerable extent on politicians at the center finding the necessary balance of selective sanctions and accommodation.

"It should now be clear," wrote Yevgenii Yasin, a respected liberal economist and later economics minister, in December 1992. "Russia in the foreseeable future cannot be simultaneously united and democratic" (quoted in Sakwa 1993, 179). Despite the flaws in Russian democracy, and despite the practical independence of Chechnya, on balance it remained both in the late 1990s. As of late 1998, the clamor for autonomy or even secession had quietened, and Russian leaders had repeatedly submitted themselves to the voters' choice. Against the backdrop of the broadly successful federal policy of Moscow in the 1990s, the war in Chechnya stands out as not just a tragedy but a mistake.

Though it may be a temporary compromise of convenience, even the extreme opposition Communist Party leadership seemed to have become reconciled to the game of electoral politics through the sufficiently realistic hope it offered them, especially in 1995–96, of actually winning. A more revolutionary, extraparliamentary and extraconstitutional path had been conceivable. The electoral successes of various "Red" regional leaders, from Ryabov and Mukha to Tuleev and Stroyev, suggested that a communist in power in Moscow might have some help learning the importance of the game of relations with the regions.

Yet, despite the successes of the center's fiscal strategy, the mechanism by mid-1997 seemed once again to be under strain. A growing shortfall in federal revenues collected was impeding the center's ability to redistribute in stabilizing ways. The tax problems of the late 1990s owed more to evasion by enterprises and less to direct fiscal challenges by the regions—though some of these did occur as well, as the center increasingly failed to make promised payments to finance federal programs and as elections of governors encouraged a surge of mobilizational confrontation.[22] In part, the leaders of regions with populations relatively *loyal* to Moscow were finding ways, through colonizing regional branches of the tax collection agencies, to conceal and divert revenues secretly rather than to demand them openly. The greatest challenge for the Russian government by 1998 had become to regain administrative control over lower branches of the State Tax Service and to prevent progressive bureaucratic decay from undermining the past achievements of political bargaining.

APPENDIX A

Appendix to Chapter 1: A Formal Analysis

The following is an adaptation of Timur Kuran's formal analysis of the way revolutionary activity spreads, sometimes rapidly and unexpectedly, among previously docile populations (1989).[1] The logic of bandwagons and deterrence in such cases resembles that observable in the interactions between center and regions in multilevel states such as Russia. Besides adapting Kuran's model to the case of intergovernmental relations in a divided state, I suggest two natural extensions. These are to incorporate central strategies of fiscal appeasement into the analysis of how protests spread, and to consider the way that imperfect information affects such central strategies.

Consider a two-level state consisting of a central government and N regional governments, subscripted i.[2] The center sets net tax (or subsidy) rates for each of the N regions, $T_i \in (-\infty, \infty)$. Next, each of the N regional governors decides simultaneously on a course of action, $X_i \in \{A, R\}$, where A constitutes accepting the center's authority and paying the tax (accepting the subsidy), and R constitutes rejecting the center's authority and withholding the tax (refusing the subsidy). Assume that at a given moment the center has a fixed stock of resources it can use to sanction recalcitrant governors, and that it is irrevocably and incorruptibly committed to punish all defectors to the limit of its ability, splitting the punishment between them. Thus, if $X_i = R$, the governor of i will be subjected to a central punishment that decreases his utility by an amount negatively related to the number of regions choosing R (denoted N_R).[3]

Governors are assumed to derive positive utility from both income and local political support. They suffer utility losses when they remit taxes to the center, since any revenue remitted either reduces the governors' own tax take or his local support (since constituents do not like paying more tax and expect their governor to negotiate a favorable deal with the center). However, support of local constituents does not depend just on the level of tax they are required to pay. It also depends on how historical, cultural, and other factors predispose constituents to respond to conflicts between their regional governor and the center, independent of the impact such conflicts may have on tax rates. Populations of different regions have different propensities to "rally round" behind a local leader in confrontations with the center. Let σ_i ($\in [0, 1]$) denote region i's "rallying-round" factor—the exogenous propensity of its population to support a regional leader who defies the center *because of the act itself, regardless of instrumental calculations*. A high value of σ_i—i.e., a population prone to rally behind the governor—suggests that a provincial leader can earn a high support premium by defying the center. Assume that σ_i varies across regions, but that its distribution is common knowledge.

Governor i's choice of action, then, depends on the balance between three factors.

$$V_i(R|\sigma_i,T_i) = M(T_i) - P(N_R^e) + S(\sigma_i) \tag{1}$$

$$V_i(A|\sigma_i,T_i) = 0. \tag{2}$$

As noted, T_i represents the net tax or subsidy that the center has assessed to region i. N_R^e is the number of regions governor i expects to choose R. Assume $M(\cdot)$ and $S(\cdot)$ are monotonically increasing in T_i and σ_i respectively, and $P(\cdot)$ is monotonically decreasing in N_R^e. That is, the governor's expected utility of choosing R increases as the region's tax assessment and the anti-center predisposition of the population increase. It also rises as the expected number choosing R rises—and, therefore, the expected cost of central punishment falls. Note that the utility of not paying tax (disutility of not receiving a subsidy) enters as a positive term in the expected value of rejecting the center's authority, but the tax term does not enter in the expected value function of accepting the center's authority to avoid double counting.

From (1) and (2), governor i will just be indifferent between A and R when

$$M(T_i) - P(N_r^e) + S(\sigma_i) = 0. \tag{3}$$

From this, it follows that for a given level of T_i, the value of σ_i that makes governor i just indifferent between choosing A and choosing R declines with increases in N_R^e. This is illustrated in figure A1, in which the governor prefers to choose R if the ordered pair (σ_i, N_R^e) lies above the function depicted, and prefers to choose A if it lies below the function. Intuitively, for any given expected level of regional defection, there will be a threshold level of regions' "rallying-round" factor above which governors will choose to build support through mobilizational confrontation even knowing that they can expect to be punished by the center.

For simplicity, following Kuran, I assume that all governors form the same point expectations of the number of regions defecting, N_R^e, and that they all have the same functions translating σ into utility when R is chosen, $S(\cdot)$, and higher tax levels into dissatisfaction, $M(\cdot)$. I assume, in addition, that the center's punishment function is common knowledge and that each governor is equally sensitive to central punishment (i.e., $P(\cdot)$ is the same for all). These assumptions make it possible to focus on how differences in the values of σ_i, N_R^e, and T_i affect the nature of possible equilibria. They imply that all governors share the same boundary in figure A1.

Note that the boundary curve in figure A1 has a horizontal segment at $\sigma_i = 1$. This indicates that when the expected number choosing R is below $N_R^e{}_1$, even the regions most predisposed toward confrontation with the center (those for which $\sigma_i = 1$) will still choose A. Because the fear of central punishment is so great, N_R^e must pass above $N_R^e{}_1$ to provoke even these firebrands into rebellion. It is also possible for there to be a horizontal segment toward the bottom right at $\sigma_i = 0$. This would indicate that above a certain level of N_R^e, all regions—even those maximally loyal to the center—would join in a rebellion. Following Kuran, I call the boundary curve in figure A1 the *threshold function,* denoted $x(N_R^e)$. It assigns to each possible expectation about the number of defections a range of values of σ_i for which choosing R is optimal.

Figure A2 superimposes on figure A1 a curve, $g(\sigma)$, that represents the *cumulative density* of regions' values of σ. It measures across the top axis the number of regions

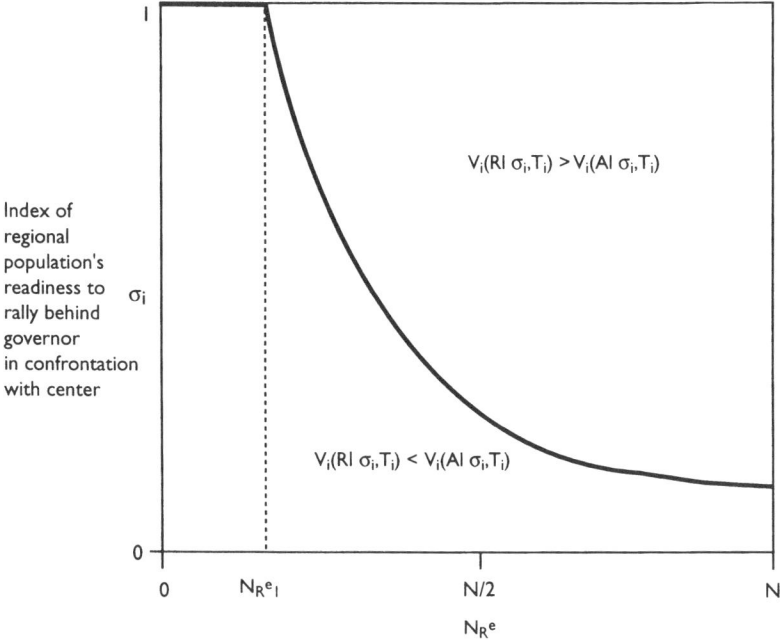

Fig. A1. The threshold function for regional rebellion

with values of σ greater than the value on the vertical axis. The relatively steep shape of the curve as drawn implies that most regions have relatively low values of σ. A curve that was concave upward throughout would indicate a larger proportion of high values.

At equilibrium, the expectations of governors and the center about how many will choose R are correct: $N_R^e = N_R$. This implies that $x(N_R^e) = g(\sigma)$; i.e., equilibrium occurs where the two curves in figure A2 intersect. In figure A2, there is only one equilibrium, at $N_R^e = N_R = 0$. To see why other points represent disequilibria, imagine that expectations started higher: 15 regions were expected to choose R. From the graph, this implies that only regions with a value of σ greater than σ_1 would actually choose R. From the cumulative distribution function, however, there are only 11 regions with σ > σ_1. Since expectations were too high, this will lead to a downward revision of expectations. If, based on this experience, 11 regions are expected to choose R next round, no regions will actually choose R since even at σ = 1, regions require a higher level of expected defection to defect themselves. At the point where $N_R^e = N_R = 0$, the top left-hand corner, expectations will correspond to actual choices, representing an equilibrium. It will also be a stable equilibrium, since any shock that leads to higher expectations will set off a similar process of downward revision. While any point where the two curves

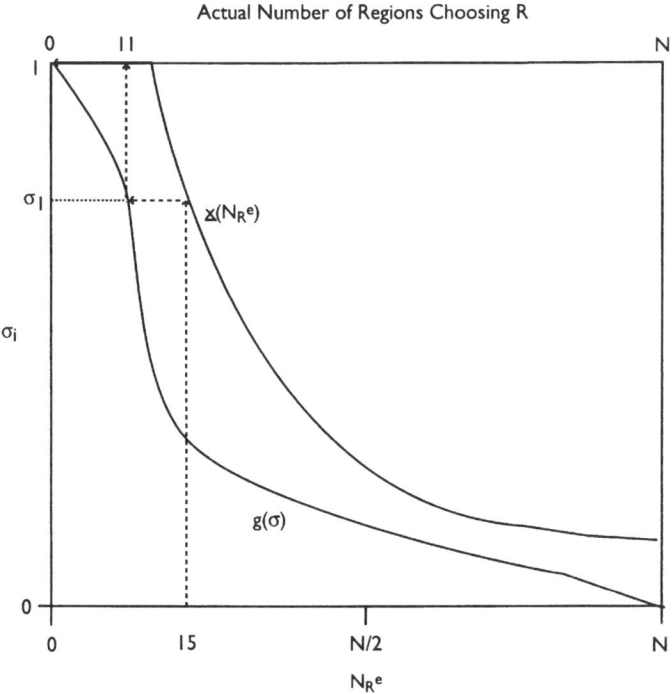

Fig. A2. Threshold function and cumulative density of σ

cross constitutes an equilibrium, stable equilibria will occur where the cumulative density function, $g(\sigma)$, crosses the threshold function, $x(N_R^e)$, from above.

Consider now how tax policy can affect the nature of equilibria. In figure A3, three equilibria exist given the two solid curves as drawn. A full-compliance equilibrium exists at the top left corner; a full-defection equilibrium exists at the bottom right corner. Both of these are stable—i.e., the system will return to these equilibria after small perturbations. There is also an unstable equilibrium at the point where the two curves cross. It is unstable because if expectations are slightly too high, a process of revision will occur that leads to the full-defection equilibrium, and if expectations are slightly too low, revisions will lead the system to full compliance. Up to this point, the center's tax assignments to the regions have been assumed fixed. In fact, an increase in all regions' tax assignments will lead to a downward shift in the threshold function: the higher the tax, the more attractive defection becomes regardless of one's level of σ_i and the level of N_R^e. A decrease in all regions' tax assignments, by contrast, will shift $x(N_R^e)$ upward.

Imagine that a state begins at the full-compliance equilibrium, where $N_R^e = N_R = 0$. All regions are paying tax and acknowledging the center's authority. But then the cen-

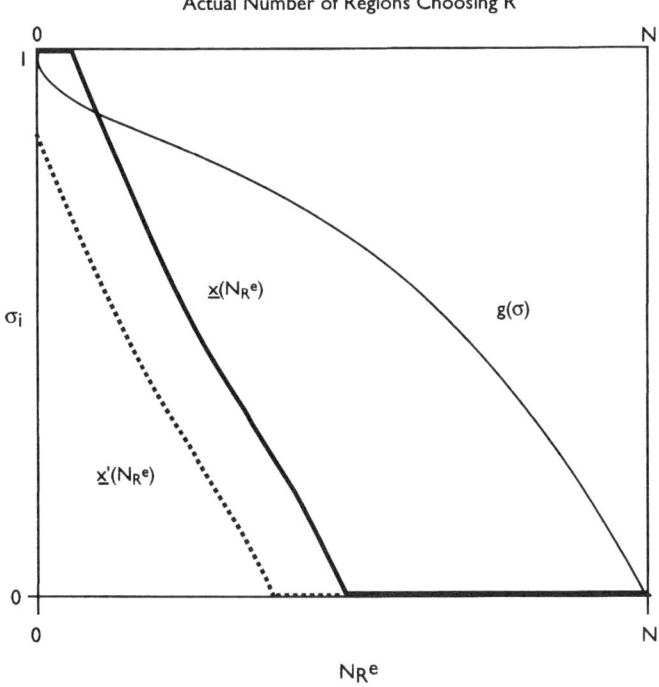

Fig. A3. Increasing tax

ter raises all regions' tax assignments slightly, shifting $x(N_R^e)$ down to $x'(N_R^e)$. Now full compliance is no longer an equilibrium; the only equilibrium lies at universal defection. The slight tax increase sets off a spiral of challenges that quickly forms into a bandwagon of regional protest, leading eventually to complete collapse of the state's fiscal capacity. At any value of σ_i greater than 0, the number actually choosing R, $g(\sigma)$, will turn out to be greater than the number expected, $x'(N_R^e)$.

There is a way, however, for the center to avoid such a fiscal meltdown if it is able to assign different T_i's to the various regions and if it knows each region's value of σ_i.[4] Suppose that instead of increasing taxes equally for all regions, the center concentrates the tax increases on those with the lowest values of σ_i and uses the gains to reduce the tax increases for those at the highest values of σ_i (the n_1 regions with $\sigma_i > \sigma_1$, in fig. A4), thus achieving the same final value of ΣT_i. This could preserve the full-compliance equilibrium by making the slope of the threshold function steeper (replacing $x'(N_R^e)$ with $x''(N_R^e)$ in fig. A4). And since the only equilibrium in the previous case was at $N_R^e = N_R = N$, yielding an actual total tax take of zero, the actual tax take under $x''(N_R^e)$ would

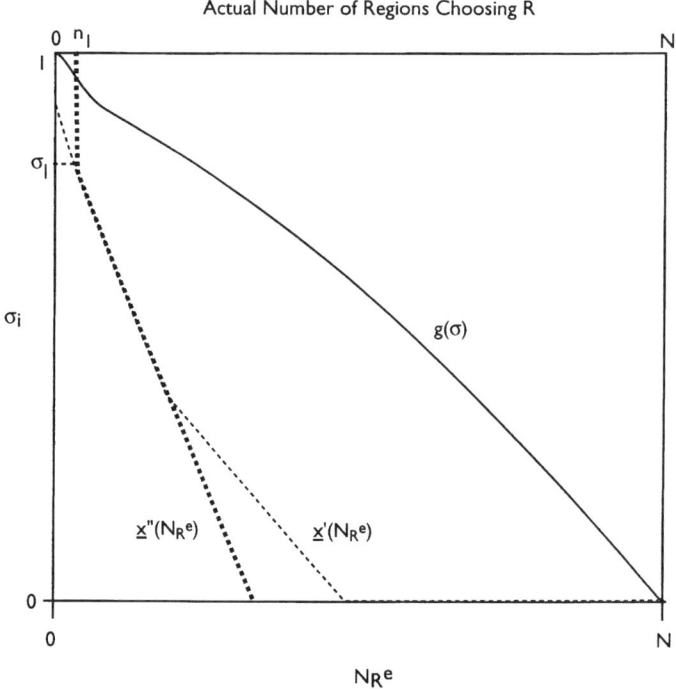

Fig. A4. Tax increase with selective appeasement

be much higher (assuming expectations of defections had not risen too fast, undermining the strategy). Thus, a strategy of redistributing via the tax system in favor of those regions where populations are more predisposed to favor conflict with the center, at the expense of more loyal regions, may prevent spirals of noncompliance and increase the center's total tax take. Such a strategy may require just charging lower tax to the confrontation-prone, or it may require paying them a positive subsidy. Either way, it will sometimes be the center's optimal strategy to maximize net receipts.

Finally, what if the center wishes to adopt such a redistributive strategy but does not know which regions are the most confrontation-prone. Suppose that while it (and all the regions) knows the distribution of σ, only the regions themselves know their particular value, σ_i. In such a situation, it may be optimal for the center to redistribute each round to try to demobilize those that have chosen R in the previous round. Imagine a state faces a threshold curve $x'(N_R^e)$ and a cumulative distribution $g(\sigma)$, as in figure A3. Expectations start at $N_R^e = 0$. This implies, in this example, that five regions will choose R (see fig. A5). If the center has time to alter tax assignments before regional governors adjust their expectations to this new baseline, it can appease these five defiant regions by re-

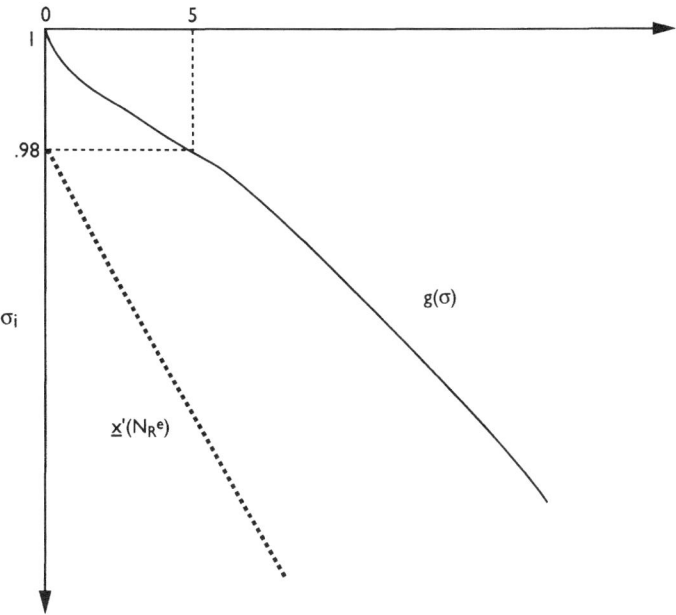

Fig. A5. Appeasement with imperfect information

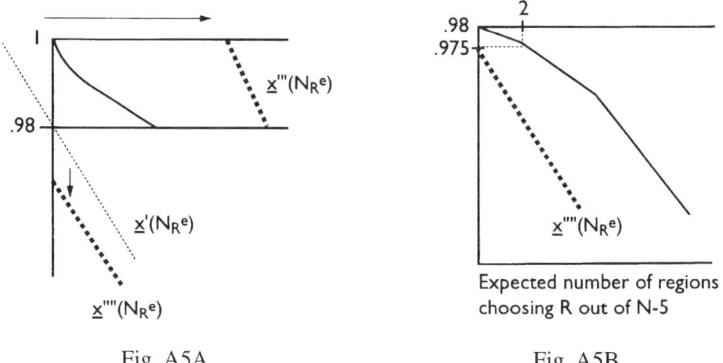

Fig. A5A

Fig. A5B

ducing their tax assignments, so that their threshold function shifts right to $x'''(N_R^e)$ (fig. A5A). Each of these regions is now expected *not* to protest in the future, unless a certain number of others have already broken the ice. Assuming the center must finance these payoffs domestically, it must then increase the tax assignments on other regions. Since it does not know which of the remaining regions have high and which have low values of σ_i, its best bet is to increase all other regions' taxes by a small, equal amount. This shifts the threshold function for these regions down to $x''''(N_R^e)$ (fig. A5A). As can be seen, while the appeasement strategy succeeds in demobilizing the protests of the five regions with the highest values of σ, the additional tax burden prompts two of those regions with slightly lower σ values to rebel, even though they do not expect any other regions to join them (fig. A5B). If the center wishes to prevent this stimulating a bandwagon in future rounds, it must in turn appease these two regions, financing their tax cuts with money from those that still have not defected.

Such a process of appeasement stimulating additional protests may go on for several rounds—or may continue indefinitely, depending on the shape of the functions. If the cumulative density of σ slopes downward sufficiently steeply in the region near the top left corner, then each successive increase in the tax level to finance appeasement of protesters will probably provoke a smaller number of additional defections, leading relatively sooner to an end to the cycle of protest. If, on the other hand, large numbers of regions have high σ values, then the center's appeasement attempts may never catch up with the bandwagon, merely slowing rather than halting the escalation. If the general tax increase stimulates a large number of defections, this may even threaten to return regions already appeased to protest strategies. But for a range of values of the parameters, appeasement will lead to a deescalation of protest and return the system to the full-compliance equilibrium. The model, therefore, demonstrates how rational choices on the part of a central government with imperfect information might lead to a pattern of selective appeasement, starting with the most exogenously defiant regions, and moving down gradually to regions predisposed to greater loyalty to the center that are provoked into protest by the accumulating tax burden they are required to pay to support the appeasement of other regions. It also explains why even some previously appeased regions may jump back onto the bandwagon if the number protesting continues to increase, or if they too are required to finance part of the appeasement payments to more recent defectors.

APPENDIX B
Appendix to Chapter 3

Notes on Data and Construction of the Variables

The experience of the Soviet era, in which statistics were deliberately distorted for purposes of propaganda, along with the general confusion and dislocation of the transition years, provide good reason to be cautious in using statistics collected in Russia by official sources. Nevertheless, in the 1990s the availability and quality of published statistics has risen. One OECD economist even writes of "spectacular improvements" at the main statistical agency, Goskomstat Rossii (Koen 1996, 321). The data used in this study have been cross-checked wherever possible, and attempts are made to test hypotheses more than once, using different data streams and different years. The persuasiveness of claims should not depend on any one particular coefficient estimate, but rather on the accumulation of supportive evidence, both statistical and derived from other kinds of analysis.

Some types of data are thought to be particularly vulnerable to error in postcommunist economies. The postreform decline in output is likely to be overstated for several reasons (Fischer et al. 1996, 48–49; Koen 1996). Quality improvements induced by competition often go unmeasured. The collapse of planning reduces incentives for inflated production reporting, and incentives for tax evasion or goods withholding for barter may lead to subsequent underreporting (Noren 1993, 421). In addition, state statistical services in communist countries were set up to measure output from the state sector, and in the Soviet case used a complete enumeration method rather than sampling. Lack of resources and experience may impede broadening the scope to include growth of output in the private sector initially; and deliberate evasion by semilegal or illegal private enterprises will also probably lower the estimates (Koen 1996; Plyshevskii 1996, 135–40). Some adjustments were made by Goskomstat to better capture private sector output in 1994, but these were probably still insufficient (Koen 1996).

Price data may also contain error. Since "price increases in the previous controlled price regime may have been disguised as quality improvements and inflation in the black markets simply ignored, inflation during the transition may have been overestimated" (Fischer et al. 1996, 49). In the transition, the prices of individual items in Russia moved at very different speeds, complicating index construction (Koen 1996). Foreign trade figures, especially in the early period of transition, were thought to be underreported, as statistical reporting lagged behind the liberalization of the old system of special exporters (Noren 1993, 422). Banking and financial statistics have also been subject to question (Grigori Khanin, in *EKO*, no. 6, 1992, cited in Noren 1993, 421). According to

TABLE B1. Center-to-Region Transfers and Regional Tax Share, Russia 1994

	Region's Share of Tax Revenue		Federal Budget Transfers to Region		Subsidies Paid to Region in First Quarter	
	(1)	(2)	(1)	(2)	(1)	(2)
A. Bargaining Power						
Recent Protest or Opposition						
Vote for "Russia's Choice" December '93	−.34 (.25)		−7.96* (4.35)	−5.55** (2.71)	−.56 (.93)	
Log (1 + man-days lost to strikes, 1993)	−.73 (2.21)		51.14 (38.51)		11.42 (8.25)	5.45 (7.61)
Region's governor publicly opposed Yeltsin Sept. 1993	5.21** (2.11)	4.14** (1.82)	40.91 (36.66)		7.63 (7.85)	
Political Weight						
Population	.00 (.00)		−.01 (.01)		−.00 (.00)	
Estimated regional output per capita	.01 (.00)	.01*** (.00)	.19** (.08)	.18*** (.06)	.02 (.02)	.03** (.01)
Republic status	6.41** (2.65)	7.33*** (1.84)	−131.52*** (46.06)	−84.01** (33.80)	−9.34 (9.86)	
B. Alleviating Need						
Social infrastructure more developed	−.07 (.10)		6.66*** (1.69)	7.43*** (1.17)	.82** (.36)	.52** (.23)
Classified in federal budget as "needy"						
Classified in federal budget as "especially needy"[a]						
Profits per capita 1993	−49.13*** (14.43)	−48.37*** (9.72)	−1273.48*** (250.89)	−1087.43*** (183.66)	−137.17** (53.73)	−172.40*** (37.09)
% of population under 16	.69 (.78)		12.16 (13.61)		6.79** (2.92)	5.29*** (.79)
% of population of pension age	−.01 (.50)		−24.70*** (8.78)	−34.04*** (3.59)	1.39 (1.88)	
Estimated real income 1993	.00 (.01)		.28 (.19)		.05 (.04)	
Degrees latitude north	.25 (.22)		−6.04 (3.87)		−1.26 (.83)	
C. Other Central Objectives						
Advanced pace of economic reform	.29 (.22)		7.96* (3.87)	7.70** (3.29)	.90 (.83)	
% of work force in agriculture	−.11 (.22)		−7.28* (3.79)		−.98 (.81)	

	Types of Central Transfers to the Regions, 1994							
	Direct Transfers From Regional Support Fund in II–IV Quarters		Total Transfers from RSF, including Added Reductions From VAT Remissions		Net Mutual Payments		Federal Budget Investment	
	(1)	(2)	(1)	(2)	(1)	(2)	(1)	(2)
	−1.18*	−1.49***	−3.63**	−3.16***	−4.70		−1.07	
	(.68)	(.40)	(1.41)	(.82)	(2.98)		(1.78)	
	10.23*		17.08	21.31*	29.96		15.05	
	(5.74)		(11.96)	(11.69)	(26.35)		(15.75)	
	9.33*		18.01		6.33		21.86	
	(5.44)		(11.34)		(25.09)		(15.00)	
	−.00		.00		−.02	−.02**	.00	
	(.00)		(.00)		(.01)	(.01)	(.01)	
	.01		.03	.05***	.29***	.31***	−.11***	−.10***
	(.01)		(.02)	(.02)	(.05)	(.05)	(.03)	(.02)
	−6.99		−16.11		−51.45		−50.04**	36.12**
	(6.92)		(14.42)		(31.52)		(18.84)	(14.02)
	.68***	.56***	.91*	.71*	3.12***	2.90***	1.17*	.93**
	(.25)	(.19)	(.52)	(.37)	(1.16)	(.92)	(.69)	(.46)
	−.21		16.07					
	(6.79)		(14.13)					
	25.94***	21.88***	56.05***	63.44***				
	(7.71)	(6.58)	(16.07)	(12.55)				
	−86.67*	−62.93***	−236.98**	−323.86***	−1038.68***	−970.32***	52.33	
	(43.85)	(14.94)	(91.33)	(58.90)	(171.69)	(134.60)	(102.64)	
	5.13**	2.82***	3.98		6.47		2.17	
	(2.04)	(.67)	(4.25)		(9.31)		(5.57)	
	1.98		1.38		−14.82**	−14.82***	−6.16*	−6.80***
	(1.31)		(2.74)		(6.01)	(2.09)	(3.59)	(1.30)
	−.01		−.06		.15		.09	
	(.03)		(.06)		(.13)		(.08)	
	−.39		.98		−5.92**	−6.56***	−1.23	
	(.58)		(1.20)		(2.64)	(1.96)	(1.58)	
	1.66***	1.44***	1.41		3.28	2.90	.69	
	(.59)	(.48)	(1.22)		(2.65)	(2.23)	(1.58)	
	−.43		−1.88		−2.47		−4.61***	−3.20***
	(.58)		(1.21)		(2.59)		(1.55)	(.83)

(continued)

TABLE B.1. Center-to-Region Transfers and Regional Tax Share, Russia 1994

	Region's Share of Tax Revenue		Federal Budget Transfers to Region		Subsidies Paid to Region in First Quarter	
	(1)	(2)	(1)	(2)	(1)	(2)
Region's share in RF output of raw materials	.05 (.28)		−6.85 (4.94)	−6.82* (3.76)	−.74 (1.06)	
Tax collection effort	−.77 (2.42)	−3.35** (1.65)	30.13 (42.12)	−12.67 (51.68)	−4.61 (9.02)	
D. Access and "Pork"						
Chairman (or deputy) of Budget Commission is from region	−.94 (3.93)		26.35 (68.41)		−18.35 (14.65)	
Chairman (or deputy) of parliament is from region	−4.27 (3.29)		47.98 (57.17)		−12.12 (12.24)	
Representatives per capita in State Duma (smc)	−.13 (2.58)		31.58 (44.85)		−4.45 (9.61)	
Yeltsin visited region in 1994	−2.40 (2.04)		−4.79 (35.49)		−4.08 (7.60)	
Chernomyrdin visited region in 1994	2.35 (2.42)		17.88 (42.15)		−7.05 (9.03)	
Region had perm. rep. in Moscow	−1.78 (1.99)		−83.92** (34.60)	−105.06*** (31.00)	−6.97 (7.41)	
Constant	51.78* (28.46)	73.35*** (2.29)	874.84* (494.78)	1007.70*** (114.57)	−88.09 (105.97)	−104.11*** (23.06)
R^2	.65538	.59896	.84423	.80439	.57661	.59785
Adjusted R^2	.50375	.57032	.77570	.77688	.39032	.56952
N	72	75	72	73	72	76

Note: standard errors in parentheses. Federal Budget Transfers to the regions include direct payments from the support fund, additional indirect subsidies via later exemptions from VAT sharing, federal subventions, net mutual payments, net budget loans, federal budget investment, and payments to the closed cities. For sources, see notes on data. One extreme outlier, the Koryaksky Autonomous Okrug, was excluded from the data except that for the regional tax share since its value for all the other dependent variables was more than 5 standard deviations greater than the mean. The Koryaksky Autonomous Okrug, a

Central Bank Chairman Viktor Gerashchenko, the Russian Central Bank did not in 1992 have a reporting system that extended to the rayon level, comparable to that of the former State Bank, Gosbank (Noren 1993, 421).

I have, therefore, exercised particular care when using these types of statistics. Not much emphasis is placed upon the analysis of figures on bank credits. Measures of var-

	Direct Transfers From Regional Support Fund in II–IV Quarters		Total Transfers from RSF, including Added Reductions From VAT Remissions		Net Mutual Payments		Federal Budget Investment	
	(1)	(2)	(1)	(2)	(1)	(2)	(1)	(2)
	.83		.96		−8.22**	−6.80**	1.79	3.55**
	(.82)		(1.72)		(3.38)	(2.80)	(2.02)	(1.57)
	−4.27		−5.93		18.82		13.72	23.64*
	(6.31)		(13.14)		(28.82)		(17.23)	(12.85)
	.24		−10.71		−34.51		37.15	54.62**
	(10.18)		(21.20)		(46.81)		(27.99)	(23.32)
	−9.48	−12.66*	−17.30		−3.67		49.41**	54.80***
	(8.62)	(6.77)	(17.96)		(39.12)		(23.39)	(18.99)
	11.62*	10.08**	7.38		52.10*	55.38*	−9.40	
	(6.72)	(4.93)	(13.99)		(30.69)	(27.96)	(18.35)	
	4.94		1.54		6.87		−7.65	
	(5.36)		(11.16)		(24.29)		(14.52)	
	3.21		.73		36.52		−16.63	
	(6.41)		(13.36)		(28.84)		(17.24)	
	−4.89		−15.93		−17.42		−48.69***	−44.67***
	(5.16)		(10.74)		(23.68)		(14.16)	(11.80)
	−107.34	−39.43*	−32.25	96.11***	487.29	604.04***	361.95*	335.50***
	(73.39)	(19.77)	(153.70)	(16.63)	(338.59)	(110.31)	(202.43)	(44.45)
	.78196	.73007	.72264	.67552	.86395	.83300	.70546	.63659
	.67294	.69684	.58395	.64770	.80409	.80952	.57586	.58068
	72	73	72	76	72	73	72	75

sparsely inhabited North-Eastern territory of 35,000 inhabitants, received more than 6 million rubles per capita in 1994 central transfers.

[a]Included in regressions for FFSR, to test relationship between allocation and the specific criteria on which FFSR allocations are supposed to be based.

*$p < .10$ **$p < .05$ ***$p < .01$

ious independent variables used in the study are taken from recent Goskomstat Rossii publications. Some of these may, indeed, be problematic. Territorial statistical agencies, to the degree that they fall under the influence of local political authorities, may be pressured to inflate indicators of "need" that would justify greater transfers. Yet, if the incentive is equal in all regions, the distortions are likely to average out in cross-regional

TABLE B2. Regions' Ranks in Net Transfers Received (as % of Total Revenue Collected in Region)

Region	Rank in Net Transfers Received 1988	Rank in Net Transfers Received 1992
Karelia	3	13
Komi	22	4
Archangl	20	42
Nen AO	.	.
Vologda	69	47
Murmansk	2	27
St. Peter	42	68
Leningra	48	20
Novgorod	51	32
Pskov	14	26
Bryansk	37	15
Vladimir	71	59
Ivanovo	70	66
Kaluga	25	29
Kostroma	53	35
Moscow C	18	57
Moskovsk	30	52
Orlovska	44	37
Ryazan	56	64
Smolensk	27	55
Tverskay	60	49
Tulskaya	61	38
Yaroslav	67	67
Mari El	13	16
Mordovia	23	12
Chuvashi	28	28
Kirovska	40	53
Nizhegor	59	62
Belgorod	35	65
Voronezh	43	58
Kursk	38	63
Lipetsk	64	36
Tambov	24	70
Kalmykia	8	5
Tatarstan	68	8
Astrakhan	17	21
Volgogra	66	46
Penza	33	40
Samara	72	71

TABLE B2.—*Continued*

Region	Rank in Net Transfers Received 1988	Rank in Net Transfers Received 1992
Saratov	50	44
Ulyanovs	62	56
Adygeia	.	.
Dagestan	4	2
Kab-Balk	21	11
Kar-Cher	.	.
N. Osset	45	1
Chechnya	31	6
Krasnoda	46	60
Stavropol	49	61
Rostov	32	50
Bashkort	54	19
Udmurtia	65	.
Kurgan	26	33
Orenburg	58	39
Perm	63	69
Komi-Per	.	.
Sverdlov	55	48
Chelyabi	41	30
Gorn Alt	.	.
Altai Kr	29	22
Kemerovo	57	23
Novosib	1	51
Omsk	52	43
Tomsk	10	45
Tyumen	73	72
Khant-Ma	.	.
Yam-Nen	.	.
Buryatia	5	7
Tyva	7	3
Khakassi	.	.
Krasnoya	47	25
Taimir	.	.
Evenki	.	.
Irkutsk	39	9
Ust-Orda	.	.
Chita	6	10
Ag-Burya	.	.
Sakha	15	18

(continued)

TABLE B2.—*Continued*

Region	Rank in Net Transfers Received 1988	Rank in Net Transfers Received 1992
Primore	36	41
Khabarov	19	34
Yevreiskaya	.	.
Amur	9	14
Kamchatka	11	17
Koryaksky	.	.
Magadan	12	24
Chukotka	.	.
Sakhalin	16	31
Kaliningrad	34	54

regressions. The weakness of some statistics suggests one should be cautious in ruling out hypotheses that might fail primarily because of inadequate data sources. Yet, the strong positive results reported seem quite unlikely to be caused by data distortions.

The data on fiscal transfers and taxes were obtained from several sources. Those for 1992 on tax payments and receipts of central transfers (other than budget investments) are based on figures published by Leonid Smirnyagin, an adviser to President Yeltsin on political geography and a member of the Presidential Council, in the newspaper *Segondnya* (Smirnyagin 1993a). A fuller accounting than the one published was provided to me by Smirnyagin. According to Smirnyagin, the data on tax remittances by the regions in 1992 were taken from the President's Budget Message (*Byudzhetnoe poslanie*), which circulated in the spring of 1993. The statistics on receipts of central financial resources were prepared by the Regional Politics Department of the Council of Ministers, using information from the Ministry of Finance. (Smirnyagin has said that these data were rechecked by the Ministry of Finance and corrected before he was allowed to present his findings to President Yeltsin. I, of course, use the corrected version.) The figures on central budget investments were obtained from Goskomstat Rossii. Most data for 1994, 1995, and 1996 come from the Ministry of Finance and State Tax Service and were provided by Aleksei Lavrov, of the President's Analytical Administration. Figures on transfers to closed cities come from the corrected federal budget for 1994 and investment figures for 1994 come from Goskomstat.

One issue of obvious concern is whether incentives to misreport data might lead to distortions. In the case of this data, such problems are unlikely to arise, since the figures were obtained from central agencies. While regional governments might have an incentive to exaggerate the amount of tax they pay to the center, the central Tax Service, from which the data were obtained, has no such incentive, as it would be required to account for any shortfall between its reported collections and the actual amount remitted. Nor does it have any obvious reason to underreport the amount of tax specific regions have paid, and thus reveal itself to be failing in its tax collection responsibilities. Likewise, though regions might underreport the levels of central transfers they receive in the attempt to lobby for more, the central agencies making these transfers have no incentive not to report them in full, since again they would be liable for diversions between Finance Ministry and recipients. The only figures where such distortions might plausibly play a part are those for the level of regional tax collection and the proportion of total tax collected in a region remitted to the center. Regional leaders might seek to conceal part of regional revenue, to keep certain flows off-budget, and hence to exaggerate the proportion sent to Moscow. This is likely to lead to some overestimation of Moscow's share across the board, which should not affect the relative differences between regions too greatly. In any case, the results for revenue share retained are only one of many fiscal variables analyzed separately, and the main conclusions do not rely on these particular results.

While caution is merited in using Goskomstat statistics, the emerging consensus in the field is that, with certain exceptions, they are sufficiently reliable to be informative in works of this kind when used carefully. Citations of Goskomstat Rossii data are virtually universal in studies of post-Soviet Russian economic, political, and social developments. (For a few recent examples, see Hanson 1996; Sutherland and Hanson 1996; Hough, Davidheiser and Lehmann 1996; IMF 1992b.) Where possible, alternative indicators and specifications should, of course, be attempted. I have done my best to do so in this study.

Sources of Data

Dependent Variables

Main data compiled from State Tax Service and Ministry of Finance accounts. Provided to the author by Leonid Smirnyagin and Aleksei Lavrov of the President's Analytical Administration. Data on federal budget investments in the regions in 1992 and 1994 calculated from Goskomstat, *Rossiisky Statistichesky Yezhegodnik 1995,* 842–50; figures for payments to closed cities 1994 taken from the 1994 (corrected) Russian Budget.

For 1992, the Smirnyagin aggregate transfers data differs slightly from the sum of the separate transfer streams for which data were available (in 13 of the 72 cases, the Smirnyagin transfers variable is slightly larger). In table 3.3, the 1992 net transfers variable is constructed from the original Smirnyagin aggregate variable. However, results are almost identical if the sum of separate transfer streams is used instead. For 1996, the net transfers variable used is that estimated by Alexei Lavrov, and apparently includes estimates of part of federal spending in the regions.

Independent Variables

Bargaining Power

  Recent vote for pro-reform party or presidential candidate

    1992:   vote for Yeltsin in 1991 presidential election (McFaul and Petrov 1995).

1994 and 1995: vote for Russia's Choice in 1993 parliamentary election (official results from Central Electoral Commission).
1996: vote for Yabloko or Russia's Choice in 1995 parliamentary election (Moscow Carnegie Center, *Parlamentskie vybori 1995 goda v Rossii*, Moscow, 1996, 19).

Region declared sovereignty by end of 1990

(Sheehy and other sources: see table B5)

Governor opposed Yeltsin September 1993

(Teague 1993 and reports in FBIS). "Governor" here taken as head of administration of oblasts and krais, and president—or if none, chairman of Council of Ministers—of republics.

Governor did not support Chernomyrdin's Our Home Is Russia bloc 1995

Variable set at -2 if governor ran on OHIR electoral list; at -1 if governor did not run, but another high official from regional administration did; at 0 if no high official from regional administration ran on OHIR list (Official party lists).

Log Strike Variable

1992: Log of 1,000 man-days lost to strikes in 1991 (from Goskomstat Rossii, *Narodnoe Khoziaistvo RF*, 1992). Adjusted, so that those regions with less than 1,000 man-days lost coded as zero.
1994: Log of 1,000 man-days lost to strikes in 1993 plus one (Goskomstat Rossii, *Rossiisky Statistichesky Yezhegodnik* 1994, 475). I assume all strikes given as in Tyumen in fact occurred in Yamalo-Nenetsky AO (gas industry).
1995: Log of 1,000 man-days lost to strikes in 1994 plus one (Goskomstat Rossii, *Rossiisky Statistichesky Yezhegodnik* 1995, 577–79).
1996: Log of 1,000 man-days lost to strikes in 1995 plus one (Goskomstat Rossii, *Rossiisky Statistichesky Yezhegodnik* 1996, 780).

Population

1992: Population 1992 (Goskomstat Rossii, *Sotsial'noe Razvitie Rossiiskoi Federatsii. 1992,* Moscow: Goskomstat Rossii, 1992, 17–21).
1994–96: Population 1994 (*Rossiisky Statistichesky Yezhegodnik 1994,* Moscow: Goskomstat Rossii, 1994).

Estimated economic output
All years: estimate of 1993 industrial output plus agricultural output plus services output, all per capita (Goskmostat Rossii).

Republic

Goskomstat Rossii, *Rossiisky Statistichesky Yezhegodnik 1996*

Access

Visited by President or Prime Minister that year

1992: tally of official visits constructed on the basis of reports in *Nezavisimaya Gazeta*.
1994: tally constructed from FBIS.
1996: visits by president in period up to June 16, 1996, compiled from Moscow Carnegie Center, *Prezidentskie Vybori v Rossii*, no. 9, June 1996, and press reports.

Region had member on parliament's budget committee

1992: member on Supreme Soviet's Commission on Budgets, Planning, Taxes and Prices (Carroll Publishing, *Russian Government Today,* spring 1993 and fall 1993 editions).

Chairman of parliamentary budget committee (or deputy) from region

1994–95: membership of commissions (either lower or upper house) from *Russian Government Today,* spring 1994.
1996: Panorama Publishing, *Telefonnaya Kniga Rossii*, April 1997, and election results. (1 if chairman or a deputy chairman of either house's budget committee was elected from that region—i.e., in Duma, not on party list).

Chairman (or deputy) of one house of parliament from region

1994–95: *Russian Government Today,* spring 1994.
1996: Panorama Publishing, *Telefonnaya Kniga Rossii,* April 1997.

Parliamentary deputies per capita

1992: Supreme Soviet representatives per million inhabitants (official listings).
1994–95: Duma representatives elected in single-mandate constituencies per million inhabitants (McFaul and Petrov 1995).
1996: Duma representatives elected in single-mandate constituencies per million inhabitants (official 1995 election results).

Region had permanent representative in Moscow

Russian Government Today, fall 1993; Panorama Publishing's *Rossiskaya Federatsia: Telefonnaya Kniga* (July 1993 and April 1997 editions).

Alleviating Need

Social infrastructure underdevelopment

In each case, an index of social infrastructure underdevelopment was tried, as well as the elements of this index, and some additional indicators of social infrastructure underdevelopment. The one most significant was used in the final specification. 1992: index; 1994: telephones (or access to them) per 100 urban families in 1992; 1995: telephones (or access to them) per 100 urban families 1995; 1996: doctors per 100,000 residents 1994. (Signs changed so that higher value indicates greater need.)

1992: Index constructed using factor analysis from four indicators of social need:[1] (a) average housing space per inhabitant in 1991; (b) the number of doctors per thousand inhabitants in 1991; (c) the number of hospital beds per thousand inhabitants in 1991; and (d) the number of home telephones per hundred urban families in 1991. The first factor extracted explained 39 percent of the variance, and was used as the index. Factor loadings are shown in table B3.

1994: proportion of urban households with a telephone or access to one in 1991 (from *Sotsial'noe Razvitie Rossiiskoi Federatsii. 1992.* 1992. Moscow: Goskomstat RF, 235–36).

1995: telephones (or access to them) per 100 urban families 1995 (Goskomstat Rossii, *Rossiisky Statistichesky Yezhegodnik 1996*).

1996: Doctors per 10,000 residents 1994 (Goskomstat Rossii, *Rossiisky Statistichesky Yezhegodnik 1995,* 643-45).

Proportion of population under 16

As of 1994 (Goskomstat Rossii, *Demograficesky Yezhegodnik RF 1993,* 1994, 32).

TABLE B3. Index of Social Infrastructure Underdevelopment

	Factor Loadings
Telephones per hundred urban families	.894
Doctors per thousand residents	.873
Housing space per capita	.086
Hospital beds per thousand residents	−.029

Source: Goskomstat Rossii, *Sotsialnoe Razvitie Rossiiskoi Federatsii, 1992* (Moscow: Goskomstat Rossii, 1992, 122–24, 165–67, 175–77, 235–36).

Proportion of population of pension age

Percentage of population over 60 for men, over 55 for women, 1994 (Goskomstat Rossii, *Demograficheskiy Yezhegodnik RF 1993*, 1994, 32).

Profits per capita previous year

1992: region's total profits in 1991 divided by its population (Goskomstat Rossii, *Finansy v Rossiiskoi Federatsii 1992*, Goskomstat Rossii, Moscow, 1992, 18–20).
1994: profit in 1993 divided by population (*Sotsialno-Ekonomicheskoe Polozhenie Rossii 1994*, Goskomstat Rossii, 318–19).
1995: profit in 1994 divided by population (*Sotsialno-Ekonomicheskoe Polozhenie Rossii*, Goskomstat Rossii, January 1995, 204–7).
1996: profit in 1995 divided by population (Goskomstat Rossii, *Rossiisky Statistichesky Yezhegodnik 1996*).

Estimated average real income previous year (1992 same year)

1992: average monthly money income as percentage of cost of 19 basic food commodities end 1992 (Goskomstat Rossii, *Tseny v Rossii* 1996, 139).
1994: average monthly money income previous year as percentage of cost of 19 basic food commodities end 1993 (Goskomstat Rossii, *Tseny v Rossii* 1996, 139).
1995: per capita monthly money income as percentage of per capita monthly subsistence minimum 1994 (Goskomstat Rossii, *Rossiisky Statistichesky Yezhegodnik 1996*, 786–88).
1996: per capita monthly money income as percentage of per capita monthly subsistence minimum 1995 (Goskomstat Rossii, *Rossiisky Statistichesky Yezhegodnik 1996*, 789–91).

Degrees latitude north
Times Atlas.

Other Central Objectives

Advanced economic reform

1992: index of economic reform constructed from: (a) percentage of enterprises included in the privatization program that had in fact been privatized in 1992 (Goskomimmushchestvo Rossii, *Panorama Privatizatsii* 2 (4), January 1993, 66–67 (variable labeled "Ipr")); (b) the percentage of apartments privatized by January 1993 (calculated from Goskomstat Rossii, *O Razvitii Ekonomicheskykh Reform v Rossiiskoi Federatsii (1–6 1993)*, Moscow, Goskomstat Rossii, 1993, 100–101); (c) the number of private farms per thousand rural residents (for

Moscow and St. Petersburg set to mean for other regions, since no rural population or private farms) (calculated from Goskomstat Rossii, *Razvitie Ekonomicheskykh Reform v Regionakh Rossiiskoi Federatsii,* 1993, 6, 98–100); (d) number of commodity exchanges per thousand residents in 1993 (Goskomstat Rossii, special report); and (e) a variable measuring the extent to which regional governments continued to regulate local prices even after central price liberalization (Yasin 1993b, 24).[2] These five variables were combined by factor analysis.[3] The first factor extracted, which explained 27 percent of the variance, was positively correlated with the prevalence of commodity exchanges and private farms, with the degree of achieved privatization of both enterprises and apartments, and negatively correlated with the extent of regional price regulation. It was used as the index of economic reform. Factor loadings are shown in table B4.

1994: percentage of 285 goods with controlled prices (Goskmostat Rossii, provided to me by Andrew Warner).

1995: private farms January 1994 per 1,000 inhabitants (Goskomstat Rossii, *Ekonomicheskoe Polozhenie Regionov RF 1994,* 290–91 (set at mean for Moscow, St. Petersburg).)

1996: percentage of 285 goods with controlled prices (Goskomstat Rossii, provided to me by Andrew Warner).

Percentage of work force in agriculture

Percentage of work force in agriculture 1993 (Goskomstat Rossii, *Ekonomicheskoe Polozhenie Regionov RF 1994*).

Region's share in RF raw materials output

Percentage of Russian Federation output of raw materials industries accounted for by region 1993 (Goskomstat Rossii, *Ekonomicheskoe Polozhenie Regionov RF 1994,* 49–50).

Index of tax effort

Constructed by method of Roy Bahl (Bahl 1994, 177–79), using most appropriate available data for each year. It measures the ratio of the tax actually collected in the

Table B4. Index of Pace of Economic Reform

	Factor Loadings
Private farms per 1,000 rural residents	.616
Percent of eligible enterprises privatized	.535
Commodity exchanges per 1,000 residents	.334
Percent of apartments privatized	.187
Extent of regional price regulation	−.737

region to an estimate of that region's "taxable capacity," derived by regressing tax collected on per capita gross value of industrial output, the average monthly wage, the percentage of the population living in urban areas, and the population size. For 1992, Bahl's original index is used: it ranges in value from .49 to 2.53 and is calculated for 67 of Russia's regions.

TABLE B5. Sovereignty Declarations, August 1990–May 1991

Region	Date of Declaration	Source
Karelia	Aug. 10, 1990	Anne Sheehy, "Fact Sheet on Declarations of Sovereignty" Radio Liberty *Report on the USSR,* Nov. 9, 1990, 23–25.
Komi	Aug. 30, 1990	Sheehy
Tatarstan	Aug. 30, 1990	Sheehy
Udmurtia	Sept. 19, 1990	Sheehy
Yakutia	Sept. 27, 1990	Sheehy
Chukotka	Sept. 29, 1990	Sheehy
Adygeia	Oct. 7, 1990	Sheehy
Buryatia	Oct. 8, 1990	Sheehy
Koryaksky	Oct. 9, 1990	Sheehy
Bashkiria	Oct. 11, 1990	Sheehy
Komi-Perm	Oct. 11, 1990	Sheehy
Kalmykia	Oct. 18, 1990	Sheehy
Yam-Nen	Oct. 17, 1990	Yuri Perepletkin, "Yet Another Republic," *Izvestia*, Oct. 17, 2. Sheehy.
Mari El	Oct. 22, 1990	Sheehy
Chuvashia	Oct. 24, 1990	Sheehy
Altai Rep	Oct. 25, 1990	Sheehy
Irkutsk	Oct. 26, 1990	TASS, 2011 GMT, Oct. 26, 1990. Declares region an "equal and independent subject of the federation" RL *Report on the USSR,* Nov. 2, 1990, 37.
Nenetsk	Nov. 1990	RL *Report on the USSR,* Nov. 23, 1990, 35.
Kar-Cherk	Nov.–Dec. 1990	RL *Report on the USSR,* Nov. 30, 1990, 22.
Chech-Ing	Nov. 27, 1990	RL *Report on the USSR,* Dec. 7, 1990, 23–24.
Mordovia	Dec. 1990	RL *Report on the USSR,* Dec. 21, 1990, 28. (watered down sovereignty declaration without word 'sovereignty'—on the state-legal status of the Mordvinian SSR).
N Ossetia	Dec. 1990	RL *Report on the USSR,* Jan. 4, 1991, 65.
Kab-Balkar	Jan. 1991	Ali Kazikhanov, "A Step Toward Sovereignty," *Izvestia,* Feb. 1, 1991, 2.
Dagestan	May 15, 1991	RL *Report on the USSR,* May. 24, 1991, 38.

TABLE B6. Characteristics of the Independent Variables Used in Final Regressions

Continuous Variables	Mean	Standard Deviation	Min	Max
A. Bargaining Power				
Pro-Yeltsin Vote 1991 Elections (%)	52.29	12.47	15.25	84.80
Vote for Russia's Choice Dec. 1993 (%)	14.5	5.8	1.7	34.7
Vote for Yabloko or Russia's Choice 1995 (%)	8.4	4.8	2.5	28.5
Population 1992 (mn)	1.7	1.5	.03	9.0
Population 1994 (mn)	1.7	1.5	.02	8.8
Estimated Regional Output per capita (1,000 Rs per capita, 1993)	969.3	455.9	210.4	2,567.1
Log Man-Days Lost to Strikes 1991	.21	.60	.00	3.21
Log Man-Days Lost to Strikes 1993	.16	.40	.00	1.85
Log Man-Days Lost to Strikes 1994	.31	.56	.00	2.40
Log Man-Days Lost to Strikes 1995	.72	.66	.00	2.65
B. Need				
Social Infrastructure Development Index 1992	0	1.0	−1.40	5.53
Access to phone per 100 urban families 1992	34.80	12.80	13.50	96.40
Access to phone per 100 urban families 1995	40.81	15.19	3.80	105.10
% of Population Under 16	25.10	4.10	18.90	36.50
% of Population of Pension Age	17.99	5.69	3.80	26.90
Degrees North	54.32	5.78	42.59	69.27
Real Income end 1992 (% cost of 19 products)	223.26	69.57	101.01	526.32
Real Income 1993 (% cost of 19 products)	363.83	102.18	212.77	714.29
Real Income 1994 (% subsistence minimum)	197.45	69.82	99.00	641.00
Real Income 1995 (% subsistence minimum)	167.80	54.64	84.00	520.00
Profits per capita 1991 (1,000 rubles p.c.)	2.33	.74	.52	4.38

TABLE B6.—*Continued*

Continuous Variables	Mean	Standard Deviation	Min	Max
Profits per capita, 1993 (m rubles p.c.)	.24	.14	0	.77
Profits per capita, 1994 (1,000 rubles p.c.)	328.83	378.80	−1511.94	1625.43
Profits per capita, 1995 (1,000 rubles p.c.)	997.68	1398.73	−4093.72	6972.42
C. Access				
Deputies to Supreme Soviet per mn inhabitants	3.52	5.59	0	40.00
State Duma SMC Reps. per mn inhabitants 1994	3.09	6.13	.64	44.25
State Duma SMC Reps. per mn inhabitants 1996	3.08	6.14	.64	44.25
D. Other Objectives				
Index of Advanced Pace of Economic Reform 1992	0	1.0	−2.17	3.37
% 285 goods with controlled prices	4.43	3.88	.00	14.74
Private Farms per 1,000 rural inhabitants 1995	6.60	3.83	.18	18.48
Employment in Agriculture 1993 (% work force)	14.79	7.16	.30	35.30
Region's Share in RF Raw Materials Output (%)	1.3	4.0	0	33.8
Index of Region's Tax Collection Effort 1992	1.02	.27	.49	2.53
Tax Collection Effort 1994	1.1	.4	.6	3.3
Tax Collection Effort 1995	.97	.72	.20	5.48

Dummy Variables	Yes	No	N
Declared Sovereignty, 1990	22	66	88
Yeltsin visited 1992	13	74	87
PM visited 1992	10	77	87
Yeltsin visited 1994	15	73	88
Chernomyrdin visited 1994	11	77	88
Yeltsin visited first half of 1996	23	66	89
Region had permanent representative in Moscow 1992	63	25	88
Region had permanent representative in Moscow 1994	60	28	88

(continued)

TABLE B6.—*Continued*

Dummy Variables	Yes	No	N
Region had permanent representative in Moscow 1995	79	10	89
Republic Status (AO's excluded)	21	58	79
Region's Governor Publicly Opposed Yeltsin Sept. 1993	15	73	88
Representative on the Parliament's Budget Commission 1992	6	82	88
Chairman (or Deputy) of Budget Comm. from Region 1994	5	84	89
Chairman (or Deputy) of Budget Comm. from Region 1996	7	82	89
Chairman (or Deputy) of Parliament from Region 1994	7	82	89
Chairman (or Deputy) of Parliament from Region 1996	8	81	89

	-2	-1	0	N
Reg. Admin. Support for "Our Home Is Russia" 1995	5	24	59	88

TABLE B7. Correlation Coefficients for Independent Variables Used in Same Long Regression in Table 3.3 (only those with $r > .50$ shown)

	% of Population Pension Age	Republic Status		
% of Population Under 16	−.753	.636		
	Share of RF Raw Materials Production	Estimated Economic Output 1993	1991 Profits per Capita	1993 Profits per Capita
Estimated Real Income 1992	.647	.696	.607	
Estimated Economic Output 1993	.563	.747		.798
Estimated Real Income 1993				.538
	Degrees Latitude North	% of Work force in Agriculture	Population 1994	
1991 Profits per Capita	.508	−.555		
Vote for Russia's Choice 1993	.622	−.721		
Vote for Yabloko + Russia's Choice 95		−.655	.502	
	Population 1994	Profits per Capita 1995	Vote for Yabloko + RC 1995	
Estimated Real Income 1994	.514			
Estimated Real Income 1995	.528	.568	.504	

TABLE B8. Breakdown of the Dependent Variable, 1992 (all figures given per capita)

	Mean (1,000 rs)	Standard Deviation	Min	Max	Coefficient of Variation
(1) Total Central Transfers	11.36	12.99	1.27	95.59	1.14
Subventions	3.45	6.95	0	50.14	2.01
Investment Grants	3.38	2.28	.95	12.44	.67
Government Reserve Fund Payments	.06	.18	0	1.03	3.0
Supreme Soviet Reserve Fund	.26	.71	0	4.60	2.73
Credits (Subset for which data available)	2.48	1.36	.08	8.25	.55
Special Benefits	3.66	12.07	0	81.60	3.30
(2) Tax Payments to the Center	14.75	9.89	.03	74.75	0.67
(3) Net Central Transfers	−3.14	15.17	−57.66	64.34	−4.83

TABLE B9. Breakdown of the Dependent Variable, 1994 (all figures given per capita, Koryak AO outlier excluded)

	Mean (1,000 rs)	Standard Deviation	Min	Max
Total Central Transfers	419.96	532.43	17.6	3,939.5
Subsidies, QI	43.56	83.96	0	549.1
Federal Subventions	3.35	31.60	0	298.15
Direct Transfers from Support Fund	42.31	87.69	0	622.9
Total Payments from Support Fund (inc. indirect subsidy via VAT reduction)	78.7	117.1	0	711.6
Net Mutual Payments	226.12	371.72	0	2,774.0
Federal Investment Grants	100.7	71.8	7.7	429.8
Payments to Closed Cities	3.21	11.17	0	68.1
Budget Loans	4.4	29.2	0	265.3
Regional Share of Tax Revenue, %	70.1	9.6	52.0	100.0
Net Center-Region Budget Transfers	122.04	543.60	−1,348.9	3,144.7

Note: First Quarter subsidies not included in total transfers, since they were likely included in year-end figures for support fund payments. Indirect subsidies via VAT reductions are included in total transfers, but not in net transfers, since this represents transfers minus tax payments and to include them would constitute double counting.

APPENDIX C

Appendix to Chapter 4

Notes on Variables in Tables 4.1–4.7

Dependent Variables

April 1993: percentage voting yes to question 1 on April 1993 referendum, from McFaul and Petrov (1995).
December 1993: vote for Yabloko, Russia's Choice and RDDR, from official results as reported by Central Electoral Commission, Moscow (1995).
December 1995: from Orttung and Parrish, *Transition,* Feb. 23, 1996.
1996: from Moscow Carnegie Center, *Prezidentskie Vybory v Rossii* June 1996, No.9; second round 1996 voting official results from printout from Central Electoral Commission, Moscow.

Dependent variables for regional administration official elections compiled from official election results, McFaul and Petrov 1995, and press reports.

Estimated Output Per Capita

1993 for all. From Goskomstat Rossii, *Ekonomicheskoe Polozhenie Regionov RF,* 1994, 9–11; and Goskomstat Rossii, *Rossiisky Statistichesky Yezhegodnik* 1994, 557–59. All in 1,000 Rs per capita.

Estimated Recent Real Income Change

1993 regressions: estimated change in real incomes of the population June 1992–June 1993, money incomes from Goskomstat Rossii, *O Razvitii Ekonomicheskykh Reform v RF (dopolnitel'nie dannie za I polugodie 1993 goda),* 1993, 38–39; deflated by estimated average inflation first half of 1992–first half of 1993, calculated from *O Razvitii Ekonomicheskykh Reform,* 1993, 14–15.
1995 and 1996 regressions: change in average income 1994–95 as percentage of subsistence minimum in region, from TACIS, *Analiz Tendentsii Razvitia Regionov Rossii v 1992–1995 gg,* Moscow, March 1996, 84–87.

Unemployment

1993 regressions: unemployment level in August 1993 as percentage of work force,

Goskomstat Rossii, *Razvitie Ekonomicheskykh Reform v Regionov RF* 1993 (10): 122.
1995–96 regressions: unemployment in percentage in September 1995, from TACIS, *Analiz Tendentsii Razvitia Regionov Rossii v 1992–1995 gg,* Moscow, March 1996, 92.

Inflation

April 1993 regression: regional CPI December 1992 divided by regional CPI December 1991, in times, from Goskomstat, electronic transfer.
December 1993 regression: regional CPI December 1993/regional CPI December 1992, from Goskomstat, electronic transfer.
1995–96 regressions: most recent inflation data available were change in CPI 1993–1994, average for year, from Le Houerou 1995, table A11.

Proportion of Enterprises Insolvent

April 1993 regression: proportion of regional enterprises insolvent in January–May 1993, from *O Razvitii Ekonomicheskykh Reform v RF (dopolnitel'nie dannie za I polugodie 1993 goda),* 1993, 5–6.
December 1993 regression: proportion of enterprises insolvent in January–August 1993, from Goskomstat Rossii, *Razvitie Ekonomicheskykh Reform v Regionakh Rossiiskoi Federatsii* (10) 1993, 61–62.
1995–96 regressions: percentage of enterprises insolvent in 1995, from TACIS, *Analiz Tendentsii Razvitia Regionov Rossii v 1992–1995 gg,* Moscow, March 1996, 116.

Wage Arrears

April 1993 regression: index of overdue payments for consumption per worker on 1/10/92, from Goskomstat Rossii, *Razvitie Ekonomicheskykh Reform v Regionov RF* 1993 (10): 67 (Russian Federation average = 1).
December 1993 regression: index of overdue payments for consumption per worker 1/10/93, (Russian Federation average = 1), Goskomstat Rossii, *Razvitie Ekonomicheskykh Reform v Regionov RF* 1993 (10): 67.
1995 regression: index of overdue payments for consumption per employee on 1/1/96 (RF average = 1), from TACIS, *Analiz Tendentsii Razvitia Regionov Rossii v 1992–1995 gg,* Moscow, March 1996, 113.
1996 regressions: overdue payments for consumption per employee as of June 1996, Goskomstat Rossii, *Sotsial'no-ekonomicheskoe Polozhenie Rossii,* 1996, presented in Yitzhak Brudny, "How and Why Russian Regions Vote: Regional Voting Patterns, 1991–96," Yale University, manuscript, 1996.

Percentage of Work Force in Agriculture

All regressions: percentage of work force in agriculture 1993, from Goskomstat Rosii, *Ekonomicheskoe polozhenie regionov RF,* 1994.

Region's Share in RF Raw Materials Output

All regressions: percentage of RF output of raw materials industries accounted for by region, from Goskomstat Rossii, *Ekonomicheskoe Polozhenie Regionov RF,* 1994, 49–50.

Exports Per Capita

April 1993 regression: region's exports per capita in 1992 (1,000 Rs per cap), from Goskomstat Rossii, *Rossiisky Statistichesky Yezhegodnik* 1995, 869.
December 1993: region's exports per capita in 1993 (1,000 Rs per cap), from Goskomstat Rossii, *Rossiisky Statistichesky Yezhegodnik* 1995, 869.
1995–96 regressions: region's exports in 1994 in 1,000 Rs per capita, from TACIS (op. cit., 142).

Value of Enterprises Privatized

April 1993 regression: value of privatized enterprises as of 1/1/93, in 1,000 Rs per regional inhabitant, calculated from Goskomimushchestva Rossii, *Panorama Privatizatsii,* January 1993, 70.
December 1993: charter capital of enterprises privatized in 1993, per regional inhabitant (1,000 Rs per cap), from Goskomstat Rossii, *Rossiisky Statistichesky Yezhegodnik* (1994).
1995–96 regressions: charter capital of enterprises privatized in 1993 and 1994, per regional inhabitant (1,000 Rs per cap): Goskomstat Rossii, *Rossiisky Statistichesky Yezhegodnik* 1994 and *Rossiisky Statistichesky Yezhegodnik* 1995, 694–96.

Proportion of Apartments Privatized

1993 regressions: calculated from *Razvitie Ekonomicheskykh Reform v Regionov RF* 1993 (6) 108–9.
1995–96 regressions: from Goskomstat Rossii, *Sotsialno-Ekonomicheskoe Polozhenie Rossii, ianvar-aprel 1995 g,* 1995, 296–97.

Percentage of Population Russian

New World Demographics, *The First Book of Demographics for the Republics of the Former Soviet Union, 1951–1990,* Shady Side, MD (1992).

Proportion of Population Above Working Age

All regressions: percentage of population 60 or older (for men), 55 or older (for women), as of 1994, Goskomstat Rossii, *Demograficheskiy Yezhegodnik RF 1993* 1994, 32.

Proportion of Population Below Age 16

All regressions: percentage of population 15 or younger as of 1994, Goskomstat Rossii, *Demograficheskiy Yezhegodnik RF 1993* 1994, 32.

212 Appendixes

Proportion of Population With Higher Education

All regressions: percentage of economically active population with higher education, as of Nov. 1, 1994, Goskomstat Rossii, *Rossiisky Statistichesky Yezhegodnik 1995* 1996, 550.

Pollution

All regressions: emission of pollutants from stationary sources into air 1994, in tons per thousand inhabitants, Goskomstat Rossii, *Rossiisky Statistichesky Yezhegodnik 1995* 1996, 676–78.

Crime

1993 regressions: crimes registered per thousand inhabitants, January–September 1993, Goskomstat Rossii, *Razvitie Ekonomicheskykh Reform v Regionov RF* 1993 (10): 130–31.
1995–96 regressions: crimes registered per 100,000 inhabitants in 1994, Goskomstat Rossii, *Rossiisky Statistichesky Yezhegodnik 1995* 1996, 625–27.

Recent Change in Life Expectancy

All regressions: change in life expectancy 1991–93; from *Demografichesky Yezhegodnik RF 1993* 1994, 84.

Refugees and Forced Migrants Per Capita

1993 regressions: number of refugees (forced migrants) registered, per 1,000 residents, July 1, 1993, from Federalnaya Migratsionnaya Sluzhba Rossii, *Vynuzhdennie pereselentsy v Rossii* 1995, 13.
1995–96 regressions: number of refugees and forced migrants as of April 1, 1995; from Federalnaya Migratsionnaya Sluzhba Rossii, *Vynuzhdennie pereselentsy v Rossii* 1995, 9.

Regional Budget Expenditures Per Capita

1993 regressions: regional budget expenditure per capita in 1991, from Philippe Le Houerou 1993, Annex 5, table 1.
1995 regression: regional budget expenditure per capita 1993, data provided by Aleksei Lavrov from Ministry of Finance and State Tax Service.
1996 regression: regional budget expenditure per capita 1994, data provided by Aleksei Lavrov from Ministry of Finance and State Tax Service.

Recent Change in Regional Budget Expenditure Per Capita

1993 regressions: estimated real change in regional budget expenditure per capita, 1991–92, deflated using change in CPI December 1992 over December 1991, expressed in 1992 1,000 Rs per capita, calculated from Le Houerou 1993, Annex 5.

1995 regression: estimated real change in regional budget expenditure per capita, 1993–94, deflated using change in average change in monthly CPI 1993–94, expressed in 1994 1,000 Rs per capita, from data provided by Aleksei Lavrov from Ministry of Finance and State Tax Service.

1996 regression: estimated real change in regional budget expenditure per capita, 1994–95, deflated by nationwide CPI December 1995/December 1994 (= 2.31 times), since data were not available on changes in CPI 1994–95 broken down by region, from data provided by Aleksei Lavrov from Ministry of Finance and State Tax Service.

Bilateral Power-Sharing Agreement Signed

Yeltsin had signed bilateral treaty with region by time of second round of 1996 presidential election, compiled from Federal Broadcast Information Service Daily Reports and other sources.

At Least One Presidential Decree or Government Resolution Passed on Economic Aid to Region

Up to June 16, 1996, for presidential decrees, and to June 11, 1996, for government resolutions; compiled from official publications of normative acts (*Sobranie Zakonodatel-nykh Aktov*). A presidential decree or government resolution (*postanovlenie*) was included if it mentioned a specific region (i.e., oblast, republic, etc.) in its title, with the following exceptions: acts on appointment or dismissal of the head of administration or other personnel changes, on the organization of elections in the region, on technical changes in the wording of housing law, on the Chechen war, on canceling local decrees, or on transferring shares to regional governments. These exceptions were made to ensure that decrees and resolutions reflected aid to the regions (also does not include decrees providing aid to broader areas such as Siberia or the Central Chernozem).

Pro-Yeltsin or Pro-Reform Vote Previous Time

1993 regressions: regional vote for Yeltsin in 1991 presidential election, from McFaul and Petrov 1995.

1995 regression: vote for Russia's Choice in December 1993 election (official results from Central Electoral Commission).

1996 election: vote of support for Yeltsin on question one in April 1993 referendum, from McFaul and Petrov 1995, 657–58.

TABLE C1. Characteristics of Russia's Regions

	Mean	Std. Dev.	Minimum	Maximum
Estimated change in average real income (June 92–June 93)	1.45	.30	.82	2.77
Change in average income as % of subsistence minimum, 1994–95	−65.85	34.61	−233.50	36.70
Unemployment August 1993 (%)	1.01	.87	.00	3.92
Unemployment 1995 (%)	3.28	3.39	.49	28.05
Proportion of enterprises insolvent Jan.–May 1993 (%)	19.4	8.8	6.8	50.9
Proportion of enterprises insolvent 1993 (%)	18.07	8.60	5.70	48.80
Proportion of enterprises insolvent 1995 (%)	40.88	13.26	15.00	75.00
Increase in CPI Dec. 1992/Dec. 1991, times	25.9	8.1	11.9	52.7
Increase in CPI 1993/92	10.0	2.09	6.70	17.80
Increase in CPI 1994/93	3.11	.28	2.63	4.01
Wage arrears 1992	1.15	1.44	.02	8.23
Wage arrears 1993	1.16	1.02	.01	6.23
Percent of working age population employed in agriculture	5.54	3.94	0	16.5
Region's share in total raw materials output (%)	1.28	4.02	0	33.80
% of apartments privatized 1993	9.2	6.9	.7	38.2
% of apartments privatized 1995	33.3	11.6	2.0	74.0
Regional budget expenditure 1991 (Rs p.c.)	1,338	733	663	4,488
Exports per capita 1992 (1,000 Rs p.c.)	9.6	13.5	.01	69.2
Exports per capita 1993	89.3	129.3	0	825.0
Exports per capita 1994	292.2	335.0	0	1,769.7
Regional budget expenditure 1993 (1,000 Rs p.c.)	340.1	462.4	127.6	4127.0
Regional budget expenditure 1994 (1,000 Rs p.c.)	935.8	1,068.3	386.4	7,639.0
Change in estimated real regional budget expenditure 1991–92	−19.7	27.0	−168.3	9.6

TABLE C1.—*Continued*

	Mean	Std. Dev.	Minimum	Maximum
Change in estimated real regional budget expenditure 1993–94	−116.0	634.7	−5,360.9	1,192.9
Change in estimated real regional budget expenditure 1994–95	−282.1	1,016.6	−8,462.2	1,020.4
Value of privatized enterprises as of Jan. 1, 1993 (1,000 Rs per cap)	1.41	2.13	.02	17.06
Value of enterprises privatized in 1993 (1,000 Rs per cap)	3.47	4.56	0	37.18
Value of enterprises privatized in 1993–94 (1,000 Rs per cap)	7.82	12.54	.59	91.15
Percent of population Russian	75.6	21.3	9.2	97.4
Percent of population above working age	18.0	5.7	3.8	26.9
Percent of population below age 16	25.1	4.1	18.9	36.5
Percent of economically active population with some higher education	16.5	4.1	10.1	38.4
Change in life expectancy 1991–93	−3.6	1.3	−6.6	.4
Refugees per 1,000 residents 1993	2.02	2.05	.03	10.72
Refugees per 1,000 residents 1994	5.23	8.17	0	69.82
Crimes registered per 1,000 residents 1993	13.8	4.4	6.8	24.9
Emission of pollutants 1994 (tons per 1,000 inhabitants)	177.0	224.5	1.6	1,194.5
Estimated output 1993 (1,000 Rs per cap)	969.3	455.9	210.4	2,567.1

	% Yes	% No	N
Region Predominantly Christian	83	17	76

APPENDIX D

Appendix to Chapter 5

Note: What Determined How Regional Delegates to the National Parliament Voted?

Chapter 5 examined the constraints and objectives of regional executive officials. But how do these differ from those of regional deputies to the national parliament? One might expect such regional representatives to be more loyal to the legislative branch and the national parliamentary leadership than to President Yeltsin and his government. On the other hand, a parliamentary delegation that contained the region's governor might be influenced by him to take positions closer to those of the national executive branch. But most of the same factors that seemed plausible determinants of governors' strategies—local public opinion, personal background, institutional factors, fiscal dependence, and administrative status of republic—might be expected also to influence regional deputies' political behavior.

The Russian political scientist Alexander Sobyanin and colleagues compiled ratings for the regional delegations to the different meetings of the larger parliament, the Congress of People's Deputies, on the basis of how their members voted on roll-call votes (see Sobyanin et al. 1993). He calculated an index of political "temperature," which measures on average how a region's deputies broke down between the president's and opposition sides on different issues. It ranges from +100, indicating unwavering support for Yeltsin's side, to −100, indicating unwavering opposition.[1] This index makes it possible to calculate in relative terms the degree to which each delegation's voting behavior changed between 1991 and 1993. The mean rating of regional delegations in 1991 was −7 (i.e., opposing Yeltsin's side slightly more often than supporting it); by 1993 it had dropped to −37.

I used ordinary least squares regression to explore which factors were associated with changes in the "temperature" of the region's deputies to the central parliament. The 1993 roll-call voting rating was regressed on a range of independent variables, controlling for the 1991 rating. Results are shown in table D1. Column 1 shows the estimates when all relevant factors are included; column 2 gives estimates when all independent variables that do not significantly improve the fit of the regression (as judged by an F-test, at the .10 level) are excluded.

Looking at these estimates, it is striking how similar the determinants of regional delegation voting appear to have been to those of regional governor strategy analyzed in chapter 5. Again, recent changes in the regional population's voting seemed to influence politicians. The delegates from regions where voters' approval of Yeltsin had recently increased were very significantly more likely to vote on the side supported by Yeltsin on

TABLE D1. Which Regional Delegations to the 1993 Congress of People's Deputies Voted with Yeltsin's Side? (OLS regression coefficients: Dependent variable is degree to which regional parliamentary delegation voted with the president's side, 1993.)

	(1)	(2)
Regional Public Opinion		
Yeltsin vote June 1991	.52	
	(.28)	
Pro-Yeltsin vote *rose* June 91–	21.55***	16.76**
April 93	(5.86)	(4.89)
Background of Deputies		
Percentage who were (still)	−20.63	
Communist Party members,	(19.17)	
Feb. 91		
Percentage of Russian	11.43	
nationality	(16.64)	
Relations with Regional Executive		
Governor was a member of the	15.26**	13.87**
delegation	(5.08)	(4.90)
Region's Dependence on Central Subsidies		
Central subventions as percentage of	.25	
total regional tax revenue, 1992	(.17)	
Republic Status	−18.25*	−22.59***
	(8.95)	(5.34)
Degree to which Parliamentary	.40***	.53***
Delegation voted with Yeltsin's	(.10)	(.07)
side, 1991		
Constant	−71.48*	−43.17***
	(32.01)	(4.64)
Adjusted R^2	.544	.535
N	78	78

Note: standard errors in parentheses.
*$p < .05$ **$p < .01$ ***$p < .001$

roll-call votes in the Congress. This provides some quite impressive evidence of democratic influences at work.[2] As before, the evidence suggested different political processes in regions of different administrative status. Delegations from the republics, regardless of their ethnic composition and the recent voting history of their constituents, were very significantly more likely to vote against Yeltsin's side. This seems to add evidence for the hypothesis that regional political elites in the republics are more conservative, or they have political resources that make it more rational for them to oppose Yeltsin than for the leaders of oblasts and krais.

The background of delegates—whether their levels of Communist Party membership or ethnicity—did not bear any significant relationship to their voting. But their institutional integration did: those delegations that included the region's governor, and therefore had closer ties to the regional level executive branch, were more likely to vote with the side supported by the head of the nation's executive. While insignificant, the coefficient estimate for subventions suggests that dependence on central transfers may have reduced the likelihood the delegation would vote against Yeltsin.

So the way a region's parliamentary representatives vote seems to be shaped by some of the same factors that determine whether its governor sides with Yeltsin or his opposition; and among them are the expressed positions of the region's voters.

Explanation of Variables in Table 5.1

Voting Data. Both for 1991 and 1993 expressed as percentage of total ballots cast (i.e., including spoiled ballots). Data available in McFaul and Petrov 1995, 655–58.

Governors' Backgrounds. Compiled from Barsenkov 1993 and other sources.

Governor's Institutional History. Compiled from Barsenkov 1993 and other sources.

Fiscal Dependence of Region. Data on 1992 subventions from Ministry of Finance, provided to author by Leonid Smirnyagin; data on regional tax revenue, from Le Houerou 1993.

Explanation of Variables in Table 5.2

Voting Data. Source and classification of reform parties from Clem and Craumer 1995b. Reform parties in 1993: Russia's Choice, Russian Movement for Democratic Reform (RDDR), Party of Russian Unity and Accord (PRES), Yabloko; Reform parties in 1995: Russia's Democratic Choice, RDDR, PRES, Yabloko, Our Home Is Russia, Worker's Self-Government, Pamfilova/Gurov/Lysenko, Forward Russia, Common Cause, CD Union. 1993 Referendum data in McFaul and Petrov 1995, 655–58.

Governors' Background. Compiled from Barsenkov 1993, McFaul and Petrov 1995, and other sources.

Governor Popularly Elected. Listing prepared by Robert Orttung, OMRI.

Central Budget Transfers and Regional Tax Revenues. From data provided to author by Aleksei Lavrov, from Ministry of Finance and State Tax Service.

Yeltsin Regional Visits during 1996 Campaign. Compiled from Moscow Carnegie Center, *Prezidentskie Vybory v Rossii,* June 1996, no. 9, and press reports.

Bilateral Power-sharing Agreement, Aid Decrees. See appendix C (to chap. 4).

Notes on Data Used in Table D1

Voting Data. See above.

Sobyanin Ratings. Sobyanin et al. 1993.

Fiscal Dependence. See above.

Governor Elected to 1990 Parliament. See above.

Percentage of Congress Delegation Party Members as of February 1991. Supreme Soviet RSFSR, *Spisok Narodnykh Deputatov RSFSR na 12 Fevralya 1991 g,* Moscow, 1991.

Percentage of Congress Delegation Russian Nationality. Supreme Soviet RSFSR, *Spisok Narodnykh Deputatov RSFSR na 12 Fevralya 1991 g,* Moscow, 1991.

Notes

Chapter 1

1. Remarks of Rafael Khakimov, an adviser to President Shaimiev, reported in Rutland 1996.
2. Russia in the mid-1990s was divided administratively into 21 ethnically defined republics (20 if one does not include Chechnya), 10 ethnically defined autonomous okrugs, one ethnically defined autonomous oblast, and 57 non–ethnically defined units—oblasts, krais, and the two capital cities of Moscow and St. Petersburg (see chap. 2).
3. *Moskovskie Novosti,* Sept. 19, 1993, A2. See also Wallich 1994.
4. See, for example, Sachs (1995), who argued in 1994 that the kind of competitive tax withholding that had undermined the Yugoslav federal government in 1989 and that of the Soviet Union in 1991 "could still threaten the Russian Federation."
5. On "tipping" games, see Schelling 1978, 101–2.
6. For instance, Layard and Parker 1996, 317–18; Moltz 1996.
7. *Integration* is a term used by different writers in different ways. I use it in a relatively narrow sense synonymous with state survival, and as an antonym for *disintegration.* In what follows, *integration* refers to the absence of secession by a territorial unit within the state, or of violent conflict involving a significant proportion of the population over the issue of secession. Thus, the United States in the 1860s, Spain since 1975, and Russia in the mid-1990s faced problems of integration of differing degrees of severity (Spain with regard to ETA, Russia with regard to Chechnya). Nevertheless, none of them disintegrated.
8. For instance, Birch 1989, 8.
9. Polanyi 1957a, 1957b, chap. 4. Polanyi also discusses another mode of integration that does not require central organization—reciprocity (1957b, chap. 4). But this mode of integration requires a high degree of symmetry in the structure of society, less likely to be found in modern, complex systems.
10. For a useful review, see Bolton, Roland, and Spolaore 1996.
11. See, for instance, Oates 1972.
12. For instance, Lemco 1991.
13. For instance, Young 1976, 65; Stuart Woolf, "Introduction," in Woolf 1996, esp. 29–32; Hobsbawm and Ranger 1983; Barth 1969; Przeworski et al. 1995, 20.
14. As Washbrook writes of South Asia: "Communities form and unform, define and redefine themselves, in relation to this struggle. They exist, essentially, for the purpose of opposing and demanding a share of the privileges seen to be enjoyed by 'others' and

dissolve or reconstitute themselves as the context changes and throws up new 'others' for them to oppose. . . . In Tamil society, then, all categories of community and identity and, related to them, all evaluations of culture and history are permeated by politics and exist in flux" (Washbrook 1989, 230–31, quoted in Mitra 1992, 145.) For an interesting exploration of how different Russian diaspora communities in several former Soviet republics make such identity choices, see Laitin 1996.

15. See, for instance, Mazrui 1972; Hobsbawm and Ranger 1983; Brass 1974.

16. It is possible that respondents felt such an answer more prudent, but it is highly unlikely that at this point, after several years of glasnost they felt any fear of reprisals should they have said they thought of themselves as "Russian."

17. The Russian saying "Scratch a Russian and you find a Tatar" long ago became a cliché.

18. White Southerners were not ethnically distinct from white Northerners.

19. The exact vote was 138,653 to 70,706. See Birch 1989, 187.

20. Carrère d'Encausse 1981; Donald Horowitz (1992) also anticipated particularly severe separatist pressures in Central Asia, though for somewhat different reasons.

21. Figures are reported in *Pravda,* Mar. 27, 1991, 1–2. The vote may certainly have been less free in the Southern republics than in the more developed ones, so this may indicate the preferences of the political leadership to a greater extent than the population.

22. Ordeshook 1996; also see Riker 1987, chap. 11, for a slightly different view of the importance of party structure in federations.

23. Tarrow draws a similar distinction between administrative, growth-oriented integration through the state bureaucracy in France and clientelistic integration through parties in Italy (Tarrow 1977).

24. *OMRI Russian Regional Report,* Oct. 30, 1996.

25. *Federal Broadcast Information Service Daily Report: Eurasia,* Nov. 1, 1993, 37–39 (FBIS-SOV-93-209).

26. *Kommersant-Daily* Nov. 4, 1993, 4, translated in *Federal Broadcast Information Service Daily Report: Eurasia,* Nov. 4, 1993, 56 (FBIS-SOV-93-212).

27. Author's interview with Ramazan Abdulatipov, Moscow, July 8, 1996.

28. Average of imports and exports of goods between constituent units, from IMF 1992b, table 1, 37.

29. OMRI *Russian Regional Report,* Mar. 26, 1997.

30. Institute for East-West Studies, *Russian Regional Report,* Apr. 24, 1997.

31. Interestingly, the Soviet Union's political institutions *have* been considered by some to have been consociational, rendering its disintegration even more surprising.

32. See, for instance, Yeltsin's own account in Yeltsin 1994.

33. Was this a deliberate, consciously adopted strategy or one that evolved out of a series of improvisations? There were elements of both, but I would emphasize the latter. Analyzing Yeltsin's thinking at any given time is a challenging task, and on this point he was particularly ambivalent in public statements. On the one hand, he did grasp intuitively (where Gorbachev had not) that accommodating most of the demands of regions and ethnic republics would alleviate tensions far more effectively than attempting to intimidate them. There was definitely an element of political strategy and quite acute judgment in his courting of the more mobilized regions and in his assessment of regional politicians' credibility. He was skilled at combining "carrots" with the threat of a "stick," and at judg-

ing just how large the carrots had to be. On the other hand, while most of the time playing this game skillfully, he seems at times to have felt personally embarrassed by it. He expressed something close to shame at his own acts of monetary largesse and seemed to accept the arguments that such a strategy was economically inefficient. He described his regional policy as "papering over the cracks" and flirted with ideas of a more drastic consolidation of regions. In Chechnya in 1994, he blundered so dramatically, completely reversing his previously successful strategy, that one cannot help wondering how much he understood about the successes he had earlier achieved by instinct. In Yeltsin's entourage, there were deep disagreements over regional strategy. Some would probably recognize the logic of the argument I present. Others would be exasperated by the suggestion that the apparent chaos concealed a functional logic. Similar disagreements could be found in the parliament and in most of the inner circles of Moscow officialdom.

34. Tatarstan was the first to sign a bilateral power-sharing agreement with Moscow in February 1994. It was soon followed by North Ossetia, Kabardino-Balkaria, Sakha, Buryatia, and Bashkortostan. By early 1996, the center had also signed pacts demarcating divisions of jurisdiction and powers with several oblasts (Kaliningrad, Sverdlovsk, Orenburg, and Krasnodar Krai). See Orlov 1996 and *OMRI Daily Digest,* Jan. 30, 1996.

35. The chairman of Tyva's parliament was also a leader of a Tyvan nationalist organization, but not the republic's president.

36. *OMRI Daily Digest,* Feb. 14, 1996.

37. Interfax, Kazan, Feb. 2, 1996, published in FBIS-SOV-96-024, Feb. 5, 1996, 47. At rallies in Tatarstan in May, Shaimiev reportedly observed numerous communist flags with the hammer and sickle, but no exemplars of the green, white, and red flag of Tatarstan (Gershaft 1996).

38. Interfax, Moscow, Feb. 9, 1996, published in FBIS-SOV-96-028, Feb. 9, 1996, 43–44.

39. RIA, June 5, 1996.

40. *Rossiiskie Vesti,* "Compact with the Urals Is a Guarantee of the Federation's Stability (Interview with Eduard Rossel, governor of Sverdlovsk Province and leader of the Transformation of Russia movement)," Jan. 19, 2, translated in CDPSP 48 (3) (1996): 21.

41. Two caveats are important. While the study examines empirically the goals and strategies of regional and central leaders, it treats regional populations nonstrategically. I do not explicitly examine the rationality of individuals' voting or protest actions, nor do I consider how individuals reach decisions about political participation. A second omission concerns the structure of the central and regional state. The book's analysis of conflict and cooperation between the executive and legislative branches at both the central and regional levels is limited. While I believe that competition between the two branches—empirically, a very important aspect of Russia's political history in the early 1990s—increased the incentives for their leaders to act in the ways I describe, I do not demonstrate this. A more comprehensive—and much longer—study would also incorporate this part of the political process.

Chapter 2

1. This reflected the situation as of late 1998 (Chechnya is counted as one of the ethnic republics, though its status was actually unresolved). For useful discussions of the

administrative status of the various regions, see Slider 1994; Wallich 1994, 23. In what follows, I use the word *regions* to refer to republics, oblasts, krais, autonomous oblasts, autonomous okrugs, and the two federal cities of Moscow and St. Petersburg. In this, I depart from common usage, which more often classifies the oblasts and krais as "regions" and contrasts them with the "republics," other ethnically defined units, and the two cities. Where I wish to draw narrower distinctions, I use the specific units' names (e.g., *oblast, krai*).

2. This is based on details provided in McFaul and Petrov 1995. For one example, see Fainsod's account of administrative reform in Smolensk and surrounding regions (1958, 52, 61). Some additional details are in Ushkalov and Khorev 1989.

3. These were called "autonomous republics" to distinguish them from the 15 "union republics" (Kozlov 1988, 32–35).

4. According to the RSFSR Constitution, state and administrative bodies of the autonomous oblasts had the right to communicate with corresponding bodies of the RSFSR either through the superior krai bodies or directly. In the Council of Nationalities of the USSR Supreme Soviet, the central parliament's upper house, each union republic received 32 deputies, each autonomous republic 11, each autonomous oblast 5, and each autonomous okrug 1 (*The Soviet Constitution: A Dictionary,* 1986, 20, 274.)

5. See, for instance, Remnick 1994, chap. 10. On more criminal aspects of these local cartels, see Vaksberg 1991.

6. For a good discussion, see Paretskaya 1996.

7. Author's interview with Yuri Blokhin, deputy governor of Tambov Oblast, June 26, 1996.

8. *Moscow News,* 1992, no. 10, quoted in Solnick 1995, 57.

9. Teague 1994a, 31; Sakwa 1993, 127. Similar ideas periodically re-emerge. The proposals of the extreme nationalist Vladimir Zhirinovsky to eliminate ethnic republics are widely reported. However, he is not alone in advocating such reforms. Anatoli Sobchak, then mayor of St. Petersburg, proposed in February 1995 reorganizing the administration of Russia to re-create the *gubernii* of imperial Russia (Tolz 1996, 44). Presidential adviser Sergei Shakhrai suggested (also in February 1995) "merging the 89 currently existing republics and regions into a dozen larger administrative formations, each combining prosperous as well as poor federation members" (Tolz 1996, 44).

10. Author's interview with Ramazan Abdulatipov, Moscow, July 8, 1996.

11. Interview with Leonid Smirnyagin, July 9, 1996, Moscow. Smirnyagin said he had opposed the selective granting of special benefits associated with such an approach, but had become reconciled to it as the lengthening list of regions thus favored eroded the particular advantages.

12. Interview with Anatoly Moiseev, adviser to the chairman of the government of Karelia, Petrozavodsk, July 2, 1996.

13. Interview with Yuri Blokhin, first deputy head of administration, Tambov Oblast, June 26, 1996, Tambov.

14. Abdulatipov, interviewed in *Pravda,* Feb. 19, 1992, 1–2; translated in *Central Digest of the Post-Soviet Press* 44 (8) (1992): 1–3.

15. By late October 1991, practically all the Soviet republics had accumulated large arrears in remittances to the Union budget: Russia owed 29 billion rubles, Ukraine 8 billion, Kazakhstan 1.5 billion, Uzbekistan 985 million, and Lithuania 720 million. The

same month, the Russian Finance Ministry froze the bank accounts of several central ministries, and in November President Yeltsin announced that Russia would stop funding the operations of more than 70 Union ministries. See Diuk and Karatnycky 1993, 37.

16. "*Ya uveren v svoey Pobede*" (interview with President Yeltsin), *Delovie Lyudi,* May 1996, 8–11.

17. Author's interview with Ramazan Abdulatipov, July 8,1996, Moscow.

18. Laba 1996, 5. Or, as Ruslan Aushev, the president of Ingushetia put it in the context of Russia's internal order: "We are a little republic which would of course be easily conquered by Russia. But I do not think that the Russian Army has the power to put down all the other republics if they rise up" (FBIS *Daily Report Central Eurasia,* Jan. 23, 1995).

19. An example of the mixed interests and shifting positions of the Siberian leaders was presented by the remarks of Krasnoyarsk governor Valerii Zubov when deputy premier Anatoli Chubais visited in 1997. First, Zubov reportedly "warned that if the federal government did not stop giving preferences to such regions as Tatarstan, Bashkortostan, Sakha, Moscow, and Ingushetiya, it could not count on the support of the Siberian governors." Later, he found time to attack the privileges received by some of these same Siberian governors, complaining "that Tyva and Altai [also members of Siberian Agreement] received the most generous subsidies from Moscow, while his Krasnoyarsk Krai was a donor—giving more than it received in return." Institute for East-West Studies, *Russian Regional Report,* May 15, 1997.

20. Personal pique may also have played a role, though it is hard to evaluate its significance. President Mintimer Shaimiev of Tatarstan met with Yeltsin in early 1994 and discussed Chechnya. In Shaimiev's account: "It was as if he was asking himself the question, as we were talking. He said to me: 'What do you think? Probably I should negotiate with Dudaev.' Then Boris Nikolaevich said: 'I want to meet with Dudaev. But not all in the Security Council share my inclination.' Two or three weeks passed. There were sharp attacks on Yeltsin from Dudaev's side. At the end of May Yeltsin came to [Tatarstan], and I asked him: 'You wanted to meet, but the situation is getting worse. What happened?' 'You can see,' he replied. 'It's not possible to meet. It has come to insults toward the President of Russia'" (interview with Shaimiev, Russian television, "*Moment Istiny,*" Aug. 2, 1997).

21. The Yeltsin regime in Moscow reportedly also hoped that because of his weak links to local power structures Dudaev would prove more clubbable than his predecessor, Doku Zavgayev, who had played the nomenklatura nationalist strategy quite ably until the August 1991 coup attempt (Shoumikhin 1996, 8). See also Khazanov 1995, 216.

22. Interview with Shaimiev, Russian television, "*Moment Istiny,*" Aug. 2, 1997.

23. Author's interview with Ramazan Abdulatipov, July 8, 1996, Moscow. Dudaev may, of course, have been putting a brave face on a situation of obvious weakness. In President Shaimiev's interesting formulation, Dudaev found himself by this point "a general in whose hands remained nothing but weapons" (interview with Shaimiev, Russian television, "*Moment Istiny,*" Aug. 2, 1997).

24. *Nezavisimaya Gazeta,* Aug. 12, 1, translated in CDPSP 46 (32) (1994): 12.

25. The phrase is from *The Economist,* "Why Chechnya Matters," Dec. 17, 1994, 50.

26. *The Economist,* "Why Chechnya Matters," Dec. 17, 1994, 49.
27. On these various ideas, see Thomas 1995a; Shoumikhin 1996.
28. *Segodnya,* Jan. 12, 1995, 1, translated in CDPSP 47 (3) (1995): 14.

Chapter 3

1. Interview with Leonid Smirnyagin, July 1993, Moscow.
2. This was claimed by a Finance Ministry report, cited in Hanson 1994, 19.
3. This chapter draws upon work reported in Treisman 1996b and 1998c. I am grateful to the *British Journal of Political Science* and Cambridge University Press for permission to excerpt from these.
4. While the State Tax Service was nominally under complete federal control from 1991 and local branches were in theory subordinate to the headquarters in Moscow, in practice local tax officers retained loyalties to and dependence on the oblast administrations (Wallich 1994, 27; author's interviews).
5. This may merely have accelerated a process of decentralization of fiscal authority noted since Stalin's death (Bahry 1987a, chap. 1).
6. From World Bank operational data; see table 3.1. These figures do not include transfers between the federal and regional/local budgets.
7. The Finance Ministry discontinued using expenditure norms in 1988, according to Martinez-Vazquez 1994, 111; however, oblast and rayon governments continue to use them to make a case for greater tax retention or transfers. In any case, the norms traditionally employed were only for recurrent—not capital—expenditures and represented estimated operating costs of running existing facilities. They, thus, reinforced whatever pattern of distribution had resulted from past capital investment.
8. Unfortunately, no comprehensive official accounting is available. In what follows, I draw on the estimates and analysis of Freinkman and Titov 1994; Le Houerou 1995; and Lavrov 1995a, 1995b, 1995c; as well as World Bank operational data as of April 1997.
9. Calculated from Freinkman and Titov 1994 and Le Houerou 1995, table A4. In 1992, total transfers are estimated by Freinkman and Titov at 19.44 percent of GDP. However, this only includes a Central Bank credit total of 1.98 trillion rubles. The IMF estimates total Central Bank credits for the year at 2.8 trillion rubles (Le Houerou 1995, table A1). When its credit figures are used, the transfer total rises to 23.98 percent of GDP. Federal off-budget fund spending is estimated at 9.56 percent of GDP (territorial off-budget fund spending has been subtracted from the totals in Le Houerou 1995, table A4. Unlike the figures in table 3.1, this does not include import subsidies). Federal tax revenues remitted by regions were estimated at 13.48 percent and federal off-budget fund revenues at 12.27 percent. (Unlike the revenue figures in table 3.1, these estimates of federal tax and off-budget fund revenues do not contain tax revenues of foreign trade, not remitted by the regions, or nontax revenues.) The 13.48 percent figure is calculated from Le Houerou 1995, table A1, as total tax revenues plus intergovernmental transfers minus taxes on foreign economic activities.
10. Center-region transfers estimated at 7.8 percent of GDP. Federal off-budget fund spending is estimated at 7.92 percent.
11. Calculated from Le Houerou 1995, tables A3–4, and World Bank operational

data. Federal tax revenues remitted by regions in 1994 are estimated at 9.4 percent of GDP (from World Bank operational data); intergovernmental transfers to federal budget and federal off-budget fund revenues are estimated at 9.3 percent. (Unlike the revenue figures in table 3.1, these estimates of federal tax revenues do not contain revenues from foreign trade taxes, which are not remitted by the regions, or nontax revenues.)

12. If additional tax breaks to specific regions extended by the Ministry of Finance after the budget had been enacted are included among center-region budget flows, the 1994 total comes to 3.9 percent of GDP. The total budget transfers dropped somewhat in 1995 and 1996.

13. Estimates from Freinkman and Titov 1994 and Le Houerou 1995.

14. According to the Russian Agricultural Bank, of 120 billion rubles provided in soft credits for the spring 1992 sowing season, only 71 billion rubles were returned (Yasin 1993a, 29–30). In the run up to the 1996 presidential election, Yeltsin wrote off the entire debt of the agroindustrial complex on all kinds of centralized credits extended since 1992—a sum assessed at about 21 trillion rubles (Bekker 1996).

15. Yasin et al. put the total value of export-import benefits for regions and enterprises for the year at 700 billion rubles, or 3.9 percent of GDP (1993a, 29).

16. In discussing "winners" and "losers" from central fiscal transfers, an important complication is the impact that regional transfers (and spending) may have *outside* the recipient region. Public finance specialists note that spillovers often lead to patterns of "benefit incidence" that differ from the actual pattern of transfers (see, for instance, Bennett 1980, chap. 9). This is probably also the case in Russia. This study, however, focuses on the observable relationships between the parts of transfers that do not "spill over," rates of regional spending, regional voting, and political strategies. The significance of transfers might be even greater were there no spillovers. Yet, even with them, relationships between transfers and other variables can be observed.

17. This equaled about $220 per capita at the average exchange rate for the year.

18. The coefficient of variation, a measure of dispersion, is the standard deviation divided by the mean.

19. If Alaska is excluded, the coefficient of variation is only .19. Russian figures from Le Houerou 1995.

20. For example, Johnston 1978; Gottschalk 1981; Friedland and Wong 1983; and the other studies cited in Rich 1989.

21. Liebowitz found that while there was some redistribution of investment funding to less developed parts of the USSR in the 1950s through mid-1970s, after that investment priorities focused on more resource-rich and industrially developed regions (1996, 159–84). Of course, there is considerable evidence that, both in socialist and market systems, much redistribution that is publicly justified in terms of alleviating need in fact favors less needy groups (see Szelenyi 1978, 1983; Kornai 1992, chap. 13; Tullock 1983).

22. On tax collection effort, see, for instance, works of Roy Bahl (1994) and James Tong (1994).

23. For one example of such claims, see an interview with the finance minister, Boris Fyodorov, in mid-1993 (Bekker 1993b). Fyodorov accuses the agrarian lobby of pressing for credits and subsidies with "hysterical speeches" and "picket lines of people with pitchforks."

24. In the rueful account of one Economics Ministry department head, "what gener-

ates the most force is not logical arguments but lobbying—who phoned whom, who put pressure on whom" (Yanovsky 1993). According to former Finance Minister Boris Fyodorov: "our budgets are always made by lobbies" (Ostankino television, Apr. 10, 1994, quoted in Hanson 1994, 19).

25. See, for example, Bekker 1993a. A considerable lore has developed around the logistics of such visits in Russia. Indeed, one political geographer says special teams of handlers accompanied Yeltsin on visits to the regions in the early 1990s, with instructions never to leave him alone with local officials. Yeltsin himself has regretfully acknowledged his role as an "ambulance," flying to troubled regions with shipments of cash (*Trud* 1994). Southern regions such as Krasnodar, where government leaders like to vacation, are rumored to do particularly well. During a vacation in Sochi, Yeltsin reportedly agreed to a series of measures proposed to him by the region's governor, ranging from financial aid to a bid to host the 2002 Winter Olympics. "If the state's top men continue to take regular vacations on our coast," one local journalist gleefully observed, "the Kuban will soon become the most prosperous region in Russia" (Alekseyeva 1994). Ivan Rybkin, the speaker of the State Duma, was quite blunt in his remarks on arriving in Petropavlovsk-Kamchatsky during a tour of Siberia and the Far East in the summer of 1994. His party of legislators had come, he said, because they wanted "advice on the best way to divide the pie which is called the budget" (Itar-Tass, Moscow, 8:02, June 26, 1994). One presumes that they got it.

26. According to Jon Elster, bargaining power is the capacity "to harm the other party without conferring excessive harm on oneself." See Elster 1992, 175.

27. On strikes, Vladimir Mau, then economics adviser to acting prime minister Gaidar, explained in July 1992 how regional leaders bargained using their leverage over local enterprises as a weapon. "The head of local administration demands this and this and this, and . . . threatens to bring his enterprises out on strike" (Mau 1992).

28. Boris Fyodorov, the former finance minister, in 1996 described the government as caving in abjectly to the demands of striking coal miners. "These guys are so afraid of the miners, the moment somebody announces a strike they promise to pay. Of course, they do not pay on time. Then in the next six months a new wave starts" (Gordon 1996b). He suggested recruiting Margaret Thatcher to overhaul the Russian coal industry.

29. The data on transfers and tax payments were obtained from Leonid Smirnyagin and Aleksei Lavrov of the President's Analytical Apparatus, who obtained them from the Russian Ministry of Finance and the State Tax Service. For full details, see appendix B.

30. For details of their construction, see appendix B. In various cases, I tried several specifications of the variable in order to reduce the chance of rejecting a hypothesis because the indicator I chose was faulty (see notes to table 3.3). It might seem strange to include such a comprehensive set of explanatory variables in the long regressions. Some early readers of the manuscript expressed surprise at the number of predictors. In fact, this is preferable on statistical grounds. To omit any variable that theoretically might explain the pattern of transfers is to risk "omitted variable bias"—i.e., biased estimates of the coefficients on independent variables that are included. On the other hand, including additional explanatory variables merely reduces the efficiency of the estimates—i.e., it makes it less likely that any estimates will be found to be significant. In this sense, by including more variables, I am in fact stacking the deck *against* my main hypothe-

ses. It may make sense to adopt a slightly higher criterion for significance when more independent variables are included to compensate for the increased chance of uncovering a spurious correlation. Most of the major results presented below are so extremely significant that they would still be significant given a much stricter criterion.

31. The individual transfer streams for which data were available in 1992 were: subventions, budget investments, payments from the government's and parliament's reserve funds, special benefits (for the first nine months of 1992), and some credits. Together, for all regions, these came to 1.45 trillion rubles, or about 41 percent of the total fiscal transfers estimated by Freinkman and Titov (1994, 15). The included transfers for 1994 were: subventions, first quarter subsidies, direct payments from the Regional Support Fund, indirect payments from the Regional Support Fund (made by subsequent increases in regions' permitted share of VAT retained), net mutual payments, short-term budget loans, and payments to closed cities made by the Defense and Atomic Energy Ministries. The transfers for both years were predominantly allocated by the central government and parliament rather than the Central Bank.

32. In fact, the volume of central credits was sharply reduced from late 1993. Descriptive statistics for the variables are provided in appendix B.

33. However, the voting variable *is* significant at the .03 level in 1996 if one controls in model 2 for the region's northerly location, itself positively, though not significantly, related to net transfers. Where not otherwise indicated, I refer to significance levels in the model 2 regressions.

34. I also tried substituting a variable measuring Yeltsin's 1991 margin of victory for the pro-Yeltsin vote in the 1992 regression. If central allocators concentrated resources on marginal constituencies, one would expect this factor to be significant. In fact, it was far less significant than the Yeltsin vote variable (coefficient of -0.17, significant at $p = .10$, in model 1) and the regression had a lower adjusted R^2-value. There was no discernible policy—either by supporters or opponents of Yeltsin—of concentrating resources on marginal constituencies.

The association between anti-Yeltsin or antireform voting and higher transfers might have two explanations: (1) Yeltsin and the reformers might be trying to shore up support in hostile regions, or (2) the opposition parliamentary leadership might be trying to reward its supporters. In 1992, the fact that anti-Yeltsin voting was most significantly related to "special benefits," a category of transfers most controlled by the president and government, suggests the first interpretation (see table 3.4). There was not a significant relationship between voting and payments from the Supreme Soviet Reserve Fund. In 1994, a lower vote the previous year for Russia's Choice was followed by higher payments from the Regional Support Fund. Since allocations under this fund were first calculated and adjusted by the Ministry of Finance and then voted on by the parliament, it is harder to disentangle the effect of pressures in the different institutions.

35. A nonlog formulation of the strike variable is even more significant if one extreme outlier, Kemerovo, is excluded from the data. In 1991, the coal-mining region of Kemerovo lost about eight times more man-days to strikes than the next most strike-prone region. Not surprisingly, it did not receive eight times more in net transfers.

36. Regression analysis is, of course, insufficient to prove a causal relationship. But it suggests a strong hypothesis, especially when other theoretically plausible causes are

controlled for and previous-year values of independent variables are used where possible and appropriate to reduce problems of endogeneity.

37. Variables were constructed to measure the relevant population proportions in the ethnic republics and autonomous okrugs and coded zero in the nonethnic oblasts and krais.

38. Details of the dates of sovereignty declarations are provided in appendix B.

39. Under the regulations, regions qualified for aid from the Regional Support Fund if they met one of two criteria. "Needy" regions were those that had per capita budget revenues the previous year lower than 95 percent of the country's average. "Especially needy" regions were those whose expenditures the previous year exceeded the budget revenues of the average region (see Le Houerou 1995, 20; Lavrov 1995b; Treisman 1998c).

40. This is taken from the model 2 estimate for total RSF transfers in appendix B, table B1. Since the criterion for classification as "especially needy" was simply to have spent a lot in the base year, fiscal transfers under the Fund actually favored big spending regions.

41. Transfers under the Fund may also have responded to strikes or governor opposition to Yeltsin, though these results are only marginally significant.

42. Politicians were quite blunt in suggesting that arbitrary political adjustments were frequently made, concealed by the technical complexity of the formula calculations. Oleg Morozov, head of the Russian Regions faction in the State Duma, complained, "People from the Ministry of Finance have explained many times how the calculations are made, and even with a Ph.D. in political science I did not understand anything" (author's interview, State Duma, Moscow, July 7, 1997). Mikhail Motorin, head of staff of the Duma Budget Committee, was quite categorical: "There isn't any formula—just a certain balancing of interests, first in the Ministry of Finance and then here [in the Duma]" (author's interview with Mikhail Motorin, State Duma, Moscow, Aug. 14, 1997).

43. The apparently lower 1992 transfers to agricultural regions may have been compensated by targeted agricultural subsidies and credits, for which regional breakdowns were not available.

44. The lack of clear signs of the influence of access recalls Bahry's pre-perestroika conclusion that fragmented institutions of government provide a range of alternative niches for would-be lobbyists. Rivalry between central ministries and departments, and the increasing complexity of national leaders' goals, created a "multitude of windows— and the 'art of being a successful advocate in Soviet politics is to find them'" (Bahry 1987a, 159; her quotation is from Gustafson 1981). This reflected "not the uselessness of connections but the fact that there are so many connections that can be of use." Such an interpretation would echo the prevailing view of pork-barrel allocation in the United States—that it results in a universalistic spread of benefits. (For a recent discussion of this literature, see Stein and Bickers 1994 and Weingast 1994.)

45. See Treisman 1996c for more details on the campaign. The disaggregated regressions do suggest one other possible confirmation of the image of a largesse-dispensing president, traveling with pen and checkbook at the ready. Those regions visited by President Yeltsin in 1994 did get significantly larger investment grants that year. These benefits, however, were canceled out by the larger share of tax revenue that these regions tended to remit to Moscow.

46. The regions varied quite widely in the scale of their representation. While the average region got one single-member electoral district per 324,000 inhabitants, the Republic of Sakha's 1.1 million residents had only one representative between them. Their neighbors in the Evenkiisky Autonomous Okrug were rather more fortunate, with one representative for 23,000.

47. As one would expect, parliamentary overrepresentation did not cut much ice with the government. While having more Supreme Soviet representatives per capita was associated with larger transfers under the Supreme Soviet's reserve fund, it was actually correlated with *lower* transfers from the government's reserve fund.

48. Examining tables 3.4 and B1 suggests a trade-off: more populous regions tended to retain larger shares of tax revenue (at least in 1992), but to receive smaller transfers. The net impact was negative.

49. Author's interview, Moscow, July 8, 1996.

50. One alternative view might nevertheless explain such allocative policy as a means by which Yeltsin repaid his supporters; in 1990–91, Yeltsin in fact encouraged both strikes and autonomy movements within Russia as a way of putting pressure on President Gorbachev and the Union level of power. Such explanations would not, however, account for the greater allocations to regions that voted *against* Yeltsin.

51. Rankings are shown in appendix B.

Chapter 4

1. The results of the other candidates also show no very clear pattern.

2. For more on the context of this election, see, for instance, Colton and Hough 1998; Treisman 1998b. In all regions where the election occurred, voters were presented with at least four ballots: a proportional representation national party-list ballot; a single-member-district ballot for their local constituency; a two-vote ballot for the upper house of parliament, the Council of the Federation; and a referendum ballot on Yeltsin's proposed constitution. Some regions supplemented these four with additional regional ballots.

3. For previous, useful studies of Russian electoral geography, see Clem and Craumer 1995a, 1995b, 1996; Slider, Gimpelson, and Chugrov 1994.

4. The voting data analyzed in this chapter are those published by the Central Electoral Commission. Some analysts have expressed doubt about the veracity of official figures as reported for at least one of the elections in question (Sobyanin and Sukhovolsky 1995). Most notably, Sobyanin and Sukhovolsky claimed that up to nine million votes were added in December 1993, mainly in favor of the LDP and the proposed constitution. These allegations were based on a statistical analysis of the official results rather than direct evidence of falsification. However, two political scientists who examined the statistical arguments on which Sobyanin's claims were based were not able to substantiate them (Filippov and Ordeshook 1996). The notion that local officials—who tended to be associated with either Russia's Choice or the Communists—would inflate the vote of the LDP as was claimed seems somewhat implausible (White, Rose, and McAllister 1996, 127–29). A nationally representative opinion survey taken around the time of this election found support levels for the national party lists similar to the official vote tallies (Colton and Hough 1998). Whether the turnout on the constitutional referendum

reached the required 50 percent is far less clear, and I do not include analysis of that vote. In general, however, I share the opinion of various scholars that while substantial falsification cannot be ruled out, the minor falsification or errors that undoubtedly did occur would probably balance each other in the aggregate (White, Rose, and McAllister 1996; Colton 1997; Filippov and Ordeshook 1996). The likelihood of falsification would seem greatest where the interests of local officials were involved—e.g., in the 1993 Council of Federation election and the single-member district races—and then in matters of central presidential concern such as the constitutional referendum. Organizing a systematic, nationwide falsification of the results in favor of one party or presidential candidate in the other votes, however, would have been extremely difficult, given the large number of monitors—50,000 representatives of different parties and thousands of candidates in the 1993 poll (see White, Rose, and McAllister 1996, 129). In 1996, not even the defeated candidates publicly questioned the Central Electoral Commission's figures. Finally, the analyses presented in this chapter examine voting behavior in a given election controlling for voting in the previous one. If the degree and political objectives of any falsification in a given region did not change between elections, it should not affect the results.

5. In brief, fuel and raw materials industries won lucrative export opportunities, while a shift in relative prices severely worsened profitability in agriculture. During 1992, while the prices of basic industrial inputs used by farms rose by 26 times, procurement prices for agricultural goods increased by only 10 times (Wegren 1994, fn. 70).

6. Alternatively, privatization might spark antipathies toward reform if the change results in less security for workers, harder working conditions, or downward pressure on wages, and it is perceived as enriching an unmeritorious minority.

7. Lipset and Rokkan 1967; Putnam 1993; Johnston 1990. For discussions of the implications of Lipset and Rokkan's model for electoral geography, see Johnston 1990 and Lijphart 1990.

8. The agricultural concentration of a region may thus affect political attitudes in two ways: by altering prospective evaluations of the region's economic well-being in conditions of market reform, and through the distinct cultural traditions and social organization of rural life. For discussions of rural conservatism, see Lipset 1963; Wegren 1994.

9. Smith 1987, 11–12. For discussion of construction of multiple indices of inequality and "standard of living," see Smith 1987, chap. 1.

10. Thirteen blocs ran in this election, representing all parts of the ideological spectrum.

11. Again, including explanatory variables to capture all theoretically plausible determinants of regional voting behavior is statistically preferable and stacks the deck *against* the key hypotheses being confirmed. See chap. 3, note 30.

12. Despite the variation, some continuity did remain between elections. In three out of the four cases, the level of a region's pro-Yeltsin or pro-reform vote in the previous election was significantly related to the vote the next time around. Controlling for all the other factors, for every 10 percentage points of a region's vote that supported Yeltsin in the April 1993 referendum, the president could expect 6 or 7 percent of the vote in the first round of 1996.

13. This might mean that ethnic minority and non-Christian voters were more likely to vote for the party of power—or it might mean that ethnic Russians and Christians in

ethnic minority or non-Christian regions were more likely to do so. No direct inference can be drawn.

14. It might seem that a more direct way to demonstrate this relationship would be to regress the voting variables on net central transfers rather than on regional spending. I use spending variables in the regressions because on theoretical grounds it is the spending that is expected to affect voting, not transfers per se. If part of the transfer ends up in the governor's pocket rather than financing government programs, this would reduce the correlation between transfers and voting. In fact, however, the significant results in table 4.1 suggest that such leakages were quite limited. And a similar positive relationship *can* be identified statistically between central transfers and voting for central incumbents. When the spending variables in the short models of tables 4.2 and 4.3 are replaced by a variable measuring the level of center-region transfers per capita in the previous year, along with a control variable for the region's domestic tax revenues, transfers are significant at $p < .03$ in the 1995 and both 1996 regressions, and at $p < .14$ in the 1993 regression (using the level of subventions—i.e., direct central aid to finance regional budget deficits). Controlling for the level of regional tax revenue is necessary since if transfers go disproportionately to fiscally poorer regions, the positive impact of the transfers might be obscured by the negative impact of relative fiscal poverty.

15. These estimates are calculated from the coefficients in table 4.2, models 1 and 2.

16. Oddly enough, both also polled particularly highly in regions with high levels of exports. Perhaps high levels of exports polarize political attitudes, creating a sharper division between those who benefit from them (who become more pro-reform) and those who feel excluded from the benefits derived from their region's industrial or resource wealth (who vote more for the opposition).

17. The result is only marginally significant (at $p < .07$) for the elderly population variable in the Communist Party regression (model 1).

18. The Communists also received a lower vote in regions where inflation was high. However, this may actually reflect the fact that in regions where both voters and political leaders were more Communist, regional administrations were more likely to impose regional price limits, which did initially slow the jump in prices (for instance in Ulyanovsk). This would explain an association between low inflation and high Communist support.

19. On the other hand, the same survey found that pension-age respondents were less likely to say they had voted for Yeltsin.

20. Survey results provided to author by Timothy Colton.

21. Author's interview with Yuri N. Blokhin, first deputy head of administration, Tambov Oblast, June 26, 1996, Tambov.

22. Author's interview with Valery Koval, mayor of Tambov city, June 26, 1996, Tambov.

23. I also tried including a variable reflecting the month in which the gubernatorial election had taken place, on the assumption that either anti-incumbent or pro-incumbent sentiment might have been growing over time. This dummy variable was not significant and lowered the significance of the equation's chi-square. Including it increased the estimate of the coefficient on the regional budget spending variable slightly (to .12), but reduced its significance to $p = .076$. The other coefficient estimates were not much changed.

24. Again, the number of variables included was limited on both theoretical and practical grounds. But as a check, I tried adding each of the excluded economic performance or quality of life variables to the final regression. None of these was significant, and none caused a major change in the main results.

25. In fact, if agricultural employment, agricultural output, or rural share of the population is added to the regression, each has a *negative,* though insignificant coefficient.

26. In elections in which members of the regional executive branch were running, there is particularly strong reason to be concerned about possible falsification. This could invalidate the results of the analysis if the degree of falsification was correlated with the factors found to be significant. It seems unlikely, however, that governors of more developed, higher output regions would have a greater ability or propensity to falsify: the conventional wisdom is that such problems are far more prevalent in less developed, more easily controlled regions. Similarly, there is no obvious reason to believe that falsification of results in gubernatorial elections or the Council of Federation vote would be greater in regions where budget expenditures recently increased relatively more.

27. The mean regional spending that year was 925,000 rubles per inhabitant.

28. Author's interview with Yuri Blokhin, first deputy head of administration, Tambov Oblast, June 26, 1996, Tambov.

29. Author's interview with Viktor Stepanov, chairman of the government of Karelia, Petrozavodsk, July 2, 1996.

Chapter 5

1. Meeting of President Yeltsin with regional leaders in Cheboksary in September 1992. See Respublika 1992.

2. Reports of this come mainly from Barsenkov 1993.

3. Tallies were compiled from reports in Teague 1993 and the *Federal Broadcast Information Service* Daily Reports.

4. It may be assuming too much to view these two soundings of regional leaders' positions as indicators of the trend in regional leaders' behavior between December 1992 and September 1993. However, it is interesting to note which coefficients are similar in the two regressions. This might be because the same leaders tended either to support or oppose Yeltsin on both occasions, rather than revealing any deeper underlying common causes. However, there was some variation in leader response in the two cases. Of the 70 regional governors for whom data is available on both occasions, 47 adopted the same course in the two crises, either supporting or opposing Yeltsin in both. However, 21 of those who failed to support Yeltsin in December supported him in September; and two who had supported him in 1992 opposed him the next year.

5. This is based on the antilog of the coefficient, -2.43. Another way of making this point is that, even without controlling for the other determinants of regional leader strategy, 30 percent of leaders in regions where the vote for Yeltsin had fallen chose to oppose him overtly during the crisis, compared to 11 percent of leaders in regions where the vote for Yeltsin had risen.

6. Of course, it is also possible that causality runs in the reverse direction: governors influence the change in vote totals in their region rather than opinion constraining gov-

ernors. Claims are frequently made that regional administrations falsify election results or pressure voters to support their favored candidates. There is no clear-cut way, with data available, to test for the direction of causation. However, if causation runs from regional leadership preferences to votes rather than the reverse, one might expect earlier indicators of regional leadership preferences to help predict subsequent changes in reported voting behavior. In particular, the governors' positions in December 1992 might affect how regional electorates were reported to have voted in the April 1993 referendum. To test this, I tried including the December 1992 governor strategy dummy variable in the short regression of April 1993 referendum voting from table 4.2, second column from the left, in chapter 4. It proved to be highly insignificant. Whether or not a region's governor opposed Yeltsin in December 1992 bore no relation to the level of voter support for Yeltsin in April 1993, controlling for the Yeltsin vote in 1991 and other factors. However, the direction of change in voting between 1991 and April 1993 *was* significantly related to whether or not the region's governor supported Yeltsin in September 1993. So the evidence suggests that causality ran from voting to leadership action.

7. The antilog of the estimated coefficient from model 2, 3.17, is about 24.

8. This might merely reflect coincidence: that more conservative regions *held* elections. But the result already controls for the region's vote for Yeltsin in 1991 and for whether the governor is a former apparatchik. More elections for regional executive were held in the republics than in the oblasts and krais, but the regression results control for republic status, so this too cannot explain the outcome.

9. He added, however, that Yeltsin had asserted by decree the authority to fire any governor, regardless of whether he or she was elected or appointed, which in practice reduced the difference.

10. Nine of the 15 oppositionist regional leaders were from ethnic republics, while six were from oblasts or krais.

11. In appendix D, I present evidence that regional delegations to the national parliament were swayed in their voting choices by many of the same factors as determined the strategies of regional governors. Where the pro-Yeltsin vote rose within the region, its parliamentary delegation tended to vote more often on Yeltsin's side.

12. In another analysis I did find that among Russia's ethnic republics and districts, more fiscally dependent regions were less likely to demonstrate high levels of separatist activism. See Treisman 1997.

13. To be more sure of all the causal links in the argument would require comparable data covering several years, and some form of causal modeling. But these results, which do isolate relationships from many possible confounding factors and which find relationships that are significant using timed data that fits the hypothesized intertemporal causal links but not significant if the timing is reversed, suggest some quite powerful evidence for the hypothesized links. In addition, the interpretation presented is supported by various other types of empirical evidence: see the discussion of specific cases below.

14. The real spending drop appears to have continued the following year, though a change in the budget classification system used makes it difficult to compare 1994 and 1995 levels.

15. *Segodnya,* July 25, 1995, 9, translated in CDPSP 47 (30) (1995).

236   Notes to Pages 135–57

16. *Rossiiskaya Gazeta,* Dec. 9, 1995, 4.
17. For more on Sakha, see, for instance, Balzer 1994.

Chapter 6

1. For instance, Milanovic 1994; Lynch and Lukic 1996.
2. Russia in 1993 had inflation of 900 percent, compared to 588 percent in Yugoslavia in 1990, 91 percent in the USSR in 1991, and 11 percent in Czechoslovakia in 1992. Its reported real GDP had dropped 38 percent in the preceding four years, compared to 22 percent in Czechoslovakia, 4–8 percent in Yugoslavia, and 7 percent in the USSR, for the four years preceding their disintegration. Calculated from: IMF 1992a, 1994; OECD reports (Dec. 1992, 1993, 1995); Fischer and Frenkel 1992; Goskomstat Rossii 1994; Uvalic 1993.
3. It is also possible that such policies were not tried because leaders knew that their political systems currently lay outside the boundary conditions in which they could be effective.
4. Important differences between Russia and the other three include the larger number of subunits (89 compared to 15, 8, and 2), the far longer history of Russian statehood, and the higher proportion of the largest nationality (Russians constituted 81.5 percent, compared to 63 percent Czechs in Czechoslovakia, 51 percent Russians in the USSR, and 36 percent Serbs in Yugoslavia).
5. The 12.5 percent figure is from World Bank operational data. *Russian Economic Trends* 5 (2) (1996): 11, gives an estimate of 12.4 percent for the first half of 1996. The figure with foreign exchange sales excluded is from this source.
6. All figures calculated from the *Europa World Yearbook* (1995).
7. At the same time, republic and local revenues and expenditures also increased as a share of GSP; so the change represented not so much recentralization as an increase in tax collection at all levels.
8. Calculated from Aleksashenko 1992, 446.
9. Revenues of the "available" general government (including the federation, republic, local governments, extrabudgetary funds, and operations of the State Financial Assets and Liabilities account) dropped from 62.2 percent of GDP in 1989 to 47.2 percent in 1992.
10. For a discussion of fiscal developments in Czechoslovakia in the early 1990s, see Prust 1993.
11. Of course, Czech and Slovak republic expenditures may not all have been made in the same republics, but it seems safe to assume the majority would have been. Per capita republic expenditures still remained slightly higher in Slovakia than in the Czech Republic, though the gap narrowed.
12. After Slovakia's secession, Klaus "remarked that an optical illusion had disappeared from the map" (Rév 1994, 167).
13. While Slovenia's share of Yugoslav exports and imports and retail sales were above average (2.5 times and 2.1 times the national average, respectively), so was its share of Yugoslav GDP (1.7 times the national average) and manufacturing income (2.6 times the national average), other bases on which tax could have been assessed.
14. Latvia and Lithuania seem to have been paying (increasing) positive net transfers to the center, while Estonia received a (decreasing) net transfer from the center.
15. *Pravda,* Apr. 11, 1990, quoted in Khazanov 1995, 34.

16. For another estimate of these implicit subsidies, calculated for 1987 (and expressed in rubles rather than share of GDP), see Austin 1996, table 2.

17. The account of negotiations in 1989–90 between the Baltic republics and the center given in Bahry 1991 suggests a central strategy of insincere concessions, manipulation, and stalling, explained in part by divisions and disorganization of the central bureaucracy.

18. The net transfer to Uzbekistan, for instance, doubled between 1990 and 1991.

19. As noted, it is not certain whether this was the case for the USSR.

Chapter 7

1. Zaslavsky notes the greater incentive for mobilization provided by central redistribution in ethnically divided states: "In multiethnic countries in which territorially based nationalities exhibit profound differences in economic and cultural development, the redistribution of resources by the state creates the conditions for the rise of nationalist or separatist movements" (1992b, 114).

2. In a similar vein, Przeworski argues that the collapse of communist regimes in Eastern Europe was caused by an ideological crisis combined with a failure of repression. "The reasons the system collapsed so rapidly and so quietly are to be found both in the realm of ideology and in the realm of physical force. . . . By 1989, party bureaucrats did not believe in their speech. And to shoot, one must believe in something. When those who hold the trigger have absolutely nothing to say, they have no force to pull it. . . . Moreover, they did not have the guns. In no country did the army, as distinct from the police forces, come to the rescue" (1991, 5–6).

3. According to Rokkan and Urwin: "The dilemma for centres is that even the slightest concession might be taken to be, and might become, the thin end of a wedge that might ultimately threaten these regime imperatives, for at the furthest edge peripheral demands challenge the unity of the state" (1983, 166).

4. This is one view of the Roman leadership's strategy to preserve its empire. As Mellor describes it: "They gambled on trouble always being limited to a few spots in the Empire rather than any general insurrection, for they had inadequate resources to maintain a proper strategic reserve. By tolerance and fairness, but a fierce and ruthless response to any troublemakers, they maintained a level of peace not previously experienced" (1989, 162).

5. Axelrod also extends the logic to empires trying to deter revolts by their provinces or by external aggressors and notes that Britain's ability to deter aggression against Gibraltar and Hong Kong was enhanced by Whitehall's decision to respond with force to the Argentine invasion of the Falkland Islands (1984, 150–51).

6. In a discussion of individual tax evasion, Margaret Levi also suggests that "side payments are most effective for appeasing those with significant bargaining resources—especially those constituents from whom it is better to get some tax than no tax. Relative bargaining power can determine the kinds of tax reductions, cutbacks, extra services, or other concessions a constituent receives" (Levi 1988, 64). However, unlike the argument of this book, her account of "quasi-voluntary compliance" assumes that the free-rider problem is overcome in part by a normative motivation of individuals to pay tax as long as they believe others will do the same.

7. The emphasis here is on *questions*. I do not pretend to offer answers or make broader claims based on one case study. It does, however, suggest hypotheses that might be worth examining more thoroughly in other contexts.

8. Another scholar has described the treaty of peace Theodosius made with the Visigoths in 382 and other subsequent treaties with Germanic and Hun war bands as "no more than legal affirmations of the *status quo* and Roman self-deceptions" (Christ 1984, 231). Nevertheless, the same writer acknowledges that the "long duration of the agony and the complexity of its development are to be explained by the fact that the Germans in question were not always destructive in their effects but for a long time exerted their military strength on behalf of Roman interests" (232).

9. See Kann 1979, 100–101: "As the Austrian prime minister, Count Eduard Taaffe (1879–93) put it, the best way to govern was to keep all Austrian national groups in a moderate state of dissatisfaction. . . ."

10. According to Barkey:

> Traditional historians who do not see the calculated aspect of state policies at this time argue that the Ottoman state was weak. Accordingly, the deals the Ottoman state made with bandit leaders are described as originating from a position of weakness rather than of strength. Ottoman rulers had no other choice, say historians, because they had to fight their foreign enemies. The position I take differs. . . . The Ottoman policies of incorporation of bandits were policies of strength. They originated from a need to incorporate more armies into the war effort against the Habsburgs or the Persians, as well as from the need to undermine the regional strength these bandits could acquire if left to their own devices. The state in the Ottoman Empire was strong since it was able to preempt potentially disruptive action by the bandits as well as exploit it when it became important. (Barkey 1994, 239–40)

11. Quoted in Root 1994, 229; from Jean-François Solnon, *La Cour de Paris,* 523 (Paris: Fayard, 1987).

12. In an interesting article, Lijphart has argued that Indian political institutions actually constitute a variant of "consociational" democracy (1996).

13. For another interesting discussion of how central fiscal policies have helped to moderate conflict within divided federations, see Bird 1986.

14. See Hirschman 1995 for an elegant review of this tradition. He traces the idea that conflict can play a constructive role in social relationships to, among others, Heraclitus, Machiavelli, Georg Simmel, Lewis Coser, Ralph Dahrendorf, Max Gluckman, Michel Crozier, Marcel Gauchet, and Helmut Dubiel.

15. For a formal demonstration of this point, see Weingast, Shepsle, and Johnsen 1981.

16. The British electorate was about 250,000 (Root 1994), which was probably between 2 and 5 percent of the total population (based on population estimates in Plumb 1950). The Chinese party nomenklatura in 1982 has been estimated at a little less than 1 percent of the population (Greer 1989, 50).

17. Of course, there is no reason to assume that central governments would prioritize efficiency. However, the public good characteristics of financial restraint and other efficiency-enhancing policies suggest that the center's encompassing interest will give it greater incentives than the regions.

18. Haggard and Webb consider a number of institutional factors that may influence how economic and political reforms interact—the party system, timing of elections, organization of bureaucracies, strength of interest groups, program design, and international involvement (1994). Geddes considers how the number of political parties, their internal discipline, and the balance of power between them affect the likelihood of reforms to increase state capacity—an often crucial aspect of economic reform (1994).

19. Pereira et al. 1993; Hellman 1996; Bates and Krueger (1993, 466) argue that technocratic insulation of the government can reduce confidence in its programs.

20. While some economists have certainly noted the important political dimension of economic policy in federal states (e.g., Bird 1986), the usual economic reform advice has been to liberalize more or less indiscriminately.

21. "Yeltsin Discusses Republics' Sovereignty, Health," Moscow Television, FBIS SOV-90-212, Nov. 1, 1990, 79, quoted in Laba 1996, 9.

22. Nikolai Sevryugin, the governor of Tula Oblast, issued such a challenge to the center, threatening to cut off tax remittances, during his unsuccessful bid for reelection in early 1997.

Appendix A

1. For other recent formal analyses that explore aspects of the same problem, see Kuran 1991; DeNardo 1985; Lohmann 1994.

2. In order to focus on the interactions between the levels, I make the large assumption that each of these is unitary; in reality, many important complications arise from the interaction between different actors *within* a given level of government.

3. It would be possible to make this a function not just of the number choosing R, but a function that weights different defectors differently (perhaps larger regions that defect absorb more of the center's punishment resources, lowering the risk more for others). For simplicity, I assume that all are equally effective at reducing the risk for others of defying the center.

4. Obviously, another way for a central government to avoid such a fate is to increase its enforcement capacity. But at times the center may not be able to do this or may prefer not to. Indeed, the threshold function may also shift downward because of a fall in enforcement capacity, as the result of decay in the state apparatus, the decline of national parties, or democratization of vertical relations. These changes may be difficult or undesirable to reverse. In such situations, changes in tax policy may be able to make full compliance once more an equilibrium.

Appendix B

1. The terms were combined in an index to economize on degrees of freedom. For a similar approach to index construction, see Putnam 1993.

2. This was a discontinuous variable, based on the classification provided in Yasin 1993b, 24. This study divided Russia's regions into three groups on the basis of the degree of price regulation in the period March 1992–June 1993: those with active price regulation (more than 9 of 19 food products surveyed subject to price controls); those with a "mixed strategy" (3–8 of the 19 products subject to price controls); and those

with little or no price regulation (controls on 2 or fewer of the 19 products). For much of the period, the price of bread remained regulated at the federal level.

3. They were combined in an index to economize on degrees of freedom. Including discontinuous variables, such as that measuring the extent of price regulation, in a factor analysis is often viewed as problematic. However, when the correlations between the underlying variables are believed to be moderate (no greater than .6 or .7), the technique can still be expected to perform well (see Kim and Mueller 1978, 75). Given the generally moderate observed correlations between different measures of commitment to economic reform, it is likely that this condition is met in this case.

Appendix D

1. The index is calculated for each roll-call vote as the percentage of the deputies in the delegation voting with the president's side minus the percentage voting against it. Thus, if they are split 50-50, the rating is zero. The authors say the temperatures are calculated from several dozen key roll-call votes in the 3d Congress (1991) and 9th Congress (1993).

2. It is conceivable that the opinions of the parliamentary delegation influenced voters, rather than the opinions of voters influencing the parliamentary delegation. However, some evidence suggests otherwise. The roll-call voting temperature of a region's delegation in 1991 was not a significant predictor of regional public voting in the April referendum (the 1991 temperature is insignificant when included in the regression in table 4.2, second column from left, in chap. 4). But public voting in the April referendum (whether included in absolute terms, or broken down into the 1991 level of support for Yeltsin and the 1991–93 change) *was* a highly significant determinant of the parliamentary delegation's 1993 temperature (even controlling for the 1991 temperature).

References

Aleksashenko, Sergei. 1992. "Macroeconomic Stabilisation in the Former Soviet Republics: Dream or Reality?" *Communist Economies and Economic Transformation* 4 (4): 439–67.

Alekseyeva, S. 1994. "Benefits of a Vacation in Sochi." *Sovetskaya Rossiya,* March 29, 3, translated in FBIS-SOV-94-060, 31.

Alesina, Alberto, and Allan Drazen. 1991. "Why Are Stabilizations Delayed?" *American Economic Review* 81:5.

Andrews, Josephine, and Kathryn Stoner-Weiss. 1995. "Regionalism and Reform in Provincial Russia." *Post-Soviet Affairs* 11:4.

Antonov, Anatoly. 1993. "Russia's Disintegration Is Inevitable." *Megapolis-Express,* Feb. 10, 13, translated in CDPSP 45 (7): 23.

Ash, Timothy Garton. 1990a. *The Magic Lantern: The Revolution of '89 Witnessed in Warsaw, Budapest, Berlin, and Prague.* New York: Random House.

———. 1990b. "Eastern Europe: Après Le Déluge, Nous." *New York Review of Books,* Aug. 16, 1990, 51–57.

Austin, D. Andrew. 1996. "The Price of Nationalism: Evidence from the Soviet Union." *Public Choice* 87:1–18.

Aven, Petr. 1992. "Economic Reform in a Bargaining Economy." In Janos M. Kovacs and Marton Tardos, eds., *Reform and Transformation in Eastern Europe: Soviet-Type Economics on the Threshold of Change.* London: Routledge.

Aven, Petr, and V. Shironin. 1987. "Reforma khoziasistvennogo mehkanizma: realnost' namechaemick preobrazovanii." *Izvestia SO AN SSSR,* ser. ekonomiki i prikladnoi sotsiologii, 3.

Axelrod, Robert. 1984. *The Evolution of Cooperation.* New York: Basic Books.

Bahl, Roy. 1994. "Revenues and Revenue Assignment: Intergovernmental Fiscal Relations in the Russian Federation." In Christine Wallich, ed., *Russia and the Challenge of Fiscal Federalism*, 129–80. Washington, DC: The World Bank.

Bahry, Donna. 1987a. *Outside Moscow: Power, Politics, and Budgetary Policy in the Soviet Republics.* New York: Columbia University Press.

———. 1987b. "Politics, Generations and Change in the USSR." In James Millar, ed., *Politics, Work and Daily Life in the USSR: A Survey of Former Soviet Citizens.* New York: Cambridge University Press.

———. 1991. "The Union Republics and Contradictions in Gorbachev's Economic Reform." *Soviet Economy* 7 (3): 215–55.

Baldersheim, Harald, and Michal Illner. 1996. "Local Democracy: The Challenges of

Institution-Building." In Baldersheim et al., eds., *Local Democracy and the Processes of Transformation in East-Central Europe.* Boulder: Westview.

Balzer, Marjorie Mandelstam. 1994. "From Ethnicity to Nationalism: Turmoil in the Russian Mini-Empire." In James R. Millar and Sharon L. Wolchik, eds., *The Social Legacy of Communism*, 56–87. New York: Cambridge University Press.

Barkey, Karen. 1994. *Bandits and Bureaucrats: The Ottoman Route to State Centralization.* Ithaca: Cornell University Press.

Barnwell, P. S. 1992. *Emperors, Prefects and Kings: The Roman West, 395–565.* London: Duckworth.

Barsenkov, A. S. 1993. *Politichesakaya Rossiya Segodnya.* Moscow: Moskovsky Rabochy.

Barth, Fredrik. 1969. *Ethnic Groups and Boundaries: The Social Organization of Cultural Differences.* Boston: Little, Brown.

Bates, Robert H., and Anne O. Krueger. 1993. *Political and Economic Interactions in Economic Policy Reform: Evidence from Eight Countries.* Cambridge, MA: Blackwell.

Baumol, William J. 1952. *Welfare Economics and the Theory of the State.* Cambridge, MA: Harvard University Press.

Bekker, Aleksandr. 1993a. "Premer obeshchaet regionam lgoti u derzhit slovo." *Segodnya,* Oct. 19, 3.

———. 1993b. "Boris Fyodorov: 'The Next Two Weeks Will Be a Time of Political Choice.'" *Segodnya,* Aug. 24, 11, translated in *Current Digest of the Post-Soviet Press* 34 (1993): 11–13.

———. 1996. "Vserossiiskaya doika." *Segodnya,* July 10, 2.

Bennett, R. J. 1980. *The Geography of Public Finance: Welfare Under Fiscal Federalism and Local Government Finance.* London: Methuen.

Berkowitz, Daniel, and Beth Mitchneck. 1992. "Fiscal Decentralization in the Soviet Economy." *Comparative Economic Studies* (summer): 1–18.

Birch, Anthony H. 1989. *Nationalism and National Integration.* London: Unwin Hyman.

Bird, Richard M. 1986. *Federal Finance in Comparative Perspective.* Toronto: Canadian Tax Foundation.

Bolton, Patrick, Gérard Roland, and Enrico Spolaore. 1996. "Economic Theories of the Break-Up and Integration of Nations." *European Economic Review* 40:697–705.

Brass, Paul. 1974. *Religion and Politics in North India.* Cambridge: Cambridge University Press.

Brewer, John. 1989. *The Sinews of Power: War, Money and the English State, 1688–1783.* New York: Alfred A. Knopf.

Brubaker, Rogers. 1994. "Nationhood and the National Question in the Soviet Union and Post-Soviet Eurasia: An Institutionalist Account." *Theory and Society* 23:47–78.

Carrère d'Encausse, Hélène. 1981. *Decline of an Empire: The Soviet Socialist Republics in Revolt.* New York: Harper and Row.

Central Electoral Commission. 1994. *Byuleten' No. 1.* Moscow: Central Electoral Commission.

Christ, Karl. 1984. *The Romans: An Introduction to Their History and Civilisation.* Berkeley: University of California Press.

Cingranelli, David L. 1984. "The Effects of State Lobby Offices in Washington on the Distribution of Federal Aid to States." Manuscript, cited in Rich 1989.

Clark, Susan L., and David R. Graham. 1995. "The Russian Federation's Fight for Survival." *Orbis* 39 (3): 329–51.

Clem, Ralph S., and Peter R. Craumer. 1995a. "The Politics of Russia's Regions: A Geographical Analysis of the Russian Election and Constitutional Plebiscite of December 1993." *Post-Soviet Geography* 36 (2): 67–86.

———. 1995b. "The Geography of the Russian 1995 Parliamentary Election: Continuity, Change and Correlates." *Post-Soviet Geography* 36 (10): 587–616.

———. 1996. "Roadmap to Victory: Boris Yel'tsin and the Russian Presidenial Elections of 1996." *Post-Soviet Geography and Economics* 37 (6): 335–54.

Colton, Timothy J. 1998. "Introduction." In Timothy J. Colton and Jerry Hough, eds., *Growing Pains: Russian Democracy and the Election of 1993.* Washington, DC: Brookings Institution Press.

Colton, Timothy J., and Jerry Hough, eds. 1998. *Growing Pains: Russian Democracy and the Election of 1993.* Washington, DC: Brookings Institution Press.

Comfort, Nicholas. 1993. *Brewer's Politics: A Phrase and Fable Dictionary.* London: Cassell.

Coulson, Andrew, ed. 1995. *Local Government in Eastern Europe: Establishing Democracy at the Grass Roots.* Aldershot, UK: Edward Elgar.

Cox, Robert Henry, and Erich G. Frankland. 1995. "The Federal State and the Breakup of Czechoslovakia: An Institutional Analysis." *Publius* 25 (1) (winter): 71–88.

Crick, Bernard R. 1962. *In Defence of Politics.* London: Weidenfeld and Nicolson.

Crozier, Michel. 1977. *The Governability of West European Societies.* University of Essex: Noel Buxton Lecture.

Cvikl, Milan, Evan Kraft, and Milan Vodopivec. 1993. "Costs and Benefits of Independence: Slovenia." *Communist Economics and Economic Transformation* 5:295–315.

De Waal, Thomas. 1995. "Chechen Myth of the Year." *Moscow Times,* Dec. 8, 9.

DeNardo, James. 1985. *Power in Numbers: The Political Strategy of Protest and Rebellion.* Princeton: Princeton University Press.

Deutsch, Karl. 1964. "Communication Theory and Political Integration." In Philip E. Jacob and James V. Toscano, eds., *The Integration of Political Communities,* 46–74. Philadelphia: Lippincott.

———. 1966. *Nationalism and Social Communication.* Cambridge: MIT Press.

Dewatripont, Mathias, and Gerard Roland. 1991. "Economic Reform and Dynamic Political Constraints." *Review of Economic Studies* 57:703–30.

Diamond, Larry. 1994. "Toward Democratic Consolidation." *Journal of Democracy* 5 (3) (July).

Diuk, Nadia, and Adrian Karatnycky. 1993. *New Nations Rising: The Fall of the Soviets and the Challenge of Independence.* New York: John Wiley and Sons.

Dmitrieva, Oksana. 1996. *Regional Development: The USSR and After.* London: UCL Press.

Dubravcic, Dinko. 1993. "Economic Causes and Political Context of the Dissolution of a Multinational Federal State: The Case of Yugoslavia." *Communist Economies and Economic Transformation* 5 (3): 259–72.

References

Dudaeva, Alla. 1996. "Dzhokhar ochen khotel mira" (Dzhokhar wanted peace very much). *Izvestia,* June 8, 6.

Dunlop, John B. 1997. "Russia: In Search of an Identity?" In Ian Bremmer and Ray Taras, eds., *New States, New Politics: Building the Post-Soviet Nations.* New York: Cambridge University Press.

Eismont, Maria. 1996. "The Chechen War: How It All Began." *Prism,* Jamestown Foundation, Mar. 8.

Elster, Jon. 1992. *Local Justice: How Institutions Allocate Scarce Goods and Necessary Burdens.* New York: Russel Sage.

Fainsod, Merle. 1958. *Smolensk Under Soviet Rule.* Boston: Unwin Hyman.

Fearon, James D. 1993. "Ethnic War as a Commitment Problem." University of Chicago, manuscript.

Fedorchenko, Sergei. 1994. "Customs Post on Border with Khakassia." *Segodnya,* Sept. 1, 3, translated in CDPSP 46 (35): 19.

Felgengauer, Pavel. 1994. "They Love the Army in the Provinces: Governors Are Interested in Military Bases." *Segodnya,* Sept. 15, 3. Translated in CDPSP 46 (37): 19.

Fernandez, Raquel, and Dani Rodrik. 1991. "Resistance to Reform: Status Quo Bias in the Presence of Individual-Specific Uncertainty." *American Economic Review* 81:5.

Filippov, Mikhail, and Peter C. Ordeshook. 1996. "Fraud or Fiction: Who Stole What in Russia's December 1993 Elections." California Institute of Technology, manuscript, January.

Fiorina, Morris P. 1981. *Retrospective Voting in American National Elections.* New Haven: Yale University Press.

Fischer, Stanley. 1992. "Stabilization and Economic Reform in Russia." *Brookings Papers on Economic Activity* 1:77–126.

Fischer, Stanley, and Jacob Frenkel. 1992. "Macroeconomic Issues of Soviet Reform." *AEA Papers and Proceedings, American Economic Review* 82 (2) (May): 37.

Fischer, Stanley, Ratna Sahay, and Carlos A. Végh. 1996. "Stabilization and Growth in Transition Economies: The Early Experience." *Journal of Economic Perspectives* 10 (2) (spring).

Fisher, Ronald C. 1991. "Interjurisdictional Competition: A Summary Perspective and Agenda for Research." In Daphne A. Kenyon and John Kincaid, eds., *Competition Among States and Local Governments: Efficiency and Equity in American Federalism.* Washington, DC: Urban Institute Press.

Fitzpatrick, Sheila, ed. 1978. *Cultural Revolution in Russia, 1928–31.* Bloomington: Indiana University Press.

Fondahl, Gail A. 1996. "Contested Terrain: Changing Boundaries and Identities in Southeastern Siberia." *Post-Soviet Geography and Economics* 37:1.

Freinkman, Lev, and Stepan Titov. 1994. *The Transformation of the Regional Fiscal System in Russia: The Case of Yaroslavl.* Internal Discussion Paper IDP-143. Washington, DC: The World Bank.

Friedland, Roger, and Herbert Wong. 1983. "Congressional Politics, Federal Grants, and Local Needs: Who Gets What and Why?" In Alberta M. Sbragia, ed., *The Municipal Money Chase: The Politics of Local Government Finance.* Boulder: Westview.

Garvy, George. 1977. *Money, Financial Flows, and Credit in the Soviet Union.* Cambridge, MA: Ballinger Publishing Co.
Geddes, Barbara. 1994. *Politician's Dilemma: Building State Capacity in Latin America.* Berkeley: University of California Press.
———. 1995. "Challenging the Conventional Wisdom." In Marc F. Plattner and Larry Diamond, eds., *Economic Reform and Democracy.* Baltimore: Johns Hopkins University Press.
Geertz, Clifford. 1963. "The Integrative Revolution: Primordial Sentiments and Civil Politics in the New States." In Geertz, ed., *Old Societies and New States: The Quest for Modernity in Asia and Africa.* New York: Free Press.
Gelman, Vladimir, and Olga Senatova. 1995. "Sub-National Politics in Russia in the Post-Communist Transitions Period: A View from Moscow." *Regional and Federal Studies* 5 (2): 211–23.
Gershaft, Mikhail. 1996. "Will Russia's Economy Turn into a 'Crazy Quilt'?" *Prism,* Jamestown Foundation 2 (16) October.
Goffart, Walter. 1980. *Barbarians and Romans, AD 418–584: The Techniques of Accommodation.* Princeton: Princeton University Press.
Gorbachev, Mikhail. 1995. *Zhizn' i Reformy.* Moscow: Novosti.
Gordon, Michael. 1996a. "Three Die in Blast in Chechnya; Protesters Insist That Russians Leave." *New York Times,* Feb. 10, 5.
———. 1996b. "Woes of Modern Russia Mirrored in the Decline of its Coal Mines." *New York Times,* Feb. 29, 8.
Goskomstat Rossii. 1994. *Rossiiskii Statisticheskii Yezhegodnik.* Moscow: Goskomstat.
———. 1995. *Rossiiskii Statisticheskii Yezhegodnik.* Moscow: Goskomstat.
Goskomstat. 1995. E-mail data transfer to author.
Gottschalk, Peter T. 1981. "Regional Allocation of Federal Funds." *Policy Analysis* (spring): 183–97.
Gouré, Leon. 1994. "The Russian Federation: Possible Disintegration Scenarios." *Comparative Strategy* 13 (4): 401–18.
Gras, Solange. 1982. "Regionalism and Autonomy in Alsace since 1918." In Stein Rokkan and Derek W. Urwin, eds., *The Politics of Territorial Identity,* 309–54. London: Sage.
Greenfeld, Liah. 1992. *Nationalism: Five Roads to Modernity.* Cambridge, MA: Harvard University Press.
Greer, Charles E., ed. 1989. *China Facts and Figures Annual 1988.* Gulf Breeze, FL: Academic International Press.
Gregory, Paul R., and Robert C. Stuart. 1990. *Soviet Economic Structure and Performance.* 4th ed. New York: Harper and Row.
Grossman, Gregory. 1990. "Sub-Rosa Privatization and Marketization in the USSR." *Annals of the American Academy of Political and Social Science* 507 (January): 44–52.
Gudkov, Lev. 1994. "Natsional'noe soznanie: versiya Zapada i Rossii." *Rodina* 2:14–18.
Gustafson, Thane. 1981. *Reform in Soviet Politics: The Lessons of Recent Policies on Land and Water.* New York: Cambridge University Press.
Haggard, Stephan, and Robert R. Kaufman. 1995. *The Political Economy of Democratic Transition.* Princeton: Princeton University Press.

Haggard, Stephan, and Steven B. Webb. 1994. "Introduction." In Haggard and Webb, eds., *Voting for Reform: Democracy, Political Liberalization, and Economic Adjustment,* 1–36. Oxford: Oxford University Press.

Hanson, Philip. 1994. "The Russian Budget Revisited." *RFE/RL Research Report* 3 (18) 6 May.

———. 1996. "Economic Change and the Russian Provinces." In J. Gibson and Philip Hanson, eds., *Transformation from Below: Local Power and the Political Economy of Post-Communist Transitions.* Cheltenham, UK: Edward Elgar.

Hardgrave, Robert L., Jr. 1993. "India: The Dilemmas of Diversity." *Journal of Democracy* 4 (4) (October): 54–68.

Harrop, Martin, and William L. Miller. 1987. *Elections and Voters: A Comparative Introduction.* Basingstoke, UK: Macmillan Education.

Hayek, Friedrich A. 1948. *Individualism and Economic Order.* Chicago: University of Chicago.

Hellman, Joel. 1996. "Competitive Advantage: Political Competition and Economic Reform in Postcommunist Transitions." Harvard University, unpublished paper.

Hirschman, Albert O. 1994. "The On-and-Off Connection Between Political and Economic Progress." *American Economic Review* 84 (2) (May): 343–47.

———. 1995. "Social Conflicts as Pillars of Democratic Market Societies." In *A Propensity to Self-Subversion.* Cambridge: Harvard University Press.

Hobsbawm, Eric, and Terence Ranger, eds. 1983. *The Invention of Tradition.* Cambridge: Cambridge University Press.

Horowitz, Donald. 1992. "How to Begin Thinking Comparatively about Soviet Ethnic Problems." In Alexander J. Motyl, ed., *Thinking Theoretically About Soviet Nationalities.* New York: Columbian University Press.

———. 1993. "Democracy in Divided Societies." *Journal of Democracy* 4 (4) (October): 18–38.

Hough, Jerry F. 1990. *Russia and the West.* 2d ed. New York: Simon and Schuster.

Hough, Jerry F., Evelyn Davidheiser, and Susan Goodrich Lehmann. 1996. *The 1996 Russian Presidential Election.* Washington, DC: Brookings Institution Press.

Huang, Yasheng. 1995. "Why China Will Not Collapse." *Foreign Policy* 99 (summer): 54–68.

Hueglin, Thomas O. 1986. "Regionalism in Western Europe: Conceptual Problems of a New Political Perspective." *Comparative Politics* (July): 439–57.

Hughes, James. 1993. "Yeltsin's Siberian Opposition." *RFE/RL Research Report* 2 (50) (Dec. 17): 29–34.

———. 1994. "Regionalism in Russia: The Rise and Fall of Siberian Agreement." *Europe-Asia Studies* 46 (7): 1133–61.

———. 1996. "Moscow's Bilateral Treaties Add to Confusion." *Transition* 2 (19) (Sept. 20): 39–43.

Huntington, Samuel P. 1968. *Political Order in Changing Societies.* New Haven: Yale University Press.

———. 1991. *The Third Wave: Democratization in the Late Twentieth Century.* Norman: University of Oklahoma Press.

Ignatev, Sergei (deputy chairman of Russian Central Bank). 1993. Author's Interview, Moscow, Central Bank of Russia, July 29.

Illarionov, A. 1996. "Attempts to Carry Out Policies of Financial Stabilization in the USSR and Russia." *Problems of Economic Transition* 39 (2) (June).

Ilyumzhinov, Kirsan. 1993. Letter to Deputy Chairman of the Russian Government, Boris Fyodorov, May 10.

IMF. Various years. *IMF Economic Reviews.* Washington, DC: International Monetary Fund.

———. 1992a. *The Economy of the Former USSR in 1991.* April. Washington, DC: IMF.

———. 1992b. *Economic Review: Common Issues and Interrepublic Relations in the Former USSR.* April. Washington, DC: IMF.

———. 1994. *Economic Review: Russian Federation.* Washington, DC: IMF.

———. 1995. *IMF Economic Reviews, 1994, 16: Russian Federation.* Washington, DC: IMF.

IMF, World Bank, OECD, EBRD. 1991. *A Study of the Soviet Economy.* Paris: IMF et al.

Jennings, Kent, and Richard Niemi. 1981. *Generations and Politics: A Panel Study of Young Adults and Their Parents.* Princeton: Princeton University Press.

Johnston, Ronald J. 1978. "The Allocation of Federal Money in the United States: Aggregate Analysis by Correlation." *Policy and Politics* 6:279–97.

———. 1990. "Lipset and Rokkan Revisited: Electoral Cleavages, Electoral Geography, and Electoral Strategy in Great Britain." In R. J. Johnston, F. M. Shelley, and P. J. Taylor, eds., *Developments in Electoral Geography,* 121–42. London: Routledge.

Jones, A. H. M. 1966. *The Decline of the Ancient World.* New York: Holt Rinehart and Winston.

Judt, Tony. 1994. "The End of Which European Era?" *Daedalus* 123 (3) (summer): 1–19.

Kann, Robert A. 1979. *The Habsburg Empire: A Study in Integration and Disintegration.* New York: Octagon Books.

Kedourie, E. 1961. *Nationalism.* London: Hutchinson.

Keller, Edmond J. 1983. "The State, Public Policy, and the Mediation of Ethnic Conflict in Africa." In Donald Rothchild and Victor A. Olorunsola, eds., *State Versus Ethnic Claims: African Policy Dilemmas.* Boulder: Westview.

Kempton, Daniel R. 1996. "The Republic of Sakha (Yakutia): The Evolution of Centre-Periphery Relations in the Russian Federation." *Europe-Asia Studies* 48 (4): 587–613.

Kennedy, Paul. 1987. *The Rise and Fall of the Great Powers.* New York: Random House.

Key, V. O. 1966. *The Responsible Electorate.* New York: Vintage.

Khasbulatov, Ruslan. 1993. *The Struggle for Russia: Power and Change in the Democratic Revolution,* ed. Richard Sakwa. London: Routledge.

Khazanov, Anatoly M. 1995. *After the USSR.* Madison: University of Wisconsin Press.

Khodorovich, M. I. 1991. "Budgets of the Union Republics in the Period of Transition to the Market." *Finansy SSSR* 6:3–10.

Kiewiet, D. Roderick. 1983. *Macroeconomics and Micropolitics: The Electoral Effects of Economic Issues.* Chicago: University of Chicago Press.

Kim, Jae-On, and Charles W. Mueller. 1978. *Factor Analysis: Statistical Methods and Practical Issues.* Beverly Hills: Sage.

Kirkow, Peter. 1997a. "Russia's Regional Puzzle: Institutional Change and Economic Adaptation." *Communist Economies and Economic Transformation* 9:3.
Klyuchevsky, V. O. 1995. *Russkaya istoria: polny kurs lektsii v trekh knigakh.* Moscow: Mysl.
Koen, Vincent. 1996. "Russian Macroeconomic Data: Existence, Access, Interpretation." *Communist Economies and Economic Transformation* 8:3.
Kolakowski, Leszck. 1992. "Amidst Moving Ruins." *Daedalus* 121 (2) (spring).
Kordonsky, Simon. 1991. "Otkuda v SSSR Mafia?" Moscow, mimeo.
———. 1992. "Pressure Groups in the Social Structure of Reforming Society." *Communist Economies and Economic Transformation* 4 (1): 85–95.
Kornai, Janos. 1992. *The Socialist System: The Political Economy of Communism.* Princeton: Princeton University Press.
Kozlov, Viktor. 1988. *The Peoples of the Soviet Union.* London: Hutchinson.
Kraft, Evan. 1992. "Evaluating Regional Policy in Yugoslavia, 1966–1990." *Comparative Economic Studies* 34 (3–4): 11–33.
Kraft, Evan, and Milan Vodopivec. 1992. "How Soft Is the Budget Constraint for Yugoslav Firms?" *Journal of Comparative Economics* 16:432–55.
Kuran, Timur. 1989. "Sparks and Prairie Fires: A Theory of Unanticipated Political Revolution." *Public Choice* 61:41–74.
———. 1991. "Now out of Never: The Element or Surprise in the East European Revolution of 1989." *World Politics* 44 (October).
Laba, Roman. 1996. "How Yeltsin's Exploitation of Ethnic Nationalism Brought Down an Empire." *Transition* (Jan. 12): 5–13.
Laitin, David D. 1996. "Language and Nationalism in the Post-Soviet Republics." *Post-Soviet Affairs* 12 (1): 4–24.
Lapidus, Gail W., and Edward W. Walker. 1995. "Nationalism, Regionalism, and Federalism: Center-Periphery Relations in Post-Communist Russia." In Gail Lapidus, ed., *The New Russia: Troubled Transformation.* Boulder: Westview.
Laqueur, Walter. 1994. *The Dream that Failed: Reflections on the Soviet Union.* New York: Oxford University Press.
Lavrov, Aleksei. 1995a. "Rossiiskiy Byudzhetny Federalizm: Pervie Shagi, Pervie Itogi." *Segodnya* 104 (June 7): 5.
———. 1995b. "Problemy Stanovleniya i Razvitiya Byudzhetnogo Federalizma v Rossii." Moscow: Analytical Administration of the President of the RF, September.
———. 1995c. "Problemy i Perspektivi Razvitiya Mezhbyudzhetnykh Otnoshenii v Rossii." *Obshchestvo i Ekonomika* 3:3–23.
———. 1995d. Data provided to author, Moscow.
———. 1996. "Mify I Rify Rossiiskogo Byudzhetnogo Federalizma." December. Moscow: Institut Otkrytoe Obshchestvo.
Layard, Richard, and John Parker. 1996. *The Coming Russian Boom: A Guide to New Markets and Politics.* New York: Free Press.
Lazarsfeld, Paul F., Bernard Berelson, and Hazel Gaudet. 1968. *The People's Choice.* New York: Duell, Sloan and Pearce.
Le Houerou, Philippe. 1993. "*Detsentralizatsionnye i nalogovo-byudzhetnye disproportsii v regionakh rossiiskoi federatsii* (Decentralization and Fiscal Disparities among Regions in the Russian Federation)." Moscow: The World Bank, mimeo.

———. 1995. *Fiscal Management in the Russian Federation,* 14862-RU, Washington, DC: World Bank.
Lemco, Jonathan. 1991. *Political Stability in Federal Governments.* New York: Praeger.
Levi, Margaret. 1988. *Of Rule and Revenue,* Berkeley: University of California Press.
Lewin, Moshe. 1988. *The Gorbachev Phenomenon: A Historical Interpretation.* Berkeley: University of California Press.
Lewis-Beck, Michael S. 1988. *Economics and Elections: The Major Western Democracies.* Ann Arbor: University of Michigan Press.
Liebowitz, Ronald. 1996. "Russia's Center-Periphery Fiscal Relations During Transition." In Michael Kraus and Ronald Liebowitz, eds., *Russia and Eastern Europe After Communism: The Search for New Political, Economic, and Security Systems.* Boulder: Westview.
Lijphart, Arend. 1990. "The Cleavage Model and Electoral Geography: A Review." In R. J. Johnston, F. M. Shelley, and P. J. Taylor, eds., *Developments in Electoral Geography,* 143–50. London: Routledge.
———. 1993. "Consociational Democracy." In Joel Krieger, ed., *The Oxford Companion to Politics of the World,* 188–89. Oxford: Oxford University Press.
———. 1996. "The Puzzle of Indian Democracy: A Consociational Interpretation." *American Political Science Review* 90 (2) (June): 258–68.
Linz, Juan J., and Alfred Stepan. 1992. "Political Identities and Electoral Sequences: Spain, the Soviet Union, and Yugoslavia." *Daedalus* 121 (2) (spring): 123–39.
Lipset, Seymour Martin. 1963. *Political Man: The Social Bases of Politics.* Garden City: Anchor Books.
Lipset, Seymour Martin, and Stein Rokkan. 1967. "Cleavage Structures, Party Systems, and Voter Alignments: An Introduction." In Lipset and Rokkan, eds., *Party Systems and Voter Alignments: Cross-National Perspectives.* New York: Free Press.
Lohmann, Susanne. 1994. "The Dynamics of Informational Cascades: The Monday Demonstrations in Leipzig, East Germany, 1989–91." *World Politics* 47 (1): 42–101.
Lowenhardt, John. 1995. *The Reincarnation of Russia.* Durham, NC: Duke University Press.
Lustig, Nora. 1996. "Mexico: The Slippery Road to Stability." *Brookings Review* (spring): 4–9.
Lynch, Allen, and Reneo Lukic. 1996. "The Russian Federation Will Remain United." *Transition* (Jan. 12): 14–17.
Maravall, José Maria. 1995. "The Myth of the Authoritarian Advantage." In Marc F. Plattner and Larry Diamond, eds., *Economic Reform and Democracy.* Baltimore: Johns Hopkins University Press.
Martinez-Vazquez, Jorge. 1994. "Expenditures and Expenditure Assignment." In Christine Wallich, ed., *Russia and the Challenge of Fiscal Federalism.* Washington, DC: The World Bank.
Matlock, Jack F., Jr. 1995. *Autopsy on an Empire: The American Ambassador's Account of the Collapse of the Soviet Union.* New York: Random House.
Matsnev, D. 1996. "Will We Maintain the Integrity of the Russian Economic Space?" *Problems of Economic Transition* 38 (11) (March).
Mau, Vladimir. 1992. Author's Interview, July 6, Moscow, Russian Government.

Mazrui, Ali A. 1972. *Cultural Engineering and Nation-Building in East Africa.* Evanston, IL: Northwestern University Press.

McFaul, Michael, and Nikolai Petrov. 1995. *Politichesky Al'manakh Rossii 1995.* Moscow: Carnegie Endowment for International Peace.

Medvedev, Oleg. 1996. "Federation Council Plays Stabilizing Role." *Business in Russia* 69 (Sept.): 16–18.

Mellor, Roy E. H. 1989. *Nation, State, and Territory: A Political Geography.* London: Routledge.

Mencinger, Joze. 1993. "The Slovene Economy." *Nationalities Papers* 21 (1) (spring): 81–87.

Migranyan, Andranik. 1991. "Can Yeltsin's Russia Survive?" *Moscow News* 40:8.

Mihaljek, Dubravko. 1993. "Intergovernmental Fiscal Relations in Yugoslavia, 1972–90." In Vito Tanzi, ed., *Transition to Market: Studies in Fiscal Reform,* 177–201. Washington, DC: IMF.

Milanovic, Branko. 1994. "Why Have Communist Federations Collapsed?" *Challenge* 37:2.

Miller, W. E., and D. E. Stokes. 1963. "Constituency Influence in Congress." *American Political Science Review* 57:45–56.

Mitra, Subrata K. 1991. "Room to Manoeuver in the Middle: Local Elites, Political Action and the State in India." *World Politics* 43 (3): 390–413.

———. 1992. *Power, Protest and Participation: Local Elites and the Politics of Development in India.* London: Routledge.

Moltz, James Clay. 1996. "Core and Periphery in the Evolving Russian Economy: Integration or Isolation of the Far East?" *Post-Soviet Geography and Economics* 37 (3): 175–94.

Motyl, Alexander J. 1987. *Will the Non-Russians Rebel? State, Ethnicity, and Stability in the USSR.* Ithaca: Cornell University Press.

Muir, Richard, and Ronan Paddison. 1981. *Politics, Geography and Behaviour.* London: Methuen.

Naishul, V. A. 1991. *The Supreme and Last Stage of Socialism.* London: Centre for Research into Communist Societies.

———. 1993. "Liberalism, Customary Rights and Economic Reforms." *Communist Economies and Economic Transformation* 5 (1).

Necak, Dusan. 1993. "A Chronology of the Decay of Tito's Yugoslavia, 1980–1991." *Nationalities Papers* 21 (1) (spring).

Nelson, Joan M., ed. 1990. *Economic Crisis and Policy Choice.* Princeton: Princeton University Press.

Neshchadin, A. A. 1995. *Lobbizm v Rossii: Etapi Bol'shogo Puti.* Moscow: Russian Institute of Industrialists and Entrepreneurs Expert Institute.

Noren, James H. 1993. "The FSU Economies: First Year of Transition." *Post-Soviet Geography* 34:7.

North, Douglass C. 1981. *Structure and Change in Economic History.* New York: Norton.

North, Douglass C., and Barry R. Weingast. 1989. "Constitutions and Commitment: The Evolution of Institutions Governing Public Choice in Seventeenth-Century England." *Journal of Economic History* 49 (4) (Dec.): 803–32.

Oates, Wallace E. 1972. *Fiscal Federalism.* New York: Harcourt Brace Jovanovich.

O'Donnell, Guillermo. 1988. *Bureaucratic-Authoritarianism: Argentina 1966–1973 in Comparative Perspective.* Berkeley: University of California Press.
OECD. 1990. *OECD Economic Surveys: Yugoslavia.* Paris: OECD.
———. 1994. *OECD Economic Surveys: The Czech and Slovak Republics, 1994.* Paris: OECD.
Olcott, Martha Brill. 1997. "Kazakhstan: Pushing for Eurasia." In Ian Bremmer and Ray Taras, eds., *New States, New Politics: Building the Post-Soviet Nations.* New York: Cambridge University Press.
Ordeshook, Peter C. 1996. "Russia's Party System: Is Russian Federalism Viable?" *Post-Soviet Affairs* 12 (3): 195–217.
Orlov, Dmitri. 1996. "Equal Rights for Federation Members." *Rossiiskie Vesti,* Jan. 17, 2, translated in CDPSP 48 (3): 21.
Orlov, V. E. 1991. "The Union Budget: Problems of Implementation." *Finansy SSSR* 8 (1991): 3–8.
Orlowski, Lucjan T. 1993. "Indirect Transfers in Trade Among Former Soviet Union Republics: Sources, Patterns and Policy Responses in the Post-Soviet Period." *Europe-Asia Studies* 45 (6): 1001–24.
Page, Benjamin I., and Robert Y. Shapiro. 1983. "Effects of Public Opinion on Policy." *American Political Science Review* 77:175–90.
Paretskaya, Anna. 1996. "Regional Governors Could Offset the 'Red Duma.'" *Transition* 23 (Feb.): 34–35.
Pashkov, Aleksandr. 1993. "Byudzhetnaya voina possisskikh territorii nachalas. Yest pervie zhertvy." *Izvestia* 121 (July 1): 1.
Payin, Emil. 1995. "Separatism and Federalism in Contemporary Russia." In Heyward Isham, ed., *Remaking Russia,* 185–202. Armonk, NY: M. E. Sharpe.
Payin, Emil, and Arkady Popov. 1995. "Da zdravstvuet revolutsia." *Izvestia* (Feb. 7): 4.
Pelissero, John P., and Robert E. England. 1980. "Washington Grantsmen: A Study of Municipal Representatives in the Nation's Capital." Norman: University of Oklahoma Bureau of Government Research.
Pereira, Luiz Carlos Bresser, José María Maravall, and Adam Przeworski. 1993. *Economic Reforms in New Democracies: A Social-Democratic Approach.* New York: Cambridge University Press.
Petrov, N. V., S. S. Mikheyev, and L. V. Smirnyagin. 1993. "Russia's Regional Associations in Decline." *Post-Soviet Geography* 34 (1): 59–66.
Petrovsky, Viktor. 1993. "Prizyv k zdravomysliyu." *Rossiskaya Gazeta* (July 8): 2.
Pipes, Richard. 1957. *The Formation of the Soviet Union: Communism and Nationalism, 1917–1923.* Cambridge, MA: Harvard University Press.
———. 1974. *Russia Under the Old Regime.* New York: Collier Books.
Plumb, J. H. 1950. *England in the Eighteenth Century.* London: Penguin.
Plyshevskii, B. P. 1996. "Territorial Statistics in the Russian Federation: Problems of Development." *Studies on Russian Economic Development* 7 (2): 135–40.
Polanyi, Karl. 1957a. "The Economy as Instituted Process." In Karl Polanyi, Conrad M. Arensberg, and Harry W. Pearson, *Trade Market in the Early Empires.* New York: Free Press.
———. 1957b. *The Great Transformation: The Political and Economic Origins of Our Time.* Boston: Beacon Press.

Posen, Barry. 1993. "The Security Dilemma and Ethnic Conflict." *Survival* 35:27–47.
Prust, Jim. 1993. "The Czech and Slovak Federal Republic: Government Finances in a Period of Transition." In Vito Tanzi, ed., *Transition to Market: Studies in Fiscal Reform.* Washington, DC: IMF.
Przeworski, Adam. 1991. *Democracy and the Market: Political and Economic Reforms in Eastern Europe and Latin America.* Cambridge: Cambridge University Press.
Przeworski, Adam, et al. 1995. *Sustainable Democracy.* Cambridge: Cambridge University Press.
Putnam, Robert D. 1993. *Making Democracy Work: Civic Traditions in Modern Italy.* Princeton: Princeton University Press.
Radvanyi, Jean. 1992. "And What If Russia Breaks Up? Toward New Regional Divisions." *Post-Soviet Geography* (Feb.): 69–77.
Ramet, Sabrina. 1992. *Balkan Babel: Politics, Culture and Religion in Yugoslavia.* Boulder: Westview.
Remmer, Karen L. 1995. "New Theoretical Perspectives on Democratization." *Comparative Politics* (October): 103–22.
Remnick, David. 1994. *Lenin's Tomb.* New York: Vintage.
Respublika. 1992. *Vserossiiskoe Soveshchanie Rukovoditel'ey Organov Gosudarstvennoi, Predstavitel'noi i Ispolnitel'noi Vlasti Respublik v Sostave Rossiiskoi Federatsii, Kraev, Oblastei, Avtonomnoi Oblasti, Avtonomnykh Oblastov, Gorodov Moskvy i Sankt-Peterburga,* Sept. 11, Cheboksary. Moscow: Respublika.
Rév, István. 1994. "The Postmortem Victory of Communism." *Daedalus* 123 (3) (summer): 159–70.
Reznik, Boris. 1995. "Far East Gives the Center an Ultimatum." *Izvestia,* Feb. 3, 1, translated in CDPSP 47 (5): 20.
Rich, Michael J. 1989. "Distributive Politics and the Allocation of Federal Grants." *American Political Science Review* 83 (1) (March): 193–213.
Riker, William. 1987a. *The Development of American Federalism.* Boston: Kluwer Academic Publishers.
Riker, William, and Jonathan Lemco. 1987b. "The Relation Between Structure and Stability in Federal Governments." In Riker, *The Development of American Federalism,* 113–30.
Roeder, Philip. 1991. "Soviet Federalism and Ethnic Mobilization." *World Politics* 43:196–232.
Rokkan, Stein, and Derek W. Urwin. 1983. *Economy, Territory, Identity: Politics of West European Peripheries.* Beverly Hills: Sage.
Root, Hilton L. 1987. *Peasants and King in Burgundy: Agrarian Foundations of French Absolutism.* Berkeley: University of California Press.
———. 1994. *The Fountain of Privilege: Political Foundations of Markets in Old Regime France and England.* Berkeley: University of California Press.
Rose, Richard. 1996. *New Russia Barometer 6: After the Presidential Election.* University of Strathclyde, Centre for the Study of Public Policy.
Rosenberg, David. 1989. *Accounting for Public Policy: Power, Professionals and Politics in Local Government.* Manchester: Manchester University Press
Rupnik, Jacques. 1994. "Europe's New Frontiers: Remapping Europe." *Daedalus* 123 (3) (summer): 91–114.

———. 1995. "The Post-Totalitarian Blues." *Journal of Democracy* 6 (2) (April): 61–74.
Rustow, Dankwart. 1970. "Transitions to Democracy: Toward a Dynamic Model." *Comparative Politics* 2:337–64.
Rutland, Peter. 1994. "Has Democracy Failed Russia?" *National Interest* (winter): 3–12.
———. 1996. "Tatarstan: A Sovereign Republic Within the Russian Federation." *OMRI Russian Regional Report* 1 (5) (Sept. 25).
Sachs, Jeffrey D. 1995. "Russia's Struggle with Stabilization: Conceptual Issues and Evidence." In The World Bank, *Proceedings of the World Bank Annual Conference on Development Economics 1994,* 57–89.
Safire, William. 1993. *Safire's New Political Dictionary.* New York: Random House.
Sakwa, Richard. 1993. *Russian Politics and Society.* London: Routledge.
Satter, David. 1996. "The Darkness Spreads from Primoriye." *Prism,* Jamestown Foundation, December.
Schelling, Thomas C. 1978. *Micromotives and Macrobehavior.* New York: Norton.
Schöpflin, George. 1994. "Postcommunism: The Problems of Democratic Construction." *Daedalus* 123 (3) (summer).
Sheehy, Ann. 1990. "Fact Sheet on Declarations of Sovereignty." *Report on the USSR,* Radio Liberty, Nov. 9, 23–25.
———. 1993. "Russia's Republics: A Threat to its Territorial Integrity." *RFE/RL Research Report* 2 (20) May 14.
Shils, Edward. 1975. *Center and Periphery: Essays in Macrosociology.* Chicago: University of Chicago Press.
Shirk, Susan L. 1993. *The Political Logic of Economic Reform in China.* Berkeley: University of California Press.
Shome, Parsatharasi. 1993. "Transition and Transformation: Fiscal Sector Issues in Kazakhstan." In Vito Tanzi, ed., *Transition to Market: Studies in Fiscal Reform,* 177–201. Washington, DC: IMF.
Shoumikhin, Andrei. 1996. "The Chechen Crisis and the Future of Russia." *Comparative Strategy* 15:1–10.
Shue, Vivienne. 1988. *The Reach of the State: Sketches of the Chinese Body Politic.* Stanford: Stanford University Press.
Simon, Gerhard. 1991. *Nationalism and Policy Toward the Nationalities in the Soviet Union.* Boulder: Westview.
Sinelnikov, Sergei. 1995. *Byudzhetny Krizis v Rossii: 1985–1995 gody.* Moscow: Yevrasia.
Sked, Alan. 1989. *The Decline and Fall of the Habsburg Empire, 1815–1918.* London: Longman.
Slider, Darrell. 1994. "Federalism, Discord, and Accommodation: Intergovernmental Relations in Post-Soviet Russia." In Theodore H. Friedgut and Jeffrey W. Hahn, eds., *Local Power and Post-Soviet Politics,* 239–69. Armonk, NY: M. E. Sharpe.
Slider, Darrell, Vladimir Gimpelson, and Sergei Chugrov. 1994. "Political Tendencies in Russia's Regions: Evidence from the 1993 Parliamentary Elections." *Slavic Review* 53 (3): 711–32.

Smirnov, Viktor, and Elena Kotelnikova. 1993. "Oblastnoi sovet khochet stat' verkhovnym." *Kommersant-Daily* 125, July 6.

Smirnyagin, Leonid. 1993. "Politichesky Federalizm protiv ekonomicheskogo." *Segodnya* 28 (June 25): 2.

Smith, David M. 1987. *Geography, Inequality and Society.* Cambridge: Cambridge University Press.

Sobyanin, A., E. Gelman, and O. Kayunov. 1993. "Politichesky Klimat v Rossii v 1991–1993 gg." *Mirovaya Ekonomika i Mezhdunarodnie Otnoshenie* 9 (September): 20–32.

Sobyanin, A. E., and V. Sukhovolsky. 1995. *Democracy Restricted by Falsifications.* Moscow. Manuscript.

Solnick, Steven L. 1994. "Political Consolidation or Disintegration: Can Russia's Center Hold?" Unpublished paper, Columbia University, 1994.

———. 1995. "Federal Bargaining in Russia." *East European Constitutional Review* (fall): 52–58.

———. 1996. "The Breakdown of Hierarchies in the Soviet Union and China: A Neoinstitutional Perspective." *World Politics* 48 (January): 209–38.

Solzhenitsyn, Aleksandr. 1996. "Traditsii rossiiskoi gosudarstvennosti i perspektivy federalizma" (Traditions of Russian Statehood and Prospects of Federalism). *Obshchaya Gazeta* 22 (150) (June 6–12): 3.

The Soviet Constitution: A Dictionary. 1986. Moscow: Progress Publishers.

Starovoitova, Galina. 1993. "Weimar Russia?" *Journal of Democracy* 4 (3) (July): 106–9.

Stein, Robert M., and Kenneth N. Bickers. 1994. "Universalism and the Electoral Connection: A Test and Some Doubts." *Political Research Quarterly,* 47.

Stern, Jessica. 1994. "Moscow Meltdown: Can Russia Survive?" *International Security* 18 (4) (spring): 40–66.

Stiglitz, Joseph E. 1989. *The Economic Role of the State.* Oxford: Blackwell.

Stone, Clarence N., and Heywood T. Sanders. 1987. "Reexamining a Classic Case of Development Politics: New Haven, Connecticut." In *The Politics of Urban Development,* ed. Clarence N. Stone and Heywood T. Sanders. Lawrence: University Press of Kansas.

Stone, Norman. 1984. *Europe Transformed: 1878–1919.* Cambridge, MA: Harvard University Press.

Sutherland, Douglas, and Philip Hanson. 1996. "Structural Change in the Economies of Russia's Regions." *Europe-Asia Studies* 48 (3): 367–92.

Szelenyi, Ivan. 1978. "Social Inequalities in State Socialist Redistributive Economies." *International Journal of Comparative Sociology* 19:63–87.

———. 1983. *Urban Inequalities Under State Socialism.* London: Oxford University Press.

Tarrow, Sidney. 1977. *Between Center and Periphery: Grassroots Politicians in Italy and France.* New Haven: Yale University Press.

———. 1991. *Struggle, Politics, and Reform: Collective Action, Social Movements, and Cycles of Protest.* Ithaca: Cornell University, Western Societies Program Occasional Paper No. 21.

Teague, Elizabeth. 1993. "North-South Divide: Yeltsin and Russia's Provincial Leaders." *RFE/RL Research Report* 2 (47) (Nov. 26).

———. 1994a. "Center-Periphery Relations in the Russian Federation." In Roman Szporluk, ed., *National Identity and Ethnicity in Russia and the New States of Eurasia*, 21–57. Armonk, NY: M.E. Sharpe.

———. 1994b. Comment in John W. R. Lepingwell, Alexander Rahr, Elizabeth Teague, and Vera Tolz, "Russia: A Troubled Future." *RFE/RL Reports* 3 (24) (June 17).

———. 1996. "Russia and the Regions: The Uses of Ambiguity." In John Gibson and Philip Hanson, eds., *Transformation from Below: Local Power and the Political Economy of Post-Communist Transitions*. Cheltenham, UK: Edward Elgar.

Thomas, Timothy L. 1995a. *The Caucasus Conflict and Russian Security*. Fort Leavenworth, KS: Foreign Military Studies Office.

———. 1995b. "Fault Lines and Factions in the Russian Army." *Orbis* (fall): 531–48.

Thucydides. 1972. *History of the Peloponnesian War*. London: Penguin.

Tiebout, Charles M. 1956. "A Pure Theory of Local Expenditures." *Journal of Political Economy*, 64.

Tilly, Charles. 1969. "Collective Violence in European Perspective." In Hugh D. Graham and Tedd R. Gurr, eds., *Violence in America: Historical and Comparative Perspectives*, 5–45. Washington, DC: U.S. Government Printing Office.

Tocqueville, Alexis de. 1969. *Democracy in America*. New York: Harper and Row.

Todres, Vladimir. 1993. "Primore probastovalo den." *Segodnya* (Aug. 13): 3.

Tolz, Vera. 1993a. "Regionalism in Russia: The Case of Siberia." *RFE/RL Research Report* 2 (9) (Feb. 26): 1–9.

———. 1993b. "Thorny Road toward Federalism in Russia." *RFE/RL Research Report* 2 (48) (Dec. 3): 1–8.

———. 1996. "Unease Grips Moscow and the Ethnic Republics." *Transition* (Feb. 23): 42–44.

Tong, James. 1994. "Fiscal Decentralization and its Effects on China, 1980–1994." UCLA. Paper prepared for China and Mongolia Department of The World Bank.

Treisman, Daniel. 1992. "Korruptsia: Moscow Meets Capitol Hill." *New Republic* (May 11): 14–17.

———. 1995. "The Politics of Soft Credit in Post-Soviet Russia." *Europe-Asia Studies* 47 (6): 949–76.

———. 1996a. "Why Yeltsin Won." *Foreign Affairs* 75, no. 5 (Sept.–Oct.): 64–77.

———. 1996b. "The Politics of Intergovernmental Transfers in Post-Soviet Russia." *British Journal of Political Science* 26 (July): 299–335.

———. 1997. "Russia's 'Ethnic Revival': The Separatist Activism of Regional Leaders in a Post-Communist Order." *World Politics* (January).

———. 1998a. "Fighting Inflation in a Transitional Regime: Russia's Anomalous Stabilization." *World Politics* (January).

———. 1998b. "Between the Extremes: The Moderate Reformist and Centrist Blocs." Forthcoming in Timothy J. Colton and Jerry Hough, eds., *Growing Pains: Russian Democracy and the Election of 1993*. Washington, DC: Brookings Institution Press.

———. 1998c. "Fiscal Redistribution in a Fragile Federation: Moscow and the Regions in 1994." *British Journal of Political Science* (28) (January).

Trud. 1994. "Boris Yeltsin: Danger of Russia's Collapse Has Passed." Interview with President Boris Yeltsin. Aug. 26, 1–2; translated in FBIS-SOV-94-166, 10–15.

Tsipko, Aleksandr. 1991a. "The Drama of Russia's Choice." *Izvestia* (Oct. 1): 5; translated in CDSP 43 (39): 1–4
———. 1991b. "I Don't Want to Be an Accomplice to Murder." *Literaturnaya Gazeta* (Nov. 6): 3; translated in CDSP 43 (45) (1991): 9.
Tullock, Gordon. 1983. *Economics of Income Redistribution*. Boston: Kluwer-Nijhoff Publishing.
Urban, Michael. 1996. "Stages of Political Identity Formation in Late Soviet and Post-Soviet Russia." In Victoria E. Bonnell, ed., *Identities in Transition: Eastern Europe and Russia After The Collapse of Communism*. Berkeley: Center for East European and Slavic Studies.
Ushkalov, Igor G., and Boris S. Khorev. 1989. "The USSR: Territorial and Administrative Structure." In Robert Bennett, ed., *Territory and Administration in Europe*. London: Pinter Publishers.
Uvalic, Milica. 1993. "The Disintegration of Yugoslavia: Its Costs and Benefits." *Communist Economies and Economic Transformation* 5 (3): 273–93.
Vaksberg, Arkady. 1991. *The Soviet Mafia*. London: Weidenfeld and Nicolson.
Vetrov, Ivan. 1993. "Vlasti i profsoyuzy Dalnego Vostoka vystupili vmeste." *Kommersant-Daily* (Aug. 12): 3.
Vetrov, Ivan, and Andrei Shmarov. 1993. "Ne Slishkom Dalny Vostok." *Kommersant Weekly* 33 (Aug. 16–22).
Walker, Edward W. 1995. "Designing Center-Region Relations in the New Russia." *EECR* 4 (1) (winter): 54–60.
Wallich, Christine I., ed. 1994. *Russia and the Challenge of Fiscal Federalism*. Washington, DC: The World Bank.
Wegren, Stephen K. 1994. "Rural Reform and Political Culture in Russia." *Europe-Asia Studies* 46 (2): 215–41.
Weingast, Barry R. 1994. "Reflections on Distributive Politics and Universalism." *Political Research Quarterly* 47:319–27.
———. 1995. "The Economic Role of Political Institutions: Market-Preserving Federalism and Economic Development." *Journal of Law, Economics, and Organization* 11 (1) (April): 1–31.
Weingast, Barry R., Kenneth A. Shepsle, and Christopher Johnsen. 1981. "The Political Economy of Benefits and Costs: A Neoclassical Approach to Distributive Politics." *Journal of Political Economy* 89 (4): 642–64.
White, Stephen, Richard Rose, and Ian McAllister. 1996. *How Russia Votes*. London: Chatham House.
Whitefield, Stephen, and Geoffrey Evans. 1994. "The Russian Election of 1993: Public Opinion and the Transition Experience." *Post-Soviet Affairs* 10 (1): 38–60.
Winiecki, Jan. 1991. *Resistance to Change in the Soviet Ecoomic System: A Property Rights Approach*. London: Routledge.
Wishnevsky, Julia. 1994. "Problems of Russian Regional Leadership." *RFE/RL Research Report* 3 (19) (May 3): 8.
Woodruff, David. 1995. "Barter of the Bankrupt." MIT, mimeo.
Woods, Dwayne. 1995. "The Crisis of Center-Periphery Integration in Italy and the Rise of Regional Populism: The Lombard League." *Comparative Politics* (Jan.): 187–203.

Woodward, Susan L. 1995. *Balkan Tragedy: Chaos and Dissolution After the Cold War.* Washington, DC: Brookings Institution.
Woolf, Stuard, ed. 1996. *Nationalism in Europe 1815 to the Present.* London: Routledge.
Yanovsky, Mark. 1993. Author's Interview. Moscow, Ministry of Economics, Aug. 3.
Yasin, Evgeny, et al. 1993a. *Reforms A-La Gaidar: 500 Days After.* Moscow: Russian Union of Industrialists and Entrepreneurs Institute of Experts.

———. 1993b. *Regioni Rossii v Perekhodny Period.* Moscow: Expert Institute of the Russian Union of Industrialists and Entrepreneurs, November.

Yasmann, Victor. 1995. "Boris Yeltsin's Favorite Mayor." *Prism* 1 (6), part 2. Washington, DC: The Jamestown Foundation.
Yeltsin, Boris. 1994. *The Struggle for Russia.* New York: Times Books.
Yemelyanenko, Vladimir. 1993. "The Country Will Collapse." *Moscow News,* Feb. 7.
Young, M. Crawford. 1976. *The Politics of Cultural Pluralism.* Madison: University of Wisconsin Press.
Zaslavsky, Victor. 1992a. "The Evolution of Separatism in Soviet Society under Gorbachev." In Gail W. Lapidus, Victor Zaslavsky, and Philip Goldman, eds., *From Union to Commonwealth: Nationalism and Separatism in the Soviet Republics.* Cambridge: Cambridge University Press.

———. 1992b. "Nationalism and Democratic Transition." *Daedalus* 121 (2) (spring).

Zizmond, E. 1992. "The Collapse of the Yugoslav Economy." *Soviet Studies* 44 (1): 101–12.

Index

Abdulatipov, Ramazan, 16, 34, 38, 40, 45, 75
Administrative divisions, 28–30
Adygeia, 29, 30
Afanasiev, Yuri, 10
Alexander I, 28
Altai Republic (Gorno-Altai), 30
Amur Oblast, 18, 82
Antonov, Aleksandr, 110
Appeasement, 163–66
Army, Russian, 13, 14–17
Ash, Timothy Garton, 1
Athenian Empire, 163
Australia, 11, 20, 168
Austria, 139
Avturkhanov, Umar, 43
Axelrod, Robert, 163

Bahry, Donna, 57
Balkaria, 12
Barter, 19
Bashkortostan, 16, 21, 26, 29, 34, 36, 39, 51, 54, 55, 82
Belarus, 12, 40
Belgium, 7, 139
Belgorod Oblast, 18
Blokhin, Yuri, 110
Brezhnev, Leonid, 30, 48
Britain, 5
Bryansk Oblast, 18, 71, 82
Bureaucracy, 13–14
Buryatia, 18

Canada, 11, 17
Chechnya, 2, 3, 12, 14, 16, 25–26, 30, 31, 34, 37–39, 43–46, 51, 121, 179–80

Chernomyrdin, Viktor, 15–16, 42, 46, 47, 80, 94, 98, 117, 124, 135
China, 5, 57, 174–75, 178
Chubais, Anatoli, 58
Churchill, Winston, 163
Chuvashia, 29
Consociational democracy, 7, 19–20
Constitution, 13, 29–30, 32–37
Courland, 28
Crick, Bernard, 171
Crozier, Michel, 170
Culture, 8–12, 90–92
Cyprus, 7
Czechoslovakia, 2, 4, 27, 137–51, 161

Dagestan, 12, 29, 46, 55, 75, 82, 121
Democratization, 161–63, 171–75
Deutsch, Karl, 5
Disintegration, national, 4–8, 161–63
Dudaev, Dzhokhar, 2, 16, 25, 38, 43–45, 121, 164
Dudaeva, Alla, 26, 45

Economic reform, 176–78
Elections: parliamentary, 82, 94, 100; presidential, 26, 81–82, 94, 100, 128–29; regional and local, 31, 112–15, 127, 171–75; Soviet period, 30
England, 173–74
Estonia, 157
Ethnicity, 8–12, 175–76
European Union, 7

Far East, 18
Far East Republic, 10–11, 18, 21, 38
Federalism, 7, 19, 29

259

Federation Council, 14, 35, 74, 113–15
Federation Treaty (1992), 21, 32–34, 36, 38
Finland, 28
Fiscal policy: in Russia, 47–80; in Czechoslovakia, Yugoslavia, USSR, 137–60
France, 5, 167–70, 174
Fyodorov, Boris, 2, 3

Gaidar, Yegor, 57, 124
Georgia, 40
Giscard d'Estaing, 170
Goffart, Walter, 166
Gorbachev, Mikhail, 1, 30, 37–39, 81, 156–58, 179
Gorno Republic, 29
Gosplan, 49
Gras, Solange, 170

Habsburg Empire, 167–68
Hardgrave, Robert, 169
Harrop, Martin, 90
Havel, Vaclav, 2
Hayek, Friedrich von, 172
Hungary, 2
Huntington, Samuel P., 170

Ilyumzhinov, Kirsan, 35, 80, 121
India, 5, 169
Ingushetia, 12, 30, 46, 112
Integration: national, 4–8; economic, 17–19
International Monetary Fund (IMF), 139
Ireland, 21
Irkutsk Oblast, 18, 70
Ispolkomi (executive committees), 30
Italy, 5, 11, 139, 169
Ivanov, Vyacheslav, 1

Kabardino-Balkaria, 132–34
Kaliningrad, 37
Kalmykia, 34, 35, 80, 112, 121
Karachaevo-Cherkessia, 30
Karelia, 34, 37, 71, 112, 118
Kaunda, Kenneth, 169

Kedourie, E., 8
Khakassia, 30
Khanti, 29
Khanti-Mansiisky Autonomous Okrug, 42–43, 127
Khasbulatov, Ruslan, 21, 38, 43
Klaus, Vaclav, 150–51
Kokov, Valery, 132–34
Komi, 55, 121
Koryaksky Autonomous Okrug, 55
Koval, Valery, 110–11
Kraft, Evan, 152
Krasnoyarsk, 21, 42
Kulikov, Anatoli, 15

Laba, Roman, 40
Latvia, 157
Lazarsfeld, Paul F., 90
Lebanon, 7
Lebed, Aleksandr, 46
Lemco, Jonathan, 20
Liberal Democratic Party (LDP), 103
Lijphart, Arend, 19
Lipset, Seymour Martin, 91, 117
Lithuania, 12, 21, 157, 162
Livonia, 28
Luzhkov, Yuri, 15

Magadan Oblast, 55
Magomedov, Magomed-Ali, 121
Malaysia, 7
Mansi, 29
Mari El, 29, 31
Markovic, Ante, 139
Meciar, Vladimir, 151
Melos, 163
Mexico, 5, 173
Milanovic, Branko, 162
Milosevic, 155
Mitra, Subrata, 169
Mordovia, 18, 31
Moscow City, 21
Motyl, Alexander, 39
Mukha, Vitali, 35, 42, 125, 180
Muslim republics, 16, 44

National Bank of Yugoslavia, 152
Nazdratenko, Yevgeny, 80
Nemtsov, Boris, 120
Nentsi, 29
Netherlands, 7
New Zealand, 21
Nietzsche, Friedrich, 10
Nikolaev, Mikhail, 135
Nizhny Novgorod Oblast, 18, 120
North, Douglass C., 173
North Ossetia, 46
Novikov, Vyacheslav, 42
Novosibirsk Oblast, 35, 42–43, 82, 125

Orel Oblast, 111
Orttung, Robert, 129
Ottoman Empire, 166–68
"Our Home is Russia" (OHIR), 66, 94, 98, 117, 134

Pact on Civic Accord (1994), 41
Padania, 5, 9
Panama, 21
Parties, political, 13, 179
Payin, Emil, 44
Perov, B., 21
Poland, 2, 28, 173, 178
Police, 13
Popov, Arkady, 44
Primakov, Yevgeny, 36
Primore, 18, 38, 80
Putnam, Robert, 91, 117

Quebec, 5

Rakhimov, Murtaza, 26
Regional associations, 21
Riker, William, 20
Rokkan, Stein, 90, 117
Roman Empire, 166–68
"Romantic" nationalists, 164–65
Root, Hilton, 174
Rossel, Eduard, 15, 26
Rumyantsev, Oleg, 32, 34, 40
"Russia's Choice," 71, 78, 82, 94, 98, 107–8

Rustow, Dankwart, 171
Rutland, Peter, 8
Rutskoi, Alexander, 43, 132
Ryabov, Aleksandr, 110, 180
Ryazan Oblast, 18
Ryzhkov, Nikoali, 135

Sajudis, 40
Sakha (Yakutia), 31, 32, 34, 40, 51, 135
Sakha Omuk, 135
Serbia, 21, 138, 151–55
Shafranik, Yuri, 42
Shaimiev, Mintimer, 16, 26, 31
Shakhrai, Sergei, 34, 36, 41
Siberia, 9, 10, 18, 21–22, 28, 35, 41–43
Siberian Agreement, 21, 41–43
Sked, Alan, 167
Slovakia, 138, 148–51
Slovenia, 21, 138, 151–55
Smirnyagin, Leonid, 16, 36–37
Solzhenitsyn, Aleksandr, 36
South Korea, 139
Soviets (legislative bodies), 30–32
Spain, 5, 40
Stalin, 17, 29
State Duma, 74–75
St. Petersburg, 21
Stroyev, Yegor, 36, 111, 127, 180
Supreme Soviet, 35, 72, 124
Sverdlovsk Oblast, 2, 15, 18, 38
Switzerland, 7

Tambov Oblast, 37, 110–11, 118
Tarrow, Sidney, 169
Tatarstan, 2, 16, 18, 21, 29, 31–40, 51, 54
Tax laws, 51–52
Tax sharing, 144
Teague, Elizabeth, 39
Tilly, Charles, 170
Tocqueville, Alexis de, 172
Tomsk Oblast, 71
Trade: interregional, 17–18; foreign, 17–18
Tsipko, Aleksandr, 3
Tula Oblast, 18

Tver Oblast, 18, 134
Tyumen Oblast, 42–43, 54–55, 127
Tyva, 12, 29, 36, 121

Ukraine, 12, 40
United States, 11, 20, 139
Urals, 18
"Urals Republic," 15, 21, 38
Uruguay, 21
USSR, 2, 4, 9, 11–12, 17, 20, 27, 39, 137–48, 155–59, 161–62; fiscal system of, 48–49

Vekselya (bills of exchange), 19
Vladivostok, 18
Vologda Oblast, 2, 38
Voronezh Oblast, 39

Weingast, Barry, 20, 172–73
West Indies Federation, 11

Yanovsky, Mark, 51
Yaroslavl Oblast, 134
Yasin, Yevgeny, 179
Yegorov, Nikolai, 16, 162
Yeltsin, Boris, 3, 15, 16, 25–26, 30–38, 41–47, 59–60, 65, 74, 81–82, 94, 98–135, 177–80
Yugoslavia, 4, 21, 27, 137–48, 151–55, 161–62

Zambia, 168–69
Zemli (lands), 32
Zhirinovsky, Vladimir, 92, 103
Zorkin, Valeri, 35
Zyuganov, Gennady, 100